Web Developer.com®
Guide to Creating
Web Channels

Lee Purcell

WILEY COMPUTER PUBLISHING

John Wiley & Sons, Inc.
New York • Chichester • Weinheim • Brisbane • Singapore • Toronto

This book is dedicated to Kathie, who makes it all worthwhile.

Publisher: Robert Ipsen
Editor: Robert M. Elliott
Managing Editor: Marnie Wielage
Electronic Products, Associate Editor: Mike Sosa
Text Design & Composition: Benchmark Productions, Inc.

Designations used by companies to distinguish their products are often claimed as trademarks. In all instances where John Wiley & Sons, Inc., is aware of a claim, the product names appear in initial capital or ALL CAPITAL LETTERS. Readers, however, should contact the appropriate companies for more complete information regarding trademarks and registration.

This book is printed on acid-free paper. ∞

This publication is designed to provide accurate and authoritative information in regard to the subject matter covered. It is sold with the understanding that the publisher is not engaged in rendering professional services. If professional advice or other expert assistance is required, the services of a competent professional person should be sought.

Internet World, Web Week, Web Developer, Internet Shopper, and Mecklermedia are the exclusive trademarks of Mecklermedia Corporation and are used with permission.

Library of Congress Cataloging-in-Publication Data:
Purcell, Lee
    Web Developer.com guide to creating Web channels / Lee Purcell.
       p. cm.
    "Wiley Computer Publishing."
    Includes index.
    ISBN 0-471-25168-2 (pbk. / online)
    1. Internet Programming. 2. Web sites--Design. 3. XML (Document markup language) 4. DHTML (Document Markup language) I. Title
    QA76.625.P87 1998
    005.72--DC21
                                        98-14351
                                          CIP

Printed in the United States of America.
10 9 8 7 6 5 4 3 2 1

Contents

The landscape of the World Wide Web is changing in vast and sweeping ways. Like a river cutting a course through a canyon, carving new shapes in the earth and rock, a wave of new Web standards and protocols are reshaping the way that words, images, and sound can be intermixed and presented in browser windows. Among the most striking new feature in this evolving Webscape is the appearance of Web channels—characterized in particular by the approaches used in the version 4 browsers from Netscape and Microsoft. Once part of the high-flying domain of dedicated Web servers running the latest push technology software, Web channels have come down to earth. Microsoft's Active Channels and Netscape's Netcaster employ technologies that enable small sites to deliver their content on a planned and periodic basis to subscribers. Sign up enough subscribers and you ensure a regular audience for your Web material—much like the world of broadcast media and print periodical distribution. No longer do you have to rely on sporadic visits from those journeying about the Web in search of entertainment or enlightenment.

Who This Book Is For

This book is written for the people who are planning, designing, and constructing Web channels, whether for personal use, for a small company, or for a large organization. Individual chapters describe the basic mechanisms for producing Web channels targeting three of the major delivery platforms—Netscape Netcaster, Microsoft Active Channels, and BackWeb Technologies' Infocenter. Supporting technologies, such as Dynamic HTML, are also discussed in respect to how they can be used to enhance Web channel content design and delivery.

We assume that you have some familiarity with the World Wide Web and constructing HTML pages. If you're not familiar with JavaScript, a good reference manual would be a useful complement to this book. The material is presented in such a way that it should support the efforts of beginning channel developers as well as more experienced Web developers.

How This Book Is Organized

Creating Web Channels is divided into five sections:

- Part One: Architecture
- Part Two: Active Channels
- Part Three: Netcaster
- Part Four: Case Studies
- Appendices and Glossary

Part One, *Architecture*, establishes the foundation upon which Web Channel delivery relies. The interlocking and overlapping collection of standards and protocols that form the essential architecture for presenting channel content are introduced. Dynamic HTML (DHTML), the interactive cousin to standard HTML, is looked at as the ideal vehicle for composing Web channel content.

Part One of this book also looks at the software tools that will become vital components of the Web developer's toolkit when working with channels and DHTML. By the time you're finished with these three chapters, you should have a strong understanding of the working environment that supports Web channels and Dynamic HTML.

The individual chapter breakdown is as follows:

Chapter 1, "Adding Intelligence to Push," provides a definition for Webcasting and a careful examination of how this form of Web communication differs from previous incarnations of HTML. The chapter also offers quick definitions on the plethora of supporting standards, and discusses the security issues associated with channel delivery of content, including applications that run on the desktop.

Chapter 2, "Exploring Dynamic HTML," offers an overview of the interactivity made possible through the use of Dynamic HTML. The standards and components that make DHTML possible are explained, and some simple examples of DHTML implementations are provided. Finally, the latest authoring tools that have been designed for creating platform-independent DHTML are introduced with suggestions as to how they can enhance a typical Web developer's efforts.

Chapter 3, "The Enabling Standards: CDF, DOM, and RDF," goes into additional detail on the matrix of standards that make Web channel delivery possible. The structure (and inherent simplicity) of CDF files is demonstrated. The important role of the Document Object Model (DOM) in unifying the browser's control over individual components is explained, and the means by which DOM permits full interactivity with the contents in a browser window is covered. The evolving standard for meta-information, data about Web content, known as the Resource Description Framework, is also introduced. RDF promises to become an important part of the Web information infrastructure, providing a means by which to categorize and access large quantities of information.

Part Two, *Active Channels*, focuses on the scalable Microsoft model for Web channel delivery. In this part of this book, we explain the mechanisms for creating Web channels using the Channel Definition Format file, and gaining subscribers for the newly created channel. Examples of how to incorporate elements of Dynamic HTML into Web channel content are also provided.

Chapter 4, "Creating an Active Channel," explores the various tools available for producing CDF files and walks through the process in some detail. Strategies for planning, creating, and publicizing an Active Channel are presented. This chapter also examines the methods for creating the icons and graphics that are used in Internet Explorer 4 to identify your channel to subscribers. Finally, the special features supported by CDF are discussed, with examples of how they can be used.

Chapter 5, "Using Dynamic HTML for Active Channels," shows how the rich Microsoft implementation of DHTML can be used to produce lively, interactive pages for delivery as Web channels. A number of short examples of DHTML code point out the ease with which complex interactive presentations can be constructed with a minimum amount of programming. Some of these examples are constructed using the authoring tools introduced earlier in the book to show how this kind of software can accelerate the development process. The chapter concludes with an example of how to create a preview page that can be used to showcase your work in Microsoft's Active Channel Guide.

Chapter 6, "Scaling up to IP Multicasting," examines the means by which large-volume Webcasting can be accomplished using BackWeb Technology's Infocenter 4.0 product. The discussion centers on how BackWeb's architecture can be used to enhance and extend Active Channel delivery and how it can be used as an independent client through the BackWeb client.

Part Three, *Netcaster*, demonstrates the Netscape model for presenting Web channel content. The use of JavaScript to specify the characteristics of the channel is explained, and the mechanisms by which content is presented are covered. A number of examples of Dynamic HTML pages designed for use with Netcaster are also provided.

Chapter 7, "Creating a Netcaster Channel," goes through the individual steps involved in producing a channel for use with Netcaster. The underlying concepts of this form of channel delivery are described, as well as the subscription mechanism from the point of view of the subscriber. The wizard provided by Netscape for creating a Netcaster channel is discussed in some detail. Security issues are also explored in this chapter.

Chapter 8, "Using DHTML for Netcaster Channels," shows the advantages of incorporating DHTML elements into channel content. A series of examples demonstrate how some of Netscape's unique features can be used to generate animations. Some of the examples rely on authoring tools, including mBed Interactor and Macromedia Dreamweaver, to produce effects.

Part 4, *Case Studies*, examines how various companies have implemented channel content, and provides tips and guidelines for the design and construction of your own channels.

Chapter 9, "Lightspeed Publishing Case Study," outlines the process by which I converted a portion of my own Website, the home of Lightspeed Publishing, to a channel for Web delivery. The site makeover includes specific details on how the low-level content mechanisms and DHTML were handled, and how the subscription elements for the channel were constructed.

Chapter 10, "AnyWare Ltd. Case Study," examines the site evolution of a company, AnyWare Limited, that has produced a valuable CDF file construction and maintenance tool, and how the site has been organized to provide automatic updating of software subscriptions.

Chapter 11, "*Fast Company* Case Study," focuses on the birth and life of a Netcaster channel representing one of the fastest-growing, Internet-savvy business publications: *Fast Company*. This chapter goes into considerable detail into the hardware and software architecture used to build an automated system by which writers and editors can contribute articles and content to the channel and have it incorporated into the DHTML automatically. A number of detailed scripts and a block diagram of the site organization provide a useful model for publications looking towards ongoing channel management issues.

Chapter 12, "NewsEDGE/BackWeb Case Study," shows how channel delivery can be scaled to enterprise-level systems. This chapter examines the means by which the filtered news content offered by NewsEDGE can be integrated into a BackWeb channel delivery system for use by professionals in a hypothetical high-tech consulting firm. This chapter highlights the features of the newest InfoCenter product offering from BackWeb and explains how a system of this sort can be implemented and managed.

And finally, three appendices and a glossary provide some additional resources for developers considering the technologies presented in this book.

Appendix A, "HTML 4.0 and XML," provides an overview of the two languages that are heir to Web construction duties in the near future. Those aspects of the languages that are most important to channel delivery considerations are highlighted.

Appendix B, "Resources," covers a number of tools and organizations that should prove invaluable to developers working in this new medium. Both channel development tools and authoring packages are discussed, and the appendix also examines some useful graphics applications that can simplify page design and construction tasks.

Appendix C, "The Companion Website," introduces the types of materials that will be made available to you through this book's companion website.

The Glossary provides definitions of the key terms encountered in the Web channel environment.

What Channels Bring to the Web Experience

Channels are about personalization and convenience. You can spend a lot of time on the Web actively seeking and retrieving information, firing up search engines and weeding through the responses, and revisiting those sites that you regularly depend on for news and information. When you subscribe to channels, the information comes to you in convenient, accessible packets, ready for offline viewing at your leisure. Some technologies, such as BackWeb's Polite Agent approach, perform updates in the background, grabbing idle processor cycles and refreshing your channel content while you're browsing other sites or collecting and reading your email. Other channel sites provide you with a selection of highlights of news and articles that you can scan and then jump to the longer pieces online for those topics that interest you. IDG.net, for example, lets you create a personalized page to access a range of topics culled from IDG's 220-plus Websites. If you subscribe to the channel, only the article highlights are downloaded for offline viewing, but you can quickly follow the links the next time you are online to access the detailed content.

Other online publications, such as Microsoft's *Slate*, offer both news and commentary. If you subscribe, you receive a daily briefing that scans and reports on content from the leading domestic and international newspapers, as well as leading news magazines. Publications such as *Time, Newsweek, The New Yorker, The Nation, The New Republic,* and *Esquire* appear in the Briefing, and international events are illuminated with capsule summaries from papers such as the *Corriere della Sera* of

Milan, the *Guardian* of London, and *France-Soir* of Paris. Once again, the briefing offers summaries of the content, and if you find reason to delve deeper into the topics, the full-length articles can be accessed by going back online. The content is presented in such a way, however, that in many cases, the summary may provide all the news that you need. The insights into those topics that are of interest to readers in London, Paris, or Moscow, as reported in the international papers, also provide a valuable perspective to frequently myopic American readers.

While some types of content adapt better than others to Web channel delivery, almost any Website has some content that can be effectively delivered through a channel. Channels let you communicate with an audience on whatever schedule makes sense for your business or enterprise. Some worldwide news providers, such as IDG and the Weather Channel, update their channel content on an hourly basis. Smaller, information-oriented providers, such as *Fast Company* and Microsoft's *Slate*, opt for a daily update schedule. Other content providers might have significant new content every other day or once per week. Even monthly channel updates make sense in certain circumstances, such as for software providers who distribute updates to their software products over the Web (for example, virus protection programs that regularly require additions). While channel subscriptions will probably never replace manual browsing activities, they can certainly supplement the information gathering and collection that is important to professionals as well as casual Internet users. Whether you're looking for a diet of entertainment news or cutting-edge, high-technology insights, channels can play a valuable role on your computer's desktop.

Who Is Offering Channels?

Not only major corporations and news providers are offering channels, but many smaller companies and individuals have joined the fray. To get a sense of the range of channel content available, try out the search mechanism in the Active Channel Guide offered by Microsoft, which allows you to locate channel providers in a diverse range of areas.

Through the Active Channel Guide, you can subscribe to the *Traffic Station*, a personalized guide to traffic conditions all over the metropolitan United States. Get traffic reports delivered to your desktop for a quick scan before you leave on your morning commute. A personalized map, based on your submitted telephone area code, displays color-coded routes of the major traffic regions, pointing out the slow areas to be avoided. You can supplement this info with wallpaper for your desktop delivered from the Weather Channel, featuring a full-screen weather map to cue you in on approaching storms and impending travel problems.

Some of the liveliest content comes from print publications that have decided to also maintain a strong Web presence. Among the participants in this online news-stand are noteworthy publications such as *Red Herring, Rolling Stone, Mother Jones, Wired, Fast Company*, and so on. If improving the financial condition of your business or your personal situation is important, business-oriented channels abound, including Quicken.com, Financial Times, Fortune, Bloomberg News, and many independent channels. If you're interested in MIDI music, 17 channels include MIDI as part of their description.

Netscape's equivalent guide to the Netcaster world, the Channel Finder, also includes an impressive array of established companies, as well as many startups and new enterprises. ABC News, CNN, Business Week, ZDNet, and Infoseek share the rungs on the Channel Finder first-tier ladder. Drop a level deeper into the Channel Finder and you discover channels such as EventCal, a worldwide calendar of events in the arts, business, the Internet, movies, science, technology, trade shows, travel, and so on. The Adventure and Learning section includes the WITS channel (Web Interface for TeleScience), where you can get involved with a rover simulation system as used by NASA to plan the exploration of Mars. If you're interested in news, the Fox news channels offers national and international coverage of events. The Sporting News gives insights into the players and teams in every conceivable sport, with an archive, frequent contests, and a fantasy sports area. You can also subscribe to the LYCOS Direct channel and get reviews of the top Websites and the ability to create finely tuned searches. The *Fast Company* channel, discussed in Chapter 11, offers daily advice to entrepreneurs and technology-savvy business people.

You can end up with some pretty hefty downloads if you subscribe to lots of channels. Most people should be able to find five or six that closely match their interests and information needs.

Where Are Channels Headed?

Channel technology is still too new to predict its ultimate impact on the World Wide Web. Though the benefits of channel-delivered content are apparent, the shifting fortunes and directions of the Internet defy accurate forecasting, even for those who are involved with projections as a part of their livelihood. It is clear by the major players who are represented on Netcaster channels and Active Channels (and sometimes both) that many of the leading information providers in the industry think that it is important enough to warrant their participation. As a technology that requires very little expense to introduce, enterprising small companies and independent developers are establishing their own channels and trying to carve out a niche in this area before it becomes overcrowded.

Push technology is not only active on the desktop computer, but developments in the handheld computing marketplace have brought it down to the level of mobile devices, such as Microsoft's Palm PC. The term coined for this approach is "Mobile Channels." It works like this: Content subscribers who have their Palm PC synchronized with their desktop computer can uncouple the device at the end of the day and bring the channel content along for reading on the bus, plane, or train. This approach requires nothing more than a standard Channel Definition Format file, which is initially described in Chapter 1, and content transferred through Internet Explorer 4. The integration of Internet Explorer 4, the Palm PC, and the Microsoft Windows CE operating system makes information delivery to mobile professionals a simple process. Since Microsoft has signed up more than 1000 developers who are targeting applications for the mobile PC marketplace, you can expect to see many innovative approaches to applying push technology to handheld computers.

Ultimately, the success of the Web channel marketplace will depend on the creativity and spirit of the developers, as well as the acceptance of the Internet audience, many of whom will embrace the opportunity to custom tailor the information that they receive and reduce the symptoms of information overload characteristic of the wild and chaotic Web. Channels are about getting the information you want when you want it. As a developer, you can skillfully use the tools at your disposal to deliver high-quality content through channels to a global audience of subscribers. *Creating Web Channels* demonstrates how to achieve this goal.

Part One

Architecture

Adding Intelligence
to Push

The paradigms that have guided Web development for the past several years are changing under an umbrella of new standards. The latest browsers from Microsoft and Netscape change the manner in which we interact with the World Wide Web. One of the more significant changes involves the use of Web channels coupled with redesigned browser interfaces that reduce the boundaries between locally stored content and information stored on the Web. New and emerging standards and specifications—such as HTML 4.0, Extensible Markup Language, Channel Definition Format, Resource Definition Framework, Document Object Model, and the multifold implementations of Dynamic HTML—are converging to make it possible to intelligently deliver specialized Web content to the user's desktop. By subscribing to channels, users receive custom-designed information or multimedia content according to a schedule and delivery system that they select.

As a developer, you have the tools at your fingertips to accomplish previously impossible communication tasks. Dynamic HTML and Cascading Style Sheets let you precisely control the display of information onscreen, encouraging designer-inspired layouts and better integration of graphics and text. By layering objects in a Dynamic HTML document, you can create a level of interactivity equivalent to the best CD-ROM-based multimedia without requiring complex programming or the heavy use of server-side interactions.

Documents designed to these specifications can be delivered to the desktop through channels with the regularity (but not the cost) of an express delivery service. Getting information from the Internet becomes more like receiving a package on your front porch from UPS, rather than having to jump in the car, drive to the mall, and hunt around for whatever you need. Information retrieval on the Web is evolving from a hunter-gatherer model to an agricultural model. Sow your seeds through channel subscriptions and be rewarded when the crops sprout up on your desktop.

With the data structuring offered by the Resource Definition Framework and Channel Definition Format, you have the tools to accurately define the content of your Website and make documents available to both search engines and channel delivery. To offer information to specialized audiences, these approaches to *metadata* (data about data) take the Web one more step towards becoming an organized, international repository of information—closer to an electronic library than the chaotic wired newsstand that it has been in the recent past.

Approved as a World Wide Web Consortium (W3C) recommendation in mid-February 1998, Extensible Markup Language (XML) provides the framework for developers to move beyond the bare simplicity of HTML to a more flexible, more comprehensible markup language—a streamlined, Web-oriented version of SGML. This doesn't mean that HTML is going away any time soon, but that XML will be sliding into place in complementary ways as Web development advances towards better techniques for information distribution and access. Approval as a W3C recommendation means that the specification has been found stable and that it contributes to communication on the Web; with this blessing, software manufacturers will increasingly be building XML support into Internet products (many have already included XML components).

This chapter examines the architecture that supports Web channel development and the standards that support channel delivery techniques.

What Is Webcasting?

Much of the software architecture and infrastructure being developed for the Web supports a new set of technologies generally grouped under the term *Webcasting*. Webcasting is a method of delivering content across the Internet based on the creation of Web channels that support interaction with subscribers. The movement of content is automated and it is controlled from two directions:

- Each participating Website specifies the range of content to be delivered and the normal schedule for delivery.

- Each end user subscribing to a channel specifies the method of delivery and the timing by which deliveries should be handled.

As might be expected, Microsoft and Netscape have developed different approaches to Webcasting, and each has worked to line up lists of third-party players in support of their technology. Existing push technology companies have also been working to shape their products to fit into the Microsoft or Netscape delivery mode, in some cases signing partnering deals for the inclusion of their software into the browsers or to accompany plug-ins and ActiveX modules bundled with browser products.

In the middle of the turf wars, the World Wide Web Consortium is trying to equitably deal with the proposals and standards being presented on both sides and work them into the emerging HTML 4.0 and XML standards in such a way that the Web will become more unified, rather than more fragmented by competing standards. The good news is that within those areas where agreements have been reached, there is a good deal of solid ground upon which developers can produce content in new and interesting ways. Throughout this book, we'll work to steer a course through the divergent implementations of Dynamic HTML and differing methods of Webcasting, while pointing out the areas where software producers have reached common agreement.

The Desktop Merges with the Web

Past incarnations of Web browsers used the metaphor of the voyage to describe the act of moving about the Web, stopping at points along the way to collect information and enjoy the content. Netscape's clipper ship, which appears all over its banners and pages, supports that theme, as does calling the browser *Navigator*. Images of sea captains setting off to see what beasts lurk at the unmapped fringes of the world mix with animated logos—when Navigator is working properly, the Netscape "N" floats amidst a swift-moving barrage of asteroids and comets as you download files and jump from site to site. Maybe the mixed metaphors of ancient mariner and cosmic traveler aren't really so far apart. Microsoft echoes the theme with its orbiting satellites circling a globe that regularly morphs into an "e" for Explorer, one more extension of the browser as a tool for exploration.

To experience the Web, you travel through a matrix of interconnected sites. Instead of loading your vessel with bolts of silk and jars of spices, you fill your hard drive with audio clips, Acrobat documents, saved HTML files, and downloaded images. At the end of the journey, after you've logged off from your network connection, you can sample the collected booty at your leisure.

Within the Webcasting view of information delivery, files come to you. This new model for information delivery on the Web may need a change of symbols. One way to visualize the information flow is to picture a news editor sampling a number of incoming news wire feeds; from the universe of news information, the editor just receives and sorts through the content received through subscription. With push technology and Web channels, you no longer need to deliberately set out to retrieve information. You subscribe to a channel and the content comes to you. How often and in what form you receive the content is up to you (depending on the update schedules offered by the Web channel provider and your preferences).

Network administrators in charge of handling company-wide intranets can use Webcasting to perform dynamic updates to applications installed on workgroup members' machines, as well as distribute groupware components to be used by project team members. The Netscape approach supports the use of Netcaster to maintain a set of replicated information files, customized according to users' preferences, and place them on the network server in an accessible location. Network users logged in to the server can then gain access to their email, important HTML documents, bookmarked content, and other files without needing to physically transport these files on a portable laptop or on their remote desktop machine. Netscape likens this approach to the roaming feature provided on a cellular phone. Implementing this approach requires using Netscape's SuiteSpot server software in combination with Netscape Communicator.

Administrators can also use the broadcast features of Webcasting to alert workgroup members to company-wide issues or important events. Unlike the passive approach offered by email, which requires users to open and read their email messages from an application, notices delivered through Webcasting can interact with users' computer desktops and incorporate multimedia elements to gain attention. Play a MIDI synthesizer melody to announce a department meeting or shoot an animated comet across the desktop to catch the user's eye. These kind of direct, attention-grabbing techniques make more sense in the captive confines of an intranet, rather than the more open framework of the Internet, where such desktop pyrotechnics would be considered obtrusive by most computer users.

As a Web developer, this changing model offers you a variety of possibilities, as well as abundant opportunities to go completely off track. To keep subscribers, you need to carefully consider the type of content you are offering—more so than you would in a conventional Website where users are less likely to react negatively to content as they navigate through the barely controlled chaos of the Internet. Well-polished, carefully designed HTML and XML pages with worthwhile information will encourage subscribers to keep the channel open to your site. Ill-conceived, badly designed material will be greeted with all the fondness of those supermarket flyers that get stuffed in your mailbox each week. With Web channels, users offer you open access to their desktops, giving you the opportunity to leave them informative and entertaining packages to open and enjoy.

The clarion call to action revolves around a set of interlocking standards and technologies that offer you, as a developer, the means to provide information that is highly personalized for individual users. The layout of the information can be personalized through the use of DHTML and style sheets. The content can be personalized through the subscription process and the programmability of the document's elements. Rather than providing generalized, bland Web content designed for mass audiences, you can skillfully target the precise interests and requirements of your audience in a manner that hasn't been possible before. This book demonstrates the techniques needed to accomplish this, and offers case studies of how different companies have used Webcasting through channels successfully.

Microsoft Explorer 4.0 and the Active Desktop

The version 4.0 release of Microsoft Internet Explorer comes with built-in capabilities to support Web channels. You have the option of installing the Explorer browser in standalone mode or installing the full Active Desktop, which turns your computer desktop into a seamless environment where the difference between a locally stored file and a Web-resident file becomes transparent.

Within this model, objects appear on the desktop as they are used or needed. A Channel Bar, one of the new features of this release, provides controls over the content delivery mechanism from a selection of Web channels—each channel appears as a button on the bar. You can choose from the defaults offered by Microsoft, including channels for Disney and MTV, or add your own channels to sites that provide specialized content that suits your interests. Figure 1.1 shows the desktop appearance with Internet Explorer installed and the Channel Bar visible.

Microsoft has designed Explorer v4.0 to support Channel Definition Format (CDF), a standard that has been submitted to the W3C to become a part of the Extensible Markup Language. Essentially, CDF provides file information that specifies the characteristics of a Web channel. Using Microsoft's CDF model, any Website on the Internet can create the necessary file to offer content through a Web channel. This method of delivering content is commonly called *Webcasting*. The technique employed by CDF does not require any additional server support beyond the specifications included in the CDF, making this method more accessible to Web developers than forms of push technology that require expensive server software.

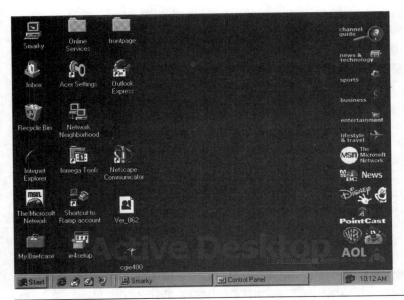

Figure 1.1 Microsoft Internet Explorer 4.0 desktop.

The meeting of the desktop and the browser as implemented in Internet Explorer is a dramatic shift in the way Web interactions take place. An equivalent shift needs to be made by developers working in this new environment. Web channels won't replace conventional Web surfing expeditions, but by gaining subscribers to a Web channel you can provide targeted, accountable proof of the popularity of your site. Building a subscription base can be as important as developing readership for a newspaper or periodical, and being able to measure the subscriber base could be an important incentive to the sponsorship of a site by advertisers and supporters.

Netscape Netcaster and the Webtop

In their own parallel universe, Netscape has also developed a model for integrating the computer desktop with extended browser functions. Their approach to this technology is a component add-on to the Netscape Communicator suite called *Netcaster*. Netscape has developed an approach that lets you create what they call a *Webtop*, basically using the computer desktop as a landing pad for incoming channel content. A navigation bar called the *Channel Finder* lets you arrange a selection of ready-made channels or define additional channel content using any provider that offers HTML documents in the appropriate format. Figure 1.2 shows the Channel Finder as it appears on the desktop.

As with the Microsoft offering, many different features are provided to allow the delivery and appearance of the channel content to be customized to a user's

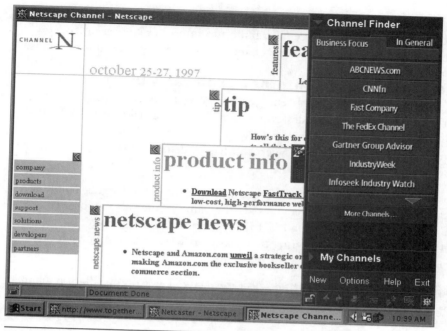

Figure 1.2 Netscape Navigator with Channel Finder displayed.

preferences. Netscape's Channel Finder also includes a built-in tuner for Marimba Castanet, so channel content can also be accepted from Castanet servers. The method for creating channels using Netscape's Netcaster uses a distinctly different approach than does Microsoft, even though many of the underlying concepts and the delivery strategy are similar. Examples of how to develop channels for both environments are provided later in this book.

Tuning in to Channels

To tune in to Web channels, you need a properly configured, current-generation browser that can be set up to receive new content directly to the desktop of your computer. Optionally, you can configure your browser to notify you of new content, which you can then retrieve at your convenience. The approaches designed into both Microsoft's and Netscape's browsers fully support online or offline viewing of content and can be set up to accept channel content in the background so that you don't disrupt other computer activities that are taking place.

The minimum price of admission for automatic Web channel access is that you must have either Microsoft Internet Explorer 4.0 or Netscape Navigator 4.0

installed, with the necessary features for each enabled. The following sections examine how channel features have been built into Internet Explorer and Communicator and how you can access channel content and set up subscriptions.

Channels in Microsoft Internet Explorer 4.0

Microsoft has invested considerable energy in creating a model for Internet interactions that converts the computer desktop into a live playing field for HTML content. Websites that have been set up to deliver content on a scheduled basis are referred to as *Active Channels*, and Microsoft has trademarked the phrase to make sure you don't forget whose idea it is.

Microsoft is still giving away its Web browser software (and forging bundling deals with Internet Service Providers all over the planet). Internet Explorer is available as a reasonably sized download (5.13Mb) from the Microsoft site. In response, in early 1998 Netscape began offering their basic browser and communications package for free, as well.

If you install Internet Explorer and select the Active Desktop installation, channel support is automatically installed, and each time you restart your computer, a Channel Bar appears on the desktop. A number of Active Channel sites appear on the bar by default, but you can modify the channels that you want to access by dragging and dropping links from a Website to the Channel Bar. Alternately, many sites include the Add Active Channel logo (provided by Microsoft) and associated code to install the site with a single click.

Installing the full Active Desktop option causes the Internet Explorer software to modify the shell for accessing your file system and to perform a number of fairly substantial configuration and setup changes to the Windows95 environment. The application does include an uninstall module; on the first system that I attempted to install Internet Explorer on I had to take advantage of the uninstall to remedy seemingly unresolvable problems with the application on an older 100MHz Pentium system. I strongly recommend that you tune and optimize your system and also remove any troublesome software components before installing Internet Explorer. A second installation to a newer 133MHz Pentium system went like clockwork, and I've detected no problems on this second system since IE4 wove its tentacles into the soft underbelly of the operating system.

The essential point is: Installing IE4 is more than just a simple browser installation. Internet Explorer 4 takes over control of different parts of your operating system. Once installed, some of the familiar parts of the OS will look different and behave differently. For example, as shown in Figure 1.3, the window that displays the directories and subdirectories on your system takes on a new Internet Explorer

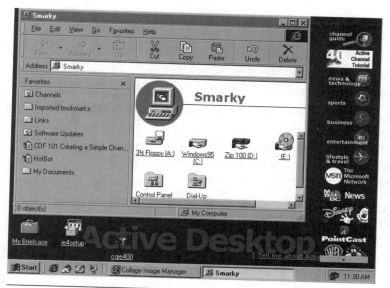

Figure 1.3 Modified File and Directory window with Internet Explorer installed.

look. You can also select the Web style desktop controls, which make your desktop elements behave more like the Web, with single-click access to files.

Since Internet Explorer 4 may be integrated into the Windows98 operating system (if Microsoft resolves its current difficulties in the court system), this should lessen the instances of conflicts and problems developing in systems running this software. In the meantime, be forewarned that older systems and systems running lots of complex software (especially earlier legacy applications) may run into problems with IE4.

Getting Listed as an Active Channel

Microsoft offers the opportunity to have your site listed in the Active Channel Guide, an online compilation of Web channels worldwide. If you join the Microsoft Site Builder Network, your membership entitles you to inclusion in the guide and the privilege of using the Microsoft Add Active Channel logo.

Microsoft emphasizes the advantages of offering your site in this manner, including the fact that through its heavily trafficked site you could potentially reach an audience of millions. Until massive numbers of sites convert their Web content to Web channel delivery, this could be an effective means for smaller sites and companies to make a major impact and add considerable momentum to their business growth.

Adding an Active Channel

Most Websites that have set up and prepared to offer subscriptions through Active Channels will place the official Microsoft Add Active Channel icon in a prominent spot on one of their initial Web pages. For example, Figure 1.4 shows *The New York Times* entry page with the Add Active Channel button ready for use.

Clicking this button gives the user a set of options to choose the appropriate subscription handling. In most cases, the minimal approach is to add an additional button to the Channel Guide bar with the new channel. In other situations, the channel content can be set up for automatic updating in the background or for providing user notification when there is new material available.

Once an Active Channel has been added to a system, it not only appears on the Channel Guide bar, but it becomes accessible through the Folder windows by opening the channel selection menus. This is one more example of Web content being merged with the conventional file system content on your system.

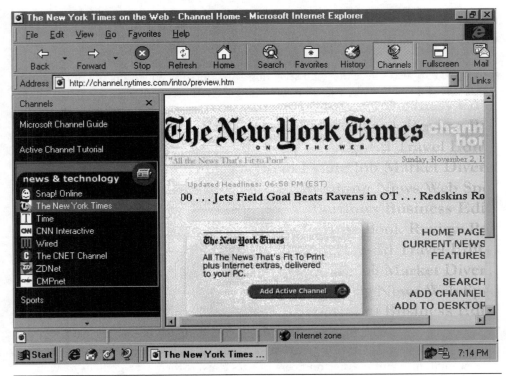

Figure 1.4 *The New York Times* **Add Active Channel.**

Pioneering Active Channel: LiveWired

The print publication *Wired* was among the first major magazines to adapt its content to the Web. It has consistently been on top of the trends in Web development and often is the first to introduce new technologies to its site. True to form, the LiveWired Active Channel was one of the first channels available through Microsoft's Channel Guide. As one option, LiveWired provides a means for displaying news and current articles on your Internet Explorer Active Desktop in the form of a screensaver. As the articles cycle through one by one, displaying teasers and quick summaries of article content, you can choose links to access the full article content. The articles displayed in the screensaver are updated from time to time when you log on to the Web.

The LiveWired content makes heavy use of Dynamic HTML to provide a genuine multimedia presentation; content options scroll across the screen, graphics are used imaginatively to draw interest to articles or present provocative statements or quotations. LiveWired employs most of the DHTML effects, including animations of graphics and text blocks, several different types of transitions, including fades and window panes, and frequent color shifts and changes. A set of navigation icons along the bottom edge of the screensaver display lets you choose among different categories of content, as shown in Figure 1.5.

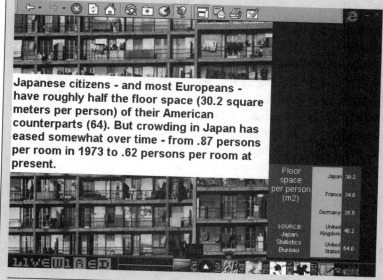

Figure 1.5 LiveWired Active Channel screensaver.

Training and Education through Active Channels

Microsoft takes advantage of the opportunity to use subscriptions through Active Channels to provide training materials and educational content to users. You can subscribe to an Active Channel tutorial series and receive updates or notifications of new content automatically. The possibilities open to developers for producing training modules and distributing them through subscription channels are considerable. Lessons and training materials can be easily packaged in DHTML format and delivered to students weekly, biweekly, or monthly.

Should You Make Your Site an Active Channel?

There are some compelling reasons that you might want to consider equipping your site for Active Channel delivery. The amount of work necessary to prepare the CDF file that becomes the link to IE4 browsers is minimal. It could require more work to update your pages to Dynamic HTML to ensure that your presentation is more lively than the typical collection of static HTML pages. But, for a minimal investment of time and effort, you can be delivering your Website through channels to an international audience. You can also still take advantage of Microsoft's listing service—the Active Channel Guide.

The Active Channel Guide is a good place to get started to see what types of sites are providing content through Active Channels and the techniques they are using to deliver material. The Active Channel Guide is one of the preinstalled options on the Channel Guide bar. Click it and you bring up a screen similar to what is shown in Figure 1.6. Notice that each site has the option of providing a brief description of its site contents.

Microsoft has the guide designed so that it automatically cycles through a list of Active Channels, periodically changing the displayed items. A thorough tour of the available Active Channels should be your first checklist item if you're considering converting your site. Offering subscriptions to customers is a very effective method to keep them linked to your site and receive updates and new content from you on a regular basis. With some work and some solid content, Active Channels offers an inexpensive and far-reaching opportunity to create a working base of interested customers. Keep them entertained and informed and they'll most likely keep their Active Channel subscription to you open.

Instructions for preparing a site for Active Channel delivery appear in Part Two of this book.

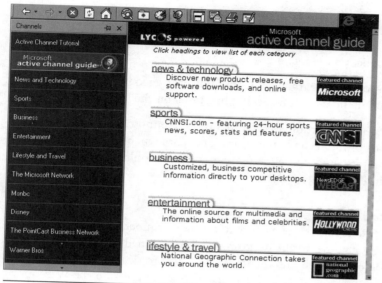

Figure 1.6 Comparing sites through the Active Channel Guide.

Netcasting with Netscape Communicator 4.0

With the release of its suite of Internet tools, referred to in their bundled form as *Netscape Communicator*, Netscape began putting together the framework for a cross-platform Internet desktop environment. The Netcaster component was added a few months after the release of Communicator version 4 and adds features that allow users to convert their computer desktops into Web channel receivers for acquiring broadcast content.

Netcaster can receive messages delivered through push technology as well as entire applications or organized collections of Website content. By setting up channel preferences, users can choose how the information is displayed and delivered. Content can be viewed while online or offline in a variety of formats.

Netscape has built the architecture for Netcaster around a set of open standards, so the developers and content producers can create material for distribution through Web channels and offer it from any conventional Web server using HTTP transfers.

Some security issues arise based on the approach that has been used, which permits the Netcaster software to perform file management operations and the launching of applications. Microsoft's Internet Explorer has similar capabilities. Both companies have taken a logical stance on security matters, as described later in this chapter. A combination of security provisions include:

- Granting rights to a trusted site to perform operating system functions.

- Requiring a specific certificate to proceed with any function involving file write operations or application launching.

For example, Figure 1.7 appears when Communicator encounters JavaScript code or a Java applet intended to run specific functions on the desktop.

While the risk of abuse is certainly a consideration, computer users who understand the implications of the security issues and take care when setting up channel access and defining rights shouldn't experience any more problems than do Internet users using pre-push technologies.

Filling the Webtop

One of the options provided by Netcaster is to create a semipermanent channel stream by anchoring a channel to the desktop. Netscape coined the term *Webtop* to describe this merging of the Web and the desktop. A Webtop can occupy all of the screen or a designated portion of it. You can also choose to position the Webtop behind other windows until you are ready to view it.

The obvious kinds of information that users might want streaming onto their Webtops through a channel are filtered news items, financial data, weather information, and so on, depending on their occupation or interests. But a channel

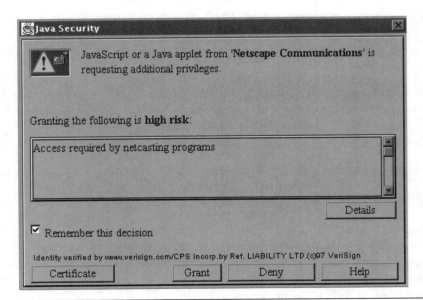

Figure 1.7 Java Security privileges when running Netcaster.

Webtop could be used for many different kinds of applications, even in an intranet environment. For example, the network administrator at a busy order-entry department could periodically push a set of relaxation and stretching exercises to order takers to cut down on the prevalence of repetitive stress injuries. Or, the desktop could be used to present short training segments to new employees to guide them through the first few weeks on a new job.

Not all channels are equally suitable for Webtop use, but Netcaster provides the flexibility of letting you make any channel a Webtop. Choose wisely. To convert a channel to Webtop use, you must first add it to the Channel Finder. You then select Options from Channel Finder and open the Display panel. The Webtop Mode display option uses the full expanse of screen real estate for the Netscape Channel and positions other windows on top, as shown in Figure 1.8.

Note that Dynamic HTML is used to control access to the sliding menus and panels that appear on the Webtop. Single-click operations can hide or display either the Channel Finder itself or the various topics (shown in a series of overlapping layers) that are provided as part of the current channel display. These topics, of course, change automatically as a part of the subscription process each day as you log on to the Internet.

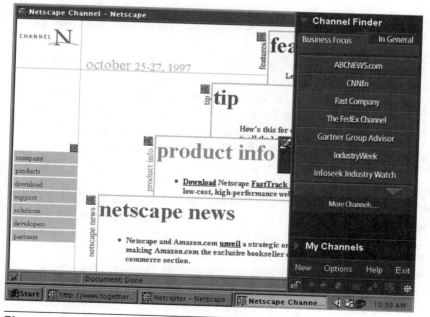

Figure 1.8 Netscape Channel as a Webtop.

Items that appear on the desktop are clearly competing for a user's active attention and this can clearly conflict with other kinds of work someone may be performing. The use of the Webtop needs to be based on respect for the viewer and awareness of basic workflow issues.

Using the Channel Finder

The Netscape Channel Finder is a tool for selecting from a range of available Web channels that have been set up for access. Figure 1.8 shows the Channel Finder as it is displayed on a typical Webtop. The Channel Finder incorporates a built-in version of the Castanet Tuner and can display any Marimba Castanet channels that have been defined and are accessible.

Subscribing to channels is a straightforward process once you have completed your obligatory registration with Netscape. Netscape also encourages you to obtain a VeriSign ID, which includes a *Digital Certificate*. The Digital Certificate verifies your identity when performing different types of interactions on the Web. Figure 1.9 shows an example of a Digital Certificate, which can be presented (digitally, as it is attached to your browser) to applications that require a positive ID. You can also request a Digital Certificate from other parties prior to downloading a file or completing a subscription.

Without a Digital Certificate, you'll be restricted to some degree as you attempt to subscribe to channels within Netcaster. In some cases, you may be prevented from performing certain operations. While Internet Explorer also uses VeriSign for a similar kind of certification process, it is more liberal in allowing subscriptions to be set up and used. In many cases, you only need to provide security validation for a particular zone (as associated with a trusted Website) to open up channel activity. Both approaches have some merit, and the degree of security you may require (or request) has much to do with the kinds of files you are downloading from different sites and your personal knowledge of the trustworthiness of the sources.

Assigning Channel Properties

When you subscribe to a channel through Netcaster, you can determine the frequency of channel updates, the manner in which channel content is displayed (including making the channel a Webtop), the caching options associated with the channel, and the time and date that channel updates occur. Figure 1.10 shows the Channel Properties panel with a selected weekly update schedule at 9:00 A.M. every Sunday. You will probably want to create a daily or even hourly update schedule for channels that you interact with for weather, news, or sports. For

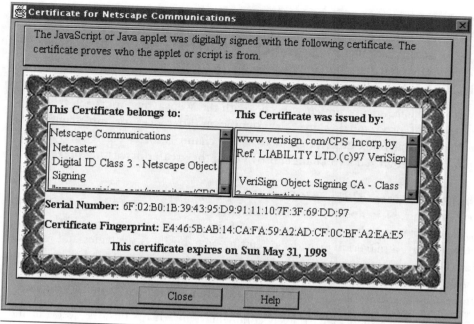

Figure 1.9 A Digital Certificate confirms your identity on the Web.

other channels that produce content that stays current for longer periods of time—such as a monthly periodical or news magazine—you can choose weekly or monthly updates as required.

Figure 1.10 Channel Properties panel in Netcaster.

Other channel options cover security and layout issues. For example, the Security tab, shown in Figure 1.11, determines the handling of Castanet items. You can choose to Accept Castanet cookies (which requires writing to your hard drive), Enable Castanet logging (to maintain a record of Netcaster interactions), and Enable Castanet profiling.

Netcaster shares many similar concepts with the Webcasting approach taken by Microsoft, but also requires some fairly significant differences for implementation. Part Three of this book describes how to set up channels for Netcaster and how to get your site recognized as a channel provider in the greater netcasting universe.

Sample Netcaster Channel: Fast Company

Like Microsoft, Netscape has formed allegiances with a number of companies to provide entertaining channel content. One of those companies is the publisher of *Fast Company*, a maverick provider of cutting-edge business strategies and philosophies. The *Fast Company* icon appears on the Netcaster Channel Finder. By clicking the Add Channel button, Netcaster guides you through registration in Netscape's Member Services, and offers you a chance to obtain a VeriSign Digital Certificate.

Fast Company provides smart, lively commentary on today's business scene, including case studies with many companies that have been willing to break the mold and try out new approaches to employee relations, customer service, company structuring,

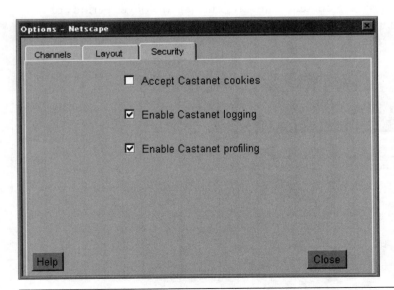

Figure 1.11 Security tab showing Castanet options.

and other aspects of business in the '90s. Its Netcaster Channel offers new content on a daily basis. A sample from one of its recent issues is shown in Figure 1.12.

Netcaster is a resource-hungry, processor-intensive application (as is Internet Explorer). My initial experience running it on a 100MHz Pentium with 16Mb of memory resulted in very slow performance and an almost constant whirring of gears as files were shuffled between disk and memory. The waits to accomplish nearly any click of a button seemed interminable—a number of times I thought the system had locked. Running Netcaster successfully requires at least 32Mb of memory and a current-generation Pentium for reasonable performance. Anything less and you will probably be disappointed.

A Convergence of Standards

The collection of new standards that makes intelligent Webcasting possible provides an interlocking set of options for the developer pondering the best way to present

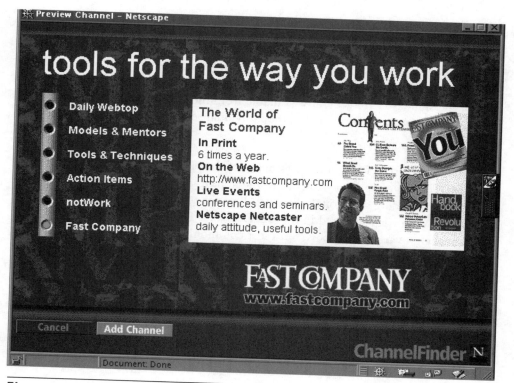

Figure 1.12 *Fast Company* **offers advice to maverick businesses.**

content through channels to users' desktops. HTML 4.0 supports a programmable document structure, called the *Document Object Model*, basically making all of the components within an HTML document available for programming through the scripting or programming language of your choice. You can use JavaScript (or JScript, in Microsoft's parlance), VBScript, Perl, or other languages in combination with typical HTML elements (such as frames, forms, or buttons) to control behavior and appearance. Everything in the HTML document can be treated as an object, allowing some impressive effects to be achieved in document presentation.

Dynamic HTML (DHTML) offers another tray in the toolbox for developers, providing a framework for manipulating the objects in an HTML document, performing animation, data handling, and other useful functions from within a downloaded HTML file—without additional server interaction. Dynamic HTML minimizes the effort required to produce a more interactive HTML document.

Other ingredients in the extensive acronym pie include RDF, CDF, XML, CSS, CSS-P, and so on. If you're not familiar with these acronyms or their practical, real-world applications, the following sections provide a capsule description for each of them.

Figure 1.13 illustrates the interrelationships between these different standards.

These Web standards are summarized in the following sections and discussed in more detail in the next two chapters of Part One. Full detailed specifications for each of the standards are generally available from the appropriate standards bodies; these contact listings are provided in the individual sections.

Dynamic HTML

Dynamic HTML (DHTML) addresses many of the problems of the earlier versions of HTML by providing a way to control the appearance of a document dynamically without downloading additional content. All of the relevant information to interact with a Web visitor is contained in the DHTML file. The interactivity can be triggered through a variety of means, but most commonly the scripting languages—such as JavaScript and VBScript—will provide the most direct means of programming the internal elements of DHTML documents.

While in its current iteration, Dynamic HTML is implemented differently by Microsoft and Netscape, the two embattled companies have pledged to support the W3C Document Object Model. This should eliminate most of the major differences between browser implementations and make DHTML a more universal standard, thus reducing developer headaches in deciding which platform to support.

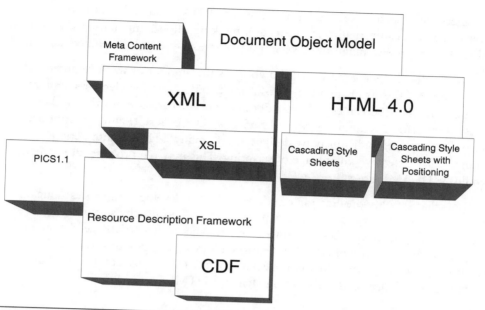

Figure 1.13 Overview of Web standards.

DHTML uses Cascading Style Sheets as the basis for determining the attributes that apply to page elements, such as text blocks, graphic positioning, and white space. To make things more interesting, these elements can be manipulated on the page in real time without further server interaction. Download times for DHTML may be initially greater than simpler HTML pages, but after the page has been downloaded, elements interact with user input almost instantly. Elements can be layered and then programmed to respond to onscreen events, such as the onMouseover event being used to create simple rollover effects (popping up a message box or highlighting the graphic beneath the mouse pointer).

One of the more interesting capabilities of DHTML is the dynamic positioning of objects. You can use this capability to apply movement to any of the objects that appear within the DHTML document, easily moving text and graphics around the screen in true multimedia fashion. You can also use this feature for the precise positioning of any of the elements on the page in combination with CSS.

Early examples of pages delivered through Web channels show excess use of this dynamic positioning feature. Menu bars and message boxes slide up and down, graphics fade in and out, text slips around the screen, the viewer gets vertigo.

Designers will hopefully relax a bit in the use of DHTML capabilities to provide screens that you can actually read instead of blinking, slip-sliding multimedia carnival rides. Dynamic positioning can be very effective if not overused; developers take heed.

Dynamic HTML's biggest initial drawback is the amount of work required to create many of the effects manually. Positioning and animating elements manually through the use of screen coordinates doesn't appeal to anyone but the hardiest (most stubborn) programming types. JavaScript (ECMAScript) and VBScript are generally only used judiciously by designers, and many DHTML interactions require fairly extensive knowledge of scripting. This may tend to discourage many would-be DHTML users.

Tools that simplify the creation of effects make the development process much more amenable to designers as well as programmers. Tools such as ExperTelligence's WebberActive, Macromedia's Dreamweaver, and Microsoft's FrontPage98 contain full support for the majority of DHTML features, allowing creation of special effects, positioning, and animation in a visual environment. These tools are discussed in greater detail in Chapter 2, "Exploring Dynamic HTML."

XML

The Extensible Markup Language (XML) bridges the simplicity of HTML with the structured benefits of SGML in a form that is specifically tailored for the Web. The limitations of HTML for supporting serious, professional-caliber, structured documentation have long been a source of frustration for technical writers, developers, information technology professionals, electronic publishers, and others. XML provides the extensibility required to provide useful functionality on the swiftly evolving Web, without the necessity for having to approve and release a new version of HTML for every additional group of tags that proves useful. XML also offers a more robust framework for large, complex document collections—an area where SGML has excelled for a number of years.

The downside of SGML, of course, has always been its complexity. Creating a cohesive document, even a simple document, is far more involved than producing an HTML document. The meticulous structuring of an SGML document is an attribute that gives the information it contains accessibility and strength, but a very lucrative consulting market rose around the creation of SGML primarily because of the difficulty in mastering the markup skills. SGML's popularity has always been highest within those kinds of organizations that produce vast and complex document collections—financial institutions, government agencies, large corporations, manufacturers of intricate machinery (such as aircraft and tanks). The structure provided by the language provides a unifying element that helps group, sort, consolidate, filter, and otherwise manipulate large bodies of information.

Unlike SGML, HTML was conceived as a quick-and-dirty method for presenting text on the Web. While it bears a family resemblance to SGML, it represents only a very tiny subset of the total capabilities of SGML. HTML succeeded well in this role, but information professionals who began trying to present more elaborate collections of interrelated information and data quickly bumped their heads on the limits of this skeletal markup language.

XML occupies the mid-ground. The fact that it is extensible means that designers and developers can tweak and adapt the markup language for specialized needs—something that has never been possible with HTML. XML bears enough of SGML's rigorous structuring to support database applications and data retrieval functions without the burdensome infrastructure of SGML (such as the necessity for specifying a DTD for even elementary documents). XML seems to be pleasing folks at both ends of the spectrum: the SGML advocates see this scaled-down language as the right way to apply SGML principles to the distribution of information on the Web. The HTML proponents see the advantages in overcoming the weaknesses of HTML and fortifying the language for more ambitious document handling. With support such as this coming from two usually forcefully opposing factions, XML appears to be destined for acceptance.

HTML succeeded to a large degree in becoming the markup language of choice on the Web because of its simplicity. Authors could easily master the limited set of tags defined for document use, and in the early rapid-growth years of the Web the tag restrictions were generally overlooked. XML will supersede HTML because it offers the flexibility of custom tag sets. Authors and designers are freed from the constraints of a one-size-fits-all model of document design and can individually construct much more elaborate forms of information delivery.

NOTE XML was developed by trimming down the features and options of the Standard Generalized Markup Language (SGML), while maintaining conformance with SGML parsers. A correctly constructed XML document, as a dialect of SGML, should be fully readable by an SGML parser. In practical use, XML documents will be accessed with software modules called *XML processors*.

XML offers the following capabilities:

- It supports the creation of individual custom tags. These tags can be used for search and retrieval functions, interactions with programming languages such as Java, and custom interactions.

- It offers a variety of ways to structure and identify data, as well as methods for interacting with databases in support of online transactions and exchanges.

- It provides a hierarchical, sequential organizational framework that can be helpful in modeling certain types of information delivery situations.

- It extends the basic framework of HTML from simple markup of text and graphics for display to providing a means for specifying types of content and logical relationships between the parts of a document.

Overall, the XML specification requires only about 10 percent of the pages necessary to codify and formalize the SGML86 standard. Document Type Definitions (DTD), a mandatory element of an SGML document, are optional for an XML document. A DTD even as an optional element opens up additional structuring options to XML developers who can use this logical, organizing framework to create and maintain sets of similarly structured documents for virtually any conceivable application.

Not everyone is wildly enthusiastic about XML. While it provides the classic, hierarchical tree-structured means for classifying and organizing information, not all information fits neatly into such a model. Ted Nelson, founder of the Xanadu Project (and the person who coined the term *hypertext*), sees the XML structure as too rigid to support many of the more interesting uses of the Web as a network of interconnected information. He favors an approach that maintains two parallel streams of data: one containing the content in textual (and graphic) form, and the other including the embedded tags that are used for displaying and categorizing the data.

The support for XML, however, seems strong enough that it will almost certainly become the successor to HTML over time. We will probably also be seeing a period where both HTML and XML documents will be prevalent. Browsers will need to include an XML parser to be able to interpret the XML content, but this capability is already present in some current browsers, such as Microsoft's Internet Explorer 4.

XML is discussed in more detail in Chapter 3, "The Enabling Standards: CDF, DOM, and RDF" and Appendix A, "HTML 4.0 and XML."

CDF

The Channel Definition Format, originally proposed to the W3C by Microsoft and supported by the release of Internet Explorer 4, draws its vocabulary from the XML standard. Essentially, CDF is an open specification that supports automated delivery of information through Internet channels. Push technologies such as Pointcast and BackWeb can be used as the delivery medium, but this standard also supports simple channel delivery of documents without requiring special server software. CDF predates the Resource Description Framework, which is described in the next section.

Microsoft adopted XML as the underpinning of CDF because it offered a natural and effective means for representing data targeted for Webcasting applications. By enthusiastically jumping aboard the XML bandwagon and integrating XML into the approach used by Channel Definition Format, Microsoft gave a big push towards industry acceptance of XML.

Microsoft's First XML Program

Even before the official approval of the working version of XML by the W3C, Microsoft was busily creating its first official XML application using the CDF specification. The approach to Active Channels incorporated into Microsoft's Internet Explorer 4.0 utilizes the Channel Definition Format as the structure to present metadata, detailed information about the contents of a Website. To interpret the information contained in a CDF file, Internet Explorer was equipped with an XML parser. The next release of Microsoft's Windows98 will include a full version of Internet Explorer 4, so the ability to interpret XML documents will be a feature of every machine that is running Windows98. In many ways, this move ensures the availability of Webcasting to the masses and will let anyone running Windows98 tune in to Active Channels. Since the simple addition of a CDF file can convert a Website to an Active Channel, developers and designers will have a simple means of distributing selected areas of their sites to anyone with a copy of Windows98 installed on his or her computer who has the Active Channels feature enabled.

The format of CDF information shouldn't look very surprising to anyone familiar with a basic HTML file. The following simple example shows how site information can be identified for channel delivery. We're not trying to launch into a tutorial this early in the book, but only wish to illustrate the elegant simplicity of a CDF file. Later chapters expand on the intricacies of CDF file creation.

```
<?XML version="1.0" RMD="NONE" ?>
<!DOCTYPE Channel SYSTEM
"http://www.lp-vt.com/delivery/channels.dtd">
<CHANNEL>
      <SCHEDULE>
            <INTERVALTIME HOUR="4"/>
            <LATESTTIME MIN="30"/>
      </SCHEDULE>
      <TITLE>Lights over the City Update</TITLE>
      <ITEM HREF="http://www.lp-vt.com/blurbs/active.htm">
            <ABSTRACT>Updates on events during the week. </ABSTRACT>
            <TITLE>Latest News from the Home Front</TITLE>
      </ITEM>
</CHANNEL>
```

This particular implementation relies on a document type definition file (channels.dtd), but use of a definition file of this type is optional for XML. If someone were to select your Active Channel based on the data that you've provided, he or she would receive any changed content indicated in the <ITEM HREF> tag every four hours.

While CDF data can be provided in concise terms in many instances, some implementations will require more complex and elaborate coding. Refer to Chapter 3, "The Enabling Standards: CDF, DOM, and RDF," for a more in-depth examination of the CDF file format.

RDF

The Resource Description Framework might at first glance appear to be a competing standard to CDF, but it actually plays a more encompassing and complementary role in the matrix of standards. RDF utilizes the syntax of XML as the transfer model, allowing a wide range of tools and code bases to be applied to defining site architecture and interactions. RDF is intended to serve as a unifying framework into which other standards, such as CDF, can be incorporated.

As an example of how RDF could be used, a developer could produce an RDF file in the form of a Java applet that could contain the entire, navigable contents of a Website. Since this file could be easily distributed, it could serve as the "keys to the kingdom" for site administrators looking for a way to make specialized content available or to provide access to certain fee-based content.

RDF was hatched within the incubator of the W3C as a part of that group's goal to incorporate more data about information content into files that are distributed across the Internet. The W3C Metadata Activity includes the RDF Working Group; some of their efforts run parallel to earlier work accomplished in setting up the PICS label, designed as a content rating system, and other attempts to establish a concise and reliable means for determining the content of Web pages.

What does all this mean to you as a developer? The architects of the RDF draft have some very specific applications in mind. Still in a working draft form, the final version of RDF will make it possible to:

- Catalog the individual items and types of information contained within a Website or on an individual Website page.

- Specify the intellectual property rights as they apply to content that appears on the Web.

- Assist intelligent software agents in retrieving customized information from the Web and exchanging that information with other parties.

- Make Internet search engines more effective by providing more precise details of site contents in a structured framework.

- Support the use of digital signature technology to open up Website activities to improved electronic commerce and private forms of collaboration.

- Offer content rating guidelines that permit both screening of material from children and identification of content for adults.

RDF enjoys wide support from leading industry companies, and as related standards and specifications are being developed, many of them are taking into account the framework that RDF provides.

DOM

The Document Object Model (DOM) takes those common elements of a typical HTML document—frames, text boxes, buttons, graphics, plug-ins, and so on—and defines them in a standard way. The goal is to create an object-oriented environment where the full range of scripting and programming languages can be brought into play to interact with these page elements. While this has been possible for some time using VBScript and JavaScript, DOM formalizes the object environment and ensures that all of these components will be accessible in a predictable and useful way. Other languages, such as Perl, Java, and so on, can interact with these elements as well.

Another of the creations of the W3C, DOM has advanced through the working draft stage and is at the final proposal stage. Since both Microsoft and Netscape have agreed to follow the Document Object Model, many of the incompatibilities that have been observed in the Microsoft and Netscape implementations of DHTML should go away.

CSS

Cascading Style Sheets are a means of specifying and changing the physical layout of an HTML document based on properties associated with particular styles. In the past, each browser had a different—though generally similar—way to display each specific element tagged with HTML code. For example, the <H1> heading tag looked almost identical as displayed by most of the major browsers, though small variations were apparent from browser to browser.

CSS, incorporated as part of the approved HTML 3.0 specification, lets the physical appearance of content appearing between tags be controlled by definitions contained in a referenced style sheet. For example, if you want to bump the point size of the <H1> heading up 6 points and color the text Cyan, you can apply a style sheet that defines the tag as such. The term *cascading* refers to the fact that if you don't specifically define an element (for example, the <H2> heading tag), a default style sheet definition will be applied to control the display of the element. In other words, if you don't define a style for something, the control cascades to the next (default) style sheet identified.

Using Cascading Style Sheets you can:

- Control positioning of elements on a page
- Define the colors that apply to fonts, rules, backgrounds, or other HTML components
- Specify and manipulate white space within a document layout
- Control margins and text columns
- Determine individual font usage within a document
- Vary font sizes

If you've used a word processor that incorporates style sheet tags (such as Microsoft Word) or a typical desktop publishing application (such as Adobe FrameMaker), you're undoubtedly familiar with the concept behind the use of style sheets. The style sheet exerts popular control over the appearance of tagged elements. Swapping one style sheet for another can radically change the appearance of a document, and most applications of this type offer a means of attaching a different style sheet or copying style sheet tag definitions from one document to another.

The same basic principles apply to the use of Cascading Style Sheets. An HTML document can reference a style sheet located at a particular URL on the Web, and the attributes associated with that style sheet will be immediately applied to a displayed document. This opens up the possibility for professional design skills to be incorporated into Web page design by simply establishing a link to a carefully crafted style sheet. It also makes it possible for users to select and apply their own style sheets according to personal preferences, essentially overriding the wishes of the original document designer. Suppose your vision isn't that great and you want to bump up all the point sizes displayed in a document by 25 percent. You can reference a custom-designed style sheet that will do this even if the original page designer thought it looked elegant to present the body text in 8-point Bodoni. Through style sheets, the content of an HTML document becomes malleable. You can shape the onscreen elements in a wide variety of ways—both for enhancement and for the possible detriment of accepted design principles.

Both Internet Explorer 3.0 and Netscape Navigator 3.0 support CSS, but Netscape also introduced a variation called *JavaScript-controlled Style Sheets* that has yet to gain approval within an HTML specification, but is supported in current-generation Netscape browsers.

As with many of the other standards and specifications discussed in this chapter, CSS works effectively with today's browsers and will also play an important role in standards such as XML. CSS provides the presentation details to shape and position content that is logically structured within an XML document; the two standards provide complementary roles in specifying Web-delivered information and determining how it will be presented onscreen. Used together, XML and CSS simplify the creation of Web documents.

CSS-P

Cascading Style Sheets are taken one step further in the form of Cascading Style Sheets with Positioning. CSS-P allows precise positioning of objects within an HTML document as specified by a number of different coordinate systems, and can also be used in combination with Dynamic HTML to move elements around a page in real time. You can animate a series of letters through DHTML controls, making them fly around a page or reassemble themselves upon a graphic object. CSS-P is defined within HTML 4.0, and Microsoft's Internet Explorer 4.0 supports CSS-P interactions.

Since the positioning of elements is very important to many different functions within DHTML, CSS-P plays an important role in determining the interaction of Web page components.

Security Issues

Both Netscape's and Microsoft's approaches to Webcasting open up significant security issues. Part of the strategy of this technology is to be able to perform application updates for users in the background—something that is controllable in an intranet environment, but far more dangerous in the open savannas of the Internet. Fears of rogue applications destroying hard disk contents after being installed through a Web channel are threatening to many users who might resist ever using this technology. In response to security concerns, both Microsoft and Netscape have taken measures to provide individual control over how downloaded applications can be run on the desktop and how file write operations will be handled.

As a developer, you need to pay careful attention to those security issues that will be of prime importance to your audience. Not everyone is going to open up their system and allow you to write to their disk drives and run downloaded applications on the desktop. By designing into your content a method for providing alternatives to information delivery to more security-conscious members of your subscriber base, you can get your message out to the broadest possible group. Using digital signatures attached to your files is another means of authenticating the validity of content from a site. Sometimes just pointing out the security considerations to Web subscribers and the protections that are built into the delivery mechanism can overcome the reluctance to allow access to an individual's system.

As part of Netscape's approach, when loading Netcaster the program informs you when any Java applet or JavaScript routine poses a potential security risk. You have the option of granting or denying the pending operation and you can instruct Netcaster to remember the selection you have made for future use.

Microsoft offers an equivalent approach to Netscape for handling security, but offers an additional option—the recognition of zones that the user specifies to determine sites that have trustworthy content. By granting the appropriate privileges through zones, you can allow applications to be run on your desktop so that content received through channels can be accessed freely.

Security will remain an important issue as a part of offering content via Web channels. The more interesting applications require fairly significant access to a user's system, and users will need assurance that receiving content from channels will not threaten their system integrity.

Digital Certificates

The use of Digital Certificates to confirm your identity and allow specific kinds of transactions to take place has also been implemented as a part of Communicator's

Netcaster. Digital Certificates are issued by VeriSign and attached to the browser through an online registration process followed by some additional setup instructions that are delivered to an email address that you provide. When the process has been completed, you will be issued a *Private Key*. With your password, selected during the registration process, and the embedded browser key, VeriSign can validate your identity. Netscape describes it as an electronic driver's license that cannot be forged.

The identity of Web parties from whom you may be receiving channel content can also be verified by the same process. A certificate can be viewed prior to granting rights for a download. This method of identification will continue to gain importance as electronic commerce becomes more prevalent and more users choose the Internet as a channel for receiving software applications and useful applets.

Summary

The current mix of standards and specifications address many of the problems that designers and developers have grappled with since the birth of HTML. You can now put carefully laid out content—courtesy of style sheets and Dynamic HTML— onto someone's desktop through push technology and Web channels, thanks to CDF and Netcaster. As XML gains acceptance, you will be able to skillfully structure collections of documents so that they are more easily retrieved and their content more accessible.

To users and Websters around the globe, this technology clearly makes it seem as though the Web is set up to respond to our bidding. If you enjoy *The New York Times* on Sunday morning, why not have it delivered to your computer desktop instead of having to haul it off the front porch covered with rain or snow or muddy paw prints? The subscriber model lets you carefully specify your interests, choose the mode of delivery that makes the most sense for you, and settle back to enjoy the flow of incoming information. Since the information can be delivered in the background while you're doing something else on your computer or doing something else in another part of your home or office, the computer becomes more like an appliance, responding to your needs without requiring active monitoring or flurries of keystrokes to initiate the retrieval of content.

Developers and Web designers now have the opportunity to appeal to their audience using more persuasive and intelligent presentation techniques than offered by elementary HTML. The caliber of design possibilities comes much closer to those time-honored techniques enjoyed by print publications, with the added benefit of interactivity. The multimedia capabilities can elevate documents delivered through

Web channels to new visual and aural heights. All of these new possibilities raise the bar a notch for those sites competing for an audience and a portion of the steadily increasing electronic commerce pie. Content alone won't make a successful Website; the presentation and aesthetic framework within which the content is delivered matter equally. And the accessibility of information—both for mainstream and physically challenged Web visitors—ranks right up there on the triad of information design. Worthwhile content skillfully presented in an accessible and customizable manner—those are the elements that will separate the most effective Websites from onslaughts of gray flannel pretenders.

The first generation of push technology splashed messages and banners over the desktop in a fairly random way—sometimes using screensaver metaphors to plaster commercial messages or news blurbs or unconnected snips of content on the screen. The model has become much more sophisticated with second-generation push technology—instead of being distracted by bits and pieces of data while you're trying to work, you can collect, organize, and store the kinds of information you're actually interested in. You don't have to look at or pay any attention to the incoming files until you're ready to. Ideally, the content you've requested is there when you're ready to use it—whether an article on alternative health care, a news announcement from a high-tech trade publication, or a catalog of products from your favorite outdoor recreation company.

Expect to see a good deal of abuse of push technology in the beginning. Companies that have not yet adjusted to the social fabric of the Web will try to use it as they've used other media for advertising. Loud music and fast-moving graphics and strident announcers compete for your attention. Attempting to infuse carbonated sugar water and sports shoes with supernatural qualities may be workable on television, but I suspect that most Web viewers will quickly tune out those channels that bombard them with thinly disguised sales pressure. Let's hope that intelligence and good taste win out. As developers, you have the opportunity to help shape this new medium.

Mastering the techniques for working in the current-generation Web requires first understanding the architecture and framework that underlies push technology and Dynamic HTML, and then becoming familiar with the tools and techniques for delivering content over Web channels. The remainder of Part One discusses the framework. Part Two, *Active Channels*, explores the applications designed for creating DHTML content and delivering it through Microsoft's channel medium, Active Channels. Part Three, *Netcaster*, offers a channel-building tour that focuses on the Netscape Netcaster model. Part Four, *Case Studies*, offers a number of case studies showcasing real-world solutions to taking advantage of the best aspects of push and Webcasting.

Exploring Dynamic HTML

This chapter introduces the basic features and characteristics of Dynamic HTML, with additional attention given to those features that can be effectively used for delivering content through Web channels. Cascading Style Sheets are examined, the Document Object Model is introduced, and basic animation techniques are explored. Some of the most capable tools for producing DHTML content are also presented.

Dynamic HTML offers a means for developers to exercise unprecedented control over the contents of an HTML page by programming the behavior of individual components. Since DHTML doesn't mandate a particular language, developers can adopt the scripting or programming language that they are most familiar and comfortable with and immediately apply their knowledge to controlling actions on the page. To simplify page setup, a number of tools have also appeared on the market that support the creation of DHTML documents without requiring scripting to control object interaction. Among the leaders, WebberActive by ExperTelligence, Dreamweaver by Macromedia, and FrontPage98 by Microsoft all provide fully interactive development environments and let you control the capabilities of DHTML in a direct and simple manner.

Web channels and Dynamic HTML go together naturally. Dynamic HTML provides an exceptionally compact way to design documents and organize content in a highly interactive manner. You can take full advantage of layered information, visual cues to guide user navigation, collapsing and expanding document structures, popup messages and rollovers, and other classic hypertext features without requiring multiple pages or excessive server interaction. For this reason, Dynamic HTML has been used heavily for delivering content through Web channels; the resulting documents open up easily on the desktop and conveniently allow offline viewing in most instances, since they are generally self-contained. There is no reason you can't use standard (HTML 3.0 and earlier) documents with Web channels, but if your audience is equipped with the requisite browsers to tune in to channel content, it makes sense to deliver DHTML files, since they are automatically supported within this framework.

Some tools, such as ExperTelligence's WebberActive, integrate channel development with the construction of DHTML pages. This integration extends through every part of the editing process and allows developers to define the channel details along with the editing of the page content. Pages can be tested with an embedded Internet Explorer preview display. The contents of a CDF file—which specifies the properties of an Active Channel—can be created within the editor and examined or modified as necessary.

Although Microsoft Internet Explorer 4 and Netscape Navigator 4 both support Dynamic HTML, critical differences exist between their implementations. This unfortunate situation should be alleviated in the near future as both Microsoft and Netscape embrace the Document Object Model (described briefly in this chapter and discussed further in Chapter 3, "The Enabling Standards: CDF, DOM, and RDF") that standardizes the object interaction within a DHTML document and specifies the mechanisms available to control these objects.

If you're developing to reach the large installed base of browsers, including the initial releases of Netscape Communicator 4.0 and Microsoft Internet Explorer 4.0, the situation is somewhat difficult. Developers have long been faced with the challenge of selecting a single platform to target development or to provide alternate content in parallel to match browser capabilities. There are trade-offs either way. In some ways, developing channel content lets you optimize your delivery specifically for the target platform. For example, if you're authoring pages for a Netscape Netcaster channel, you can choose those DHTML features that are specific to the Netscape implementation. Similarly, developers working on Active Channels often use the full range of DHTML features supported by IE4, including transitions and filters, knowing that this content is designed for playback in the Microsoft environment. You can choose to either support the native playback environment or you can author to produce channel content that can be delivered effectively on both platforms.

If you decide to support playback on multiple platforms, in many cases you will want to use one of the applications designed to construct pages that run effectively under all of the major browsers. The latest generation of Web development tools—such as Macromedia Dreamweaver and mBed Interactor—use JavaScript function libraries to generate content suitable for both platforms. Alternatively, you can program using the minimal subset of DHTML features common to both browsers, choose one platform over another for development (Navigator still enjoying the larger installed base), or develop ingenious Web pages that detect the installed browser and present only DHTML content tailored for Navigator or Internet Explorer, as is appropriate (as do the commercial applications designed for this purpose). Or, if you're patient, you can wait and target your content for the upcoming generation of browsers that will have eliminated the disparities between DHTML handling by following the Document Object Model.

Dynamic HTML Overview

Dynamic HTML, or DHTML as we'll refer to it throughout this chapter, was introduced as a means for circumventing one of the most troublesome problems of standard HTML—the inability to dynamically change content once a document file was loaded into the browser. Web-page interactivity suffered as a result of this constraint until DHTML provided avenues to work around the problem, allowing you to:

- Precisely position and layer objects on a Web page.

- Interact with styles (as defined by Cascading Style Sheets).

- Perform multimedia effects, including graphic animation and dynamic object repositioning.

- Handle data interactions from within a document using data-binding techniques.

- Respond to a variety of events, such as mouse movements and key presses.

- Alter page content in a variety of ways even after the document file has been loaded into the browser.

Many of the most powerful features of Dynamic HTML are made possible through the use of the Document Object Model, a standard that defines the means and methods by which the appearance and behavior of objects in a DHTML document can be manipulated. Simply put, this means you can put almost everything on a Web page under programmable control. The necessary elements to manage interactive behavior are embedded in the DHTML document and its associated scripts and style sheets. Reloading a page is not required to change the appearance; instead, content can be layered and the layers displayed in sequence (for effects such as rollovers and popup messages), or objects can be dynamically moved about the page under script control. The DHTML page itself becomes a dynamic multimedia engine, capable of responding to user actions, cycling through multimedia effects, performing data operations, and so on. Since all of these tasks can be performed without additional server interactions (as are necessary, for example, if you're controlling responses to user actions through a CGI server-side script), DHTML documents are ideal for offline viewing. This also makes them ideal for Web channel delivery, since the page contents and the embedded interactions exist in a single self-contained package.

Defining Dynamic HTML

Coming up with a precise definition of Dynamic HTML can be difficult. It's not a standard or a specification. It's not a product. Maybe the best way to describe it is to say: Dynamic HTML is an enabling technology that is based on several other technologies. The technology works if you have a browser with built-in support and a scripting or programming language that can be used to control the behavior of elements in a document. Several standards provide an interwoven mesh of supporting architecture to enable the use of Dynamic HTML, including HTML 4.0, the Document Object Model, CSSP, and XML. Beyond this, however, Dynamic HTML is essentially a concept, a means of interacting with HTML elements that have already been loaded by the browser. The supporting technologies make this possible. The related standards and specifications provide the framework. While this a relatively simple idea, it has far-reaching implications, as you will see in the examples throughout this book.

Drop a DHTML file onto someone's desktop—as you can with channel delivery through both Internet Explorer and Netscape Netcaster—and he or she has a fully integrated, self-running presentation vehicle. Many of the kinds of effects that used to require plug-ins or ActiveX components can be simply and compactly constructed in DHTML. The Web becomes simpler and content more universal. Bandwidth requirements are reduced since server interactions are less necessary. While not the ultimate panacea for content delivery, DHTML is a giant step forward in making the Web a more interesting and interactive place.

This section offers a fundamental introduction to Dynamic HTML, the favored tool for developing pages intended for Web channel delivery. We assume that you have some experience and background with basic HTML and script languages such as JavaScript or VBScript. Most of the examples in this book rely on Dynamic HTML techniques for constructing documents, so you should be able to learn a fair amount about the language by examining the examples and case studies provided. If you'd like a more extensive survey of the possibilities offered by Dynamic HTML, Steve Holzner's *Guide to Dynamic HTML* (John Wiley and Sons Inc., 1997) provides additional details and examples.

Web Channels and DHTML

Web channels and DHTML form a powerful and complementary technology. While neither of these technologies is dependent on the other, when combined they place a range of persuasive and highly effective tools in the hands of Web authors. Consider the types of tasks that you can accomplish with minimal programming effort using Web channels and DHTML:

- Personalize content for individual users or groups of users and deliver it directly to their desktops.

- Script the behavior of objects on a Web page so that the intelligence of the document resides completely on the client side—an important factor for presenting material for offline viewing.

- Perform data-binding operations from a Web page, opening up a wide range of online transactions, including improved forms of electronic commerce. Data retrieved from a live database can be reflected dynamically within a page.

- Create pages that interact more closely with the user so that only the information that is desired is visible. Dense and complex documents can be efficiently delivered through a channel with less bandwidth requirements and fewer files than would be necessary for conventional HTML content.

These benefits will become more apparent as you work with the examples in this book and explore the case studies that appear in Part Four, *Case Studies*.

Dynamic HTML Characteristics

While Dynamic HTML is not enormously complex, it is based on some unique concepts that provide many of its fundamental capabilities. The following sections examine the basic concepts underlying Dynamic HTML.

Using DHTML with Style Sheets to Change Page Design

One of the cornerstones of working with DHTML involves the use of Cascading Style Sheets. The definitions of attributes contained in a style sheet dictate the appearance of individual elements in an HTML document. You can abruptly change the appearance of every aspect of a document by switching from one style sheet to another. Style sheet assignments can be placed under program control through a script. For example, you could create a button on a Web page that when pushed would redefine every element of a page by attaching a different style sheet to that page. For example, an <H1> tag could be changed from black type to cyan, and a paragraph could be defined as centered rather than left-justified. Style definitions can also be changed inline using tags embedded in a document. The term *cascading* refers to the fact that style definitions can be added and subtracted from a document, composing a changing and adaptable set of definitions that can be manipulated in a variety of ways. Looked at another way, through cascading, Web authors can tinker with individual parts of a style sheet without changing the coherency of the whole. For example, a referenced style sheet in a document might only contain a half dozen new definitions for attributes. These are immediately applied to the document presentation, but all of the prior style sheet elements remain intact. Or, several partial style sheets can be referenced and combined to provide a single contiguous set of styles.

The ability to dynamically alter the elements of a page on-the-fly can be used to simply control page layout or, more ambitiously, provide a level of interactivity by modifying style sheet settings programmatically. If you want to provide a large font option for your visually impaired Website viewers, you can accomplish this by attaching a style sheet that modifies font sizes while still maintaining some aesthetic balance in your overall page layout. Or, you could create an iconized page layout to simplify navigation for visitors for whom English is a second language. If you wanted to get even more elaborate, you could save a visitor's style sheet preferences as a cookie file on his or her drive and reference this file to restore the appropriate style sheet the next time he or she visits. One aspect of providing personalized content on the Web is giving the viewer a range of options for viewing and navigating. This takes time and energy to set up, of course, but most of your Web visitors should respond positively to the opportunity to sample information according to their preferences.

Styles can be referenced on a page through each of the following means:

<STYLE> tag. Assigns styles to elements globally within complete HTML documents or sections within documents.

Embedded STYLE attribute. Assigns style options to specific individual elements in an HTML document, such as a list item, heading, or bulleted item. These inline entries override settings in an assigned global style sheet.

<LINK> tag. Accesses an external style sheet that contains definitions that will be applied to the current HTML document.

@import function. Identifies a URL pointing to a style sheet file that can be imported for use with the current HTML document.

<STYLE> Tag The <STYLE> tag identifies and defines a set of style sheet rules to apply to the current document. In a simple example, the following HTML code establishes the rules that apply to three specific HTML tags:

```
<HTML>
<HEAD><TITLE>Applying Styles with the STYLE tag</TITLE>
<STYLE>
     H1    {
          font-size: 30pt;
          font-style: italic;color: teal;
          }
     H2    {
text-align: center;
color: red;}
     BLOCKQUOTE {font-size: 40pt}
</STYLE>
</HEAD>
<BODY>
<H1>Please give us your attention!</H1>
<H2>Thanks for your time.</H2>
<BLOCKQUOTE>Styles alter properties of tags.</BLOCKQUOTE>
</BODY>
</HTML>
```

The resulting screen display, shown in Figure 2.1, demonstrates how the style sheet rules produced variations in the way the H1, H2, and BLOCKQUOTE tags displayed text.

The displayed text in the browser window uses the style definitions that were embedded within the STYLE tags. The H1 tagged text appears as 30-point text in italic. Though you can't see it in the grayscale diagram, the font is also displayed using the color teal. Similarly, the H2 tag was redefined to center the text and display it as red type. BLOCKQUOTE bumped the point size to 40-point type. Any other style sheet elements that were not included in the set of rules that appeared within the STYLE tags automatically use the default definitions.

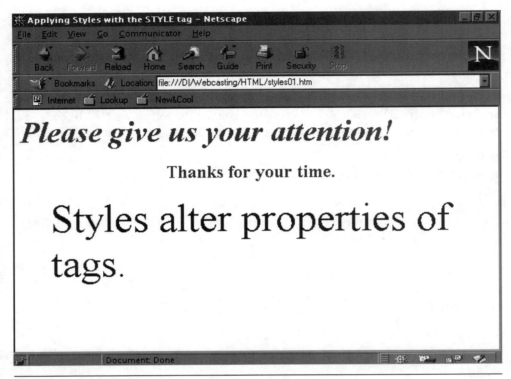

Figure 2.1 Style sheet changes to common tags.

Embedded Style Attributes For economy and expediency, you can include changes in the style sheet definitions as inline entries in your HTML code. These redefinitions of the style sheet values will be immediately applied to the designated objects as shown in the browser window. For example, the following code displays the text the same as in Figure 2.1, but in this case, the inline embedded style attributes determine the display values:

```
<HTML>
<HEAD><TITLE>Applying Styles with inline entries</TITLE>
</HEAD>
<BODY>
<H1 STYLE=font-size: 30pt; font-style: italic; color: teal>
Please give us your attention!</H1>
<H2 STYLE=text-align: center; color: red>Thanks for your time.</H2>
<BLOCKQUOTE STYLE=font-size: 40pt>Styles alter properties of tags.</BLOCKQUOTE>
</BODY>
</HTML>
```

As in the previous section, the style settings cause the H1 tagged text to appear as teal, italicized, 30-point type. The H2 tag centers and renders the text in red. The BLOCKQUOTE tag expands the font size to 40 point. These reset values will apply to any later tagged text without having to redefine the style settings. In other words, the new settings become the default values used in the document until a script or other inline attribute entry redefines the individual tag properties.

Attaching Style Sheets with the LINK Tag Style sheets can be attached to a document and used to apply a collection of properties globally by using the LINK tag. This is one of the simpler ways to produce sets of internally consistent documents. For example, if a site or designer offered a professionally produced style sheet for public access at a particular URL, you could apply the same style sheet values to your pages by referencing the URL through the LINK tag. The following example shows how you could attach a style sheet called magicsty.css to the same document we've been working with for the past two examples:

```
<HTML>
<HEAD><TITLE>Applying Styles through a LINK</TITLE>
<LINK REL="stylesheet" TYPE="text/css" HREF="magicsty.css">
</HEAD>
<BODY>
<H1>Please give us your attention!</H1>
<H2>Thanks for your time.</H2>
<BLOCKQUOTE>Styles alter properties of tags</BLOCKQUOTE>
</BODY>
</HTML>
```

This example assumes the style sheet is stored locally where it can be accessed without having to specify a path. The contents of magicsty.css could be as simple as the following listing:

```
magicsty.css
/* This style sheet includes expanded and colorized text. */
H1    {
      font-size: 30pt;
      font-style: italic;
      color: teal;
      }
H2    {
text-align: center;
color: red;}
BLOCKQUOTE {font-size: 40pt}
```

During the loading of the HTML document this style sheet file would be referenced and the style settings applied to each of the indicated tags. A similar method of bringing in a set of styles to a document is the @import function, which is described in the following section.

Using the @import Function The @import function resides between the STYLE tags, but instead of specifying tag properties item by item, it references a URL where the style sheet can be accessed and applied. For example, the following listing shows the magicsty.css style sheet being applied by means of the @import function:

```
<HTML>
<HEAD><TITLE>Applying Styles with the @import function</TITLE>
<STYLE TYPE="text/css">
     @import url(http://www.styworld.org/magicsty);
</STYLE>
</HEAD>
<BODY>
<H1>Please give us your attention!</H1>
<H2>Thanks for your time.</H2>
<BLOCKQUOTE>Styles alter properties of tags</BLOCKQUOTE>
</BODY>
</HTML>
```

Once again, the style sheet attributes imported through the magicsty.css reference are assigned to the H1, H2, and BLOCKQUOTE tags, making them display in the same manner as they did in the previous examples. Referenced style sheets define attributes throughout an entire document, but tags are overridden by any individual entries that appear within the STYLE tags. Inline embedded style definitions override both those elements that appear within the STYLE tags and referenced style sheet attributes. You can essentially supersede any active definition using an inline style sheet setting.

Using Cascading Style Sheets with Positioning

The successor to CSS1, the officially certified release of Level 1 Cascading Style Sheets, CSS-P (Cascading Style Sheets with Positioning) enjoys reasonably consistent support in the version 4 releases of both Internet Explorer and Navigator. The Positioning addition to this standard refers to the use of an x/y coordinate system to pinpoint the location of page elements.

CSS-P supports both an absolute and a relative positioning scheme. The type of positioning in effect is specified by setting the position property. Other properties that are used to precisely locate elements are left, top, overflow, z-index, visibility, clip, width, and height.

Absolute Positioning The absolute positioning coordinates state the parameters of container objects, which are essentially fixed rectangular objects that cannot be repositioned or influenced by other objects. Objects of this sort exist in a series of layers, represented by the z-order. The point of reference for positioning is the upper-left corner of the referenced object's parent. If an object doesn't have a parent—for example, a paragraph that isn't associated with other elements—the positioning by default is tied to the upper-left corner of the body. If the paragraph is contained within another element—perhaps as indicated by a <DIV> tag—the absolute positioning is based on the upper-left corner of this parent object. Absolute and relative positioning can be combined to produce fairly intricate page layouts.

Values such as left and top let you adjust the starting position of an object by specifying how far away from the upper-left corner the object is. For example, you could move an object down one inch from the top and one inch from the left by specifying left: 1in, top: 1in. CSS-P also includes other units of measurement, such as pixels (px), points (pt), and percentage (%). If the object within which the element appears is moved through a Dynamic HTML interaction, the element itself will be repositioned to maintain the same absolutely positioned reference within the parent.

Relative Positioning The relative positioning scheme organizes objects into a continuous flow of elements. These objects can interact with each other according to the flow within a document. Layers are displayed in relation to other layers. The position of each new element being displayed is based on the end point of the previously displayed element. This form of positioning is more akin to the typical HTML flow that Web authors are familiar with.

As a part of the design process, you will find circumstances where relative positioning accomplishes your goals more effectively, and others where absolute positioning will be necessary to provide precise layout positioning. Both forms of positioning can be used effectively within a single HTML document, as long as the author understands how objects interact based on the positioning method chosen.

Overflow Property The Overflow property determines what happens to text that exceeds the boundaries of the container object that it appears in. The available options are `clip`, `scroll`, and `none`.

If you assign the `clip` option to the overflow property, any text that cannot be displayed within the parent container gets cut off abruptly. The remainder becomes

Visual Positioning

Positioning elements manually using a coordinate system such as was described in the previous two sections can be tedious. A much simpler method is to employ one of the applications designed to support CSS-P in a visual editing environment. These types of applications allow you to drag, drop, and resize elements freely within the editing window, including paragraph blocks, forms, tables, images, and so on. The appropriate coordinates are automatically embedded as a part of the HTML creation. Two examples of applications that can automate positioning—Macromedia's Dreamweaver and ExperTelligence's WebberActive—are described near the end of this chapter.

inaccessible to your viewers, so in most cases, this is not a practical solution for handling an overflow situation.

The `scroll` option makes more sense. The browser automatically accommodates an overflow situation by creating vertical or horizontal scroll bars to provide access to the text that did not fit into the defined area, allowing a reader full access to the entire text.

The `none` option indicates that the text should be displayed as if the boundaries defined by the parent do not exist. The overflowing text would simply spill over into the surrounding area. This option, unfortunately, has not been consistently supported by current browsers.

Establishing Display Order with z-index With absolute positioning, you can easily specify objects that overlap one another within the browser window. The z-index value determines the order in which overlapping objects should be displayed. Objects with a higher z-index value get displayed over the top of objects with a lower z-index value. The browser also takes into account the z-index value of a parent in which an element may be contained. The display order can never be greater—in relation to other objects displayed by the browser—than the highest value assigned to the parent container.

The order of display can be used dynamically under program control to make objects appear when required. For instance, you could bring a graphic display of the floor plan of a house to the highest level to superimpose it over a photograph of the house at a click of a button. Changing and reordering the position of elements is a technique that is commonly used in some graphics applications, such as Adobe Illustrator, to accomplish different kinds of graphic effects. Now you can use the same basic technique within the browser window and use JavaScript or VBScript to determine when and how the elements are displayed. You can think of the browser window as having a third dimension beyond the flat surface—from the depths of a series of layers, you can bring items to the forefront for display as needed, or move items beneath other objects to conceal them. The z-index value can be used creatively to produce animations, create onscreen visual aids (such as pointers or navigation paths), or produce striking visual effects to increase the attractiveness of a page.

You can also use the `visibility` property to cause items to display or to be hidden, as described in the next section.

Making Elements Display on Demand The `visibility` attributes—`hidden` and `visible`—control whether an object displays in the browser or whether it is hidden. As you might suspect, you can make this behavior a means of providing script-level control over how (and when) objects appear in the browser window. The most obvious application of this feature would be popup messages that respond to onMouseOver or onscreen help where you could click a button to display a help message in the window. A number of other possibilities using this feature are also available to creative authors, as shown by examples that appear throughout this book.

ID Attribute

An addition to the HTML 3.0 specification, the ID attribute, lets a developer provide a unique identification to a line of text, which can then be referenced through scripts and then positioned or modified dynamically. The attribute is inserted within the angle brackets in the opening portion of a tag; for example: <H3 ID=gray_matterStyle>Intelligent Musings</H3>. The style sheet rule then provides the definition for how this particular section of text should be treated: #gray_matterStyle {fontsize: 18pt; color: blue}. The browser identifies the value of the ID when it detects the # symbol and interprets the value that follows; in this case, a font size of 18 points displayed in blue.

Programming Dynamic HTML

While you can accomplish a fair amount to control page layout and appearance using Cascading Style Sheets, the true interactivity available through Dynamic HTML only becomes available when you begin controlling elements through scripting and programming. JavaScript and VBScript are the logical candidates for Dynamic HTML scripting, since they operate entirely on the client side, do not require compiling (both languages are interpreted by the browser on a line-by-line basis), and scripts can be freely cut and pasted between documents. You're not limited to these languages, however; Dynamic HTML can successfully integrate program code from Java, CGI, Perl, and other languages. Of all your choices, JavaScript presents perhaps the most universal approach to providing interactive controls in HTML documents. Support for JavaScript is much more consistent in the version 4 releases of the browsers from Microsoft and Netscape. Microsoft tends to favor VBScript and uses it in many of the examples posted on its site. The Navigator browser cannot interpret VBScript without an additional plug-in, so use of VBScript in your Dynamic HTML documents limits you to the world of Internet Explorer.

If you know JavaScript, the learning curve to mastering VBScript is not extreme. Similarly, VBScript contains many similarities to JavaScript, so moving between the two languages is not that difficult. Keep your prospective audience in mind when you choose a scripting language to control DHTML page elements. Some ambitious developers, of course, create parallel paths that are optimized for specific browsers, but in most cases, you will want to develop pages that will run effectively on the widest possible range of browsers.

Cascading Style Sheet support is more robust in Internet Explorer than it is in Navigator, at least for the version 4 browser releases. Level 2 of the Cascading Style Sheet specification—CSS2—is pending approval from the W3C and may be formally sanctioned even as you are reading this. Since the style sheet elements have a significant effect on the overall programming environment, you need to be aware as a developer of the level of support for individual features of this specification. As you might expect, this is a rapidly changing situation. Some periodicals, such as *Web Review*, make a point of posting comparative tables listing support for different features among the different browsers. For up-to-the-minute comparisons of CSS properties and values between Navigator and Internet Explorer, point your browser to:

style.webreview.com/mastergrid.html

Areas for Caution While the artillery fire in the Microsoft/Netscape browser wars may be quieting a bit, you still can't seamlessly develop Dynamic HTML pages to run without problems on both platforms. Problems also exist between Macintosh and Windows versions of the same browser, a situation that has existed since the very earliest browser releases. Some of the areas where caution is advised include:

JavaScript support between Navigator and Internet Explorer is better, but not perfect. Don't expect scripts you create under one environment to run under the other without testing. It is possible to create scripts that work under both, but you need to pay careful attention to script features that you use to accomplish this.

For the widest possible document distribution, avoid including platform-specific objects in your HTML files. ActiveX can be used effectively with the Windows version of Internet Explorer, but don't expect it to work under the Macintosh version.

Netscape's approach to layers, as implemented in Netscape Communicator 4, is a proprietary technology that has been formally rejected by the W3C. If you include Netscape's layers in your DHTML documents, they will be unusable by other browsers.

Property and value definitions for Cascading Style Sheets differ between Internet Explorer and Navigator.

VBScript is not supported in Netscape Communicator. If you create DHTML pages incorporating VBScript, they will not be playable under Communicator.

The next releases of both browsers should bring us much closer to unanimity for full specification support of DOM, CSS2, JavaScript, and so on. Until then, developers bear the responsibility for bridging the differences between platforms.

DOM Event Model

Dynamic HTML's interactivity relies on an event model that is a part of the Document Object Model. The event model defines the actions that correspond to the objects composing a Web page—as specific to the browser (rather than the scripting language). Many of these are closely associated with the way users will interact with page content, such as clicking on a button and positioning the mouse pointer, but some correlate with events that occur as a natural part of navigating the Web, such as when an HTML page loads. Events drive script behavior. For example, the onMouseOver event, which occurs whenever the mouse pointer is positioned over a page element, can be used to trigger a script sequence in JavaScript. You could use onMouseOver to cause a paragraph of text to turn from black to red, pop up a message box, or start the playback of a MIDI file. Other typical events include the loading of an HTML document into the browser (onload) and the clicking of a button (onClick). The event model determines the scope of the interactivity you can utilize as a Web author, detailing those actions that can effectively direct the course of a scripted program.

Scripting Style Sheet Changes One of the most useful aspects of DHTML scripting is the ability to dynamically change the appearance of page content by modifying style sheet attributes. This can be done by attaching a new style sheet to a document, modifying the properties of an inline embedded style sheet entry, or inserting style sheet modifications into a page based on user interactions (such as clicking a button or repositioning the mouse pointer). The following example shows how a simple JavaScript segment can be used to write an additional rule to the existing rules appearing within the STYLE tags. The script is set up to respond to a mouse click anywhere in the document, which then runs the JavaScript function called redH2( ). The function creates a new rule that affects how the text tagged with H2 will appear in the browser window. The change takes place as soon as the user clicks the mouse. The example follows:

```
<HTML>
<HEAD><TITLE>Adding a Style Rule with JavaScript</TITLE>
<SCRIPT LANGUAGE="JavaScript">
function redH2(){
      document.styleSheets.neatStyles.addRule("H2","color:red");
</SCRIPT>
<STYLE ID="neatStyles">
     H1   {
             font-size: 30pt;
             font-style: italic;
             color: teal;
             }
BLOCKQUOTE {font-size: 40pt}
</STYLE>
</HEAD>
<BODY onClick="redH2()">
<H1>Please give us your attention!</H1>
<H2>Thanks for your time.</H2>
<BLOCKQUOTE>Styles alter properties of tags.</BLOCKQUOTE>
</BODY>
</HTML>
```

Note that the ID attribute within the STYLE tag (neatStyles) lets the addRule method in JavaScript identify and write the additional rule to those rules already defined by the style sheet. The change to the text tagged by H2 takes place as soon as a mouse click occurs anywhere on the page.

This example represents only a simple technique for making changes to style sheet attributes within a document. You can actually perform extensive and far-reaching changes to a document in much more sophisticated ways, allowing virtually every tag in the DHTML document to be modified on-the-fly. In other words, page content can be changed dramatically with the click of a button, the detection of a particular browser, or other forms of program control. Additional examples of using style sheet programming within DHTML to alter page layout appear throughout this book.

Scripting Animation Static HTML pages tend to be boring. You load the page and it just sits there in your browser window doing nothing. A host of workarounds have been developed to overcome the limitations of static HTML, particularly in the area of animation. Animated GIFs have become popular throughout the Web—the GIF embedded in the HTML document contains the necessary information to perform animation entirely on the client side. Server push techniques, CGI programs, embedded Java applets, and other techniques have been used to liven up static pages, but these techniques tend to require more processor power and server intervention than makes sense for most applications.

Dynamic HTML, with its ability to control movement of elements on the page through scripts, is the perfect medium for performing animation on a Web page. The animation controls are built in to the page content, so this approach works even if a document is being viewed offline. The positioning capabilities of CSSP allow intricate interactions to take place on the page, and also support the ordered layering of elements that can be used effectively in many graphic display presentations. The scripts to accomplish animation in this manner are relatively simple to design, and a variety of plug-in scripts are available to support many fundamental operations. Microsoft bundles a set of prescripted behaviors with Internet Explorer 4, enabling nonprogrammers to construct basic animations and page transitions without having to string together lengthy lines of code.

The simplicity of incorporating this form of animation has already led to its overuse. Websites of even fairly sophisticated designers often suffer from a plethora of blinking, flashing, sliding images and text, confusing the eye and making it difficult to know where to focus next. To make things worse, this technique is also often applied to banner ads that hover around the margins of page content, so these moving attention-getters are continuously fighting for your recognition. As you might suspect, this makes the rest of the page content harder to read—kind of like trying to read a book while someone nearby is twirling a flashlight beam around the room. As with other kinds of special effects and multimedia behaviors crafted into a Web page, animation should be used with discretion and tastefulness to be effective.

Using Scriptlets

By now it should be apparent that although Dynamic HTML provides a wide range of possibilities for displaying content and supports a number of multimedia-type features, obtaining these effects can require a fair amount of programming. If your Java, JavaScript, VBScript, Perl, or other language skills are not your strongest point, how can you achieve dynamic control over page elements? Microsoft's solution is to use Scriptlets—small, self-contained segments of code that can be plugged into an HTML page to accomplish specific effects. These code sequences—constructed in JavaScript or VBScript—can be quickly applied to any element of a Web page. For example, you could use one Scriptlet to make a text banner slide across a page and then alternately cycle through a rainbow of colors. You could use another Scriptlet to expand an image progressively from thumbnail to half-screen size and position it on the right-hand margin. Microsoft expects that Scriptlets will become widely available in developers' kits, on CD-ROM, from online download spots, and other locations. In theory, developers should be able to pick and choose from an assortment of self-contained scripts that perform the most commonly needed tasks in Dynamic HTML. Of course, any time you need an effect that is not provided in a canned collection, the only way to achieve it may be through an original script or through the use of third-party development tools that allow you to automate functions such as animation, rollovers, and other effects.

Experimenting with Style Sheets: Amaya

If you've become comfortable with an HTML editor or visual editing application, the prospect of having to learn a new and rather daunting set of additions to your HTML repertoire may be discouraging. You can always upgrade your favored application—most should have support for the majority of Dynamic HTML features even as you are reading this. Another approach that will cost you less money is to try out the Web client/editing tool designed by two W3C members to experiment with style sheet options and evolving versions of HTML. Amaya is available in precompiled and source code versions through the W3C Website:

www.w3.org/Amaya/User/BinDist.html (the site for the binary, precompiled version)

Since it was developed as a design and experimental tool, Amaya offers some features that make it well suited for working with the latest HTML 4.0 additions, as well as exploring new Web protocols and evolving technologies. Amaya serves as both a browser and an authoring tool with a design built around the role of active client. In this regard, Amaya can retrieve existing documents from the Web and perform modifications to them. It can also create entirely new documents and publish them to a remote server. The application interface employs a WYSIWYG model. Editing and accessing documents can include a number of linked documents with the structure and interrelationships of documents shown onscreen. The application design offers complete client functionality while working with and editing elaborate sets of documents.

Amaya's basic functionality includes these features:

- It displays documents created with style sheets compatible with CSS1 (Cascading Style Sheets Level 1) and provides tools for both creating style sheets and editing them.

- It provides access to remote sites using HTTP 1.1 protocol.

- It supports the majority of graphic formats, including the PNG format.

- It displays HTML documents and supports dynamic access to hypertext links included in documents.

- It offers a WYSIWYG interface for immediately previewing the results of style sheet additions and changes.

- It runs on several major platforms, including Windows95/NT, Unix, Linux, and others.

Amaya's approach to parsing HTML documents closely follows the Document Type Definition, but unlike other strict rules-based SGML tools, Amaya does not reject documents that do not precisely fit the structure. Instead, the program attempts to correct offending statements and repair syntax to construct a valid structure in cases where a document deviates from DTD specifications. If the structure is so far from the DTD that Amaya cannot generate appropriate HTML code, the parser only loads the document and permits only valid operations to be performed on the existing content. The resulting document may not be syntactically correct, but in most cases, it should be much closer to being DTD conformant than it was prior to loading.

In many ways, the program has been designed to mimic the typical word processor approach to text editing, but the underlying architecture is far more sophisticated. At all times as the WYSIWYG document creation is taking place onscreen, an internal representation of the line-by-line HTML code is being maintained with the structure determined by the DTD. There is no need for the Web author to enter tags or modify tags; these kinds of changes are performed transparently by Amaya beneath the surface of the editing window. Figure 2.2 shows the appearance of the main application window in Amaya as it appears running under Windows95.

A similar approach is taken in the creation and use of CSS1 entries. The Web author does not need to get involved with the syntax of specifying style sheet rules; Amaya responds to the formatting of onscreen text and produces the appropriate CSS1 syntax in the underlying HTML document. The structure of documents being created can be viewed by selecting the Show Structure option from the Views menu, as shown in Figure 2.3.

The program is organized so that you can actively be performing edits and creating links while browsing the Internet; in fact, links can be most easily created by clicking on the target document as it is displayed onscreen. Links that are embedded in HTML documents can be checked as soon as they are created while actively browsing. Amaya also supports publishing to remote servers, supporting the fundamental HTTP transfer

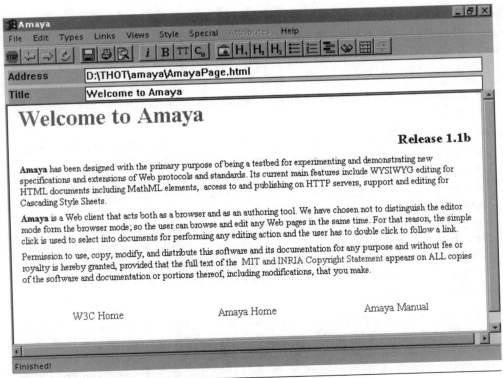

Figure 2.2 Amaya main application window.

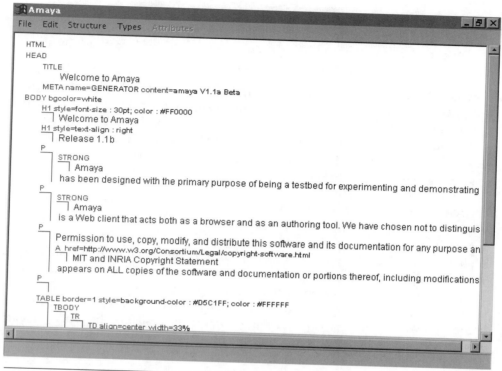

Figure 2.3 Structure displayed in Amaya.

commands (GET, POST/GET, PUT). Content negotiation is performed at the server level to maintain connections and retrieve graphics formats in an appropriate manner.

For a publicly available application, Amaya offers an impressive set of features, particularly for developers, designers, and Web authors looking for a tool that can digest and accommodate the latest protocols and standards floating about the Web, even before their final standardization. Since many of us try to stay ahead of the curve and learn these new technologies to stay competitive, an application such as Amaya can be an invaluable aid to testing and experimenting with standards.

Third-Party DHTML Tools

Not everyone enjoys the challenge of being "in the trenches," grappling with program code, even when using the relatively simple scripting languages that have evolved around HTML document programming. Manual scripting is time consuming and error prone. The introduction of several major application tools that support DHTML interactions should strengthen and broaden the use of DHTML techniques in Web pages by enabling nonprogrammers to join in the fray. Programmers may also take advantage of the opportunity to quickly craft pages and scripts before burrowing down to the line-by-line level for creating more complex scripts.

Whether you're a programmer or a nonprogrammer, DHTML tools provide some useful benefits and a carefully graduated ramp on the path to DHTML mastery. If nothing more, you may want to use one or more of these tools as a fast-path method for learning how to write effective DHTML code. This section profiles several applications that provide automated construction of DHTML content and, in some cases, one-step channel creation.

ExperTelligence WebberActive

WebberActive features both full support for DHTML as well as an integrated approach to creating Web channels within its application environment. This one application provides a means for authoring DHTML, working with Cascading Style Sheets, manipulating dynamic objects, and defining channel content. WebberActive is a robust and ambitious design tool; a great assortment of features and options are embedded into the various menus and submenus and it can take a bit of time to become fully oriented to this application. However, the design of the product makes it fairly simple to generate channel content and set up channels for use.

Text-Based Editing

WebberActive offers text-based editing with the ability to preview pages as they are being designed. The editing window features two tabs that let you flip back and forth between views. The Text Editor view, shown in Figure 2.4, uses colors to separate tags from text content, scripts, and comments. The Scripting pane shown to the left provides access to a set of methods and properties that can be inserted during HTML editing.

By clicking the Preview tab, WebberActive provides a view of the HTML code as it will appear when interpreted by a DHTML-capable browser. If the displayed content exceeds the available window parameters, scroll bars automatically appear to let you move vertically and horizontally through the page (see Figure 2.5).

One of the strengths of this program is that it can easily accommodate changes that arise as new browsers and browser features appear on the market. The use of Document Type Definitions, as described in the next section, makes it possible to plug in a small DTD file to update the editing environment for the latest HTML changes.

The program includes built-in HTML validation so that documents will conform to the selected DTD. You can choose the level of HTML support that you want to

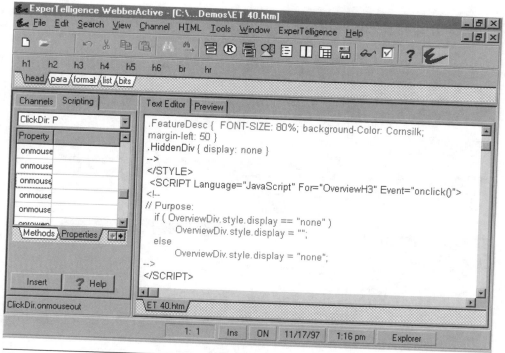

Figure 2.4 Text Editor window.

author to, selecting HTML 3.2 for wider distribution of documents or HTML 4 to incorporate the latest enhancements approved by W3C. If you like, you can even drop back to HTML 2.0 and set that editor to ensure compliance with that version of the standard. Once you select the version of HTML that you want to work with, the WebberActive program interface is modified to present only those tags that are valid for the working environment. Other selections are grayed out.

A built-in spellchecker includes the intelligence to check spelling only as it applies to the text content, not the tags, attributes, and properties embedded in a document. You can switch between a selection of available dictionaries, including U.S. English, U.K. English, German, French, and Italian. The tag bar itself can also be customized to include various tags on different tabbed panels.

Support for Multiple DTDs

WebberActive includes support for multiple DTDs. A DTD is a collection of tag descriptions that also defines the interrelationships between individual tags. While in the WebberActive editing environment, you can select DTDs that represent

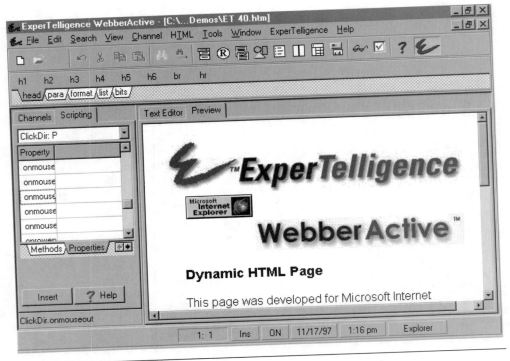

Figure 2.5 Preview window.

HTML 2, HTML 3.2, and HTML 4, which enable those tags that have been defined for the selected HTML version. In essence, an HTML version *is* a DTD. ExperTelligence's approach makes it possible to upgrade your editor simply by downloading and attaching any new DTD that comes along. Since the DTD is represented by a small text file, the upgrade process is exceptionally simple. WebberActive can also validate a document to ensure that the tags used fit a selected environment.

While version 4 of WebberActive does not yet support Netscape's Netcaster, future versions are slated to include built-in support.

Channel Creation in WebberActive

One of the major advantages of WebberActive is its ability to simplify and accelerate channel development. The options included under the Channel menu let you create and upload channel files for HTML content designated for channel delivery. The Properties option lets you determine the scheduling, longevity, channel logo, content description, and similar items for satisfying the requirements of a Channel Definition Format file. While WebberActive supports the most common channel elements, the program does not allow you to save or store unsupported channel elements (which might be included in a manually edited CDF file). The documentation warns that if you open third-party channels and then save them in WebberActive, some information may be lost (assuming less-common channel tags appear in the file). Figure 2.6 shows the Channel Properties panel.

Pages that are related to subchannels inherit the properties from the primary channel. If any channels use relative URLs, the base value displayed in the Properties box can be used to provide the complete path.

The Schedule/Logo tab of the Channel Properties panel lets you determine the scheduling characteristics of the newly created channel and specify the name of the logo (a graphic file) to identify the channel within the browser. The scheduling options let you specify the starting date for the channel and the end date, and then enter the earliest and latest dates for updating of the channel content to take place (see Figure 2.7). The cycle of the overall schedule is based on intervals that you select: the number of days, hours, and minutes. The channel is represented by an image—usually the logo of the company presenting the channel—that consists of a 16×16 pixel bitmap saved as an .ICO file. This image appears in the Internet Explorer Channel Bar at the point where the user subscribes to the channel. The channel is also represented by an 80×32 GIF image (the logo), which will be displayed in the browser following a channel subscription.

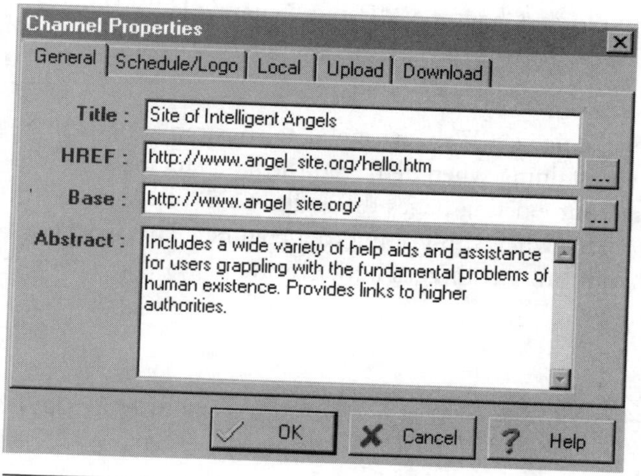

Figure 2.6 Channel Properties panel.

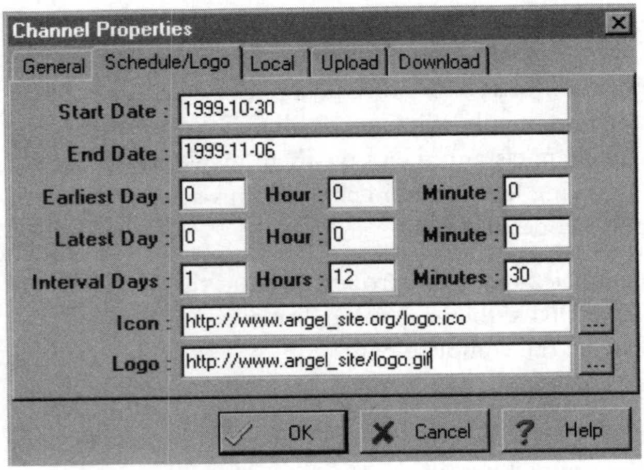

Figure 2.7 Scheduling/Logo options.

With a few additional options, specifying these channel properties is all that is necessary to turn a collection of Web pages into channel content. The information identified in the property descriptions will be pulled in by the Internet Explorer browser according to the schedule that has been established. While WebberActive makes channel creation extremely simple, it is not extremely difficult to set up these same options by manually creating a CDF file. Chapter 3, "The Enabling Standards: CDF, DOM, and RDF," provides an examination of the structure of a CDF file. Chapter 4, "Creating an Active Channel," goes deeper into the creation of channel content for Internet Explorer. Chapter 5, "Using Dynamic HTML for Active Channels," explores the Netscape equivalent to this mode of channel delivery, referred to as Netcaster.

While simply making a site available as a Web channel is fairly simple, designing site content to be effective and entertaining when delivered through channels requires more than just mapping your existing pages through a CDF file. Users expect a higher caliber of site content when subscribing to a channel. This is where Dynamic HTML can provide significant advantages in delivering pages that satisfy subscribers expectations.

Evaluation Copy

You can obtain an evaluation copy of WebberActive, which times out after 30 days, from the ExperTelligence site:

www.expertelligence.com/webbera/v40/

The evaluation version of the product is fully functional and it can be registered after the 30-day timeout through ExperTelligence for continued use.

Macromedia Dreamweaver

Macromedia has always been an active player in the Web world; its Shockwave and Flash plug-ins rate among the most effective ways to deliver multimedia content over the Internet. Millions of Websters have installed Shockwave, and it remains at the head of the pack for handling multimedia content for Web delivery.

Macromedia also wants to tap into the multimedia possibilities offered by Dynamic HTML. Dreamweaver provides a well-designed environment for managing DHTML creation. One key characteristic of this environment is that Dreamweaver is a visual design tool. Unlike many conventional Web editors that require that you jump back and forth between the code and a preview mode—which is often the view from within the browser window—Dreamweaver provides immediate visual feedback on the changes you make to page content and style sheet attributes.

The program as it appears on the Macintosh features an assortment of floating windows that provide selection of modes, access to libraries and style collections used by the program, views of the underlying HTML source code, style sheet tagging, and so on. Figure 2.8 shows the basic work environment. In many respects, the editing environment is not unlike a typical desktop publishing application, but, of course, you also gain the ability to set up and enable multimedia effects from within the editing window.

Dreamweaver also provides complete support for the Cascading Style Sheet standard, with full control over style sheet options and design. Since you can manipulate style sheet attachments on a site-wide basis, it's fairly simple to apply a globally consistent look to all of the pages stored on your site.

The program includes a library of JavaScript behaviors that can be applied to different elements on a Web page. This is the fast, economical route to creating a number of special effects, including the display of alert messages, rollover effects, complex animations, validation of forms, and audio announcements. Dreamweaver provides in-depth support of the majority of DHTML features, so if an effect is feasible within the DHTML framework, there is most likely a direct way to produce that effect in Dreamweaver.

Roundtrip HTML

Many visual editing tools do a nice job of creating page content, but they can't be relied on to handle imported HTML code without changing it significantly.

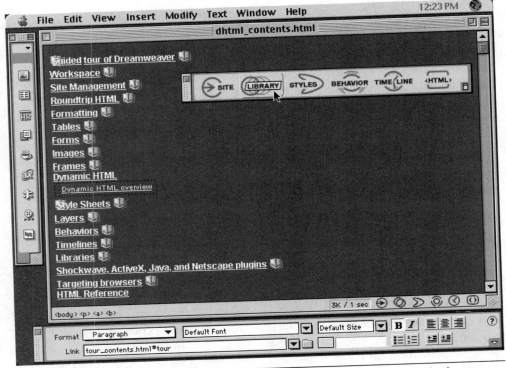

Figure 2.8 Dreamweaver application window and floating windows.

Unnecessary or unwanted tags are inserted, code is modified to fit the editor's approach to the HTML framework, and other undesirable changes often are inserted outside the control of the HTML author. Designers and developers sometimes avoid using visual tools because of the changes that are forced onto their handwritten code.

Dreamweaver uses a different paradigm. The assumption is that if you have written code by hand, you don't want it changed. HTML code that is brought into the editing environment will be exported intact and unchanged (along with any additions or changes that you made while in the visual editing mode). You can also jump back and forth between editing environments, depending on whether the visual approach or the line-by-line editing approach makes more sense for whatever function you're trying to accomplish. The product includes complete versions of BBEdit for Mac users or HomeSite for Windows users, for those times when direct text editing is preferred.

Macromedia has dubbed this approach Roundtrip HTML and trademarked it, so it's clear that Macromedia sees it as a major advantage offered by this product. The product also offers the option of controlling the Code Layout through a set of preferences, one more indication that Macromedia is positioning this product for use by serious developers who aren't afraid of getting down to the code level and looking at HTML documents on a line-by-line basis.

Cross-Browser Code Generation

Dreamweaver includes the ability to generate code that is compatible with both Netscape's and Microsoft's version 4 browsers, relieving the author of the tedious responsibility of determining which tags are implemented by which browser. If your authoring responsibilities require that you create HTML code that works for Internet Explorer and Netscape Navigator, Dreamweaver lets you concentrate on the page content instead of compatibility issues, a factor that should appeal to many frustrated designers and developers who tire of trying to keep on top of the shifting mix of standards.

Other Features

Dreamweaver also boasts a number of other high-end features to simplify DHTML authoring. The program utilizes a *score*—similar to the type that is at the heart of Macromedia Director—to control the positioning and movement of elements on a page, as shown in Figure 2.9. You can take advantage of Cascading Style Sheets with Positioning to animate and reposition any available objects. If authoring for only Netscape compatibility, you can apply score techniques to the layers feature implemented by Navigator (not supported by Internet Explorer) to accomplish similar animation feats and special effects.

Table and frame creation is managed using a fully visual construction tool. You can adjust borders and parameters with drag-and-drop mouse actions. The program also supports the precise positioning and overlapping of objects with a precision down to the pixel level. Support for Cascading Style Sheets is built in to the WYSIWYG editing window, so you can immediately view the results of attribute changes.

You can accelerate your coding by accessing a library of JavaScript behaviors that can be used to manage many common tasks and effects. The program also provides control of content on a site basis, rather than requiring page-by-page management. Any repeating content can be modified on a global basis so all the changes will ripple consistently throughout your entire site. A single style sheet can be used to control the appearance of content on a site. If you have multiple authors working

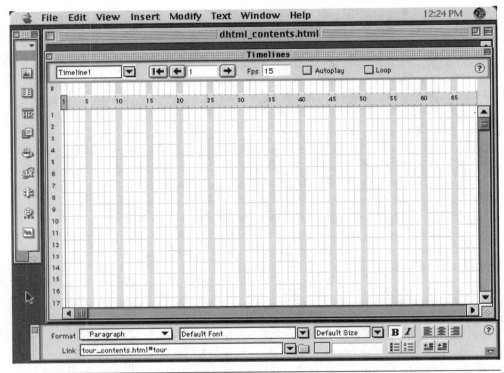

Figure 2.9 Dreamweaver score for time-based positioning of elements.

on site content, Dreamweaver includes a file-locking feature so that collaborative efforts won't result in conflicts when accessing and saving files. An FTP utility manages transfers if your site contents are stored at a remote location.

The program includes a number of tutorial sequences to guide you through the creation of documents incorporating DHTML features—many of the tutorials utilize browser plug-ins such as Shockwave to present the material, as shown in Figure 2.10. Even the preview release versions of this product included extensive descriptions of features in supporting tutorials and a clear commitment to guiding and orienting new users to the product.

Dreamweaver can help you achieve the widest possible range of DHTML effects without having to drop down to the program level. Since some DHTML features rely heavily on script-level activation, Dreamweaver can accelerate and simplify the production of DHTML documents. The animation features in particular are well-supported by the score and timeline—a feature that will make the legions of

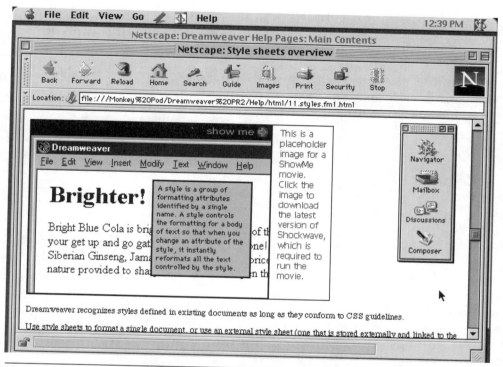

Figure 2.10 Tutorial sequence presented in Shockwave.

Macromedia Director developers feel right at home. This form of visual animation also relieves developers of the burden of having to work out the coordinates of object movement during scripted animation, a process that can be exceptionally tedious if you're trying to accomplish anything but the most primitive object movement. The features, fit, and finish of Dreamweaver should make it a popular tool for both beginning and experienced Web authors.

Summary

Dynamic HTML offers a rich, multimedia-capable environment in which to present page content. By using sophisticated page layout supported by Cascading Style Sheets, animated effects available by manipulating and positioning objects under program control, and a variety of scripting methods that tap into the Document Object Model, you can create lively page content that is both informative and entertaining. Pages crafted in DHTML can be easily delivered through Web channels, since they are essentially self-contained and can be viewed offline without requiring server interaction.

The next chapter examines the standards that make content accessible through Web channels, including CDF, DOM, and RDF.

The Enabling Standards:
CDF, DOM, and RDF

This chapter examines the Document Object Model (DOM), which is the basis of DHTML object interaction, and also looks at the Channel Definition Format (CDF). Converting a Website into a channel can be as simple as constructing a CDF file, as is illustrated in an example later in this chapter that uses Microsoft's CDF creation wizard to build a simple channel. (Part Two, *Active Channels*, goes into additional detail on the construction of Active Channels for delivery to Internet Explorer 4 browsers.) This chapter also provides an overview of the Resource Description Framework (RDF), which promises to provide a more open window to content on the Web and increase the accessibility to information for those seeking specialized topics. RDF will also make search engines more effective, including site crawlers that are used to perform channel updates for subscribers.

As you can see from the two prior chapters, an interlocking collection of standards provides the framework by which you can deliver content through Web channels. In a sense, these standards enable the technologies that make Web channel activity possible. Each of these standards deals with a different aspect of the overall process of moving information contained in a DHTML document to individual desktops through channels.

These standards provide a means for modeling and representing content in an abstract manner, creating a structure that can effectively offer solutions to the problem of linking Web applications to the vast body of resources scattered around the world. Understanding the concepts underlying these standards should help in your design and development efforts.

CDF: Webcasting for the Masses

When push technology arrived on the Web, the initial excitement was enormous, largely based on the fact that mainstream broadcasters now had a Web delivery technique that resembled conventional models of dispersing information. Within this new model, audiences were attracted to tune in to a site that was set up to handle push delivery methods. Information then flowed to the desktop on a regular basis, satisfying the user's appetite for timely, focused information. As might be expected, applying a conventional broadcast model to a medium as unique as the Web was doomed to failure. Dropping news blurbs and banner ads on desktops while people were trying to work was not a way to inspire and attract long-term viewers.

The requirements for setting up a site for push technology were also initially daunting. Many of the proprietary products could be used only through the installation of server-side software, ruling out the use of push for the thousands and thousands of sites renting server space through an Internet Service Provider (ISP). Few of the push products took advantage of multicast techniques, creating a serious concern over flooding the existing Internet bandwidth during mass scheduled events, such as a software upgrade delivery for a major software producer. Licensing of push products scaled the cost to the number of content streams being generated; the expense for high-volume content delivery under this model could be considerable.

Microsoft designed its architecture for Webcasting around a somewhat different model. Banking on the near-term acceptance of XML as the successor to HTML, Microsoft released its newest browser, Internet Explorer 4, with built-in capabilities for parsing XML files. It also incorporated a simple technique for exposing the content of a site for automated delivery: the Channel Definition Format. Designed to become an open standard, CDF was submitted to the W3C for approval, and Microsoft, confident of eventual acceptance, proceeded to design its new version of Windows98 to incorporate this technology as well.

The product design of both Internet Explorer 4 and Windows98 reduces the barriers between locally stored information and Internet-stored information, with an interface that merges the browser with the desktop. Microsoft's Active Desktop makes locally stored resources accessible in a way that is closer to accessing through a browser—paths resemble links, and files and applications can be opened with a single click, browser-style (users who prefer the more conventional display and access to files on applications on their system can select that mode of display). One significant feature of the Active Channel approach to delivering content is that channels can be updated in the background (more conveniently supporting the large file sizes that result from multimedia-rich, interactive content) and the content viewed offline at the user's convenience. It's a model akin to sending your dog out to fetch the morning paper and then reading it later at your leisure.

While Microsoft and Netscape continue to squabble and introduce different approaches to Webcasting, Microsoft justified the design of CDF on the following points:

- Locating information on the Web is difficult, and it requires too much effort to scan the multitude of sites on the Internet to find information that is pertinent to your needs.

- No easy mechanism previously existed for identifying and downloading new information from the Web when a site updated its documents.

- Web browsing at typical dial-up transfer rates is far too inefficient for everyday use.

The Channel Definition Format is designed to reduce these problems by:

- Allowing users to subscribe to those sites that offer the kinds of information most important to them.

- Letting the Web browser perform a site crawl on a scheduled basis to retrieve information in the background and present it to the user for offline viewing.

The Microsoft Webcasting approach also includes elements to meet the requirements of LAN-based users who may have a continuous connection to the Internet through their network. Rather than downloading new information from a channel when an update occurs, LAN-based users can elect to receive notifications of the updated content. In many cases, these users will access this content while online—without downloading it to their local storage.

One of the key aspects of this philosophy is that existing Website content does not have to be modified to make it available as a channel. The creation of a CDF file that contains all the essential data about channel delivery schedules, updates, and the location of channel content opens up the site for the browser site crawl that is periodically performed. Internet Explorer 4 browser users can subscribe to sites that don't have a posted CDF file, basically just setting a schedule to download site content. To make a site accessible for the simpler site crawler requires that the developer pay attention to the number of levels deep that the HTML links go. Less complex sites with fewer levels of links will download faster. Internet Explorer 4 offers the option of turning off graphics access for these types of downloads to minimize the volume of content. This basic form of Webcasting is sometimes referred to as *smart pull*, rather than push, since the content is essentially retrieved during a site crawl operation. A site becomes a *channel*, in Internet Explorer terms, only after a CDF file is created to expose its content. The simple site crawl approach, however, is sufficient to establish a subscription.

Microsoft emphasizes the fact that its approach to Webcasting is scaleable; that is, it can be designed to take advantage of multicasting techniques to distribute content in high volumes. Multicasting sends out single copies of files that can then be replicated as needed by servers at other points on the Internet to distribute to those sites closest to the destination node. This reduces bandwidth requirements considerably for mass broadcasts of information.

Because a CDF file can provide an indexed view of site contents, it reduces the number of pages that must be traversed by site crawlers retrieving keyword lists from the Web. Figure 3.1 shows the typical model where the site crawler retrieves content from a full progression of pages contained at a Website. Figure 3.2 shows how retrieving a single CDF file reduces the amount of data that has to be retrieved, ensuring faster and more effective site crawling.

Letting in the Vampire

In classic vampire lore, no matter how powerful the vampire, it could not gain entrance to its victim's chamber unless it was invited in. So is it with push technology, but with an important difference. Detractors of Web channel subscriptions liken this form of push to opening the Web to a flood of network-clogging data, much of it unneeded and irrelevant. In its earliest incarnations, technologies such as PointCast stressed network servers with a perpetual download of screensavers and data to network users, which soured many network administrators to the whole idea. Channel subscriptions are successful only if users receive what they want and need on a consistent and relevant basis. If a channel bombards them with irrelevant and useless data or information, they only need to discontinue the subscription. Savvy channel developers will remember this important point. Like a beckoned vampire, they've been invited into the chamber, but no amount of neck-biting will keep them from getting booted out if they deliver poor content or electronic junk mail.

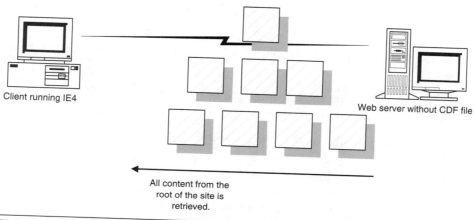

Figure 3.1 Site crawler examining unindexed pages.

Three Levels of Webcasting

When talking about its approach to Webcasting being scaleable, Microsoft is partly referring to the fact that the CDF model can be used as part of a multicasting architecture, potentially supporting thousands of simultaneous subscriber Webcasts using true push technology. However, Microsoft also divides the basic CDF approach into three separate tiers that provide different levels of functionality to subscribers. The three levels that Microsoft supports are:

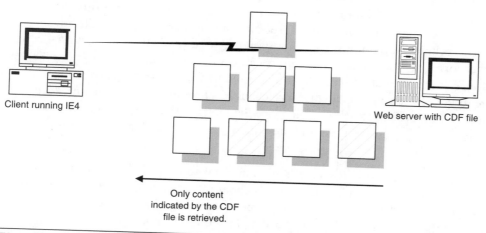

Figure 3.2 Site crawler referencing CDF file for content descriptions.

Basic Webcasting. Supports Webcasts without any site modifications (no CDF file is necessary).

Managed Webcasting. Provides control over Webcasts through the creation of a CDF file.

True Webcasting. Offers multicasting options in combination with existing push technology products.

Each of these levels is discussed in the following sections.

Basic Webcasting: Simple and Quick

As a developer or site administrator, there is a simplicity to basic Webcasting that can be very appealing. To support this approach, you don't have to do anything to your existing site contents. You can encourage subscribers to select your site through the Favorites menu provided in Internet Explorer 4, and from that point, the browser performs periodic checks of the site—using a basic site crawl technique—to identify new content. The subscriber receives notice of the changed content and can then revisit the site to view or download changed pages.

Site subscribers choose a method for receiving notification of changed pages—either a *gleam* (a red icon) that appears beside the channel name, or an email notification. See the later section titled *Illustrated Subscription Process* for insight into how selections are made during the subscription setup.

While simple, this form of Webcasting has some definite benefits. Anyone who travels can use this subscription process to stay current with the information presented on several important sites. Corporate and business users can take advantage of this technique even if a site has not been prepared for Active Channel use or for other forms of Webcasting. Home users can cut down on their connect-time charges by receiving notice of site changes, rather than having to explore each individual site to look for changed content. Since changed site content can be downloaded through Internet Explorer for offline viewing, users with laptop computers can bring Web pages on the road and view them even if a dial-up connection is not easily available.

There are several disadvantages and limitations to basic Webcasting. The subscriber must make a number of decisions about the scheduling of site crawl operations, the form of content delivery, the type of content to be retrieved, and so on. Some of these options could be better determined by the publisher of the channel information, so that the end user doesn't have to make guesses about information availability and depth of content.

Using the site crawler approach, the top page of content is downloaded and then all nested content is retrieved down to the specified level. Since it's difficult for the end user to determine how much nested content is included in the tree structure, too much information may be downloaded inadvertently. Also, this approach doesn't present any method for personalizing the type of content to be retrieved or for setting up groups of related information for easier access.

The site crawl subscription can also be subverted by those Web servers that routinely disable site crawling operations through their sites. Since site crawling can induce a heavy load on a server, some site administrators disable this feature. The subscription process will not work if site crawling is not enabled, placing some useful sites off limits to this form of Webcasting.

The managed approach to Webcasting, based on the use of the CDF file to index and organize site content and scheduling, eliminates many of these problems, as described in the next section.

Managed Webcasting: CDF Controlled

The creation of a CDF file to be associated with a Website provides control over the Webcasting process. The CDF file describes the useful content contained within a site, provides recommended scheduling options for updated content, and lets individual users take a personal approach to the type of information that they view or download. Since CDF file creation is a simple process, and this form of Webcasting does not require structural changes to the pages contained at a site, it will very likely be the choice of site administrators and developers who want to make content available through a Web channel.

This approach still uses a site crawl operation to examine Web pages and determine content, but the CDF makes the process more focused in the following ways:

- The CDF file lets the developer indicate those areas within the tree structure composing the site that the site crawler should examine to identify changed or new content.

- The CDF file specifies the anticipated scheduling of content changes so that the site crawling operation can take place according to site guidelines.

- The CDF file offers descriptive information to illuminate the useful content stored at the site to help subscribers determine those areas where pertinent topics can be located.

In a sense, the CDF file provides a layer of intelligence to the site crawl operation, revealing content in a useful way, recommending update schedules, and delineating those pages at the site that contain the content being authored specifically for channel delivery. The automated delivery of Web pages directly to a user's desktop should be managed in a careful and controlled manner. No one is going to appreciate having his or her desktop flooded with an undifferentiated mass of useless information. The CDF file lets developers and administrators select exactly the correct balance of informational content and entertainment, and control its delivery on a precisely determined schedule.

For a quick lesson in creating a CDF file using Microsoft's creation wizard, refer to the section titled *Using Microsoft's CDF Wizard* later in this chapter. For more complete details about CDF file authoring, refer to Chapter 4, "Creating an Active Channel."

True Webcasting: Extensible Multicasting

To ensure the widest possible range of applications for the Webcasting client that is built into Internet Explorer 4, Microsoft included a mechanism for plugging in to third-party client software. Products such as BackWeb and PointCast can be used to provide an alternate delivery mechanism for Web channel content that incorporates the benefits of multicast push technology. The Microsoft Webcasting architecture can also support new and emerging URL transport protocols. Since a range of third-party products can be integrated into the Internet Explorer 4 client, a single interface can be used to display and coordinate various forms of push technology and reduce scheduling conflicts that may arise between disparate push products.

The framework is also in place for implementing IP multicast techniques to direct CDF-based channel content to multiple client machines. The IP multicast approach to push technology reduces bandwidth consumption on the Internet by incorporating a one-to-many technique for distributing packets. The Microsoft NetShow product incorporates a file transfer protocol originated by StarBurst Communications—Multicast File Transfer Protocol (MFTP). This technology can be deployed either through Internet- or intranet-based equipment.

CDF files also play a role in another Microsoft endeavor: the Broadcast Architecture for Windows initiative that supports reception of Web channels through broadcast networks, both existing networks and those still in the planning stage. This form of broadcasting will make it possible to receive content through direct broadcast satellites and cable TV connections without the usual dial-up connection through phone lines. Home users who don't have the advantages of a direct Internet connection through a corporate LAN will have an alternate method for receiving channel content and updates inexpensively through several different broadcast networks.

The CDF approach to channel delivery enjoys wide support from a number of third-party vendors, who have integrated CDF support into their push technology products. Among the list of CDF-compatible software vendors, Microsoft lists: NCompass, Diffusion, Wayfarer, UserLand Software, PointCast, BackWeb, AirMedia, FirstFloor, Lanacom, NetDelivery, and a number of other companies. Microsoft is also making its own products supportive of channel delivery using CDF and providing easy-to-use techniques for generating CDF files associated with Web content. One good example of this is the new version of Microsoft FrontPage98, which provides site management and HTML authoring. A built-in CDF Wizard simplifies the creation of a fully compliant Channel Definition Format file to describe Website pages that can be flagged and included through FrontPage.

IP Multicast techniques offer the most bandwidth-efficient means of implementing push technology so that the CDF method of delivering content can be scaled to high-volume, international applications involving thousands of destination nodes. From humble, ISP-based Websites with a handful of pages to large corporations seeking a worldwide audience, Microsoft seems to have covered all the bases with its new approach to Webcasting.

Is Site Crawling Push or Smart Pull?

The most basic approach to implementing Webcasting by both Microsoft and Netscape is based on site crawling, sometimes called *Webcrawling*. Unlike push technology, this kind of Webcasting relies on a site crawler that is integrated into the browser software that periodically investigates each designated URL representing a channel and examines the content. Content that matches the criteria for downloading is then *pulled* from the site and delivered to the subscriber. The net effect is similar to push: The subscriber receives fresh content on a predetermined schedule. The mechanism, however, is more accurately called *smart pull* or *automated pull*, since the approach is completely linked to the site crawler activities. Both Microsoft and Netscape support true push technology for Web channel delivery; Microsoft's browser technology works with several third-party software products using push, and Netscape has a close partnership with Marimba and a built-in Castanet tuner in its browser.

Creating a Software Update Channel

Network administrators who oversee large numbers of workstations and who are responsible for ensuring that workgroup members have the most current software face a significant workload each time a new version of a key application is released. The upgrade process can be very time consuming.

The CDF approach to Webcasting provides an interesting alternative to the update process. Since CDF files can include Open Software Definition (OSD) elements, the upgrade operation can be carried out through a Software Update Channel created by the administrator. The Software Update Channel can either be set up to prompt users to download and install the latest network applications, or it can be designed to guide the user through an automatic installation procedure that is initiated by the downloading of an instructional Web page that includes an embedded installation routine to automate the process.

Webcasting offers a variety of useful and practical intranet applications, beyond the more commercial operations that are more likely to be used over the Internet or an extranet. With the ability to broadcast information to workgroup members on a scheduled basis and the mechanism for performing wide-scale software upgrades, network administrators have a very valuable management tool that can save time and effort.

Subscribing to a Site

If you're designing content to be made available as an Active Channel site, what means do prospective subscribers have for deciding whether or not to subscribe? What do they physically have to do within Internet Explorer 4 to initiate and maintain a subscription? Since your channel development efforts and success hinge on being able to attract and keep subscribers, it might be helpful at this point to follow the process from the point of view of the subscriber.

Two basic subscription methods are available to someone who visits a Website that is set up for delivery as an Active Channel:

- Choose Subscribe option from the Favorites menu of Internet Explorer.

- Click the hyperlink pointing to a .CDF file or the Active Channel button that appears in relation to the site.

Each of these options starts the process to guide the site visitor through the channel subscription process, which is essentially a wizard that prompts someone for his or her preferences for the channel setup.

Illustrated Subscription Process

Subscribers to Active Channels typically use a wizard approach to select channels for subscription updates on a regular basis. To locate channels, you can take advantage

Free Subscriptions

The term *subscription* applied to a Web channel seems to imply that there is some payment involved in obtaining the site content. After all, you subscribe to a newspaper or magazine—doesn't this suggest that Web channel subscriptions cost money? The term is unfortunate because in the vast majority of cases, subscribing to a Web channel is absolutely free. Some value-added sites might set up content that does require a fee to obtain access through a channel, but in the current model, most channel providers are offering their content completely free of charge. Since some users may initially respond with hesitation if they become confused about a cost being associated with a channel subscription, make it clear as a part of your site presentation that subscribing to your Active Channel is free.

of Microsoft's Channel Guide, which floats on the desktop as a Channel Bar if you have the Active Desktop feature installed. Alternatively, you can select the Channels button from the Internet Explorer tool bar and a set of Channels appears on the left side of the browser window. Suggested channels are categorized under groupings such as Entertainment, Business, Lifestyle & Travel, and so on. If you select a category, such as the Lifestyle & Travel section shown in Figure 3.3, a set of available subscription options appears onscreen. These banners correspond with the LOGO graphic specified in the CDF file. They're constructed using Dynamic HTML so that moving the mouse over a banner pops up a short description of the site contents.

If you select one of the displayed items and right-click on it, you can choose the Open Channel option to view the opening page of the site. Figure 3.4 shows the opening page when you use the Open Channel selection for the Discovery Channel.

In the upper-left corner of the window, the two buttons—Add Active Channel and Add to Active Desktop—let the subscriber select the level of interaction he or she wants with the channel content.

If you choose the Add Active Channel option, the browser displays the Modify Channel Usage dialog box, as shown in Figure 3.5. As a subscriber, you can choose to receive notification of updates and download the channel content for offline viewing (the default option), receive notice of updates only (without downloading content), or simply leave the site on the Channel Bar.

If you select the Customize button, the program guides you through the Subscription Wizard process. This lets you make decisions as to content delivery for

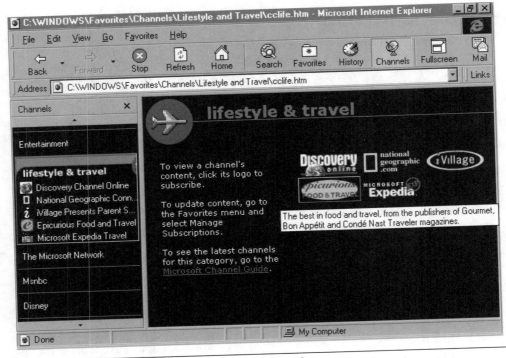

Figure 3.3 Groupings of available channels.

offline viewing. As shown in Figure 3.6, the default option is to download all the content specified by the channel. Alternatively, you can download just the opening page, which allows you to evaluate interesting content while offline and then connect to the Internet when you want to follow the actual links.

When a page that you have subscribed to changes, Internet Explorer places a small red symbol (that they call a *gleam*) on its icon on the Channel Bar to alert you. You can also choose to have an email message generated to a designated address when a content change is detected.

The next display in the wizard lets you choose the update schedule for the subscription. By default, the update will occur based on the schedule specified by the publisher of the channel (as shown in Figure 3.7). Alternatively, you can perform manual updates on a schedule that you specify.

Once you've completed all the options, the wizard returns you to the starting display. Click OK and it proceeds to download the content (if that was your choice) or open the beginning page of the channel. If you've elected to download, a

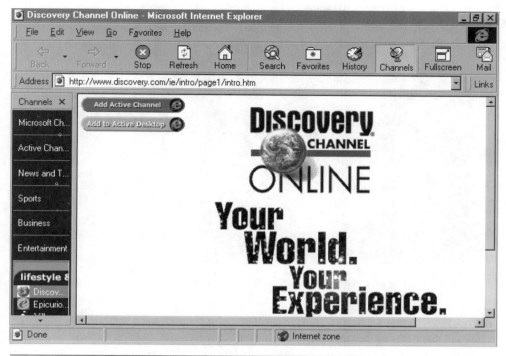

Figure 3.4 Discovery Channel opening page.

progress bar indicates the completion of the access, at which point you can log off and browse the content at your leisure. From the point that the subscription is initiated, ongoing updates will take place according to the selected schedule.

After you've set up your subscriptions, the Manage Subscriptions window (shown in Figure 3.8) gives you additional control over updates and lets you modify

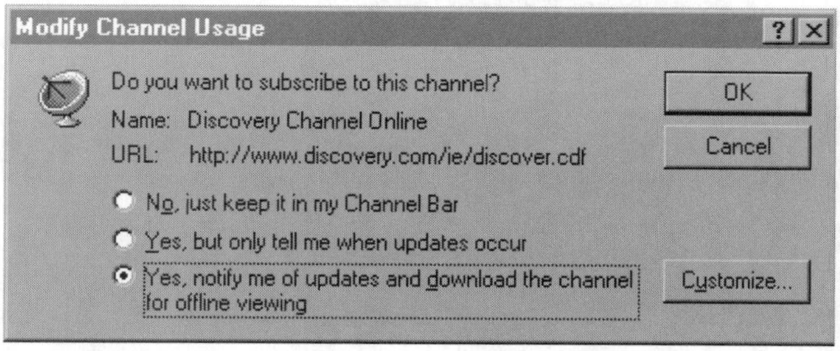

Figure 3.5 Modify Channel Usage dialog box.

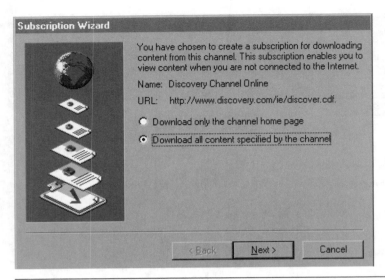

Figure 3.6 Content delivery for offline viewing.

any of your existing settings. You can choose to perform a mass updating of all your channels if you haven't done so in a while. This may take some time if you have a large number of subscriptions. Transferred documents for some of the major channels tend to range between 150K to 750K. Rather than updating en masse,

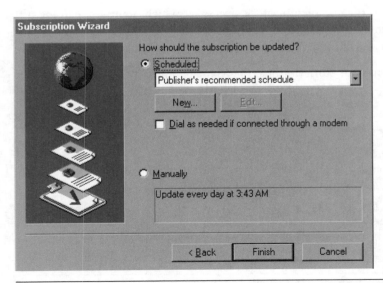

Figure 3.7 Update schedule defaults to the publisher's option.

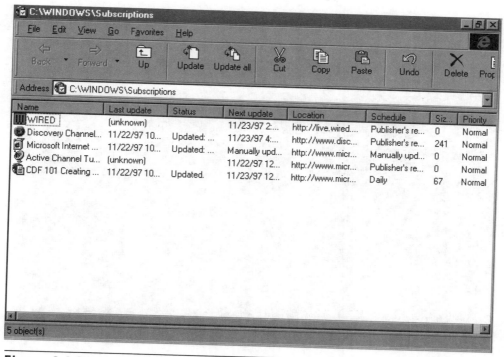

Figure 3.8 The Manage Subscriptions window can initiate updates.

many users will probably choose to let the updates be performed in the background as part of the selected schedule.

As a developer, if you specify an update schedule within the CDF file that you create, this is the schedule that will apply if the user chooses the publisher's recommended schedule when he or she subscribes to the channel. Otherwise, the update is performed on the individually selected schedule.

Site content that is designated to be downloaded for offline viewing is cached on the user's hard disk drive. When the channel is opened from the Channel Bar, if the viewer is offline, the cached copy will be used. If the user clicks on a link that is not cached locally, a dialog box appears and offers the opportunity to connect to the Internet to follow the link to the appropriate document. Ideally, you want to produce content that is reasonably self contained, including a collection of documents complete with graphics that can be accessed fully offline. If too many of the document links end up displaying a message about logging on to the Internet, odds are that the users will become annoyed pretty quickly. Figure 3.9 illustrates an article from a recent issue of the Discovery Channel, designed to run in offline mode.

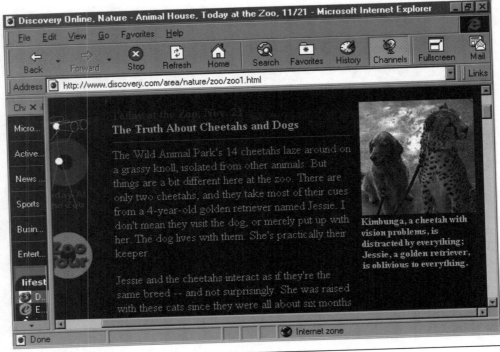

Figure 3.9 Discovery Channel article for offline viewing.

If the user chooses the Add to Active Desktop option for subscribing to a channel, the handling of content takes place somewhat differently. The Active Desktop feature generally includes some visible component, such as a built-in screensaver that cycles through a collection of content. Such an approach can work both in situations where the user is normally logged on to a network (the LAN user with a permanent Internet connection) and in situations where a dial-up connection is required. For LAN users, the screensaver provides options that are a click away by following the link. For dial-up users, the screensaver can highlight articles that can then be viewed by initiating a connection. Content that is delivered for use on the Active Desktop should be designed to accommodate both of these viewing alternatives to be effective.

Using Microsoft's CDF Wizard

While the next chapter deals extensively with the creation of CDF files, this section includes a preview that introduces the key aspects of this process. Microsoft has

Email Notifications of Updates

If a subscriber chooses to receive email updates of changes to channel content, notifications are designed to include inline HTML in the message body (using the MHTML format) for any POP3 or SMTP email applications equipped to interpret embedded HTML. For other email packages, the message notificaton appears in text format with an HTML attachment embedded within it. The attachment typically contains the top HTML page to guide the subscriber to the site content.

included a Channel Definition Wizard as a built-in feature of FrontPage98. If you have a current FrontPage Web open, the wizard guides you through the process of making the site contents available as an Active Channel. You can designate pages—called *items* in FrontPage98 terms—to be included in each scheduled update operation. Each item that is included in the CDF will be checked on the periodic basis that is specified, and either be downloaded during updates or notify the user of changes. The wizard also provides the option of letting you modify an existing CDF file that has been created either inside or outside of the program. The first page of the wizard, shown in Figure 3.10, gives you the option of creating a new CDF file or modifying an existing one.

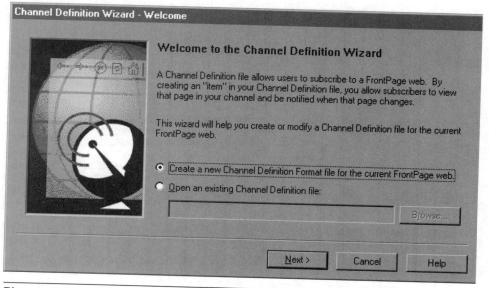

Figure 3.10 Channel Definition Wizard welcome page.

If you're not familiar with Microsoft FrontPage98, it features a set of tools for fully managing the contents of one or more Websites, from link management and verification to uploading and downloading files using an FTP utility. The program provides a number of different ways to view and access site contents, and does a good job of handling most of the frequent tasks required to keep a changing Website running without problems.

The first step in the seven-step wizard lets you enter the pertinent information to describe and identify the site to potential subscribers, including the title, an abstract that concisely describes the site contents, the page that should be displayed on the entry point for the site contents, and two graphics: one for a channel banner and the other, a more compact icon for display in the Channel pane of Internet Explorer. Figure 3.11 shows the dialog box for entering the channel description.

Step 2 lets you specify the locations of those pages that will be included as a part of the Active Channel. If you have more pages than those contained in a single folder, you can designate the use of subfolders within the primary folder, as shown in Figure 3.12.

Step 3 lists the pages to include in the channel based on the folder and subfolder that you selected. You have the option of excluding any of the pages in this listing or restoring the entire set of files that was originally selected.

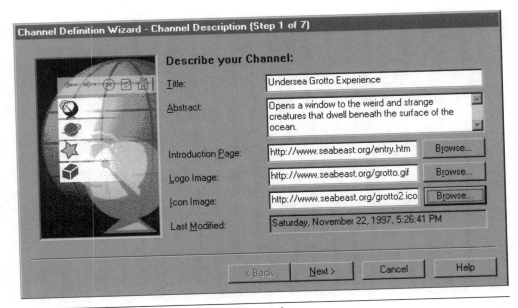

Figure 3.11 Description of the channel.

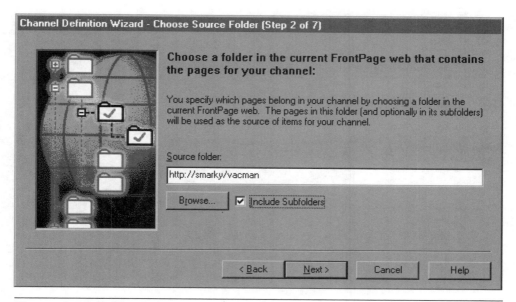

Figure 3.12 Folder location for source files.

The Channel Item Properties dialog box, shown in Figure 3.13, lets you individually describe the channel items; that is, those pages that you've selected for inclusion in the channel. The Usage portion of the dialog lets you determine how the page content will be handled. For example, a page that includes an interactive screensaver can be identified using the Screen Saver option. If chosen through the Active Desktop option when a user subscribes to the channel, the screensaver can be deployed for desktop use. You can also set up a page to serve as normal channel content, a desktop component (in the case of an application or other item that the user might want to work with frequently), or simply set up an email notification flag so that the subscriber receives a message when the designated page content changes.

The Page Cache setting determines whether pages that are downloaded will be stored in the hard disk cache for offline access. Any pages that are cached can be accessed during offline browsing; uncached pages will be inaccessible once the Internet connection is broken. Of course, the more pages that are cached, the more download time and storage space will be required. Developers should pay careful attention to the number and size of pages that are identified as content to be cached so as not to overwhelm the subscriber's available storage.

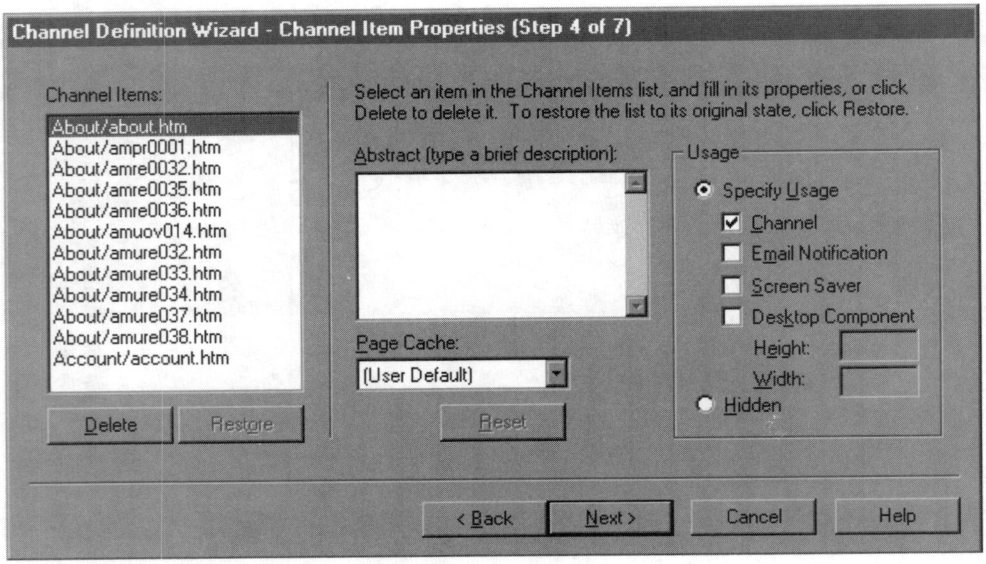

Figure 3.13 Channel Item Properties dialog box.

Step 5 lets you manage Channel Scheduling. The scheduling options provided indicate to the subscriber's browser how often the Web content included in the channel will be changing. The subscriber, of course, has the option of selecting his or her own update schedule; the defined schedule applies if the user adopts the default site schedule instead of his or her own.

A Start Date specifies the earliest point in time that site content will be available for access. The End Date specifies the date when no further connections should be made to the channel. A series of boxes let you indicate in days, hours, or minutes how often the subscriber should connect to the site to retrieve content. If you're providing a monthly newsletter to subscribers, for example, you could set this value to 30 days.

The "Delay checks between" values create a randomized time interval to offset subscriber's access, in case you are anticipating a flood of subscriber activity at a particular time each day or each week. By inserting this value, each subscriber's browser will connect at a different time based on the delay you insert. For example, if you designate to Delay checks between 1 and 6 hours (as shown in Figure 3.14), at the subscription update point (midnight on the 30th day), the browser updating process might begin anywhere from midnight to 6:00 A.M. This features staggers the

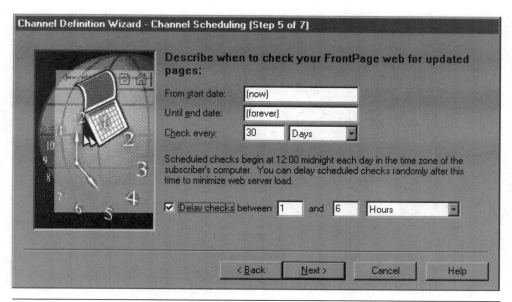

Figure 3.14 Channel Scheduling dialog box.

access times to avoid overwhelming the Web server with a massive update operation that might involve hundreds or thousands of subscribers.

Logging user browsing patterns is an important part of channel activity. Step 6 lets you designate the location of a URL that will be used to accept the log data. The logging feature is interesting in that it records user browsing activities even when the subscriber is offline; the log entries are sent the next time a connection is made to the Internet. For this feature to work, the URL should point to a form handler application—created as a CGI file or within another appropriate application—that can handle the incoming data. Data is then stored on the designated URL until the site administrator needs it. Use of a log file is optional. If you decide to use this feature, most users would probably appreciate some kind of notification that their offline activities are being monitored and relayed to you. Figure 3.15 shows the dialog box for specifying the destination for log file data.

The final step in this process is to actually create the CDF file, as shown in Figure 3.16, and determine its storage location. The wizard also gives you the option of creating a hyperlink that appears on the base of the navigation bar on your channel homepage that offers the subscription option to users. FrontPage98 is flexible in that it lets you create several different CDF files that can each access the

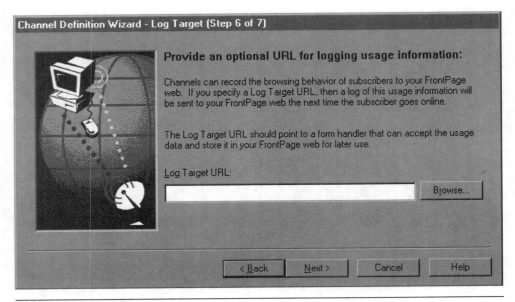

Figure 3.15 Log Destination URL.

content of a particular Website in a different way. This gives the developer the option of finding a number of ways to organize and deliver a body of content, perhaps shaping it in different ways for different audiences.

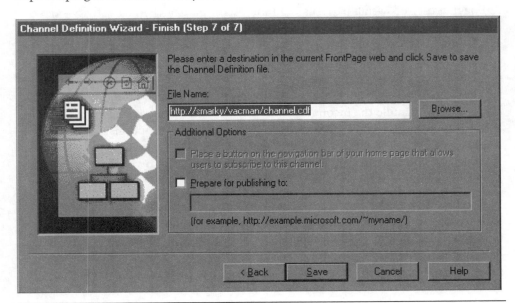

Figure 3.16 Finalizing the CDF file.

You can also choose to place a button on the navigation bar of your channel homepage that also provides the option of subscribing to the site. FrontPage98 automatically generates the code and the necessary graphics to hook up this feature and embed it in your Website content.

The resulting CDF file can be accessed and used by any browser that has CDF compatibility. Netscape's Netcaster has the basic capabilities to work with CDF content, but certain features in a CDF file are essentially overlooked by Netcaster, as discussed in Part Three of this book, *Netcaster*.

This wizard also allows you to open up an existing CDF file and make modifications to the setup values following the same step-by-step process. While you are learning the basics of CDF, the CDF Wizard provides a fail-safe method for creating properly formatted CDF files using the appropriate syntax. After generating a CDF file through the wizard, you might want to examine the file contents to gain a better understanding of how your selections are handled on a line-by-line basis. At some point, you'll probably outgrow the utility of the CDF Wizard and have reason to manually code files that have more sophisticated capabilities than the bare-bones wizard does.

Analysis of a CDF File

Examining a typical CDF file reveals the relative simplicity of setting up a site for Active Channel delivery. The embedded comments in the following example describe the most important individual entries:

```
<?XML version="1.0"?>
<!DOCTYPE Channel SYSTEM "http://www.w3.org/channel.dtd"

/* Identifies the Active Channel and associated CDF file */

<CHANNEL HREF="http://www.lp-vt.com">
  <SELF HREF="http://www.lp-vt.com/light.cdf"/>

<TITLE>Lightspeed Photon Watch</TITLE>

/* Designates the icon and banner files that showcase the channel */

<LOGO HREF="http://www.lp-vt.com/ls.ico" STYLE="ICON"/>
<LOGO HREF="http://www.lp-vt.com/ls.gif STYLE="IMAGE"/>
```

```
/* Indicates the schedule that applies to content updates. */

<CHANNEL>
<SCHEDULE>
  <INTERVAL TIME HOUR="4"/>
  <LATESTTIME MIN="60" />
</SCHEDULE>

/* Identifies subchannels that contain additional content. */

  <TITLE>Recycling Updates</TITLE>

  <ITEM HREF="http://www.lp-vt.com/recycle/news.htm">
     <ABSTRACT>News items on recycling and reduced consumption</ABSTRACT>
     <TITLE>The Recycling Bin</TITLE>
  </ITEM>

  <ITEM HREF="http://www.lp-vt.com/recycle/direct.htm"
     <ABSTRACT>Directory of recycling centers</ABSTRACT>
     <TITLE>U.S. Recycling Directory</TITLE>
  </ITEM>

  </CHANNEL>


</CHANNEL>
```

The Document Type Definition in this case (as shown in the second line of the example) is not required, but it can be added to provide additional details about the file structure that can be valuable for some applications. The pointer in this case is to a baseline Channel.dtd document residing at the World Wide Web Consortium's site.

The CDF provides indexed access to content regardless of what form that content appears in. In other words, the site being delivered as a channel can consist of documents containing standard HTML, Dynamic HTML, Java, ActiveX, JavaScript, and other content. The content representation is independent of the format of the content within documents.

Chapter 4, "Creating an Active Channel," goes into greater detail about specific types of entries that you can use in a CDF file to control how the channel delivery is handled.

Document Object Model

Netscape's introduction of JavaScript 1.0 opened up the objects in an HTML document—the windows, forms, buttons, graphics, plug-ins, and so on—to scripted program control. Rather than a conventional control-flow approach—which has been the basis for traditional programming for many years—JavaScript 1.0 relied on event handlers based on the normal types of activities that take place in the browser environment. Instead of using a main loop to coordinate the activities within a program, JavaScript 1.0 used events such as documents loading and unloading, buttons being clicked, forms being submitted, and so on, to control the progression of a script. This approach is more consistent with object-oriented programming techniques and applications that have commonly been used for creating interactive multimedia presentations, such as Macromedia Director and Asymetrix ToolBook.

The Document Object Model, currently being crafted by the DOM Working Group of the W3C, expands and extends the original JavaScript object model and reunifies the divergent courses taken by Netscape and Microsoft in implementing object controls in their recent products. The keyword for the day is *interoperability*.

Level 0 of DOM

The level of object interactivity provided in the version 3 releases of Netscape Navigator and Internet Explorer is considered Level 0 by the DOM Working Group. This was basically the foundation upon which the object model was expanded and refined. The Level 1 working draft of the DOM standard was released for public comment in October 1997. The Working Group posts regular reminders that until the standard is finalized, none of the internal specifications should be considered stable, and no effort will be made to ensure compatibility with prior *de facto* implementations of DOM. In other words, if you're a developer in the process of building something for commercial distribution, don't count on anything in the standard staying the same until it is officially approved.

Rather than the fractured, inconsistent implementations of Dynamic HTML that appeared in the version 4 browsers from Microsoft and Netscape, the Document Object Model provides an officially sanctioned, internally consistent standard upon which to base future browser releases and related products, such as HTML editors and visual programming tools.

To you as a developer, this means you don't have to spend a large part of your development and design efforts sorting through the differing approaches taken by Microsoft and Netscape in their DHTML handling. A properly structured DHTML document—if it meets the W3C guidelines—will run flawlessly on all browsers, regardless of the software producer's imprint that graces the outside of the package.

The DOM Working Group is releasing this standard in stages with a goal of encouraging software vendors to progressively incorporate all of the components of the standard. This allows the core elements of the standard to be implemented in software before some of the more complex parts of the document—such as the event model—are finalized.

In the meantime, understanding the foundation of the Document Object Model should prove helpful in constructing Dynamic HTML documents. Between the ability to control all of the basic objects in the browser window and the capability of programming the style attributes through Cascading Style Sheets, you have a framework to create compact, interactively rich documents. Many observers see these new technologies as offering the ability to create genuine crossware applications—downloadable special-purpose programs that can be run on any platform that supports a browser.

The Document Object Model is seen not just as a way of interacting with HTML and DHTML objects, but also as a core component of the evolving XML standard, so we can expect this framework to be with us for some time to come. The following sections discuss the most important aspects of DOM.

The Hierarchy of DOM

The DOM defines an object hierarchy, essentially consisting of a Document Object that includes a number of nodes—each node is an object as well. The root node of this tree structure is the Document Object itself. The organization of the tree establishes a structure and an order among all of the nodes. This basic structure provides a means of identification by which anything contained in a document can be referenced and manipulated.

The conventional relationships that are implied by tree-structured hierarchies are an important part of the naming conventions defined by DOM. The Document Object node is the parent node; all other nodes are child nodes, each of which has a parent based on its position in the tree. Naming proceeds from the root down to the lower members on the tree. Nodes are numbered sequentially as they appear in the document. References can be relative or absolute. For example, you can reference the fourth node that appears on the tree or you can reference the node that follows the current node being referenced.

If you're familiar with the naming conventions that apply to a scripting language such as JavaScript, you'll recognize the concept. If a document contains three forms and you want to reference the first button contained in the third form, you start from the parent object (the document) and work down to the button contained in the form.

```
document.form[2].button[0]
```

Objects can also be given names and referred to by name rather than by an indexed number. For example, if the form is given the name address_form and the button is named red_button, you would also be able to refer to the button in this manner:

```
document.address_form.red_button
```

Since objects can have a numerical value based on their hierarchical position in a document and can also have a name as assigned using the ID attribute, either method can be used to refer to them. Since nodes can be dynamic, using a name can sometimes be more effective than referring to an object by its position, which may change as a result of scripted operations.

Script activity can create or delete nodes, so the tree can be expanded or reduced dynamically as objects are added to or taken off the tree.

Types Recognized within the Object Model

The specification defines a core set of object model types, as shown in Figure 3.17. Each of these types is briefly defined, and as you will see, there is a deliberate intent to maintain a layer of abstraction surrounding datatypes and objects in order to maintain the necessary flexibility to make this model useful in real-world applications.

Node The most fundamental datatype in the DOM is the Node object. It is basically a single point of reference on the tree that can contain an additional collection of child nodes. Nodes exist in a hierarchy, and this hierarchy is the basis of the defining structure in the DOM.

Document Each HTML or XML document is represented by a Document object. This object is a container within which all of a document's data is organized and accessed. The Document object serves as the root of the tree structure and acts as the parent of all node objects contained in the document.

Element Element nodes are the basic units composing a document tree and the most common node type appearing within the structure. An Element node can contain and represent a collection of additional nodes. For example, the <BODY> element of a document can contain additional elements, such as <FORM> or <IMG>. All of the other elements that are between the start tag <BODY> and the end tag </BODY> are contained within it. All of the attributes that define the element are also considered within the same container. Since elements can contain other elements, the concept of nesting applies to this structure.

Attribute Element objects have a defined series of values represented by Attribute objects. The document type definition determines the range and acceptable values of attributes that can apply within the document. For example, the attributes of an <H1> element include the characteristics applied by the current style sheet values (font size, color, and so on).

Text Text objects represent the content of a document as opposed to those areas signified by markup tags. In XML documents, Text nodes are produced whenever white space is encountered between markup areas.

Comment Comment nodes consist of the entire content of a comment as indicated by the start (<!--) and finish (-->!) characters. This definition of a comment is fully supported under XML; some HTML tools may respond somewhat differently to embedded comments within a document.

PI The PI node indicates a processing instruction. The instruction is contained within delimiters, and this actual content represents the node itself.

Reference The Reference object is the base type for named entities within the body of a document. The Reference node points to another object containing the entity's value. A subtype of Reference is the NamedCharacterReference that is used to refer to alphanumeric characters that are referred to through escape strings.

NumericCharacterReference The NumericCharacterReference object represents numeric literal values, derived from radixes included in the reference itself, such as &#x33.

Establishing an Application Programmer's Interface

One of the most important reasons for finalizing the Document Object Model as a standard is to establish an Application Programmer's Interface (API) that will allow any scripting or programming language to interact with DOM components. This includes Java, C++, Perl, VBScript, JavaScript (or JScript/ECMAScript), and virtually any other language that can be used in the context of working with HTML documents. The interfaces that will provide "hooks" to the programming community are being expressed in a generalized language that has been named the

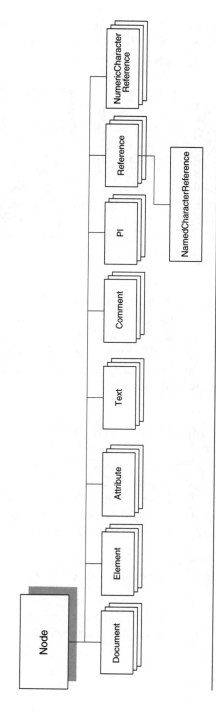

Figure 3.17 Types within the object model.

Interface Definition Language (IDL). Specific implementations of the specification in language-specific versions will be produced by the software vendors involved in browser design and accessory application toolkits.

Elements in XML

Unlike HTML with its fixed and carefully defined set of elements, XML gives authors the ability to create and define individual sets of elements. Objects can be designed according to the requirements of a particular type of document and then manipulated and accessed under script control, just as the permanent fixed objects of HTML can. The context of an object—where it appears on the document tree in relation to other objects—can be an important factor in manipulating it under program control. This is where the DOM is useful in establishing the structure by which objects are referenced.

Given a language-specific API and the DOM specification, Web developers will be working to a universal standard that offers an orderly, hierarchical model to access and control the components that make up an HTML document. As XML gains acceptance in the industry, the same DOM will provide the underlying structure and an architecture that can include newly defined elements as well as the fixed collection of elements defined for HTML.

Resource Description Framework

The Resource Description Framework (RDF) is a method for describing and categorizing information stored at any given URL on the Web. The specification, currently under development at the W3C, seeks to provide a standardized means of exchanging data about Web resources among different applications. Once established, RDF will facilitate a number of useful and practical applications, including:

- Systematize the exchange and validation of digital signatures expressed within the RDF model, improving techniques for electronic commerce and online collaboration among peers.

- Provide a framework within which intelligent software agents can seek out specialized kinds of information and share acquired knowledge with other applications.

- Simplify the cataloging and presentation of interrelated information residing at a Website, providing the means to create a digital library approach to stored data.

- Establish a model by which Web search engines can better locate resources and identify particular types of content.

- Offer a mechanism for denoting intellectual property rights as they apply to Web content.

- Lead to improved access to collections of information that are contained within large, complex Websites.

- Establish a content rating structure to allow sites to voluntarily rate their document content suitability for different age groups.

While encompassing some notably ambitious goals, the RDF specification is steadily progressing through committee meetings at the W3C and absorbing input from Microsoft and Netscape, as well as other primary players in this important segment of the market. As has been the case for other specifications that have worked their way through the W3C process, the RDF specification in final form will owe its authorship to a W3C authoring team, rather than a Microsoft or Netscape author. Though both Microsoft and Netscape have issued drafts of various parts of the RDF and worked strongly to push the specification in directions most aligned with their corporate goals, the role of the W3C is to distill the components of this specification into a workable mix for the benefit of the Web community as a whole.

Elements included in other working drafts that have been produced by the W3C have been prematurely incorporated into software applications as manufacturers rushed to gain a jump on introducing a new technology. While parts of the RDF have been finalized to the degree that manufacturers can start planning for future uses of this technology, key parts of the specification have not yet been established. Both Microsoft and Netscape are tinkering with products that incorporate their personal twist on RDF, which is unlikely to be consistent with the version that is released as a recommended standard by the W3C. One crucial component of the RDF architecture, the method for constructing a schema under RDF, has not even been issued in draft form, so developers and software engineers cannot effectively begin any serious development. A schema is the collection of properties that allows a clear content definition to be derived for Web-based material, such as the subject, the author of the content, publication date, type of document, relationship to other documents, and so on. The schema becomes the basis for exposing in detail the packaged information that is contained within a document or set of documents. In some ways, it is like the entries within a card catalog in the library. Without a working definition for this part of the RDF specification, developers can't progress very far on any kind of RDF implementations.

As with many of the other standards and specifications discussed in this book, RDF is not intended to serve as a replacement for other standards or other forms of metadata. RDF is envisioned as being a broad and encompassing content framework that incorporates and includes approaches such as Microsoft's Channel Definition Format.

Since the *smart-pull* approaches to Web channel delivery (as implemented in the basic Webcasting models for both Netscape and Microsoft) incorporate a site crawler technique for determining update schedules and evaluating the range of content, RDF can play a strong role in defining the information framework and allowing channel subscribers and client software to locate and deliver specialized kinds of content. The syntax used in RDF is also based on the XML standard; these two technologies are being designed as complementary. RDF incorporates XML conventions in naming and establishing relationships between objects.

RDF is intended to overcome one of the major obstacles to acquiring information across the Web: The lack of a machine-understandable method for extracting and retrieving data from sites. Keyword searches, the fundamental technique used by search engines, are at best a hit-or-miss approach, since the relevance of content is based on the proximity of terms that may or may not identify the topic for which the search was initiated. RDF provides a uniform descriptive mechanism that can serve as the means for automating a variety of Web activities.

While it might still be a bit early for incorporating RDF components into your development projects, we encourage developers and authors to keep a close eye on this part of the Web specifications arena. The benefits and advantages to communicating Web content through metadata are numerous and when the RDF specification is finalized, it promises to become one of the most important methods for locating, authenticating, and distributing information over the Internet.

For information on the current status of Resource Definition Framework working draft, point your browser to:

www.w3.org/TR/WD-rdf-syntax/

If you're interested in the general concept of metadata, the W3C also maintains a number of documents on this subject on their site; a good starting point is:

www.w3.org/Metadata

Knowledge Representation in PICS

The Platform for Internet Content Selection (PICS) was an early effort to provide a technique for conveying information about the content of Web pages. PICS was devised in response to fears that without some form of content rating mechanism, serious restrictions would be legislated on Internet content distribution. PICS provided the structure for developing a rating system, thereby allowing Web page content to be filtered and, if necessary, blocked from browser display. The obvious application for PICS was to allow parents to screen pages containing adult-oriented content from children, but PICS also could be used to distinguish academic content that had been through a peer-review process or ascertain that a university-based researcher had authored a particular scientific or medical paper. The work involved in developing PICS became the inspiration for RDF. PICS took a more narrow view of content classification, working more effectively when the data values associated with pages were known in advance. RDF is more open ended, providing a structural means of adapting to and describing many different types of data in a descriptively richer manner.

Summary

The industry-wide adoption of the standards that make Web channel delivery possible using DHTML components will go a long way towards making life simpler for developers and Web designers. The Document Object Model is probably the most important standard from the perspective of ensuring uniform behavior of DHTML documents downloaded into Microsoft and Netscape browsers. The ability to program the objects defined in DOM make it possible to create crossware applications for delivery through channel mechanisms, greatly increasing the potential for developers to produce engaging interactive materials to keep subscribers online and entertained.

The most important emerging standard briefly discussed in Part One is XML, which is covered in more detail in Appendix A, "HTML 4.0 and XML."

Part Two

Active Channels

Creating an Active
Channel

This chapter describes the techniques for creating Active Channels based on new or existing Websites. The material builds on the simple CDF wizard approach presented in Chapter 3 to discuss progressively more complex uses of CDF files. Each of the elements of a CDF file is discussed and defined, and special features, such as logging, logo creation, and graphics handling, are examined. The requirements for getting your site listed in the Microsoft Channel Guide are also provided. If you haven't yet read through it, Chapter 3 offers a more basic introduction to the Channel Definition Format and some simple examples to get you started. This chapter expands on the previous simple examples and leads you through some of the more elaborate CDF implementations with a number of examples.

With the creation of an Active Channel, your Website moves from being a passive roadside newsstand to becoming an active information broadcaster. Instead of spending all of your energy trying to figure out how to keep a continuous flow of traffic to your Website, you can concentrate on building a loyal subscriber base—a group of visitors who appreciate your site content so much they want to receive it on a regular basis. Attracting subscribers is a bit different than generating short-term site visitors whose click-through rates may mean nothing more than they happened to stumble across your Web pages on their way to somewhere else. While you can make conventional

HTML pages the basis of an Active Channel, most visitors will find it more rewarding if you use Dynamic HTML to produce livelier interactive content.

Automated Authoring Tools

First-generation DHTML authors and channel creators had little choice but to manually code their files. This is certainly a workable solution, but for any of the more complicated effects—such as animating objects by the use of coordinates—the amount of code necessary to produce the effect can be considerable. The authoring time can also be fairly substantial. Channel creation requires learning a new set of tags and, while similar to HTML, the chance for error when producing CDF files is also present.

Fortunately, a new generation of DHTML tools has appeared on the market that include built-in channel creation features, streamlining authoring efforts and reducing the chance of errors in CDF and Netcaster. Some of these tools can even produce parallel content that is optimized for different platforms, making it possible to create Active Channels and Netcaster channels from the same source code. DHTML differences are also handled in a similar manner. Since there are some significant differences between DHTML handling in the Microsoft and Netscape products, these authoring tools can make it feasible to create channel content using DHTML for all of the major platforms. The tools to consider include:

Pictorious iNet Developer 2.0. This tool generates different channels or Web pages dynamically by detecting the browser that the subscriber uses to connect. It also includes a number of features supporting collaboration by multiple developers; object types can be restricted to specific members of the development team. Using this tool, you can generate both Active Channels and Netcaster channels.

mBED Interactor. mBed Interactor produces multimedia content that can include a wide variety of DHTML features, including RealAudio segments synchronized with onscreen events, embedded audio clips, animations in several different forms, and interactive navigational controls. This product, however, is not set up to directly handle the channel setup.

ExperTelligence WebberActive 4.0. WebberActive authors content based on a selected DTD file, allowing the product to be easily adapted to newly introduced standards, such as the finalized release of HTML 4.0. It uses the Document Object Model as the basis for object manipulation and DHTML scripting, and can also produce CDF files associated with developed content. This program provides a highly flexible development environment capable of producing most types of DHTML content, whether the programming control is based on ActiveX controls, JavaScript, VBScript, or other languages.

SoftQuad HoTMetaL Pro 4.0. This tool includes DHTML authoring and support for the Document Object Model. It also includes a wide variety of plug-in special effects—referred to as HoTMetaL FX—that provide DHTML animation and object interactivity, as well as other types of drag-and-drop elements, such as JavaScript sequences, Java applets, animated GIFs, and basic CGI scripts.

Allaire Home Site. Allaire Home Site provides a well-organized development environment for creating Web pages and managing site contents. A collection of specialized wizards supports many different DHTML effects and multimedia handling. This program also provides extensive support for Cascading Style Sheets, letting you define and save your own style sheet attributes, fully preview style sheet changes, and assign different style sheets to precoded text.

Additional software vendors are providing support for both CDF file creation and the full range of DHTML features. Check the companion Website for this book www.wiley.com/compbooks/purcell for the most current information.

Design-Time Controls

Design-Time Controls (DTCs) are software components that guide authors through the creation of DHTML pages that include elements making them suitable for Active Channel use. These DTCs can be integrated for use with a number of the DHTML authoring applications described in this section, and also work with frontline Microsoft applications such as FrontPage98 and Visual InterDev. For example, one DTC designed to support data binding in DHTML leads the author through the process of identifying the data source for the page content, choosing the formatting attributes for the data, and specifying any interrelationships between data components. The DTC then generates an appropriate script and the supporting DHTML code to integrate it into the Web page. The idea behind DTCs is that they can accomplish fairly sophisticated functions through a step-by-step authoring sequence, freeing the author from having to create scripts by hand.

Channel Design Tool: Channel Maker

Small, third-party software vendors often step in to fill vacuums that haven't been covered by the major players. An example of this is Channel Maker, a channel creation tool designed by a small company in the United Kingdom. Channel Maker guides you through the process of properly setting up a CDF file for content that can be stored locally and verified link-by-link by the program. Containing features that go way beyond the wizard-type creation tools that are available from several sources, Channel Maker is optimized for the single task of controlling CDF file setup and options.

The program includes some features to streamline channel maintenance activities for site administrators. One useful feature is the ability to perform global updates on the Last Modified dates that are defined for Channels, Subchannels, and Items on a site. The Last Modified date provides the trigger that cues the browser that content has changed, so it is important that the listed dates be regularly changed each time the corresponding content changes. Channel Maker also lets you preview logos and icons, checks graphic formats and sizes for logos and icons, provides unattended automated channel updates, offers a "web mapping" view to visually describe site contents, and lets you control the positioning of channel items using drag-and-drop techniques.

Figure 4.1 shows the application window for Channel Maker with the General tab displayed.

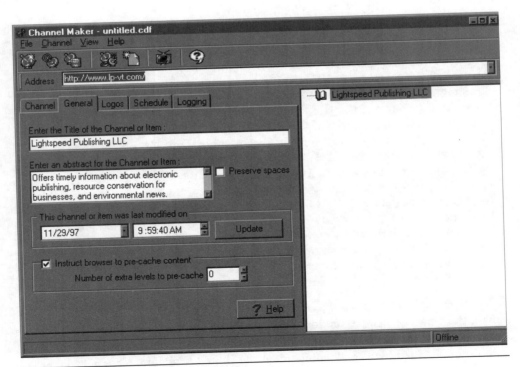

Figure 4.1 Channel Maker interface.

Channel Maker simplifies both the creation and maintenance of CDF files, so if you are performing ongoing channel activities and updates, this program can make your work easier. If you purchase the product from AnyWare Limited, you can also receive automatic software updates through the channel process, as well as updated product information through a channel subscription. Additional details about Channel Maker can be obtained from:

www.anyware.co.uk/anyware/cm/

Planning an Active Channel

The mechanical aspects of creating an Active Channel are not particularly difficult. Any Website pages can be included in a site crawl operation through the data contained in the CDF file. What does require some consideration, however, is how you redesign your content to package it for appropriate channel delivery, and how you might reorganize your site to support efficient and meaningful channel activities. The following sections examine a number of the issues surrounding the design aspects of restructuring a site for channel access.

Site Considerations

An Active Channel can include complex, nested directory structures, any multimedia content that can be embedded in an HTML document (including Java applets, plug-in movies and animation, and audio clips), and as much data as you think is appropriate for downloading.

Realistically, however, to maximize the site visits and downloads, your subscribers will appreciate it if you reorganize your site layout to make it more amenable to channel activities. If you only want to make your site accessible for the most basic site crawling operations available to Internet Explorer (without generating a CDF file), you may want to limit the depth of your nested files to two or three levels and a reasonable number of files. If you are creating a CDF file, you have the option of specifying the appropriate number of subchannels and identifying these items so that the browser can retrieve them as part of a download or updating operation. Even though the downloading process takes place in the background, don't overestimate a subscriber's generosity in granting you disk space to deliver your content. Depending on the type of content you're presenting, the combined files should fit somewhere in the range of 500Kb to 1Mb, unless you have a real reason to transfer more (maybe your company offers videotapes of digitally restored classic black-and-white movies and your channel content provides short clips in RealMedia format).

Plan your site organization and CDF file creation to be respectful of a subscriber's expectations and you will very likely be rewarded with a loyal and growing subscriber base.

Channel Overload

The CDF file that you construct does not place any kind of built-in limitations on the amount of content that you designate for channel delivery. If a subscriber accepts your basic recommendations and you create a channel definition that includes 23Mb of nested content, Internet Explorer will carry out its role of attempting to download the specified content at the indicated time. The subscriber who discovers that channel download times are taking several hours and steadily filling up all of his or her free local storage space won't think much of your delivery strategy. Keep in mind that although the CDF file doesn't place restrictions on your specified channel content, practical considerations dictate that you keep your content in easily downloadable packages of around 500Kb to 1Mb.

Scheduling Considerations

Some developers and site administrators may initially resist the idea of creating an Active Channel because of the notion that a channel requires daily or at least weekly updating. Since a significant amount of work is involved in generating new content, this notion may discourage someone from constructing an Active Channel—it might appear as if doing so would double or triple the normal workload.

In truth, though many major corporate presences may release channel information sometimes even hourly, there is no real reason why you can't select a recommended update schedule that matches the rhythm of your normal content changes. Are you a product vendor offering specialized local items for sale on the Web as gift baskets? Set your schedule to match your catalog and price updates—monthly, bimonthly, whatever works best for your business. Do you offer Web development services and attract potential clients to your site by providing news and information on emerging products and techniques for Internet information handling? Try setting a schedule of every two or three weeks to see how this works for your business. Do you publish an online Webzine with music reviews of new artists and small-label releases? Map your Active Channel to a one-month cycle and send out a highlights document that summarizes your new content and points back to your archives for more information. Creating a channel doesn't necessarily mean your normal 10-hour days developing content are suddenly going to jump to 12- or 14-hour days. The schedule should suit the content. Pay careful attention to your existing content, consider how often it changes significantly, and set your schedule accordingly. Also keep in mind that subscribers have the option of overriding your suggested schedule and instructing their browser to check for updated content whenever they feel it is appropriate. While your suggested schedule may be routinely accepted by many, other users will very likely choose their own content delivery times.

Minimum Update Schedule for Channel Guide Inclusion

If your goal is to get your site listed in the Microsoft Channel Guide, a directory of online sites that have been prepared for Active Channel subscriptions, plan to update your content on at least a weekly basis. The Channel Guide requirements state that this is the minimal acceptable update schedule to gain a listing. Since getting your site listed in this guide could result in a signficant amount of exposure for your company, it's worth considering planning for a weekly update, even if you had previously planned for less-frequent update schedules.

Content Design Issues

You may already have an impressive collection of HTML documents describing your organization or your company's products, but you should re-analyze the suitability of these pages for channel delivery. If appropriate, you might consider designing a screensaver that can be displayed by subscribers who select the Active Desktop mode. The HotWired channel, produced by the publishers of *Wired* magazine, offers a screensaver that cycles through teasers of current articles. New articles are loaded into the screensaver during update cycles for the channel. If your site involves cinema, you could design a screensaver that highlights interesting facts from film history. If your site is history oriented, you could supply a screensaver with capsule biographies of colorful figures from history.

Successful channel content authoring suggests pages that are compact and self-contained, highly interactive, visually attractive without being crowded or cluttered, and packed with information that is of prime importance to your targeted audience. Dynamic HTML has been the tool of choice for most authors working in this medium because it is so well suited to the demands of channel delivery. Other types of elements can be incorporated into Web pages composing channels, such as Java applets, Shockwave and other multimedia plug-ins, and elaborate scripts built in JavaScript or VBScript. If using Java applets, the Internet Explorer site crawler does not automatically seek out and download all of the necessary classes to run an embedded application. You can, however, create a JAR file to archive all required classes and to allow the Java applet to run even if the user is offline when viewing the page.

Ideally, your content should be constructed so that it will interact fluidly with a user even when it is being viewed offline. The majority of links should be contained within pages that are nested within the suggested number of levels for downloading. This doesn't mean that you want to completely avoid links to other outside resources that would require that the user reconnect to the Internet—such a technique can be very effective in providing pointers to valuable (but not indispensable) content. Just be sure to choose your external links carefully and recognize the fact that the person viewing the page will typically expect it to operate from his or her desktop even when offline. The key exception to this guideline is in the case of LAN-connected users who may be spending the majority of their time following links when online and who will rarely download content unless it is so essential to their work that they need it stored locally. If your primary audience is largely composed of users who have a permanent Internet connection through their LAN, you can use a more liberal linking structure, offering abundant links to any relevant content, without worrying about the importance of self-contained documents running offline.

Sites can be successfully authored for use by both Microsoft Active Channels and Netscape Netcaster, but you have to pay very careful attention to the DHTML elements that are used, since in the version 4 releases of both browsers, many incompatibilities exist. If you want to create a channel that is platform independent, you can restrict the DHTML elements to those that work on both platforms (difficult, but certainly possible with some attention to detail), or use a product that dynamically serves the appropriate content to the browser's site crawler (Pictorious iNet Developer 2.0 is one product that supports this approach).

Steps to Creating an Active Channel

Creating an Active Channel and steering traffic to it involves each of the following steps:

Planning the site contents and structuring the hierarchy at your site to easily support channel delivery (as described in the previous section). For those subscribers that choose to download the full site contents at update times, you should place a finite limit on the number of levels within the included Web pages. Two or three levels should work for many applications. Three levels should encompass even a fairly complex site, if you structure the hierarchy accordingly.

Constructing a Channel Definition Format file to expose the contents of your site to browser exploration. This can be done manually, by building the file contents line by line, using any text editor. Alternatively, you can use a CDF creation wizard, such as the one included in FrontPage98, or the standalone wizard available from Microsoft (a preview of this wizard in action is provided in Chapter 3, "The Enabling Standards: CDF, DOM, and RDF").

Designing the supporting graphics that will advertise and identify your site to subscribers. You can do this on the Channel pane and Channel Bar in Internet Explorer, and in the Microsoft Channel Guide, if you choose to have your site listed in this directory.

Enhancing any of the existing content, as is appropriate, by using Dynamic HTML techniques. Subscribers will expect a certain level of interactivity and will probably be disappointed by very basic, static HTML pages. Use DHTML as a chef uses seasoning—to enhance the existing content and to make it more accessible for your users.

Listing your site for inclusion in Microsoft's Channel Guide. Microsoft provides a free listing service for those sites that qualify in its Channel Guide. This listing could potentially open your site to thousands and thousands of subscribers. The most visible ways to attract initial attention are to provide a concise site description that highlights the most important aspects of your Active Channel and create striking graphics that attract subscribers to your banner.

These areas are discussed in the following sections.

Constructing a CDF File

Once you've structured the content on your Website to optimize it for channel delivery (as described in the previous section), the next step is to create a CDF file that reflects the site's content and other important channel characteristics. While someone can subscribe to your site in IE4 even if you don't create a CDF file, the CDF file improves channel interactions in the following ways:

- The CDF file allows the browser to present a hierarchical view of your site contents by using the <CHANNEL> and <ITEM> elements. This channel and subchannel arrangement is displayed as a series of icons nested under your channel display in the Internet Explorer 4 Channel pane.

- The CDF file contains an abstract of your site contents for a concise channel description of what you have to offer.

- The CDF file can perform page-hit logging even while offline, allowing site administrators to acquire a logged record of page perusals the next time a subscriber is logged in to the site. The ability to detect user activities even while they are logged off the network lets developers track and measure the effectiveness of existing page contents and evaluate the importance of different pages to the audience's interests.

- The CDF file supports a utility known as the Profile Assistant to dynamically fill in forms included in documents.

- The CDF file supports the enabling of screensavers composed of channel content.

- The CDF file enables authentication of users accessing site contents.

Many of the automated CDF creation tools support some of the CDF options, but generally not all of them. If you want to access the full range of CDF features, you will probably have to construct the file using a text editor or modify the basic CDF file that is created by one of the automated applications.

CDF File Tags

The format of a CDF file, which is based on the XML specification, includes a series of high-level elements that characterize the channel data. These elements are:

<CHANNEL>

<ITEM>

<TITLE>

<ABSTRACT>

<USAGE>

<LOGO>

<HTTP-EQUIV>

<LOGIN>

<LOG>

<LOGTARGET>

<PURGETIME>

<SCHEDULE>

<EARLIESTTIME>

<INTERVALTIME>

<LATESTTIME>

Definitions for each of these items appear in the following sections.

<CHANNEL> <CHANNEL> includes the basic description of a channel with embedded elements representing the contents contained in the channel, delivery schedules, and so on. The following code fragment illustrates its use:

```
<CHANNEL BASE="http://www.space_city.org"
    HREF="http://www.space_city.org/capsule.htm"
    SELF="http://www.space_city.org/main.cdf">
    <TITLE>Cities in Space: A Retrospective</TITLE>
    <ABSTRACT>Examines the possibilities of creating populated colonies in
space.</ABSTRACT>
    <ITEM HREF="colony/entry.htm" LASTMOD="1998.06.22" PRECACHE="YES">
    ...
    </ITEM>
</CHANNEL>
```

<ITEM> <ITEM> identifies an element that is included in a channel. Other tags that can be nested within the <ITEM> opening and closing tags include <TITLE>, <ABSTRACT>, <USAGE>, and so on. The following code fragment gives an example of how the <ITEM> tag is used:

```
<ITEM HREF="soups/recipes.htm" LASTMOD="1998.09.02" PRECACHE="YES">
    <TITLE>Vegetarian Soups Directory</TITLE>
    <ABSTRACT>Scan and access an extensive recipe database for vegetarian
soups.</ABSTRACT>
    <LOGO HREF="bin/soupdish.ico" STYLE="ICON" />
    <USAGE VALUE="Channel" />
</ITEM>
```

<TITLE> <TITLE> determines the title associated with a channel or individual item, as shown in the following example:

```
<TITLE>The Just In Time for Breakfast Channel</TITLE>
```

<ABSTRACT> <ABSTRACT> offers a concise description of the channel contents that can be used by subscribers to help decide whether to add the channel to their available selections. Whenever a user moves his or her mouse pointer over the channel logo as it is displayed in the IE4 Channel Bar, the text contained in the abstract appears in a small box called a ToolTip. A short example follows:

```
<ABSTRACT>This channel illuminates the mysteries of the universe, including the
origins of the bi-cameral mind and the best places to find fresh
pesto.</ABSTRACT>
```

<USAGE> <USAGE> identifies the manner in which an item is intended to be used; among the valid choices are channel, desktop component, screensaver, and so on. The following example indicates that an ITEM is a screensaver:

```
<USAGE VALUE="ScreenSaver" />
```

<LOGO> <LOGO> specifies an image file or an icon that should be displayed as channel identification. The following example selects an image file to represent the channel logo:

```
<LOGO HREF="images/fishface.gif" STYLE="IMAGE" />
```

<HTTP-EQUIV> <HTTP-EQUIV> provides identifying names for sending and receiving HTTP header information, as shown in the following example:

```
<HTTP-EQUIV NAME="HeaderFollies" VALUE="ParamTextValue" />
```

<LOGIN> <LOGIN> provides a means for determining the authenticity of users logging in to retrieve channel content. An example of the typical method for setting up a username and password follows:

```
<LOGIN METHOD="BASIC" PASS="weasel" USER="yancyq" />
```

<LOG> <LOG> indicates which channels or items are to be recorded to the channel activity log file. The current standard entry type is document.view, but additional log options are being developed. An example follows:

```
<LOG VALUE="document:view" />
```

<LOGTARGET> <LOGTARGET> indicates the destination of the channel activity log data. It also specifies those options that apply to the active log. Logs can be set up to monitor online and offline activity. Log entries can also be purged (sent to the destination server indicated by the logtarget) according to a specified schedule. A typical means of handling the log is shown next; in this case, the log data is purged every five days at 3:00 A.M.

```
<LOGTARGET HREF="http://www.potato_world.net/log_bin" METHOD="POST"
SCOPE="OFFLINE">
     <HTTP-EQUIV NAME="encoding-type" VALUE="zip" />
     <PURGETIME DAY="5" HOUR="3" />
</LOGTARGET>
```

<PURGETIME> <PURGETIME> indicates the interval for sending log file data to the server that is specified by the <LOGTARGET> entry. For example, the following statement sets the purge time to every seven days. The hour value is optional.

```
<PURGETIME DAY="7" HOUR="" />
```

<SCHEDULE> <SCHEDULE> determines the author-recommended schedule for updating channel content. Users can override these settings with their own preferences. The schedule data includes three additional tags (<INTERVALTIME>, <EARLIESTTIME>, and <LATESTTIME>), and also provides the STARTDATE and ENDDATE—the date range during which the schedule values apply. A typical set of schedule values is shown in the following example:

```
<SCHEDULE STARTDATE="1998.08.01" ENDDATE="1998.12.01">
     <INTERVALTIME DAY="2" />
     <EARLIESTTIME HOUR="6" />
     <LATESTTIME HOUR="10" />
</SCHEDULE>
```

<EARLIESTTIME> <EARLIESTTIME> specifies the earliest time—using DAY, HOUR, and MIN units—within the specified <INTERVALTIME> that the channel update should take place. For example, the follow entry indicates that the earliest time is three hours and thirty minutes into the designated interval period:

```
<EARLIESTTIME HOUR="3" MIN="30" />
```

<INTERVALTIME> <INTERVALTIME> indicates the appropriate interval (using DAY, HOUR, and MIN as the units) to perform channel updates. For example, the following entry indicates that updates should be performed every day:

```
<INTERVALTIME DAY="1" />
```

<LATESTTIME> <LATESTTIME> specifies the latest time—using DAY, HOUR, and MIN units—within the specified <INTERVALTIME> that the channel update should take place. For example, the following entry indicates that the latest time is six hours and ten minutes into the designated interval period. The Internet Explorer browser staggers the channel updates randomly within the available window so the server demands do not all occur at the same instant. If you're concerned about excess server activity, extend the range between the <EARLIESTTIME> and the <LATESTTIME> values to distribute the channel updates over a wider range.

```
<LATESTTIME HOUR="6" MIN="10" />
```

Improving Interactivity with Precaching

The PRECACHE value, which is one of the attributes included in the <ITEM> tag, streamlines page display by downloading the file contents of an item to a cache local to the browser at the same time the Web visitor is viewing other content. PRE-CACHE can be enabled simply by specifying YES within the <ITEM> entry, as shown in the following example:

```
<Item HREF="http://www.aviators.org/airshow.html" PRECACHE="YES">
        <TITLE>Highlights from the Washogi Air Show</TITLE>
        <ABSTRACT>Experience a VRML tour from the perspective of the pilot's cock-
pit view.</ABSTRACT>
</ITEM>
```

When content is loaded by precaching in this manner, it becomes immediately available from local storage as soon as a user follows the appropriate link or requests a cached resource. The interactivity of page content handled in this manner will be improved considerably.

Using Screensavers and Desktop Components

Designing content to be used as a screensaver or a desktop component places the associated DHTML content in a prominent position on the user's desktop, or, in the case of the screensaver, fills the entire desktop area whenever the browser-triggered screensaver kicks in. You can designate content to be treated as a screensaver or desktop component with the <USAGE> setting nested in the <ITEM> tag. For example, the following example indicates that the document located at the specified URL will be used as a screensaver by the browser:

```
<ITEM HREF="http://batworld.com/batsaver.htm">
        <TITLE>Bats emerging from a cave at sunset</TITLE>
        <ABSTRACT>Fill your screen with the sounds and sights of bats.</ABSTRACT>
        <USAGE VALUE="ScreenSaver" />
</ITEM>
```

Desktop components, as the name implies, occupy a prominent position on the computer desktop where they can display up-to-the-minute information and content for a particular audience. For example, if you run a Website for a surf shop, you could point a Web cam at the local surf conditions and provide a graphic image every few seconds for distribution through the channel. Avid surfers could watch the changing conditions from their computer desktops and be ready to bolt from the office and head for the beach when the conditions are right. The following example shows the manner in which you would specify a desktop component:

```
<ITEM HREF="http://www.world_o_surf.com/surfwatch.htm">
    <TITLE>Conditions at Laguna Beach</TITLE>
    <ABSTRACT>Offers a desktop window to current surf conditions at Laguna
Beach.</ABSTRACT>
    <USAGE VALUE="DesktopComponent" />
</ITEM>
```

Use the Desktop Component or ScreenSaver usage only when it is appropriate for the Web pages to which you are pointing in the CDF file.

Types of Channels

In its developer information, Microsoft defines the following distinct types of Active Channels:

News Channels. These channels offer frequently updated news items on a particular topic, such as international events, business news, sports scores, weather forecasts and alerts, environmental news, market events, and so on. News items are typically Webcast directly to the subscriber's desktop.

Immersion Channels. Immersion Channels present a fully self-contained environment with built-in navigation and content for offline browsing.

Notification Channels. Notification Channels alert subscribers to newly available information at a channel site and provide pointers to that information through a hierarchical sitemap.

Hybrid Channels. These combine different elements of the three previous types of channels to produce content for specialized uses.

Within these major groupings, content delivery and update techniques fit into three general categories:

Notification. Subscribers receive notice of updates in one of two ways—the red *gleam* that appears in the Channel pane or an email message that is generated when the browser detects changes.

Sitemap. Subscribers view content listings through a collapsible outline composed of channels, subchannels, and individual items. These relationships are defined through the creation of the CDF file, as described in the section titled *Constructing a CDF File.*

Content Caching. Subscribers download a range of content for offline use. This range is determined by the entries in the CDF file, including the PRECACHE attribute attached to an individual ITEM.

News Channel Design

News Channels suit the nature of Web channel delivery. Using frequent update schedules, you can place breaking stories on a user's desktop throughout the day. Subscribers will very likely be attracted to your channel on the basis of their confidence in receiving news items that are important to their interests, whether news, weather, sports, or market conditions. Active Channels that fit this basic format and are starring attractions in the Microsoft Channel Guide include *Wired, The New York Times, CNN Interactive, Time, The CNET Channel, The Wall Street Journal, Fortune,* and *The Forbes Channel.*

Most of these news channels within this genre take advantage of the three content and delivery mechanisms discussed in the previous section: content caching, sitemap organization, and notification. News items are typically organized individually in a hierarchical sitemap presentation; content is designed for downloading during updates for offline viewing from a local cache; and the notification feature alerts subscribers to new material in the preferred manner.

News stories can be categorized using the <TITLE> tag of individual subchannels and then grouping news items in nested fashion within the groups. For example, you could create a title for Local, Domestic, and International news and then cluster two or three stories beneath each category. Subchannels and items can be displayed by expanding the outline structure as it appears in the Channel pane, or hidden by collapsing it.

Typically, you'll want to make each news story a single page with the title providing the story headline and the abstract offering a concise description of the story contents. The use of Dynamic HTML helps consolidate the content and provides a means of navigating through a collection of stories. Chapter 5, "Using Dynamic HTML for Active Channels," offers examples of how to accomplish this by hiding text and then making it visible again.

Large graphics are inconsistent with the intent of a news channel, which is primarily intended to convey information in compact, easily digestible units. If you design the channel to provide information in carefully structured units, subscribers will be able to highlight those topics that are of the most interest to them and gain the news insights they want without excessive download times for the precached content.

Figure 4.2 shows an example of a news channel as published by the folks at *Wired* magazine. The subchannels shown in the Channel pane represent different groupings of information.

Sample Structure for a News Channel

Forming a hierarchy that can be displayed as a collapsible outline in the Internet Explorer Channel pane is a matter of adding additional <CHANNEL> tags in between the starting <CHANNEL> tag and the final </CHANNEL> tag. Those channels that appear in between are considered subchannels with their own titles and as many individual items as you include within each of them. The subchannels serve as organizers, somewhat similar to folders that group the items that are enclosed. You do not need to specify a BASE value for subchannels as you do for the primary channel.

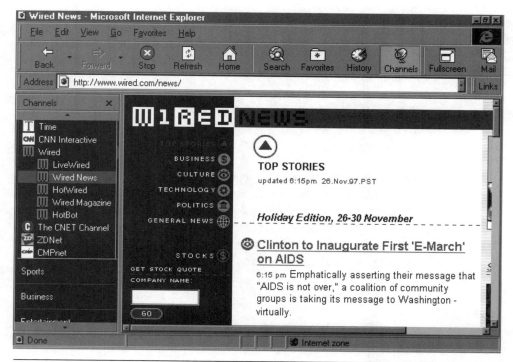

Figure 4.2 Example of a news channel with several subchannels.

The following code example shows a fictional environmental news channel that contains two subchannels, each with its own individual items; in this case, news stories that are contained within:

```xml
<?XML VERSION="1.0" ENCODING="UTF-8"?>

<CHANNEL
      HREF="index.htm"
      BASE="http://www.environews.org/articles/">

      <TITLE>Environmental News Highlights</TITLE>
      <ABSTRACT>Covers international events as they affect the environment and
planetary ecology</ABSTRACT>
      <LOGO HREF="sm_icon.ico" STYLE="ICON"/>
      <LOGO HREF="med_img.gif" STYLE="IMAGE"/>
      <LOGO HREF="lrg_img.gif STYLE="WIDE-IMAGE"/>

      <SCHEDULE STARTDATE="1998-10-23" ENDDATE="1998-12-27">
            <INTERVALTIME DAY="2"/>
      </SCHEDULE>

      <CHANNEL
            HREF="news001.htm">
            <TITLE>Activist Alert</TITLE>
            <ABSTRACT>"Alerts activists to boycotts, protests, and sit-
ins."</ABSTRACT>
            <LOGO HREF="activist.gif STYLE="ICON"/>

            <ITEM HREF="news002.htm" LASTMOD="1998-10-23T10:55">
                  <TITLE>Logging Protest in Medford, Oregon</TITLE>
                  <ABSTRACT>Demonstrators meet at steps of BLM</ABSTRACT>
                  <LOGO HREF="highlite.gif" STYLE="ICON"/>
            </ITEM>
            <ITEM HREF="news003.htm" LASTMOD="1998-10-23T10:57">
                  <TITLE>Greens Organize Boycott of Spirits</TITLE>
                  <ABSTRACT>New boycott intended to stop spirit
production</ABSTRACT>
                  <LOGO HREF="highlite.gif" STYLE="ICON"/>
            </ITEM>
      </CHANNEL>
        <CHANNEL
```

```
HREF="news011.htm">
<TITLE>News from the Field</TITLE>
<ABSTRACT>"Environmental updates from around the world."</ABSTRACT>
<LOGO HREF="updates.gif STYLE="ICON"/>

<ITEM HREF="news012.htm" LASTMOD="1998-10-23T11:55">
        <TITLE>Ocean Dumping Continues off Asian Coastline</TITLE>
        <ABSTRACT>Study indicates pollution levels increasing in Asian
coastal waters.</ABSTRACT>
        <LOGO HREF="highlite.gif" STYLE="ICON"/>
</ITEM>
<ITEM HREF="news013.htm" LASTMOD="1998-10-23T10:57">
        <TITLE>Logging Stopped in Costa Rica</TITLE>
        <ABSTRACT>Logging activities in the western region of Costa Rica
have been halted while government studies effects."</ABSTRACT>
        <LOGO HREF="highlite.gif" STYLE="ICON"/>
</ITEM>
    </CHANNEL>
</CHANNEL>
```

This organization of the channel tags results in a nesting structure that appears as shown in Figure 4.3. Since the default for precaching is YES, all of the news items contained in the subchannels will be downloaded to the user's system where they will be available for offline viewing.

Immersion Channel Design

Immersion Channels provide content that resembles an independent application or multimedia presentation. Rather than relying on the usual navigational controls included with the Active Desktop, an Immersion Channel provides its own controls. Controls might consist of a floating tool bar, embedded directional arrows, fixed button bar, or collapsible menu tree, depending on the type of content and the developer's design goals. The Immersion Channel approach gives the content designer maximum freedom to produce a well-integrated interactive platform that might consist of a multimedia game, a reference tool, an entertainment vehicle, or any other imaginative content that can be placed on the desktop for a user's enjoyment.

Possible Immersion Channel applications include:

- An educational quiz that lets children try to identify plants, animals, and astronomical objects from other galaxies. The same basic structure could be used week after week, but the quiz contents updated regularly through the subscription schedule.

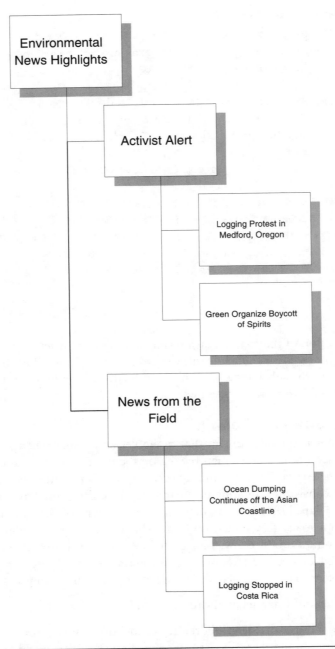

Figure 4.3 Nested structure of an environmental news channel.

- A full-screen calendar that lets users page forward or backward in time. Each individual date block on the calendar highlights an item of historical importance that appeared on that day. The calendar can be paged up to present time to use for recording notes or appointments. The subscription feature can be used to add recent events to the day blocks and add upcoming events to the future months.

- An interactive board game that takes the players into a rain forest where they interact with forest dwellers, strange creatures, and threats from the weather.

- A desktop drum simulator that lets players create polyrhythmic drum patterns by dragging and dropping objects onscreen.

The CDF file for an Immersion Channel only needs to specify the content composing the downloaded material, not those items that normally appear on the Channel Bar (which won't be visible). To identify items that are included in this type of channel, the VALUE attribute of the <USAGE> tag should be set to "None," as shown in the following example:

```
<USAGE VALUE="None"></USAGE>
```

Internet Explorer interprets this entry as meaning that subchannels and items are not to appear as part of the Channel Bar, but the content should be downloaded to the cache for offline use.

Next is an example that shows how you might deliver a calendar that appears as an Immersion Channel.

Sample Structure for an Immersion Channel

```
<?XML VERSION="1.0" ENCODING="UTF-8"?>

<CHANNEL
     HREF="today.htm"
     BASE="http://www.calendar.net/daily/">


     <TITLE>Full-screen Event Calendar</TITLE>
     <ABSTRACT>A calendar and planner that features time travel into the future
and past.</ABSTRACT>
     <LOGO HREF="blip.ico" STYLE="ICON"/>
     <LOGO HREF="blirp.gif STYLE="IMAGE"/>
     <LOGO HREF="bigblirp.gif STYLE="WIDE-IMAGE"/>
```

```
<SCHEDULE STARTDATE="1998.03.19">
      <INTERVALTIME DAY="1"/>
</SCHEDULE>

<ITEM HREF="day2day.htm" LASTMOD="1998.04.20">
      <USAGE VALUE="None"></USAGE>
</ITEM>
<ITEM HREF="more_events.htm" LASTMOD="1998.04.20">
      <USAGE VALUE="None"></USAGE>
</ITEM>
</CHANNEL>
```

Notification Channels

Notification Channels are designed for content that is primarily viewed online. The channel subscriber expects to receive notification of changes that occur on the site—through the normal notification techniques (a gleam or email)—but will normally visit the site while online to view the changes. The content, in this case, is typically items of interest to users, but not enough interest to automatically download.

Possible uses of Notification Channels include:

- Corporate intranet administrators announcing new policy and procedures manuals being posted on the server for user reference.

- Mail order companies announcing that a new color catalog in electronic format is available to those users who might want to view it.

- A multimedia game producer posting notice of a new series of downloadable demos at its shareware site.

- A government agency indicating that an updated series of sales tax forms and regulations has been posted for interested companies to inspect and download.

In all these cases, the notification alerts the user to information or content that he or she may or may not immediately want, but can examine (and download) as needed. If you are providing some type of content that fits in this category, a Notification Channel is a good way to gain the attention of your subscribers without forcing unnecessary files on them.

To prevent the content from being downloaded and cached during updates, you need to ensure that the PRECACHE attribute is set to "No," as shown in the following example:

```
<CHANNEL
      HREF="goodstuff.htm"
```

```
BASE="http://www.catalogo.com/updates/"
PRECACHE="No">
```

Hybrid Channels

Hybrid Channels, as you might expect from the name, draw on elements from any of the three previously described channel types. You can mix and match these different channel elements to create a type of channel that best matches your content presentation and delivery strategy. For example, your site might include musical samples of reviewed albums in streaming audio format for online listening, and also provide concise reviews in DHTML format for downloading and offline reading. To create this type of channel content, you only need to remember the appropriate means of assigning values to items to determine if they are to be precached, treated as immersion content without hierarchical references, or not cached at all for online viewing. Assign the necessary parameters as described in the previous three sections and you have your hybrid channel.

To successfully create a hybrid channel, you need to segregate the realistic uses of the different types of content that you offer. Keep the bandwidth considerations in mind for any material that is designated for precaching. Make sure you clearly identify those areas that have been designed primarily for online viewing—viewers can be encouraged to download content from these areas by individual selection, rather than including the material for automatic downloading during channel updates.

The Immersion Channel approach can be used to provide some interesting desktop application that might tend to draw visitors back to the site in online mode. For example, for a music-oriented site, you could create a DHTML page that displays a layered timeline of music history from the middle 1800s to present day. The timeline could summarize the different styles, show the relationships between different musical roots, showcase some of the prominent musicians in the different areas, and then offer links to your music site to sample the actual music discussed from the online catalog. The Immersion Channel in this instance would be self-contained and interesting to interact with while offline, but it would also encourage music lovers to satisfy their curiosity and increase their knowledge of music genres by supplementing the offline viewing with online visits. Since actually downloading so much musical content would present serious bandwidth problems, this approach satisfies the goal of encouraging frequent returns to your site.

Creating Graphics for Your Channel

Graphics appear in several distinct places in the Active Channel environment and play an important role in getting your site noticed and attracting subscribers.

Microsoft presents some general guidelines for the graphics that are to be used to fit in with the overall Active Desktop environment and the practical uses of the different channel navigation tools. This section explains how to prepare and reference graphics in the CDF file.

Logos Used in Active Channels

Active Channels use several different sized logos to identify sites that are set up for channel delivery, as shown in Figure 4.4.

The Channel pane, shown on the left side of the Internet Explorer application window, uses the smallest graphic—a 16-pixels high and 16-pixels wide icon, which can be produced in either GIF or ICO format. Passing the mouse pointer over the icon or its accompanying text causes a descriptive message to pop up.

The largest graphic image is used in the Channels Explorer Bar, just to the right of the Channel pane. The graphics shown in this area of the window appear in response to opening one of the categories shown in the Channel pane—in Figure 4.4, the News

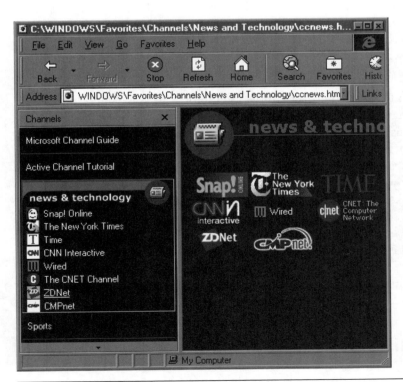

Figure 4.4 Different sized logos used.

& Technology category. If you move the mouse pointer over one of these graphics, the browser displays a popup message that contains the text specified in between the <ABSTRACT> tags in the CDF file; in other words, a concise description of the site contents. The graphic used in the Channels Explorer Bar should be in GIF format and precisely 32 pixels high and 194 pixels wide.

The Active Desktop Channel Bar, which appears in place by default if the Active Desktop option has been selected in the Windows Control Panel, uses a logo that is 32 pixels high and 80 pixels wide.

If you only reference a single 32×80-pixel image in the CDF file, Internet Explorer will use the same image for the Active Desktop Channel Bar as well as the bar inside the browser window.

Advice for Creating Graphics

To get the best results when creating graphics for your logo images, follow these guidelines:

Use an 8-bit Windows palette. Even if you suspect your audience is equipped with high-resolution monitors running at 24-bit depths, don't bother trying to use elaborate palettes for your logo graphic images. Internet Explorer reduces all graphics to a fixed 256-color (8-bit) image. When creating graphics, to ensure you won't see color shifts due to colors being translated to a lower bit depth, choose the stock Microsoft Windows halftone palette, if your graphic application offers this option.

Use black as the logo background color for the Active Desktop. Personal aesthetics aside, Microsoft has organized its Active Desktop environment around a black-background theme, and it recommends the use of a black background for the medium-sized logo (32×80-pixel image).

Use a colored background for the browser Channel Bar. The large (32×194 pixel) logo graphics ideally should have a colored background. While Microsoft probably won't kick you out of the Channel Guide if you violate this recommendation (at least it hasn't for several major corporate channels), it recommends the colored background—which helps the large logo stand out next to adjacent logo images when the mouse passes over it (which causes the plain white text to be replaced by the colored logo image).

Leave room for the gleam in the upper-left corner of the logo. A gleam, similar to a red asterisk, appears in the upper-left corner of the large image whenever the browser detects updated content. Avoid placing critical identifying information in that area of the image so that it won't be hidden by the gleam.

Maintain some graphic similarities between the two large logos. Creating a graphically similar presentation for both large logos lets Web visitors transition from the Channel Bar on the Active Desktop to the one inside the browser window. Without some similarities, the change will be too abrupt and confusing.

Indicate item relationships in some manner. Use similar colors or some distinct graphic element to indicate relationships between individual items. Containers for several nested items might be shown in a bright color with a slightly more subdued shade to indicate the nested items. Try to provide visual cues to guide users through your site contents as they appear in the Channel pane.

Favor simplicity over flashiness. While your logo may be positioned on the Channel Bar with the high-power corporate logos from Time, Warner Brothers, or Disney, don't try to attract attention by overpowering the surrounding graphics. Your site will receive more positive recognition if you use simple, tasteful graphics carefully rendered to fit the minuscule confines of the logo areas. If you try to get too flashy, your logo will end up looking like a Hawaiian shirt at the Emmy Award ceremonies.

Don't use animated GIFs. If you think it might liven up your icon or logo display by employing an animated GIF in this role, don't bother trying. Neither the Channel Bar or the Channels Explorer Bar support animated GIFs. If you try to include one, Internet Explorer displays only the first image in the animation.

Referencing Graphics

The CDF file <LOGO> tag recognizes three style values to identify the logo graphics used in the browser display: Image, Image-Wide, and Icon.

To specify the location of the Active Desktop Channel Bar image, use an entry similar to the following:

```
<LOGO HREF="spiffy.gif" STYLE="Image">
```

To specify the location of the browser window Channel Bar image, use an entry similar to the following:

```
<LOGO HREF="mungo.gif" STYLE="Image-Wide">
```

To specify the location of the small icon used in the Channel pane, use an entry similar to the following:

```
<LOGO HREF="frogbits.gif" STYLE="Icon">
```

The No-Logo Option

If you don't specify logo and icon image information in the CDF file, Internet Explorer supplies a generic image with your site label attached to it. Since you're probably seeking a higher-level identity than is offered by a bland, generic image, we recommend that you supply your own unique graphics to ensure a distinictive channel identity. Users who see that you don't even have the energy to create graphics to represent your site probably won't be encouraged to even take a peek at your content.

Attracting Subscribers

Once you have created a CDF file for your site contents, there are several methods that you can use to set up the mechanism for attracting new subscribers to your site. You can:

- Create a text link within the entry page of your site that includes a pointer to the CDF file.

- Embed an image with a link to the CDF file. Microsoft's Add Channel graphic can be used for this purpose if your site meets its criteria.

- Send email to potential subscribers providing a pointer to the CDF file for the site (for example: `http://www.cool_guys.org/cooler.cdf`).

Simple CDF File Link

The Internet Explorer 4 browser includes some built-in capabilities that support subscriber interactions. The simplest technique for using the CDF file for soliciting subscriptions is to place a reference to it in a link on your primary Web page—the entry page to your site. The link can be associated with either a text entry or an image. The following example shows it as a text item:

```
<A HREF="http://www.yow.net/yow.cdf">Let Yow! into your life: subscribe now!</A>
```

When a Web visitor clicks on this link, the Internet Explorer 4 browser displays a subscription dialog box, as shown in Figure 4.5. The dialog box guides the new subscriber through the process of establishing the channel as an addition to those channels featured in the Channel pane.

Since the browser does all the work of putting up the dialog box and handling the subscription details, as author, you only have to create the link. Once the new item is in the Channel pane, the subscriber receives automated updates based on the

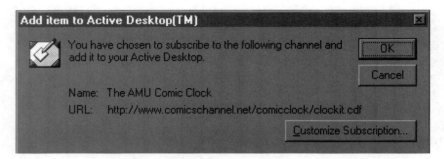

Figure 4.5 Subscriber dialog box.

schedule determined in the CDF file, or can connect to the channel at any time by clicking on the entry shown there.

Graphic CDF Link

Instead of using a text link to point to the CDF file for your channel, you can embed an image and use that image to launch the Channel Subscription Wizard. The Microsoft Add Active Channel graphic can be used by those sites that agree to the terms posted by Microsoft. These terms specify that if you use the logo, you must use the accompanying script that directs anyone who is not using Internet Explorer 4 to download the browser.

The same script also initiates the installation of the channel for those users who already have Internet Explorer 4 installed.

The HTML code for embedding and linking a graphic is similar to the text example that appeared in the previous section.

```
<A HREF="http://"www.yow.net/yow.cdf">
<IMG BORDER=0 SRC="http://www.yow.net/addChan.gif">
Let Yow! into your life: subscribe now!
</A>
```

Email Update Notification

When a new user subscribes to your channel using the Channel Subscription Wizard, he or she has the option of selecting email notification as the means of being alerted to new channel content. Once again, the email message is generated automatically by the browser whenever the site crawler detects new content on one of its regularly scheduled visits to the site. Once the subscriber gets the message, he or she can perform a manual update of the channel content on his or her system by choosing the Update All Subscriptions option from the Favorites menu.

Getting Noticed: A Listing in the Channel Guide

After you've done all the work of creating channel content and preparing a CDF file to describe the site contents, how do you get noticed in the fathomless world of the Internet? Channels are still a relatively new technology, and your audience may not be sure how to look for new and emerging channels.

One sure-fire way of getting noticed is to get your channel included in the Microsoft Active Channel Guide, a directory listing of all the channels that meet the Microsoft criteria. Everyone who is running Internet Explorer 4 or Windows98 has single-click access to the Microsoft Channel Guide, so this focal point on the Web is a good initial place to plant your signpost on the block to attract would-be channel subscribers.

Microsoft lists some conditions to make your site valid for inclusion in the Active Channel Guide, but they're not too rigorous and you probably can satisfy the requirements without an enormous amount of work. The basic requirements to obtain a listing are:

- Your site must use a CDF file to expose its channel content, and the content must include at least one Dynamic HTML feature.

- You should post the Microsoft-provided graphic—*Add Active Channel Logo*— to your entry page, with the underlying code attached to it. This allows subscribers to set up a subscription to your site with the push of a button.

- You must schedule content updates for at least once a week. Channel subscribers typically expect at least that level of activity on a site, and Microsoft is apparently trying to ensure that the Active Channel Guide doesn't end up pointing to a lot of inactive channels.

To obtain the Add Active Channel Logo and underlying code, Microsoft requires that you register with its Site Builder Network and agree to the logo-use terms. Registration can be accomplished online; you need to choose an identification name and password for future access to the Site Builder area on Microsoft's server. Microsoft will check your site contents to determine whether you're eligible for a Level 1 or Level 2 membership to the Site Builder Network.

You might also want to include the Get Microsoft Internet Explorer logo to encourage those users with other browsers who want Active Channel access to your site to download the necessary software. A number of conditions also apply to the use of the Microsoft Internet Explorer logo; for a full description of the terms, point your browser to:

www.microsoft.com/sbnmember/levels/getielogo.asp

The Active Channel Guide has the potential of exposing your site to a huge audience, so you should be prepared to keep a steady flow of worthwhile content flowing through the channel from the time you make your initial posting. At press time, this was a free listing service being provided to developers by Microsoft, but there's no guarantee it will continue to offer listings when channel use becomes extremely popular and the guide becomes bigger than the New York City telephone book.

Netscape offers a similar listing service for developers of Netcaster channels, as described in Chapter 7, "Creating a Netcaster Channel."

Using Special Features Supported by CDF

A number of special features supported by the Channel Definition Format are not typically included in third-party applications that automatically generate CDF files to turn Websites into channels. These features generally require that you set up the parameters by manually editing the CDF file and, in some cases, create additional code to handle the feature—such as constructing a routine in Perl to handle log file data that is returned to your site server as a result of browser activity logging. Several of these features are discussed in the following sections.

Enabling Password Protection

Microsoft Internet Explorer has the built-in capability to store a user's name and password when a subscription is initiated. The LOGIN element in the CDF file is a cue that Internet Explorer should prompt the subscriber for a username and password; this information is then stored with the rest of the channel subscription details. The username and password can be used to authenticate a user's identity during subsequent interactions.

Internet Explorer can use HTTP authentication for Web pages when using each of the different form types, including NTLM, RPA, Basic, and HTML.

Internet Explorer can retrieve the name and password from the channel's subscription properties while processing the form information as long as you ensure that the form uses the POST method, provides an input text box that identifies the name as either "user" or "username," and includes a password field with the name "password."

For example, the form method should be specified in a manner similar to the following line:

```
<FORM METHOD="POST" ACTION="http://www.grackle.org/log_processing">
```

The input text box should be defined as follows:

```
<INPUT TYPE-TEXT NAME="user" SIZE=14>
```

The password should be identified in the following manner:

```
<INPUT TYPE-PASSWORD NAME="password" SIZE=14>
```

Logging User Activities

Tracking the navigation paths followed by visitors to your Website can be accomplished in a number of ways, but how do you get an idea what areas are most interesting to your site visitors when they download channel content and view it offline? Internet Explorer 4 provides a built-in mechanism for tracking the page hits, even during offline activities. This feature, when enabled, can be used to return a log file indicating user activities to a designated area on the Web server handling your site. The page-hit log files can be processed by a Perl script on the server, or, if your pages are served by a Microsoft Internet Information Server (IIS), you can handle log file contents using the ISAPI DLL, which will parse and extract the relevant data.

To activate the logging feature for your channel, specify the LOG element in the site CDF file. You can indicate particular items to be included in the log and define a target destination for the data using the LOGTARGET entry pointing to the appropriate URL. Each time Internet Explorer detects a change in the CDF file for the site (when connecting to the channel), it uploads the log file contents to the LOGTARGET. Users or network administrators who are squeamish about collecting this kind of information can disable the feature at the browser level, but most Web visitors should not object to this kind of logging if you inform them ahead of time and make it clear that the information collected is for analyzing the degree of interest in different pages included in the channel.

Following is a typical log file collected during site browsing of a channel. Log file information is compiled using the Extended Log File Format, a standard that was developed by the World Wide Web Consortium. To get a better sense of what the log file entries mean, let's take a closer look at a sample file:

```
#Fields: s-URI
http://www.grackles.org/articles/musings.htm
#Fields: c-context c-cache c-date c-time c-duration
T 1 10-12-1998 12:04:37 00:09:22
N 1 10-13-1998 09:22:20 00:02:01
N 1 10-14-1998 09:30:12 00:01:45
```

The #Fields entry is based on the SCOPE= attribute that is included in the LOG-TARGET entry. As shown in this sample file, the log file includes five separate fields—each represented as a column—with the following definitions:

Context. Indicates the type of view option that was active in the browser window when the document was displayed. N indicates the normal browser window, T indicates the full-screen view (otherwise known as Theater View), D indicates the viewing of an Active Desktop object, and S indicates the Screensaver mode.

Cache. A 0 indicates the content was retrieved from the actual site; a 1, from the local browser cache.

Date. The date value, presented using a MM-DD-YYYY format, specifies what day the HTML file was viewed.

Time. The time value, presented using a HH:MM:SS format, records the time (using a 24-hour clock) when the HTML document was viewed.

Duration. Indicates the number of hours, minutes, and seconds that the page was actively displayed in the browser window.

Looking at the first line logged in the sample file indicates that on October 12, 1998, the indicated HTML document was displayed in Theater View at 12:04 P.M. The file was active in the browser window for 9 minutes and 22 seconds.

Log files are not much use unless you set up some kind of server-side processing to handle the incoming flow of information as Internet Explorer transfers the logged data during channel updates. However, with a bit of work to enable the sever-side parsing and extraction of data, you can gain valuable insights into the use of your Web pages—information that can help you refine and improve your site contents over time.

Summary

Constructing a properly compliant CDF file to expose your site contents to the universe of Internet Explorer browsers can change the nature of your Website strategy. Webcasting involves significant differences in the way material is presented and offered to users, but the physical aspects of turning your site into an Active Channel are relatively simple—as you can see from this chapter. Through careful organization of your Active Channel page content to a specific portion of your site, you can continue to offer material for conventional browsers and also provide a subscription area with items for delivery highlighted in the CDF file.

Chapter 5, "Using Dynamic HTML for Active Channels," deals with the design side of the equation—how to effectively use Dynamic HTML to create pages that will communicate well with your subscribers, take full use of the interactive features of DHTML, and have impact on Web audiences.

5

Using Dynamic HTML
for Active Channels

This chapter explores the ways you can use DHTML to create content that will keep subscribers tuned in to your channel just to see what you're going to do next. The material includes guidelines for producing DHTML documents for delivery through channels, special features available through Internet Explorer, and several examples of effective approaches to DHTML page construction.

Using the capabilities of DHTML documents delivered through Active Channels, you have all the tools necessary to build interactive presentations or even full applications and drop them onto your user's desktop. With the programming power of JavaScript or VBScript, and the page layout control offered by Cascading Style Sheets with Positioning, you can produce impressive page designs that include built-in intelligence, with components that respond to key presses, mouse movements, and so on.

Dynamic HTML Design Guidelines

When handed a new set of rules for controlling page layout and user interaction, exuberant developers often try to squeeze every possible trick into their Web page design efforts. Given an easy method for animating onscreen objects, many ambitious designers start arrows flying around onscreen, text headings whirling across the page as they change colors, images flashing and spinning, and so on. The net result is the multimedia equivalent to those early days of desktop publishing when every page had 40 different fonts, 6 columns, and 4 embedded cartoons from the latest clip art collection. Until DHTML becomes commonplace, many designers will cross the barriers of good taste without inhibition and enter into those regions inhabited by strip mall architects and Las Vegas sign designers. Sometimes, less is more.

As you begin to incorporate DHTML elements into those Web pages intended for channel delivery, consider the following guidelines:

As the first of your channel Web pages is displayed, you can use multimedia effects to focus attention and suggest the tone and character of your material. Pay attention to the way that television shows and films use the first few seconds to gain your interest, often using animated titles and graphics in artistic ways to draw you in and get you involved with the presentation. If your Web pages open with a captivating special effect, subscribers will be interested in seeing what other surprises you have for them. Use discretion, however; no one is going to want to wait two minutes for your dazzling, spinning, multicolored satellite to spin across the screen just to present the title of your page. Web attention spans are short; don't lose your audience before you even get started.

Channel content fits naturally into full-screen and Active Desktop modes (or Webtop modes for Netcaster subscribers), but when you use the full screen in this manner, you need to devise a cohesive, easily followed navigation system for your users. This can be as simple as an expandable outline with topic choices or as elaborate as a three-dimensional, repositionable toolbar with images mapped to the content, but however you go, remember that ease of navigation is probably the most important single aspect of your page design. Cast a critical eye at other hypertext and multimedia presentation tools (online help systems, Macromedia Director projects, Folio VIEWs infobases, and so on) and examine the way that navigation is handled. Users should be able to easily locate all available topics, be able to skip forward and backward or return to the beginning, and should be able to stay oriented through some type of visual guide or content tracking display.

Develop your own individualized style sheet that can be applied to all the pages on your site. By developing a distinctive, recognizable style, you can establish an identity for your site—whether you're trying for super cool, conservatively formal, hyper-modern futuristic, or classically elegant, every aspect of your page design can be encapsulated in a good style sheet. Unlike designers working with print media, you don't have to pay a premium (for color separations and extra printing costs) to use color for both text and graphic elements. Look at the way that seasoned designers use color on the Web effectively (the pages at *Wired* and HotWired are instructive, even if lime green and fuschia aren't your favorite shades). Invest some time in structuring the layout and refining the page presentation. If you don't have a good deal of page design experience, style sheets produced by professional designers are beginning to appear, and these can be applied to your pages by the simple referencing of an external style sheet file. Only do this, of course, if the style sheet is being offered for public use.

Consider the planned delivery mode when designing the DHTML content. For example, if you're building a page to present as a screensaver for Active Channel subscribers, the graphics and animation should be at the forefront of the design, with text and links less dominant. If your page is to be delivered in a window and contains several levels of news items, focus on making the page design highlight the available content and present clear paths to navigate through the information.

The examples in this chapter explore the different ways you can apply DHTML techniques to solve design problems.

Design Features of IE4

Internet Explorer provides some unique features, as discussed in the following sections, that enable a developer to accomplish various feats with a minimum of difficulty. These are, of course, platform-specific effects, but worth considering if you are producing content targeted for a single platform, such as Active Channel content for delivery to subscribers.

Using ActiveX Controls

If you're developing solely for an audience running Internet Explorer 4, you can use a wide variety of ActiveX objects within your DHTML documents. These objects can do everything from opening up an Adobe Acrobat document to updating the contents of a database. Microsoft Internet Explorer includes several ActiveX objects that are installed with it when you perform the typical installation; other ActiveX objects can be obtained through third parties. One nice feature about using ActiveX objects and controls is that they can be preprogrammed; in other words, they can be set up to create a certain effect or perform a specific function and then just dropped into an HTML document. The result is that many kinds of effects that would be difficult or time-consuming to program can be introduced into scripts where they will immediately become functional. For example, complex animations that move objects around on a page and transition graphics through dissolves and wipes can be added in the form of an ActiveX DirectAnimation sprite and path object. Manipulating these kinds of objects and controls becomes a matter of modifying their methods, properties, and behavior to events (such as mouse clicks and button presses).

Current-generation DHTML editors are beginning to include built-in facilities for inserting and managing various types of objects and ActiveX controls. ExperTelligence WebberActive uses an Object Assistant, as shown in Figure 5.1, to select from a range of available objects.

Once the object has been inserted into a document, WebberActive gives you the ability to manipulate its methods, properties, and events that control it, as shown in

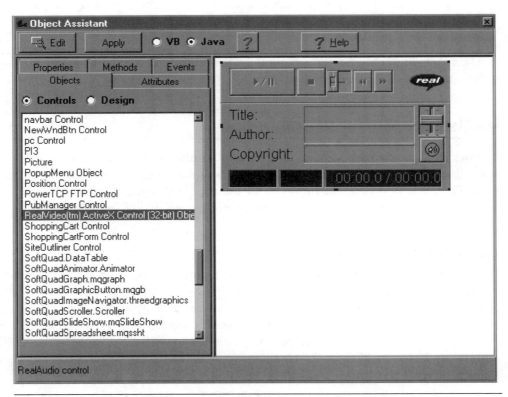

Figure 5.1 Selecting a RealVideo ActiveX control object in WebberActive.

Figure 5.2. This provides a streamlined way to create and manage a wide variety of objects available to you as a developer when working on the IE4 platform.

Using the controls available through ActiveX components, you can integrate different types of content into your page display. For example, you may have a graphic of a television screen on a page with a tuner that the viewer can click to display different QuickTime movies. Or, you could integrate a stream of RealAudio content by clicking on a radio dial graphic. Or, you could link into a live database and display portions of the database content on a real-time basis.

Programming HTML Tags

Since the introduction of JavaScript 1.0, which provided programming control over many of the elements of an HTML document, the programmable object model has been progressively expanded by both Microsoft and Netscape to include many additional objects. With the introduction of Internet Explorer 4, Microsoft has

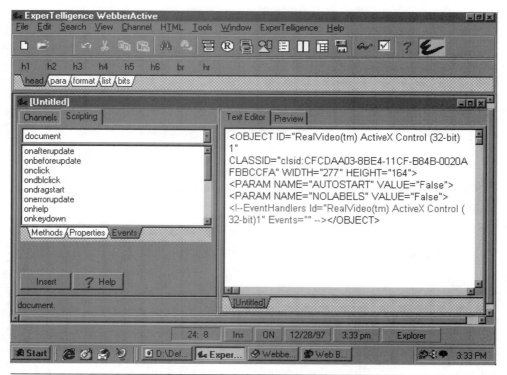

Figure 5.2 Script-level object controls.

made the entire range of HTML tags—as well as all the other elements of the document—accessible through script-level controls.

Tags have individual properties and, as is the case for all the other HTML elements that can be controlled through Dynamic HTML, you can change these properties in response to events that occur within the browser environment or style sheet definitions.

For example, the <H1> tag features the following properties:

- className
- docHeight
- docLeft
- docTop
- docWidth
- parentElement
- sourceIndex
- tagName
- align
- id
- style
- title

The <H1> tag also features its own methods, behaviors that can be applied to it, including:

- removeMember
- scrollIntoView
- contains
- getMember
- setMember

The text that appears between tags can be changed dynamically by means of an inline event handler. When using dynamic content in this manner, you have three options as to the methods that apply:

- **inner[HTML|text]:** Replaces the HTML code between the start and end tags of the element.

- **outer[HTML|text]:** Replaces the enclosed HTML code and the outer tags as well.

- **insertAdjacent[HTML|text]:** Used to add text that appears in a specified position. To place text before the beginning of the start tag, use beforeBegin. To place text after the start tag, use afterBegin. To place text before the end tag, use beforeEnd. To place text after the end tag, use afterEnd.

Only text elements can be modified using these methods, and their use depends on their actual position within a sequence of code. You cannot use these methods in combination with tables and table content.

As a simple example of how this works, let's take a heading and give it an ID value that is equal to "poe."

```
<H1 ID=poe>Raven Droppings</H1>
```

Using the heading ID, you can manipulate the text that appears within these two tags. To insert additional text that appears after the existing title, but before the end of the tag, you use the insertAdjacentHTML method with the beforeEnd parameter selected. For this example, we'll create a simple function that carries out the insertAdjacentHTML method that is called when a button is pressed. The script for this operation follows.

```
<HTML>
<HEAD>
<TITLE>The Amazing Expanding Heading</TITLE>
</HEAD>
<BODY>
<H1 ID=poe>Raven Droppings</H1>
<INPUT TYPE=BUTTON Value="Expand Heading" onClick="changeHead()">
<SCRIPT LANGUAGE=VBSCRIPT>
Sub changeHead()
     poe.insertAdjacentHTML "beforeEnd",": Hilarious Out-takes from Poe's Works"
End Sub
</SCRIPT>
</BODY>
</HTML>
```

When the page first loads, it appears as shown in Figure 5.3.

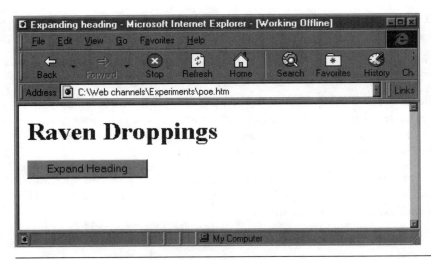

Figure 5.3 Original H1 tagged text.

When you click the Expand Heading button, the `changeHead()` function is called, which uses the insertAdjacentHTML method to insert the indicated text just before the </H1> tag (using the beforeEnd parameter). The resulting display is shown in Figure 5.4.

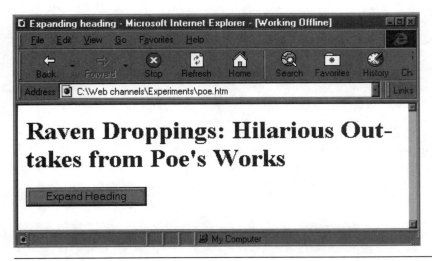

Figure 5.4 Expanded H1 heading.

Used creatively, this capability allows you to change not only the text contained within a set of tags, but the tags themselves, providing significant flexibility when manipulating content in an HTML document.

Assigning Filters to Visual Objects

Internet Explorer 4 supports a number of different filters, which produce specific effects when applied to any of the HTML objects that support the Filter property. Tags such as <DIV>, <IMG>, and <OBJECT> can be controlled by any of the following filters:

Alpha. Determines the opacity of an image, based on a percentage value (for example, alpha 70%).

Blur. Creates an illusion of motion by averaging a group of pixels in an indicated direction with a specified strength.

Chroma. Makes a specified color display as transparent. This effect can be used when layering images, much the way chromakey effects are used in television to insert images into backgrounds.

Drop Shadow. Produces a silhouette around an image of text that resembles a shadow.

Flip Horizontal. Flips an object from side to side, producing what is essentially a mirror image of the original source.

Flip Vertical. Flips an object from top to bottom, making it appear upside down.

Glow. Adds a radiance around the perimeter of an object in whatever color you specify.

Gray. Removes all color from an object, resulting in a grayscale image.

Invert. Inverts the hue, color, and saturation of an object, producing an effect that looks somewhat like a negative image.

Mask. Creates a transparent mask from a selected visual object, using pixels that are a specific color.

Shadow. Produces the illusion of a shadow by painting a solid silhouette behind an object. This effect can't be varied like a drop shadow, but the intensity is automatically varied to create a more natural-looking shadow effect.

Wave. Creates a rippling effect upon the specified image.

Xray. Produces an effect similar to a black-and-white inverted image of the source object.

Swapping Image Sources

One of the simplest effects you can achieve using DHTML in IE4 is a simple image swap—you change the source file referred to within an <IMG> tag in response to an event; for example, the onmouseover event. The new image that you specify immediately replaces the original source each time the mouse pointer passes over the region.

To show how this works, let's take an image of a caterpillar and then use the onmouseover event to change it into a butterfly. The simple line of code to accomplish this would read as follows:

```
<IMG src="caterp.gif" onmouseover="this.src = 'monarch.gif';">
```

As shown in Figure 5.5, when the source for the image is initially loaded, the file caterp.gif (the caterpillar image) appears in the browser window. This source is then dynamically changed when the onmouseover event occurs. When the mouse is detected over the image, the image source is immediately changed to monarch.gif, the image shown in Figure 5.6.

The investment in coding is minor for a fairly impressive effect that can be used in a number of different ways in HTML documents.

Using Event Bubbling

Using event handlers has been a very common method for incorporating programmability into objects, even before the popular acceptance of object-oriented languages

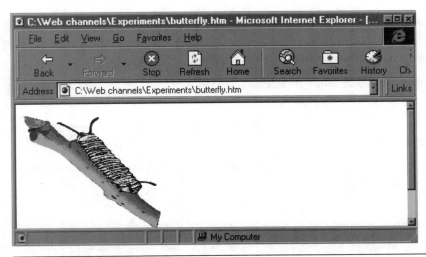

Figure 5.5 The initial SRC points to the caterpillar image.

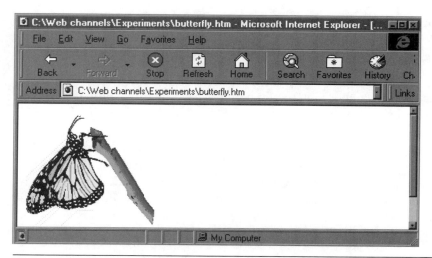

Figure 5.6 The onmouseover event changes the source to the monarch.

like Java and C++. An *event handler* is a routine that responds by running an appropriate sequence of code whenever a particular event takes place, such as the loading of a file or the press of a key. The earliest multimedia programming applications, such as Asymetrix ToolBook and Macromedia Director, applied this concept to the interactions that control multimedia presentations. By building the architecture for DHTML around an event model, pages can be made to respond to a variety of occurrences that take place within a browser.

Internet Explorer 4 supports a greater collection of elements that can be affected by events than has any other previous or current browser. Literally, any of the HTML elements contained in a document can be used to trigger an event. Earlier browser implementations limited event handling to only the following elements:

- Anchors

- Image maps

- Form elements

- Applets

- Objects

With the ability to associate events with other elements through IE4, the developer can achieve interactivity throughout the entire contents of the document. For example, a heading can be made to glow (using the Glow filter) when the mouse pointer moves over it. Or, clicking on a block of text marked with the <BLOCK-QUOTE> tag could trigger the audio playback of a reading of the text appearing in the block.

The events that apply under Internet Explorer 4 are primarily mouse-related events, but some keyboard-specific events are also included, as shown in Table 5.1.

Event Bubbling Behavior

Normally, with applications that rely on event handlers to control the program flow, if an event takes place and there is no handler registered to deal with the event, the action is essentially lost. In other words, if a user clicks on an image and that image is not set up to respond to a mouse-click event, nothing happens.

With *event bubbling* as it is handled in Internet Explorer, each event that occurs gets passed up through the document hierarchy until an appropriate handler is located or the event reaches the highest object in the tree: the document itself. This feature makes possible several interesting capabilities. It allows designers to create documents where the interactivity can be expressed in smaller amounts of code, it

Table 5.1 Events Recognized by All Elements in IE4

Mouse Event	Event Produced by
onmouseover	Positioning the mouse pointer directly over any part of the element
onmouseout	Moving the mouse pointer outside the area of an element
onmousedown	Pressing any of the mouse buttons (whether two or three are present)
onmouseup	Releasing any of the mouse buttons (whether two or three are present)
onmousemove	Repositioning the mouse pointer once it is over an element
onclick	Clicking the left mouse button on an element
ondblclick	Double-clicking the left mouse button on an element
onkeypress	Pressing and releasing a key on the keyboard once (holding the key down causes multiple generations of this event)
onkeydown	Pressing a key once (holding the key down does not trigger multiple events)
onkeyup	Releasing a key

minimizes the requirements for frequent code changes if a document is modified, and it creates a central means for controlling a number of different common actions.

Each time an event takes place, Internet Explorer creates a unique property— referred to as the srcElement—that is associated with the `window.event` object. This property records one key characteristic about the event: the element on the page that triggered it. In the following example, this event can bubble up through the document where the srcElement is interpreted by the browser, tested within a function, and used to change the style attributes of each element—the individual items grouped within the <SPAN> tags—as the pointer rolls in or out of the appropriate area.

The code for this rollover effect follows:

```
<HTML>
<HEAD>
<TITLE>Points of Interest in Vermont</TITLE>
<STYLE>
.Place {
     cursor:hand;
     font-family: verdana;
     font-size: 16;
     font-style: normal;
     background-color: black;
     color: white
}
.Point {
     cursor: hand;
     font-family: verdana;
     font-size: 16;
     font-style: bold;
     background-color: blue;
     color: orange
}
</STYLE>
</HEAD>
<BODY>
<SPAN CLASS=Place>Stowe</SPAN>
<SPAN CLASS=Place>Burlington</SPAN>
<SPAN CLASS=Place>Middlebury</SPAN>
<SPAN CLASS=Place>Waterbury</SPAN>
<SPAN CLASS=Place>Waitsfield</SPAN>
```

```
<SCRIPT>
function point_at() {
      if(window.event.srcElement.className=="Place") {
         window.event.srcElement.className="Point";
      }
}
document.onmouseover=point_at;

function point_away() {
      if (window.event.srcElement.className=="Point") {
         window.event.srcElement.className="Place";
      }
}
document.onmouseout=point_away;
</SCRIPT>
</BODY>
</HTML>
```

When displayed, the individual items appear with black backgrounds and white text, as shown in the WebberActive preview window in Figure 5.7. The background changes to blue and orange characters when the mouse pointer is positioned over an item. The `point_at` and `point_away` functions serve to toggle the style attributes on and off as mouseover and mouseout events bubble up to the document level and their srcElements are used to control the script behavior.

Additional elements could be easily added to this document without the need to create additional event handlers for each one of them. As you can see, event bubbling makes it easy to manipulate all the elements of an HTML document in very effective ways.

Extending Event Behavior

You can use events based on page elements to trigger the playing of scripts. For example, you could designate a heading level with a particular ID that can play a script when clicked. To do so, use a variation of the following code; the <SCRIPT FOR> tag makes this construction possible:

```
<SCRIPT FOR=jumpingH2 EVENT="onclick()" LANGUAGE="VBSCRIPT">
      ...script for doing something interesting, like animating the heading...
</SCRIPT>
<H2 ID=jumpingH2>Click to watch this heading jump.</H2>
```

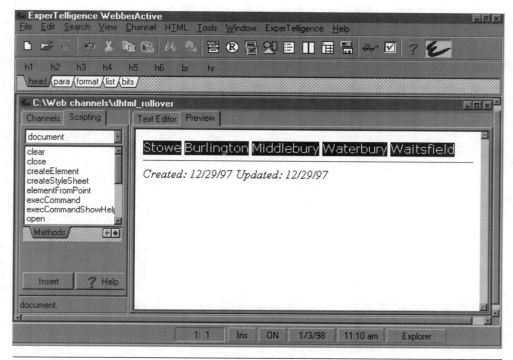

Figure 5.7 Text items used for rollover effect.

With this script in place, the text bracketed by the heading tags becomes responsive to mouse clicks. Each time it is clicked, the script included in the <SCRIPT FOR> tag is played. You could use the script to animate (or reposition) the text, display a hidden object, or apply a filter to a graphic image.

Similar uses of this technique to associate events with tagged elements on the page greatly expand the range of your options as a developer.

Controlling the Visibility of Objects

One of the most powerful features of Dynamic HTML is the sleight-of-hand offered by the Visibility property of objects. By alternately hiding objects and then making them visible under program control, you can generate pages that on the surface appear simple—with uncluttered layouts—but contain intricate and complex content beneath the surface. Using objects that can be hidden until you decide to display them—including text blocks and images—makes DHTML an ideal medium for distributing channel content, since extremely content-rich files can be compacted into the perfect form for convenient transfer and display.

As a simple example, let's design a page that displays a question and provides the answer to the question when you click on the question itself. This example demonstrates how the Visibility property of an object—in this case, a line of text—can be turned on or off under script control.

The script for this example follows:

```
<HTML>
<BODY>
<DIV STYLE="cursor: hand" onclick="magic(document.all.answer);">
Click to find out how many humans roamed the planet in 10,000 B.C.</DIV>
<SPAN STYLE="color: green" ID=answer>There were approximately 3 million homo
sapiens at this time.</SPAN><BR>
Spacing remains the same whether the item is hidden or visible.
<SCRIPT LANGUAGE=JAVASCRIPT>
answer.style.visibility="hidden"
function magic(n) {
      if(n.style.visibility=="hidden") {
         n.style.visibility="visible";
      } else {
         n.style.visibility="hidden";
      }
}
</SCRIPT>
</BODY>
</HTML>
```

When the page is first displayed, as shown in Figure 5.8, the Visibility property of the text between the <SPAN> tags (identified with the answer ID) is set to "hidden." The question itself, bracketed between <DIV> tags, has been set up so that the cursor changes to a hand when over the text. Using this style attribute makes it possible to indicate the interactivity of this text; without the Cursor option, you would have to embed the text within an anchor to cause the cursor to change in response to the mouse pointer.

Clicking the question calls the magic() function and passes it the properties of the text enclosed in the <SPAN> tags. The function then tests the Visibility property of the identified element. Since it is initially hidden, the function changes the property to "visible." The result is shown in Figure 5.9. The next time you click on the question, the function changes the property back to "hidden." Note that the following line preserves the spacing, reserving room for the question even when it is hidden.

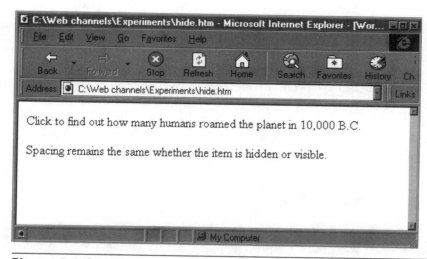

Figure 5.8 Question displayed at opening screen.

In comparison to this example, if you use the Display property of an object (which accepts the parameters none or null), the browser will reoccupy the space that was used by the previous line when it is no longer displayed. When the Display property is toggled to null, the page is dynamically reformatted to make room for the redisplayed line.

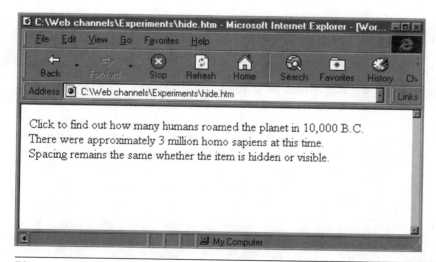

Figure 5.9 Answer displayed by clicking on the question.

Hiding lines of text or images and then displaying them at the user's command lets the developer design pages that introduce segments of text on command when they're ready to be viewed. You might, for example, design a page full of Frequently Asked Questions (FAQs) and display the answers for each question when the question is clicked. The viewer could then click the question again to hide it after reading the answer. For this example, you would want to use the Display property for the text containing each answer, rather than the Visibility property, so that the questions would remain closely grouped on the page. Formatting would then be dynamically adjusted as answers were displayed or concealed.

Creating a Preview Page

If you'd like to get your Active Channel listed in Microsoft's Active Channel Guide, Microsoft requires that you produce a preview page—an HTML document, preferably using elements of Dynamic HTML—that can be viewed as someone browses through the listed channels in the guide. The page should effectively characterize the nature and content of your site, and, of course, encourage them to subscribe.

The basic requirements for the page are as follows:

- The HTML content should be sized to 460 pixels wide and 365 pixels high for display in the guide preview window.

- The total content should occupy no more than 35K.

- The page should contain the Add Active Channel or Add Active Desktop buttons and associated scripts.

- The page should incorporate elements of Dynamic HTML.

To get a sense of how to construct an appropriate page, let's examine another DHTML production tool: Dynamite by Astound. Astound provides access to DHTML effects and integrates multimedia elements in a simple, easily understood work environment, and allows content to be generated for your choice of browser platforms. For providing a preview page for Channel Guide inclusion, there is no reason why you wouldn't want to use the full range of effects and transitions available through Internet Explorer 4, including filters, blends, and transitions. Astound gives you access to many of these effects. Another product in the same family, Astound WebCast Professional, includes the DHTML features as well as a comprehensive set of tools for managing the creation of Netcaster channels, Active Channels, or Astound's own channels that are supported with its channel server software.

Figure 5.10 shows an example of a typical preview page as it appears while cruising through the Channel Guide.

The preview page is a good opportunity to give potential subscribers a clear view of what kind of material to expect from you. Spend some time developing a striking, well-thought-out design and you'll be rewarded with a steadily expanding subscriber base.

Preview Page Planning

Astound Dynamite provides solid support for the majority of DHTML features, presented in a page-based workspace that uses a timeline to coordinate animated effects, transitions, and page progressions. Although not directly supported in DHTML, but implemented through Java applets accessible to the developer, Dynamite lets you create slide-show productions with sound backdrops that persist from page to page.

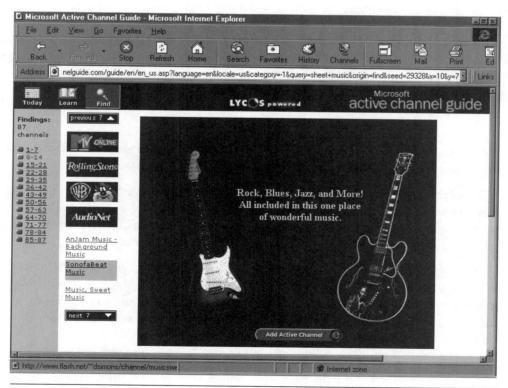

Figure 5.10 Typical preview page in the Channel Guide.

To demonstrate the capabilities of Dynamite and suggest a few ideas for preview page designs, I'll walk through the process of making a preview page for my own company—Lightspeed Publishing (which is discussed further in Chapter 9, "Lightspeed Publishing Case Study").

Transitions are a particularly nice effect, and a wide variety of them are supported in Internet Explorer 4, but in less robust fashion by Netscape Navigator. Since the preview page will be designed for viewing only in IE4, you can freely use all of the available transitions without disenfranchising your audience. Transitions such as wipe, cover, uncover, blinds horizontal and vertical, checkerboard across, fade, and dissolve, can be applied to images, animated text, objects, and so on that are presented in the preview page.

For this example, I'll use two images, one that appears initially and another with the Lightspeed Publishing information and the Add Active Channel button on it to display at the end of the presentation. Three animated text blocks will appear and move across the screen, describing the content of the site (in glowing terms, of course).

The Design Process

Dynamite has a nice utility for creating page backgrounds that includes a very interesting pattern generator. Rather than creating a background pattern, however, I'm going to use the tool to produce an opening image that will be displayed when the preview page is first introduced.

Start out in Dynamite by setting the page size to match the preview page requirements (460 pixels wide × 365 pixels high). The File menu provides access to the Page Setup values.

From the Page menu, select the Background option. The Page Background dialog box, shown in Figure 5.11, appears. You can choose a solid color for a page background (which is often preferable to using any kinds of patterns, particularly if your pages include a good deal of text), or patterns, textures, and gradients.

The textures offered can be customized for exactly the effect you need. Astound includes a fascinating collection of textures in its library, including mandelbrot images, craters, minerals, clouds, fog, strings, weaves, nebula, and so on. These textures can be tweaked and modified through a number of different controls to produce visually dramatic images for use on your pages. For example, Figure 5.12 shows the control settings available to modify the Clouds-with Stars texture.

For this example, I chose the Raindrops option and cycled through the Randomize button a few times until I came up with an image that was suitable. I initially installed the Raindrops background on the page in Dynamite, but then

Figure 5.11 Page Background dialog box.

saved the Dynamite content and brought the image into Ulead PhotoImpact and compressed it further. The resulting JPEG image weighed in at 7Kb when finished.

Returning to Dynamite, I extracted the previous Raindrops background and then dropped this new Raindrops image into place in the foreground using the Image Tool, which appears on the toolbar on the left side of the Dynamite workspace. I also dropped three text blocks into position and sized them. These will be animated and added to the timeline. At this point, the page appears as shown in Figure 5.13.

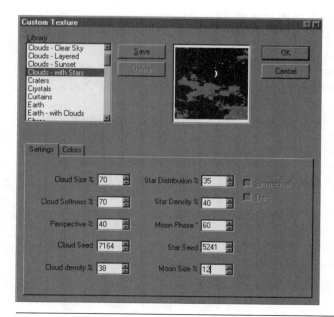

Figure 5.12 Clouds-with Stars texture controls.

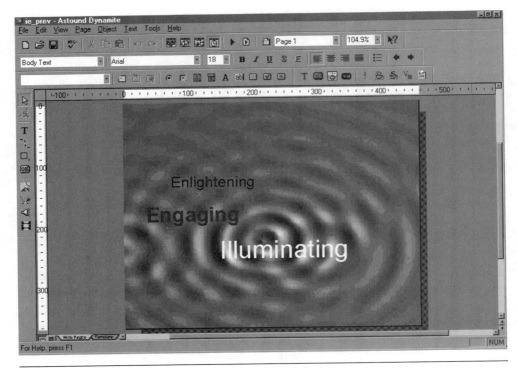

Figure 5.13 Raindrops image overlaid with text.

The next step is to select each one of the text objects in turn and create a path for it to follow during the animation. To do this, you select the text object on the page, click the Path button on the toolbar, and then point and click to select a starting point for the path. Double-clicking at the point you want the path to conclude completes the path definition. Dynamite also automatically creates a mid-position on the path to use for displaying the content for browsers that can't handle DHTML.

The concluding image that will display after the raindrops have been dissolved at the end of their transition will be the Lightspeed Publishing banner page, shown in Figure 5.14. To the right corner of the page, I added the Add Active Channel button. Once you've added the Add Active Channel button to the page, you can select it and use the Object menu to select Interaction and assign a Jump to URL that corresponds with the location of the CDF file that describes your Active Channel content (see Chapter 4, "Creating an Active Channel," for instructions on creating a CDF file).

Once you have all the key elements in place and paths assigned to each of the text blocks, you can open the Timeline window, shown in Figure 5.15, and determine

Figure 5.14 Lightspeed Publishing page with Add Active Channel button.

when each object will make its appearance in the display, and what entry and exit transitions will be associated with it.

The timeline by default is set up to a 15-second presentation. Through the Page menu Properties option, I've extended that period to 20 seconds. All of the objects that you see on the timeline will enter and exit in that time period (or, if you choose, all will be displayed at the same time). Dynamite's model supports a continuously flowing presentation that either loops or jumps to another page at the end of the time period. In this case, however, we want the presentation to stop at the end of the 20-second sequence. The Add Marker button on the Timeline toolbar lets you position a marker at the 20-second point. The dialog box that appears when the marker is positioned lets you choose to Pause Page, which will halt the events at that point.

The Lightspeed Publishing image and the Add Active Channel button, the first and second items on the timeline, are set to appear only during the last seven seconds of the presentation. The Raindrops image, the third item on the timeline, is set

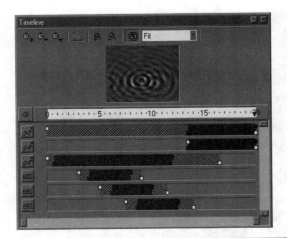

Figure 5.15 Timeline window with objects in place.

with an initial entry dissolve (the shaded area before the dark central region) that lasts for about three seconds. A similar exit area exists on the end of the Raindrops timeline entry. To set transitions for any of the images or text, select the item by clicking its icon at the beginning of the timeline and then choose Object Transition from the application menu.

The dialog box that appears, as shown in Figure 5.16, indicates the Browser Compatibility for each transition that you select. You can select different Entry and Exit transitions and control the entry and exit speeds with the slider control in the lower portion of the dialog box. You'll undoubtedly want to spend some time experimenting with the different transitions and their timing. The Preview Page button on the Dynamite toolbar lets you view the multimedia effects in Internet Explorer. For this example, I used dissolve and fade transitions on the different objects, and tweaked the entry and exit periods until the presentation seemed to be timed correctly. After experimenting a bit, I also set the background (using the Page Properties dialog box) to black so that the initial dissolve—the Raindrops appearing in the display—would be more effective.

When complete, this 20-second preview page sequence opens with a black screen, but almost immediately the Raindrops image begins appearing in a flurry of pixels. The three text objects appear one after another and follow their animated paths across the screen and vanish. Finally, the Raindrops image dissolves and the Lightspeed Publishing image fades into place in the foreground. Since there is a

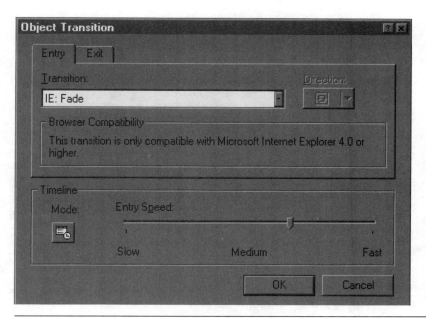

Figure 5.16 Object Transition dialog box.

Pause Page marker to halt the timeline, the presentation stops at this point and the page remains static, giving the dazed viewer a chance to subscribe.

Astound Dynamite has a Publish wizard that lets you publish your content to either a local hard disk or the final destination Web server. The playback requires a JavaScript library file, which is copied into place along with rest of the content files, and—if you use certain non-DHTML effects—a Java archive and package file. Playback of the multimedia effects is very smooth, and since you can experiment infinitely on the timing and progressions using the timeline, you can hone your production to a fine edge.

Your multimedia content will have to be carefully monitored so as not to exceed the Microsoft 35K limit. You might be able to add sound in the form of a MIDI file, but don't try to include any WAV file content along with your page content. The total storage for the files included in this example reached 33K, including the JavaScript library file (necessary for the special effects). If you use the Java features, the required JUMP.JAR and JUMP.CAB files occupy an additional 114K, which isn't excessive for a full Website presentation, since they only have to be downloaded once; however, your presentation would be over the limit for preview page use.

The features of Astound WebCast Professional (which includes the authoring capabilities of Dynamite as well as transport-independent channel creation tools) make it worth consideration for channel development. WebCast Professional is discussed in more detail in Appendix B, "Resources."

Timeline Distribution Options

Dynamite also includes a rapid-fire means of controlling the timing of multiple objects on the page. The DistributeTimelines window, shown in Figure 5.17, provides an assortment of patterns that can be applied to control the entry and exit of each object. For example, the objects can be designed to appear in sequence, one after another, or in overlapping patterns where several may remain on the screen at the same time. If you have complex presentations, this feature can simplify the object handling.

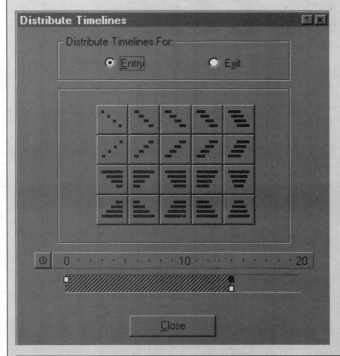

Figure 5.17 Timeline distribution controls.

Summary

Microsoft has gone way beyond Netscape in its Dynamic HTML architecture, producing an extremely fluid and highly programmable environment for presenting page content. If you take advantage of the full range of options supported by this environment, authoring pages for display in Internet Explorer 4 is not very different from creating multimedia presentations in other leading authoring applications. The additional support provided by the inclusion of ActiveX components makes it possible to embed almost any conceivable effect or multimedia element in your DHTML documents.

All of this versatility doesn't come without a cost. When using the many unique extensions offered by Microsoft—such as ActiveX components and DirectAnimation elements—you exclude a certain percentage of your audience. Depending on whose statistics you believe, Microsoft currently has anywhere from 12 to 38 percent of the browser market. Even if it has as much as 50 percent of the market, what do you do about the other 50 percent of visitors who won't be able to properly view the content?

If your goal is to provide channel-specific content—for both Netcaster and Active Channels—you can:

- Author parallel streams of documents, each set up to accommodate the features of the channel delivery mechanism selected.

- Choose to deliver content to one platform or the other.

- Use one of the applications—such as Dreamweaver or mBed Interactor—that automatically produces cross-platform content for the delivery mode of your choice.

- Author for 3.0 browsers and wait until the next generation of browser software mated to the Document Object Model reduces incompatibilities.

None of these approaches are ideal solutions; developers can only hope that there is light at the end of the tunnel as software manufacturers begin playing their instruments to the same score.

6

Scaling Up to IP
Multicasting

This chapter examines the highest level of push technology: high-volume IP multicasting. The focus is on the general architecture for supporting push and one particular product—BackWeb Infocenter 4.0—that includes support for both push technology and the Microsoft CDF Webcasting scheme.

The third tier in the Microsoft model of Webcasting is reserved for what it calls "true" push technology. Despite the shiny interface and broadcast metaphors, channel delivery through a system that relies on a site crawler to access and retrieve content is not genuine push technology. It may look like push and resemble push to the end user, but genuine push technology incorporates another level of server software and a delivery mode that downloads content using a client/server model (or, in other terms, a transmitter-to-tuner model).

Both the Microsoft and the Netscape models of Webcasting support this level of interaction—Microsoft through a variety of third-party partnering arrangements and Netscape through its integration of a Castanet tuner into Netcaster. The strongly scaleable product from BackWeb Technologies lets channel developers adapt their delivery to large-volume subscription services and incorporate the benefits of IP multicasting to reduce the bandwidth requirements of channel content.

Large-Scale Channel Delivery

The grand promise that distinguishes Web channels from the various kinds of Internet services available is the ability to offer content selectivity and personalization. Despite the growing sophistication of search engines on the Internet, and increased awareness of Web users as to the skillful use of search tools and techniques, obtaining precise information about any subject is still a time-consuming and frustrating pursuit.

At its best, a Web channel is a means of tapping into a flow of information that reflects your interests and needs. Content is delivered—the lengthy hunts through gigabytes of irrelevant information across the sprawling, unorganized terrain of the Web can be eliminated. Through channels, content can be selectively filtered, sorted, bundled, and packaged. If you want to view the interaction between the new technology and business, you can subscribe to the *Fast Company* channel. If you want a perspective on the emerging digital nation, you can tune in to the *Wired* channel. If you want the daily weather, you can have the Weather Channel deliver a complete weather map and five-day forecast to your desktop when you log on to the Internet in the morning.

This approach works well on intranets and extranets as well. With channels, network administrators have a convenient means of delivering software updates to workgroup members, brief the staff about new company developments, and publish policy and procedure manuals to coordinate corporate behavior. Products such as the BackWeb Infocenter version 4 offer a console that lets an administrator selectively push specific information through the enterprise, creating individual channels to consolidate different types of content. This channel content might include filtered news from a wide spectrum of news sources, such as the content offered by NewsEDGE, or evolving mission and policy statements of the organization to keep staff members moving in the same direction. This selectivity puts the administrator in the role of gatekeeper, allowing content to be personalized for individual staff members or specific workgroups. The administrator can push as much or as little information as is deemed appropriate, but having a key person within an organization in this role is an important step in honing and refining the flow of information within a department or a business.

Although the site crawler approach works well for many basic kinds of Web channel delivery, at some point the processing burden of satisfying thousands or tens of thousands of subscribers can overwhelm a conventional server. Subscription mechanisms offered through the "managed Webcasting" approach incorporated in the CDF file describing an Active Channel site can diminish the single point-in-time update problem. By specifying a range of time for satisfying the update delivery (whether a range of 4 hours or 16 hours), the volume of subscriber information can be more uniformly distributed over a period of time. If everyone subscribing to the Microsoft channel were to receive the latest version of the Internet Explorer browser at the same time, the Internet would probably collapse under the weight of the traffic. Staggering delivery times helps keep the traffic at more manageable levels.

As mentioned earlier in this book, IP multicasting offers one means of managing the inherent channel traffic problem, using a one-to-many distribution scheme. A single stream of packets with multiple addresses can be sent out and then replicated at the destination servers for delivery, greatly reducing the volume of data needed to distribute information. Site crawler delivery is essentially a unicast means of distributing data—the server that is servicing the channel sends out all of the information to each one of the subscribers during a channel update. Separate, identical streams of packets go out to each of the destination sites. This, as you might suspect, is an extremely wasteful method of transferring data—both from the perspective of the server, which must process and distribute the flood of data, and from the perspective of the Internet, which must deal with the distribution of large, duplicate collections of packets.

Efficiency requires a more targeted approach to distributed data. The first requirement for handling large quantities of data efficiently is using a product that supports the IP multicasting scheme.

The latest generation of push technology products offers an alternative to many of the information sorting and delivery problems associated with Internet data distribution. One product in particular from BackWeb Technologies, Infocenter v4.0, is discussed in this chapter as a means of leveraging the benefits of channel delivery in high-volume subscriber situations, while also maintaining fine-grain control over individual content. Like Microsoft's Active Channels approach, BackWeb Infocenter can employ a CDF file to describe and organize channel content and to make information more accessible to subscribers.

BackWeb Infocenter v4.0

BackWeb Technologies' acquisition of Lanacom Inc. in mid-1997 brought a collection of new tools inhouse, tools that have been integrated into the release of Infocenter v4.0. One of the core components of this product provides an application designed to scour the Internet for particular types of information, filter and extract data that fits certain parameters, and then deliver the customized content to channel subscribers. The approach can be tailored to intranet, extranet, or Internet delivery mechanisms and uses the same client/server software architecture that BackWeb had established in prior push technology products.

The goal is to step beyond simple information retrieval to more sophisticated knowledge management. Using Infocenter, companies can set up a system to collect information from a wide variety of sources and then assemble it in a central location in a form allowing business associates, customers, staff members, and others to receive it through channel delivery. The core technology has been integrated into a number of services and applications, such as Lotus's Domino.Merchant (where BackWeb's server software is bundled with the server pack that Lotus offers) and Individual's First! multiple-content news delivery service.

Channel Definition Format files can be used to define and describe other Websites, fileservers, BackWeb servers, and other Web channels. When used at the enterprise level, organizations can extend the capabilities of the BackWeb server with programs that connect to any other computer system in the enterprise. Channel content described in CDF files can be applied to query results from search engines, information culled from newsgroups, archival files in a network storage system, or application databases and then be delivered through the BackWeb server.

BackWeb Technologies offers a Channel Profiler Tool that provides a visual environment for creating and maintaining CDF files that map site content and convert Internet resources for channel delivery. Another means for simplifying content delivery is provided by BackWeb's HTML Publishing Wizard. This wizard offers a streamlined means for users to generate HTML content for channel inclusion from typical sources both internal and external to the organization.

Tuning in to Customized Information

As is common with many of the channel/subscriber models, the individual user has a large degree of control over the key aspects of information delivery, including the information display format, choice of channels, filtering options, message alerts, and so on. At the coarsest level of control, users can select those channels to receive and choose the manner in which the information is delivered. However, the system can also be set up to deliver customized information on a one-to-one basis; for example, a channel subscriber could choose to receive regular updates from Accounting as to his or her current IRA contributions, accrued vacation and sick time, or similar kinds of data. Any information stored on enterprise systems can be a source of data delivered through a generalized or customized channel.

Users running the BackWeb Infocenter client software can sort and filter through incoming information, select the most relevant items and discard the irrelevant. Most of the familiar push technology display techniques—including screensavers, wallpaper, Flashes, Tickers, and title lists—can be used to present the various types of information. Users have the ability to customize and control these display options as well.

For example, the BackWeb client can be selected as the default screensaver under Windows95. While online, the program steals cycles during idle times in Internet transmissions and downloads news headlines and other content to populate the real estate of the screensaver. When the screensaver starts up, it progressively displays the individual items, as shown in Figure 6.1, and allows the user to click and follow links online if he or she wants more in-depth information.

Additionally, users can have a ticker running across the screen with assorted headlines and news items, or popup flashes can be used to convey information. The goal is to place information in convenient desktop containers that can be easily accessed, without becoming obtrusive to the point of disrupting someone's work on the computer. A careful balance must be maintained in making information notice-

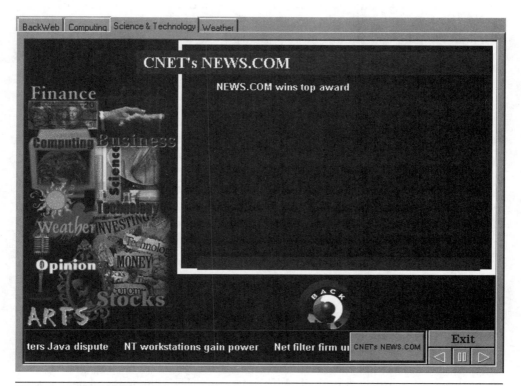

Figure 6.1 BackWeb screensaver.

able without making the presentation annoying. Content developers working to develop BackWeb InfoPaks should study this medium carefully to find the right balance for communicating with the audience.

Transmitting During Idle Times

BackWeb has developed a software technology called the Polite Agent, which is built into the Infocenter product. The Polite Agent is designed to transmit channel content during periods when a user is not actively communicating with the network (for example, when someone is reading a page of HTML content that has just been downloaded). The Polite Agents steps in during this idle time and transfers as much subscriber content as possible until it detects a sign of network activity from the user. The agent then suspends the transfer, but keeps track of how much of the downloaded file was successfully transmitted. The next idle time that arrives, the agent resumes from the previous point and continues in this manner until all of the subscriber's files have been delivered by the server. To the user, the process is transparent. Large amounts of data can be delivered quietly (and politely) in the background without interfering with other network activities or user operations. The server also uses data compression and other management techniques to minimize bandwidth requirements and download times.

IE4 BackWeb Client

In cooperation with Microsoft, BackWeb designed a version of its client software that can be integrated with Internet Explorer 4. This allows IE4 users to tap into channel content from BackWeb servers using the familiar desktop Channel Guide or browser-resident Channel Pane to display and access the individual channels. Channels that are set up appropriately can be accessed and viewed either from the conventional BackWeb interface or directly through Internet Explorer 4. To identify a BackWeb channel from the icons that are listed in the pane, you can place the mouse pointer over the item and the channel name, and its BackWeb origins appear in a tool tip. Figure 6.2 shows the appearance of the BackWeb channel controls if you select a BackWeb channel (in this case, the IDG channel, from the available selections in the IE4 Channel Pane).

Individual InfoPaks that have been downloaded for a selected channel can be accessed by double-clicking on the item as it appears in the dynamic Web page displaying the channel content. The content then appears directly within the IE4 window, as shown in Figure 6.3. Channels can exist and be accessed freely from within both environments—the BackWeb client and the IE4 browser—but if an Internet Explorer channel has the exact same name as a BackWeb channel, the BackWeb channel won't be displayed in the IE4 Channel Pane. The channel's content, however, will still be available through the conventional BackWeb client.

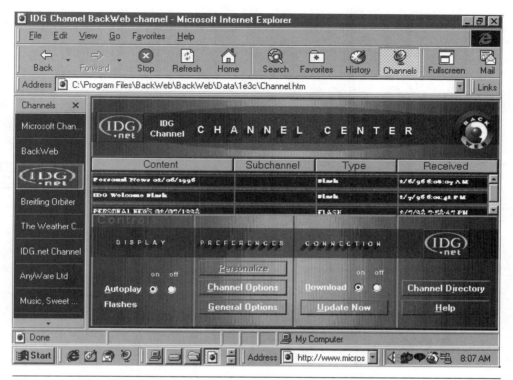

Figure 6.2 BackWeb channel controls embedded in IE4.

The level of integration that BackWeb has in relation to IE4 also extends to support for the Channel Definition Format. For native BackWeb channels, a Profiler wizard is used to define channel content and establish the characteristics of a particular channel. For channels designed for CDF directory listings, BackWeb uses a CDF Channel Agent wizard to create the CDF file and supporting information. The information compiled for channels produced in this manner include both the CDF data as well as information used by BackWeb, such as the category in which the channel should appear in the Channel Directory of BackWeb Infocenter.

The BackWeb server software includes a means for automating the delivery of replacement views of the standard BackWeb channel content display. This replacement view allows the channel to appear identically to an Internet Explorer Channel, and this technique relies on the actual CDF file data and all associated files that are referenced by the CDF information (such as HTML pages and icons). This allows IE4 channel information to be presented in a merged format that includes the appearance and behavior of an IE4 channel with the specialized functions that are

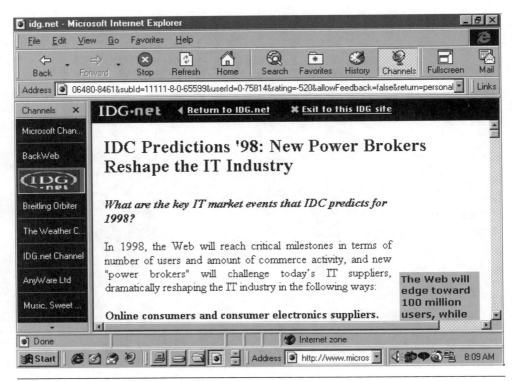

Figure 6.3 BackWeb channel content within IE4.

available through the BackWeb software, such as the Polite Agent feature that
downloads content in the background.

The IE4 client utility is available as a freely downloadable ActiveX software
component from BackWeb Technologies (www.backweb.com). The full BackWeb
Infocenter client software can also be downloaded from this same source.

Delivering Integrated Content

An alliance that was forged with two high-profile news delivery services—
Individual and Desktop Data—allows corporate customers to receive selectively filtered content using the BackWeb Infocenter v4.0 technology. Individual's First! and
Desktop Data's NewsEDGE services collect information from hundreds of different
news sources and categorize this information for subscribers. The merger of
Individual and Desktop Data (to form a company called NewsEDGE Corporation)
strengthens the ability of these companies to provide timely, relevant information
that can now be customized by means of the delivery features offered by BackWeb.

The merger will result in the largest independent news integrator in the world. Topics that have been filtered and collected by the service are presented as channels through BackWeb. Individuals can choose those channels that most closely match their interests and needs and set up a subscription through the client software. Content is then filtered and delivered directly to the users' desktops as it becomes available. The type of content is not limited to simply news items and announcements, but can also include presentations and multimedia files.

The Topic Library created by Individual includes more than 2500 categories based on industry and business news sources. Items from these sources go through both a machine-sorting process and a human editorial review process before becoming accessible as channel content that a subscriber can select.

BackWeb is offering this level of service to its Enterprise customers. Trial subscriptions are available to BackWeb users for a 30-day period by contacting BackWeb directly.

Channel Server Architecture

The following components make up the BackWeb suite of products:

Channel Server. Retrieves information and schedules it for delivery to subscribers.

Channel Server console. Controls the interaction with the Channel Server from a local or remote location.

Editor. Manages the content destined for channel delivery from a central location.

Proxy Server. Offers management of incoming content from channels being piped into a company.

Automation SDK. Facilitates automated retrieval and management of channel content stored in databases.

Client SDK. Allows Information Systems managers to design custom client utilities for use within an intranet.

Figure 6.4 shows a typical arrangement of components within a network of BackWeb servers and clients.

Although the original functionality of BackWeb software was tailored primarily to Internet push applications, the product has gradually been reshaped to fit into enterprise-level push applications where knowledge automation is the goal. Channel content can be distributed through an intranet, extranet, or the Internet, and the content can consist of a mix of internally and externally generated information.

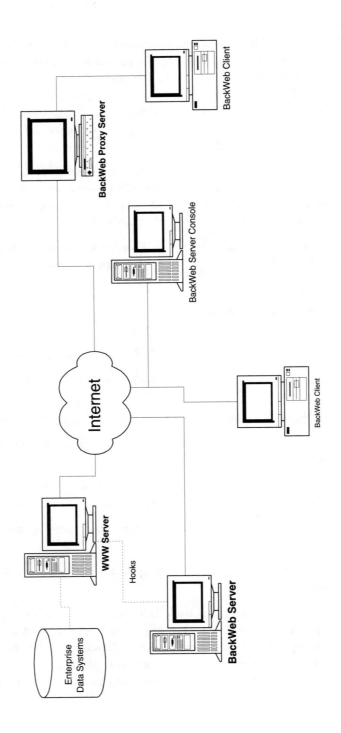

Figure 6.4 BackWeb server and client organization.

Within a typical enterprise environment, users receiving channel content might be employees, customers of a company, vendors, or the general public. Within the enterprise, however, BackWeb makes it easy to circulate news, data, and current events, keeping staff members in tune with the rhythm of the organization. The same channels can be used to perform ongoing software updates, simplifying the tasks involved at the network administration level to keep everyone in the organization running the current version of a licensed software application.

McAfee Software Updates through Channels

McAfee is one company that has heartily embraced the concept of providing software updates through a channel approach. Incorporating BackWeb Technologies software, the McAfee site can automatically deliver the most recent plug-in modules for its virus protection software through an extensive network of subscribers.

InfoPaks, the lingua franca of the BackWeb information delivery system, get circulated and delivered as a background operation, making it possible to relay even very large files or multimedia content without the user being aware of a perceptible extended download. Since the process uses spare bandwidth, the channel content slips in seamlessly between other Internet or intranet activities and then nudges the user's attention through Flashes, tickers, or screensavers. A large amount of content can be downloaded even while a user is sorting through email or browsing for information on the Web. InfoPaks are created using the BackWeb BALI editor and then uploaded to a database that resides on the designated BackWeb host.

In commercial applications dependent on advertising, the BackWeb attention-getters—Flashes, tickers, and so on—can be used to present the advertising content. The success of the advertising message depends on the approach taken by the content developer—within the framework of BackWeb, items such as Flashes can be creatively constructed. The Breitling Orbiter channel, for example, has a small-scale replica of the Orbiter float into view on the desktop where a click can launch the channel content. If this Flash is ignored, it disappears in a few seconds. Users, of course, have the option of turning off these attention-getting devices, which is important if they want to get some serious work done without distractions.

Targeting of Content

The BackWeb product offers a number of ways to target content individually to users. InfoPaks can be broadcast to the full audience, or narrowcast to a specified subset of the audience. BackWeb also supports the *segmentation* and *personalization* of content. Segmentation, a valuable tool within intranets, consists of controlling content delivery by constructing workgroup clients that have access to specific channels and channel directories. Staff members in the Human Resources department, for example, may receive a channel that contains a stream of processed résumés and job applications that have been added to a corporate database. Engineers in a group may receive a channel that provides action items and design issues that are being focused on in the course of product development. Segmentation can also be managed through the use of registration forms that characterize and separate different types of content for the end user. For example, product distributors for a corporation could complete a registration form to receive updates on particular products that are being designed and manufactured by the organization.

Personalization is another technique for controlling content distribution. Through the use of *hooks* established between a database and a BackWeb server, individuals within a group can receive specified information through a channel (Figure 6.4 shows conceptually how hooks link components in the network). Hooks function in a manner somewhat similar to CGI scripts on an Internet server, responding to input in a specific manner and providing a bridge between user responses and the host computer.

Managing from the Console

An intermediary component in the BackWeb architecture, the BackWeb Console, provides administrative control over the database on the BackWeb server that contains the InfoPaks. Through the Console, you can monitor, configure, and manipulate the properties of InfoPaks, determining who gets particular InfoPaks, when updates occur, what InfoPaks will reside in the database, and so on. The monitoring facility provides a view of how InfoPaks are being accessed and viewed. The BackWeb Console can be operated from any Window NT or Windows95 workstation with access to the Internet, allowing the server to be managed remotely even if it resides at a geographically distant location.

The basis for the whole BackWeb system is the controlled delivery of information, in the form of InfoPaks, from the BackWeb server to a collection of BackWeb clients. Since the BackWeb client software, described in the next section, is free and easily available on the BackWeb site, information residing on a BackWeb server can be channeled to anyone on the Internet who is willing to download and install the free client software.

A Look at the BackWeb Client

The BackWeb client software supports major browsers, including the version 4 releases of Netscape Navigator and Internet Explorer 4, and also has a standalone component that allows channel subscriptions to be initiated and InfoPaks (the standard unit of data exchange) to be downloaded. The download of the client utility from BackWeb Technologies' site takes just a few moments; the installation software is a little over 1Mb. Windows 3.1 users and Macintosh OS users get to come to the party too—BackWeb also has clients that run on these platforms.

You can install the software while your Internet connection is still active as long as you close the browser. Once installed, BackWeb offers you the opportunity to subscribe to a number of preexisting channels, which can be sorted by category. The channel selection window is shown in Figure 6.5.

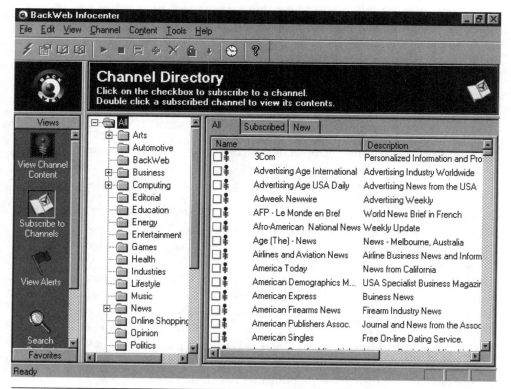

Figure 6.5 BackWeb channel selection options.

Many of the channels that you choose to subscribe to require that you fill out a short form to initiate the subscription. For example, Virgin Radio, one of the leading U.K. commercial radio stations, asks a few simple questions to initiate the subscription. A few channels, like the CommerceNet channel, require that you become a member of their organization to receive channel content. The CommerceNet membership consists largely of corporations and organizations involved in shaping the structure of electronic commerce, and memberships are pricey—plan on spending several thousand dollars to receive this channel content. Many channels, however, require no type of response at all, and the subscription begins immediately when you make the selection in the Infocenter window.

When you've completed your subscriptions, content downloads of InfoPaks, Flashes, and other BackWeb data formats begin immediately. These downloads occur in the background and can be interspersed between other Internet activity that is taking place. In other words, the BackWeb servers take advantage of idle time in the Internet connection and use those free periods to complete the subscription information transfers. This makes it fairly painless for users to receive fairly large quantities of information from channel sources—receiving this information doesn't disrupt other activities that are taking place. This is also one of the key features that separates genuine push technology from the "smart pull" technique that is used by both Microsoft and Netscape for their low-end Webcasting. When the channel content has been downloaded, the individual items are displayed in the Infocenter window. Content for the Airlines and Aviation News Channel is shown in Figure 6.6.

If you select an individual item from this content, BackWeb brings up the selected browser and displays the content within the browser window, as shown in Figure 6.7 for one of the press release items for the Airlines and Aviation News Channel.

When a new subscription begins, new information that is pushed from the channel arrives in one of a number of different forms. A *Flash* is a small notification, often animated, that appears at the edge of your display. You can acknowledge it and get more information or delete it. Some information arrives as *wallpaper*, which, as you might suspect, blankets your desktop area with an image that has been pushed from the channel. Screensavers are also a common way of delivering information. BackWeb saves the Flashes, which can be examined from the BackWeb client application either a channel at a time or en masse. Figure 6.8 shows a Flash from the Breitling Orbiter channel. Often a Flash will provide a capsule summary of a news item or longer feature article. If you choose, you can go online and access the full content of the material described by the Flash.

The BackWeb client software includes an ActiveX component so that it can work in tandem with Internet Explorer 4. For some channel content and sign-up screens, the BackWeb client brings up the browser window to handle the interaction.

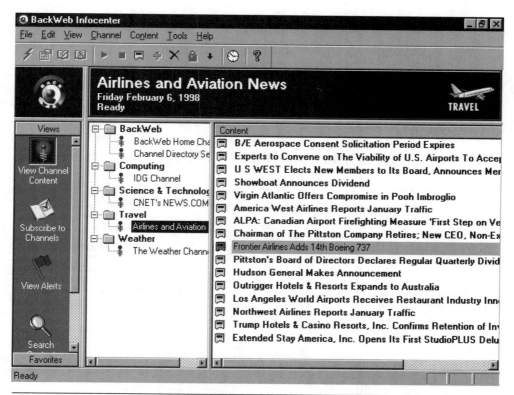

Figure 6.6 Airlines and Aviation News Channel content.

Internet Explorer 4 Channel

One of BackWeb's most prominent channels is the Microsoft Internet Explorer 4 channel, providing an easy mechanism for receiving news about current Microsoft software as well as the latest release of the software. Upgrades are managed dynamically through the subscription process. The channel also provides ongoing articles that offer technical information and practical guidelines for using Internet Explorer. Press releases on related topics are also delivered through the channel. The Internet Explorer channel can be received either through the BackWeb Infocenter client utility or through the ActiveX plug-in module that works with Internet Explorer.

Timely Information

Channels make a great deal of sense, from the subscriber's vantage point, when you're interested in following a particular event or news story. At the time that this

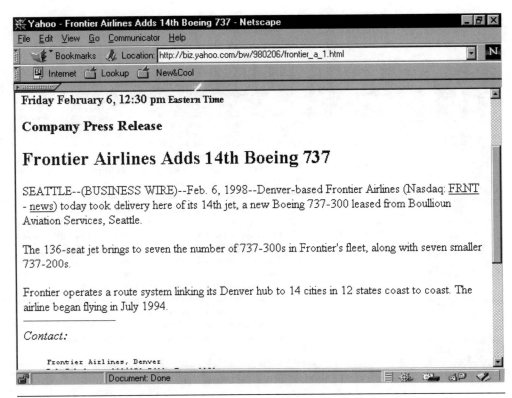

Figure 6.7 Channel content displayed in the browser window.

chapter was being prepared, BackWeb was offering a channel for the Breitling Orbiter 2, an attempt at an around-the-globe voyage by balloon. Subscribing to the channel ensured viewers of the latest information on the progress of this historic flight. Progress could also be monitored through a real-time window run by a Java applet, as shown in Figure 6.9, that displayed the current position of the balloon over a map of the world.

Channel content also is sometimes tied to real-time events that are being multicast from a server as the actual event is recorded and digitized. For such kinds of large-scale information transfer, IP multicasting is really the only practical way to distribute the information packets to a large audience. Conventional unicast techniques would quickly overwhelm the server capacity as soon as the audience reached a particular size.

Figure 6.8 A BackWeb Flash usually appears at the edge of the display.

IP Multicasting with BackWeb

In a strategic partnership with TIBCO, BackWeb channel content can be distributed through IP multicasting techniques. TIBCO, a company that gained its fame by devising a means to rapidly handle and deliver changing data from the floor of the stock market, contributes the mechanism by which channel content can be multicast. TIBCO, based in Palo Alto, California, supplies digital trading systems to financial services internationally and also provides methods to integrate these technologies into computer systems.

As a part of this partnership, TIBCO has integrated its technology, The Information Bus (TIB), into the BackWeb client/server architecture. The modified server software is being offered as a part of a joint sales agreement between the two companies. This partnership permits BackWeb customers to enjoy highly efficient, real-time delivery of content to audiences that range upwards from 10,000 users.

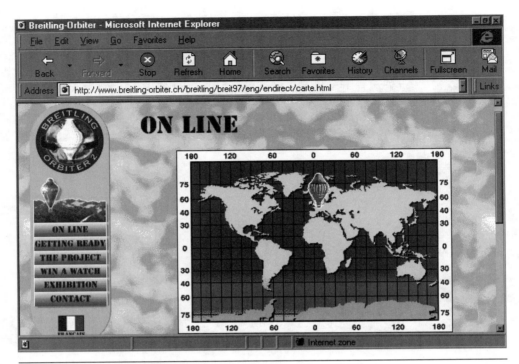

Figure 6.9 Breitling Orbiter 2's progress in real time.

Handling Push through the BackWeb TIBCO Connection

The BackWeb TIBCO connection manages the multicast push of content through BackWeb. This technology differs from BackWeb's conventional content delivery; the nature of the multicast content favors immediate push by the server—the client relinquishes control over the content delivery (BackWeb's normal Polite Agent approach is superseded by the immediate push).

The Rendezvous component of the TIBCO software module oversees the IP multicasting of content. The content provider publishes data under a descriptive subject name and this information is posted through the Rendezvous API. Clients tuned to the multicasting source receive data as it is generated, whether the content is a standard InfoPak or a multimedia presentation. With IP multicasting enabled, the data is sent a single time on the physical line and replicated as necessary to accommodate individual subscribers at multiple locations.

To facilitate this method of IP multicasting, additional software has to be installed for both the BackWeb server and client. The three necessary components

Four Requirements for IP Multicasting

Four basic requirements must be satisfied to allow the use of IP multicasting from a host computer to the multitudes in the prospective audience. The requirements are:

1. The operating system running on the host computer must support IP multicasting. Windows NT, Windows95, and recent versions of Unix all have this capability. The TCP/IP stack for the OS must also be multicast-enabled with support for the Internet Group Management Protocol (IGMP).

2. The network adapter and network drivers must be capable of supporting IP multicasting. Specifically, the network adapter must be able to filter any data link layer addresses mapped from the IP multicast addresses at the network layer.

3. The network architecture in the path of the IP multicast transmission must be designed to accommodate IP multicasting at the IP layer. This includes the routers, bridges, switches, and similar equipment in the path of the transmission.

4. Applications that are being used to perform the data transmission must be designed to support IP multicasting.

TIB/Rendezvous Software

In response to the need for a workable development environment for producing distributed information systems, TIBCO devised a software package, the TIB/Rendezvous software, to simplify development and improve the management of distributed systems. The TIB/Rendezvous software relies on an object-oriented model that depicts each individual transmission as an object with attributes that define its source and destination. This self-describing data architecture becomes the framework through which the TIB/Rendezvous software can coordinate interactions among other applications, such as the client/server software from BackWeb Technologies. Applications incorporating the TIB/Rendezvous software model exchange messages that include data structures with built-in information describing the datatypes, identifiers, and sizes. The mechanisms by which the TIB/Rendezvous software handles these interactions makes it possible to perform data transmissions through IP multicasting.

are the Rendezvous software, the BackWeb TIBCO Server Connector (BTSC), and the BackWeb TIBCO Client Connector (BTCC). The Rendezvous software must be enabled on both the client and server computers involved in a multicast transfer. The Server Connector and Client Connector are installed individually on the server and client, respectively. Once the client is so equipped, it can actively tune to any TIBCO-enabled servers, receiving InfoPaks as quickly as they are generated.

If a single BackWeb server is set up to provide conventional InfoPaks and IP multicast InfoPaks, careful attention must be paid to the network bandwidth use to ensure that it is not overtaxed if simultaneous transmissions are being generated. Sufficient bandwidth should be reserved for both forms of transmission. The IP multicast content requires a different approach then with push material typically produced through BackWeb. Besides the bandwidth concerns, certain users within an organization—such as dial-up users or those without the Rendezvous license—cannot normally receive the multicast content. In such a situation, these clients can rely on conventional BackWeb protocols to obtain InfoPaks that have been stored in the server database after an IP multicast operation has concluded.

Both BackWeb and TIBCO are active members in the IP Multicast Initiative (IPMI), working to develop and refine the standard by which data can be delivered to large numbers of recipients in real time. The increased interest in scaleable push solutions by Internet publishers, corporations interested in intranet development, and broadcasters has spurred the movement in the industry to embrace IP multicasting in its products.

Hosting Multicast Content Delivery

Medium-sized companies wanting to gain the benefits of IP multicasting without investing large amounts of money in the necessary server hardware and software can now use a hosting service provided by UUNET. UUNET is the world's largest Internet provider and has designed the service to support companies that want to reach a large audience economically. Streaming audio and video can be distributed using multicast methods—both Microsoft's NT NetShow server and RealNetwork's RealSystem server are included as a part of the hosted environment.

Summary

The smart pull techniques offered through Active Channels and Netcaster provide a reasonable entry-level means for content providers to reach an audience through channels, but only up to a point. As that audience increases and the need for real-time transmissions becomes more acute, IP multicasting provides a workable solution to information delivery. While the equipment and software investments required to perform IP multicasting are significantly more expensive than entry-level channel delivery, this investment can effectively set up a system to support very large international audiences using the basic framework of the Internet as the delivery medium. The nature of IP multicasting makes it feasible to deliver richer, more complex information—such as multimedia content, audio, and video—in real time without imposing unnecessary transmission burdens on Internet resources. With the work of the IP Multicast Initiative yielding results in producing an industry-supported open standard, IP multicasting will become a much more visible component of the Internet channel picture.

More information on the IPMI can be obtained from:

www.ipmulticast.com

Part Three

Netcaster

Creating a Netcaster
Channel

It would have been nice if Microsoft and Netscape had gotten together and said, "Let's put the browser wars behind us and build a single, unified way to present channel content on the Web for audiences throughout the world." They didn't, and there isn't. Instead, Netscape has produced an application called Netcaster that installs independently as a part of the Netscape Communicator 4 product suite. Netcaster interacts with some new objects that have been added to JavaScript 1.2, allowing the built-in site crawler to identify channel content and retrieve it for subscriber use. If the notion of tinkering with JavaScript to create a channel makes your palms kind of sweaty, Netscape has simplified the process with an Add Channel wizard that fields the answers to a series of prompts and then generates the appropriate JavaScript code to support the Netcaster channel. Netcaster also works in combination with a dedicated push server using Castanet channel technology. The integrated Castanet tuner in Netcaster can receive push content delivered through Castanet channels by a transmitter. Using a transmitter can effectively deliver your channel content to hundreds of thousands of subscribers daily; Castanet channel content can include HTML, standalone Java applications, and Java applets.

This chapter discusses the creation of Netcaster channels, from the use of the Add Channel wizard through the JavaScript components that make it all possible.

Netcaster Channel Concepts

As with Microsoft's Active Channels, the intent behind Netscape Netcaster is to provide a means for delivering customized packages of information to a channel subscriber's desktop, carrying out the work of retrieving and downloading this information behind the scenes. Information accessed in this manner can be viewed when the subscriber is online or offline; delivery schedules and content definitions can be set and modified by each individual user.

Channel content is constructed using conventional Web components, such as JavaScript, Java, HTML, and Dynamic HTML. As with Active Channels, DHTML excels in this role because of its ability to produce self-contained, interactive pages that can be designed to run offline in reasonably compact packages. To view Netcaster channel content, Netscape Communicator 4 users must install Netcaster—an add-on component to the standard Communicator software. Preexisting channels can be accessed through Netscape's Channel Finder, which uses a sliding toolbar approach to display a list of available channels. Users can expand the canned list to include their own channel favorites.

Through a series of settings in Netcaster, subscribers can personalize the use of any channel to which they subscribe. Channels can be regularly updated without user intervention on a predetermined schedule. The number of levels of content to retrieve during channel accesses can be set, and the manner in which incoming information is cached can be specified by the individual user.

A channel can also be anchored to the desktop using a feature that Netscape calls *Webtop mode*. Content designated as a Webtop typically occupies the entire display area positioned behind all the current open windows. To make sense for Webtop use, the channel content should be something that a user would find valuable to have on his or her desktop—a changing assortment of news stories or a weather map that is periodically updated, or an interactive directory with specialized content. To maintain this design model, links that are built into Webtop displays should open new content in a separate window, rather than make changes to the appearance of the Webtop. A Webtop can be seen as a customized work environment tailored to a user's requirements or needs. By embedding links from the Webtop to additional content, the range of usefulness can be extended. Since a Webtop is something that will occupy a prominent position within a user's personal workspace, careful attention to the aesthetics and presentation of Webtop content will encourage users to keep the Webtop in place. Simple, aesthetically pleasing designs are favored over complex, cluttered approaches.

Netscape's Webtop is the conceptual equivalent to Microsoft's Active Desktop. Both of these environments provide a platform for the display of incoming channel content and a live interface to resources on the Internet. Microsoft's approach is more fully integrated into the operating system, but the Webtop provides the same basic functionality—a place to display dynamic channel content where it is immediately accessible. When you're creating the channel definitions in JavaScript, you have the option of choosing the default display mode as being the Webtop. While it may be tempting to select this option—ensuring your content a prominent place within a user's workspace—make sure your content is suitable for Webtop use before you define it as such.

The easiest way for a developer to make Web pages available for channel delivery is to run Netscape's Add Channel wizard. Doing this produces a number of lines of JavaScript code that can be attached to an animated button encouraging a Web page visitor to "Add Netcaster Channel." This utility is described in the next section.

Running the Add Netcaster Channel Wizard

If you've organized your site content so that it is appropriate for channel delivery, you can use Netscape's easy-to-run wizard for creating a Netcaster channel. Before you rush into channel creation, though, take a close look at your site structure and page design to see if they fit these guidelines:

Are the channel-specific pages relatively self-contained and, ideally, constructed using Dynamic HTML? Static HTML pages can be used, but they will appear flat and uninteresting to many users interested in channel content.

If your pages rely on Java applets, have you archived the required classes in a JAR file? Classes won't be automatically downloaded for use unless they are properly archived, so without this step, your Java applications may not run.

Have you organized the nesting and structure of your site to be neatly contained within two or three levels? While users can specify the depth of content retrieved during channel delivery, you should organize the site for the optimal download situation, generally two or three levels of content and somewhere between 1 to 8Mb of content. Larger file downloads are acceptable in some circumstances, as long as the user is geared to expecting them.

If you intend to define the default for your pages as the Webtop mode, have you designed a streamlined, content-rich page to occupy the desktop? If not, perhaps you should go back and redesign the channel content to meet acceptable Webtop standards.

Is there genuine informational or entertainment value to the pages you've constructed for channel use? Subscribers are freely opening up their machines to the pages you are transmitting; don't abuse the privilege of having access to someone's desktop by providing lame content.

The mechanical aspects of creating a channel aren't as demanding as the design issues, as described in the following procedure. For more information on the most important design issues, refer to Chapter 8, "Using DHTML for Netcaster Channels," and the examples offered in the case studies in Part Four of this book.

The Developer's Edge section of the Netscape site offers many different programming and development guidelines and examples; the Netscape Add Channel Button wizard can be accessed from the following URL:

developer.netscape.com/library/examples/index.html?content=
netcast/wizard/index.htm

The initial screen of the wizard indicates that the objective is to produce an Add Channel button that automatically lets users subscribe to the content you designate as a Netscape channel. As you start the wizard, by clicking the Next button, a dialog box lets you enter the name of the channel being created and the address where it is located on the Web. As you can see from Figure 7.1, you can enter Marimba Castanet channels using their server prefix (castanet://), as well as standard HTTP 1.0 channels.

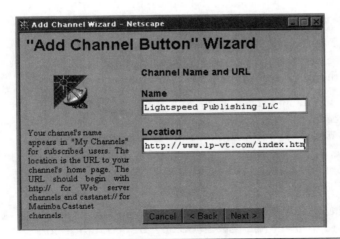

Figure 7.1 Specifying the channel name.

The next dialog box, shown in Figure 7.2, determines the interval between channel updates. The value you enter here is basically the suggested update interval. Each individual user can override your recommendations and set up Netcaster to perform the update at any interval specified by the subscriber. The built-in site crawler in Netcaster will check the channel content at the time and date indicated and download changed content, as specified.

The Channel Cache and Crawl Depth settings, shown in Figure 7.3, indicate the manner in which the site crawler in Netcaster will handle the content. By specifying a depth, you can indicate the level to which the site crawler will retrieve pages, starting at the base page. The Maximum Cache Size value denotes the size of the cache maintained by Netcaster for downloaded content. The Navigator browser and the Netcaster component each use their own separate caches. This is different from the approach used by Internet Explorer 4, which uses a single cache for both browser and Active Channel components.

Choosing the Display Mode, as shown in Figure 7.4, determines how your channel content will appear as it is downloaded. The Default Window displays channel content in a standard Navigator-style window; the Webtop display mode anchors the incoming content to the computer desktop, forming a dynamic surface upon which other windows appear. Authoring content for the Webtop mode of displays requires additional consideration for the page design and content to be effective.

Optionally, you can provide parameters, as shown in Figure 7.5, to indicate where the window containing the channel content will appear using coordinates

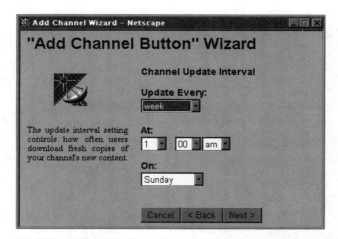

Figure 7.2 Determining the Channel Update Interval.

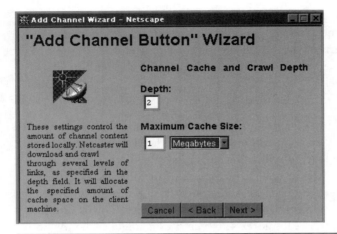

Figure 7.3 Indicating cache size and crawl depth.

that specify an offset from the upper-left corner of the window. The width and height values let you determine the initial size of the channel content window. If you don't provide entries for these settings, the channel wizard makes no entries in the JavaScript code, and the browser uses built-in defaults when the window is opened.

The next dialog box, shown in Figure 7.6, lets you specify the text to include for the Channel Creation button. This is the button that new subscribers will click to have a channel added to their available selections in Netcaster. The button graphic

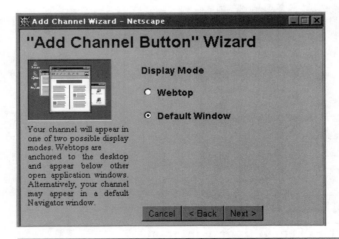

Figure 7.4 Selecting the Display Mode.

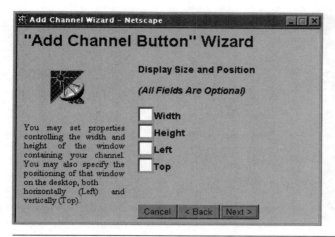

Figure 7.5 Positioning and sizing the window.

shown is also added as an element to be retrieved from the Netscape site and dropped onto the DHTML page. The one-click approach to channel selection makes it easy for users to subscribe. Subscriptions can also be initiated for any site from within Netcaster using menu options.

The last dialog box in the wizard, shown in Figure 7.7, creates the JavaScript code and accompanying HTML tags to be inserted into the page that you want to serve as the channel entry point. The wizard gives you the option of backing up through your previous entries and making any necessary edits at this point. If you

Figure 7.6 Creating button text for the channel.

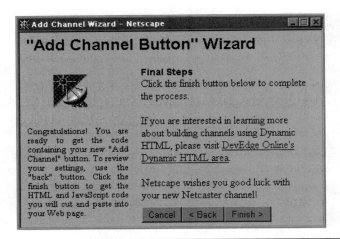

Figure 7.7 Finishing the channel creation.

click the Finish button, the wizard proceeds to convert your selections into code that appears in a Navigator window, from which it can be copied and pasted into your favorite HTML editor or DHTML design application.

The resulting JavaScript code, which you can cut and paste into the DHTML page representing your base channel page, appears as:

```
<SCRIPT LANGUAGE="JavaScript">

 function needNetcaster() {
        window.open("http://netcaster.netscape.com/finder/need_netcaster.html",
 ᴥ"need_netcaster","width=629,height=400,titlebar=yes,toolbar=no,location=no,
 ᴥdirectories=no,status=yes,menubar=no,scrollbars=yes");
        }

function addChannelAPI() {
 needNetcaster(); }
</SCRIPT>
<SCRIPT LANGUAGE="JavaScript1.2">
        var chanURL = "http://www.lp-vt.com/index.htm";
        var chanName = "Lightspeed Publishing LLC";
        var chanIntervalTime = -6;
        var chanAbsoluteTime = 60;
        var chanMaxCacheSize = 1048576;
```

```
        var chanDepth = 2;
        var chanActive = 1;
        var chanMode = "window";
        var chanType=1;

        var getChannelObject = null;
        var addChannel = null;
        var nc = null;
        var ncActive = 0;
        var poller = null;


function activateNetcaster() {
        nc.activate();
        }


function netcasterSniffer() {
        if (!components["netcaster"]) {
        alert("This page requires the Netcaster component.");
        needNetcaster();
    }
    else {
        nc = components["netcaster"];
        if (nc.active == false) {
                alert("Please click the Add Channel button once\nagain after
Netscape Netcaster has completed\nloading to subscribe to this channel.");
            activateNetcaster();
        }
        else {
            ncActive = 1;
            addChannelAPI();
        }
    }
}
function addChannelAPI() {
    if (ncActive == 0) netcasterSniffer();
    else {
        nc = components["netcaster"];
        import nc.getChannelObject;
        import nc.addChannel;
```

```
            var chan = getChannelObject();
            chan.url = chanURL;
            chan.name = chanName;
            chan.intervalTime = chanIntervalTime;
            chan.absoluteTime = chanAbsoluteTime;
            chan.maxCacheSize = chanMaxCacheSize;
            chan.depth = chanDepth;
            chan.active = chanActive;
            chan.mode=chanMode;
            chan.type=chanType;
            addChannel(chan);
        }
        ncActive = 0;
    }
</SCRIPT>
<TABLE><TR><TD ALIGN="CENTER">
<A ="#" onClick="addChannelAPI(); return(false);">
<IMG NAME="ncnowimage" SRC="http://home.netscape.com/inserts/images/ncnow.gif"
WIDTH=117 HEIGHT=55 BORDER=0 ALT="Add Lightspeed Publishing LLC Now!"><br>
Add Lightspeed Publishing LLC Now!
</a></td></tr></table>
```

To provide the necessary hooks for Netcaster to interact with JavaScript, Netscape added some proprietary extensions to the JavaScript interpreter in Netcaster. In other words, the flavor of JavaScript you'll be using to produce Netcaster channels differs from the standards-body approved ECMAScript in a number of ways. These proprietary extensions are necessary to provide basic channel interactions.

Netscape also has maintained the use of its hotly controversial <LAYERS> tag, which is supported only by Netscape Communicator. The use of <LAYERS> can produce some valuable DHTML effects, but these effects can't be accessed beyond the membership of the Navigator browser community. If you're producing a Netcaster channel, you may not be concerned about ensuring a universal audience. In this case, the more proprietary approach to DHTML authoring may make sense to you.

If you're determined to create channels for cross-platform/cross-browser use, keep the following points in mind:

CDF files can be used by the site crawler software in both the Internet Explorer browser and in Netcaster. Netcaster provides less functionality and does not use the full range of CDF file options.

The proprietary version of JavaScript used to implement Netcaster (with the new channel object and netcaster component) can't be properly interpreted by Internet Explorer or other non-Netscape browsers. If you produce pure Netcaster-enabled channels, focus on the Navigator community and provide a means by which to filter out other potential viewers. This could be done with a script that detects the browser type and redirects the path of the site visitor in an appropriate manner, or by posting notice on your Web pages of the appropriate paths to follow depending on the user's browser type.

Third-party applications, such as Macromedia Dreamweaver and Pictorius iNet Developer, can help resolve the disparities between different approaches to DHTML and scripting languages. If you don't want to get intimately involved in the low-level details of browser differences, use one of these applications to handle content issues.

Using VBScript or ActiveX components to control DHTML interactions restricts your content to the Internet Explorer audience. Use JavaScript 1.2 (or JScript in Microsoft terms) if you want cross-platform delivery of content.

Support for the Document Object Model, which has been pledged by both Netscape and Microsoft, should bring a higher order of consistency to the next release of browser software that reaches the market.

JavaScript Components

The dynamic capabilities of a Netcaster channel depend heavily on the underpinnings provided by JavaScript 1.2. The Netcaster program recognizes several distinct channel-specific objects and methods that identify the key characteristics of the channel and determine its behavior. One of the Channel object's methods installs the channel into the Channel Finder that is a part of Netcaster, where it is then displayed on the bar and can be accessed by a single click.

The Channel Object

The Channel object has a series of properties that specify its name, description, and URL.

To create a Channel object as a part of the script to initiate a Netcaster subscription, you first create a variable for a Netcaster component (named nc in the example) and then build an instance of the new Channel object, assigning a unique name for the channel, using the `getChannelObject()` method. The following two lines of code accomplish this:

```
var nc = components["netcaster"]
var greatChannel = nc.getChannelObject();
```

Once this new Channel object has been created—in this case, a channel named greatChannel, you can refer to the properties by appending them to the channel name in dot-separated format. For example, to refer to the channel URL, name, and description, you would use the following references:

```
greatChannel.url
greatChannel.name
greatChannel.desc
```

To assign values to these properties, simply use the assign statement (indicated by an equals sign) to specify the appropriate values. The URL should point to the entry page for the channel, the name identifies the channel as it appears in the Netcaster Channel Finder, and the description offers a concise account of the channel contents (a tool tip pops up with this description). The following code shows how you would make these assignments:

```
greatChannel.url = "http://www.greatness.net/channels/entry.html";
greatChannel.name = "World's Greatest Literary Channel"
greatChannel.desc = "Home of the greatest literary content on the Web."
```

Once you've specified these key characteristics of the channel, the remaining lines of JavaScript define additional information about the appearance and behavior of the channel. For example, you can define the interval time, which is the suggested update interval for the channel content.

```
greatChannel.intervalTime = 30
```

The 30 value—which uses minutes as the default units—indicates a channel update schedule of every 30 minutes. You can also specify additional intervals using a minus sign as a prefix for each of the following sequences:

```
-2    //Every 15 minutes
-3    //Every 30 minutes
-4    //Every hour
-5    //Once daily
-6    //Once weekly
```

If you use once daily (-5) or once weekly (-6), you also need to specify an absolute time value that indicates the number of minutes from midnight to perform the update (for the weekly option, it is the number of minutes from midnight on

Sunday). For example, to specify 1:00 A.M. daily for an update schedule, you would use the following two lines:

```
greatChannel.intervalTime = -5
greatChannel.absoluteTime = 60
```

Indicating the channel maxCacheSize and depth controls how much of the content in bytes can be cached and how many levels into the site the crawler will delve as it is retrieving content. The depth is based on links starting from the base page that is indicated in the channel URL entry.

The following entries indicate a maximum cache size of 1,024,000 bytes and a depth of three levels for site crawling:

```
greatChannel.maxCacheSize = 1024000
greatChannel.depth = 3
```

Channel content can be displayed in one of three modes:

- **webtop:** An immersion form of display that is anchored to the desktop and provides its own navigation.

- **window:** A standard Navigator window that occupies a defined portion of the screen.

- **full:** A full-size Navigator window that occupies the whole desktop, but includes standard browser controls.

To indicate the appropriate mode, just assign the selected mode, surrounded by quotation marks, to the channel name, as shown in the following entry:

```
greatChannel.mode = "window";
```

If you select the "window" mode, Netcaster recognizes width and height settings you specify; you can also provide a suggested placement position for the window (which may be overridden by Netcaster depending on display conditions).

For example, the following four lines create a window 160 pixels wide and 140 pixels high that is to be positioned 10 pixels down and to the right from the upper-left corner of the display:

```
greatChannel.widthHint = 160;
greatChannel.heightHint = 140;
greatChannel.leftHint = 10
greatChannel.topHint = 10
```

Netcaster also lets you specify these values using percentages. For example, you could set the window width and height to 50 percent of the current width and height of the display by using the following entries:

```
greatChannel.widthHint = screen.width/2
greatChannel.heightHint = screen.width/2
```

The channel type is specified using a value of 1 for an HTTP channel and a value of 2 for a Castanet channel. Castanet channels, of course, can only be indicated if the channel content is being delivered through a Castanet server. For most circumstances, you would use the following line to indicate an HTTP channel:

```
greatChannel.type = "1";
```

All of the lines from the various examples in this section could be combined inside a JavaScript function called `subscribe()`, which could then be called from a button or text link in the HTML document to initiate the subscription process. The AddChannelObject method when used with a Netcaster component accesses the Netcaster dialog box that finalizes the channel subscription. The final entry in the script would be as follows:

```
nc.AddChannelObject(greatChannel);
```

The resulting function would appears as follows:

```
<SCRIPT LANGUAGE="JavaScript1.2">

//This function defines a Netcaster channel and initiates subscriptions
function subscribe()
    var nc = components["netcaster"]
    var greatChannel = nc.getChannelObject();

    //Indicates the URL, name, and content of the channel
    greatChannel.url = "http://www.greatness.net/channels/entry.html";
    greatChannel.name = "World's Greatest Literary Channel"
    greatChannel.desc = "Home of the greatest literary content on the Web."

    //Specifies a daily update at 1:00am
    greatChannel.intervalTime = -5
    greatChannel.absoluteTime = 60

    //Sets the maximum cache at 1024000 bytes; crawling to 3 levels
    greatChannel.maxCacheSize = 1024000
    greatChannel.depth = 3
```

```
    //Defines a window display mode with suggested position and size
    greatChannel.mode = "window";
    greatChannel.widthHint = 160;
    greatChannel.heightHint = 140;
    greatChannel.leftHint = 10
    greatChannel.topHint = 10


    //Indicates an HTTP channel (not a Castanet)
    greatChannel.type = "1";


    //Accesses the Add Channel dialog box
    nc.AddChannelObject(greatChannel);
}
</SCRIPT>
```

As you can see, creating a channel in Netcaster requires a bit more work than defining a channel using a CDF file for Internet Explorer, but it is still a reasonably simple process and one that can be mastered by most Web authors without too much difficulty.

The Netcaster Component

JavaScript interacts with Netcaster through the `netcaster` component, which is one of the elements included in the `components` array. The `netcaster` component has its own method—`activate`—that is used to begin execution of the component.

As shown in the script in the previous section, activating the `netcaster` component for use within the script requires that you create a variable name for the component and then associate it with a channel object.

```
var nc = components["netcaster"]
var greatChannel = nc.getChannelObject();
```

You can also import the methods of the `netcaster` component to make it available for use within a JavaScript, using the following import statements:

```
import components["netcaster"].getChannelObject;
import components["netcaster"].addChannel;
```

In other words, you gain access to the channel object through the `netcaster` component. The `getChannelObject` method actually creates a new channel object; the `addChannel` method performs the task of setting up a new subscription to the channel.

The `netcaster` component also has some accessible properties:

name: Identifies the assigned name of the component.

componentVersion: Returns the version of Netcaster that is installed.

active: Specifies whether the netcaster component is available and running.

Netscape provides full documentation for what it refers to as the Netcaster application programming interface (API) at:

developer.netscape.com/library/index.html

Many of the documents at this site are now available in Adobe Acrobat format for easier offline viewing and more compact downloads.

Retrieving Content from Channels

Netcaster is designed to retrieve all the necessary content from an updated Web channel to the depth indicated, including external JavaScript code, plug-ins, Java applets, audio files, video files, and so on. However, there are a few considerations that should be followed to ensure that the necessary content is delivered for offline viewing. Subscribers will expect to receive fairly self-contained documents that don't require reconnecting to the Internet every few minutes to link with additional content, so you should spend some of your design time shaping the structure and content to this purpose. You should also look at the types of content that you want to embed in a document and follow these guidelines when setting up the channel content for effective delivery.

Delivering the Right Amount of Content

One of the key questions faced by a developer working on channel content is how much information to deliver to subscribers. Netcaster doesn't offer the same level of control over what material gets downloaded as does the CDF file used with Microsoft Active Channels. Rather than selecting individual pages for subscription delivery (as you do by defining Items in the CDF file), Netcaster relies on determining the amount of content based on the number of levels traversed by the site crawler. This, of course, doesn't take into account how much content is contained on each page. If the initial page of channel content contains an embedded video file that requires 3Mb of storage, even a single page will require significant download time. If, however, individual pages consist primarily of text and simple DHTML effects, three levels of site crawling might retrieve a total of 3Mb of documents.

Beyond the level of site crawling that is selected by the subscriber, the amount of cache allocated for channel storage will affect how much content can be retrieved for offline viewing. Keep in mind that although the channel developer can suggest appropriate values for the maximum cache size and the estimated cache size, as described in the previous section, each individual subscriber can set his or her own limits for caching. If those limits are lower than what is required for the complete downloading of all the content for a channel update, Netcaster will only download what the subscriber specifies (regardless of what the developer recommends). Subscribers are in control of the process, so all of your development work should be performed with an awareness that every one of your recommendations—as specified in the JavaScript file that sets up the channel object—can be ignored.

It might help to visualize the process by which the site crawler operates. When Netcaster is started up and it detects a scheduled update for a currently active subscription, its site crawler component accesses the base page of the channel (as indicated in the Channel properties). From this initial URL, the site crawler follows all of the links from the base page to each subsequent page, burrowing down to the level that is specified by the Depth property of the channel. The depth setting is another parameter that can be overridden by an individual subscriber. If you recommend two levels of site crawling and the individual user sets the channel depth level to one level, Netcaster will only retrieve one level of content.

The priority of downloading used by Netcaster places HTML documents over embedded objects or graphic images. In other words, Netcaster will retrieve all of the HTML documents through the indicated depth before it starts grabbing images, Java applets, multimedia plug-ins, and so on. If it runs out of cache before it collects all of the embedded content, it at least has the HTML material. If it runs out of cache before it retrieves all of the HTML documents, the user browsing the pages will have a disjointed offline experience.

The amount of content to include in the channel should be set according to user expectations. The type of content that you offer will vary according to the nature of your individual channel. If you're offering information about the tools and techniques for multimedia design, users will expect whiz-bang graphics, animation, plug-ins, high interactivity, audio—all of which adds up to fairly sizeable storage requirements. User expectations for a channel of this sort might range from 1Mb to 5Mb per update; in some circumstances, even larger volumes of content would not be out of the question.

On the other hand, someone who is anticipating receiving short news updates of technology advances to read over morning coffee expects shorter download times and more compact content. A range of 500Kb to 1Mb would be more appropriate for this type of channel.

Many users—perhaps most users—will have subscriptions to several channels. If these are all updated on a frequent schedule—daily or every three or four hours—the update times required for each channel back to back could be significant. If a user subscribes to four channels and each channel includes 5Mb of daily updates, several hours of connect time will be required for a 28.8Kbps modem to retrieve this content.

To ensure that you don't disappoint user expectations, make sure that your channel description provides an accurate sense of how much content will be delivered during updates. For example, if your site plans to deliver audio clips of rising independent music groups interspersed with RealVideo segments, describe your site accordingly: "Audio and video highlights of exciting new bands—average update: 7Mb." Without this kind of warning, you run two risks: One, that the subscriber will be annoyed at the quantity of files you dump on his or her disk; and two, that he or she may unrealistically set the maximum cache size appropriately to receive all of the content that is contained in the channel. Either way, the result won't inspire user confidence and will probably result in lost subscriptions and disgruntled viewers.

Hard-and-fast rules are difficult to come by in this situation. You don't know how fast subscriber's dial-up connections are, what balance of multimedia to text they prefer, how many other channels they subscribe to, and what they're expecting to receive from you. In response, you can let them know ahead of time what you plan to deliver through the channel, aim for the mid-range, dial-up modem crowd (somewhere between 28.8Kbps and 33.6Kbps), and put your most important content in the HTML pages, realizing that the embedded material may get excluded by maximum cache size overflows. If it sounds like you're going to have to use a good degree of intuition to shape content delivery, you're right.

Scheduling Considerations

As with most of the other Channel properties, the individual subscriber has the last word when it comes to scheduling updates. You can make your recommendations, as the channel author, and include these recommendations in the Channel object properties, but each subscriber is free to go to the Channel Properties dialog box in Netcaster and set his or her own schedules to suit personal whims.

Netcaster uses a number of minutes from a fixed point in time to calculate update times. This can make it less than obvious how to specify offsets unless you sit down with a calculator and work out the numbers.

The Channel object has two properties that indicate the scheduling of channel content:

`intervalTime:` (providing the update interval in minutes, hours, or days).

`absoluteTime:` (indicating the number of minutes after midnight on Sunday to initiate a download). Whenever intervalTime is used with a value of daily or weekly, absoluteTime must be used to specify the time of the day or the day of the week to initiate the operation.

The intervalTime indicates the number of minutes between channel updates. You can either specify a positive integer indicating the exact number of minutes or use one of the preset negative values recognized by Netcaster:

- 15 minutes is represented by –2

- 30 minutes is represented by –3

- 60 minutes is represented by –4

- Daily is represented by –5

- Weekly is represented by –6

For example, to specify a channel update every 15 minutes, you would use the statement:

```
channelObject.intervalTime = -2
```

Alternatively, you could use the actual number of minutes in the statement:

```
channelObject.intervalTime = 15
```

Whenever the Daily (–5) or Weekly (–6) presets are used, you need to also include an absoluteTime value to define the amount of offset from a base starting time.

Table 7.1 shows the number of minutes to offset from midnight Sunday to specify a particular day of the week. You then add however many minutes from the selected day of the week to indicate the time of the day, as indicated on the second table. The total number of minutes corresponds with the day and time that the update will occur.

For example, assume that you wanted to set a weekly update schedule for Wednesdays at 6:00 A.M. From Table 7.1, you take the number of minutes indicated for Wednesday: 4320. To that value, you add the number of minutes for 6:00 A.M. as shown in Table 7.2: 360. The total is 4680—this becomes your absoluteTime.

Table 7.1 Minutes to Each Day of the Week

Day of the Week	Number of Minutes Offset
Sunday	0
Monday	1440
Tuesday	2880
Wednesday	4320
Thursday	5760
Friday	7200
Saturday	8640

When used in combination with the intervalTime value (−6 for weekly), the schedule would be set by these two statements:

```
channelObject.intervalTime = -6
channelObject.absoluteTime = 4680
```

Table 7.2 Time of Day Offsets in Minutes

Hour	Offset	Hour	Offset
Midnight	0	Noon	720
1:00 A.M.	60	1:00 P.M.	780
2:00 A.M.	120	2:00 P.M.	840
3:00 A.M.	180	3:00 P.M.	900
4:00 A.M.	240	4:00 P.M.	960
5:00 A.M.	300	5:00 P.M.	1020
6:00 A.M.	360	6:00 P.M.	1080
7:00 A.M.	420	7:00 P.M.	1140
8:00 A.M.	480	8:00 P.M.	1200
9:00 A.M.	540	9:00 P.M.	1260
10:00 A.M.	600	10:00 P.M.	1320
11:00 A.M.	660	11:00 P.M.	1380

If your intervalTime is set to a daily update (–5 for daily), you only need to select the appropriate offset from Table 7.2. For example, to schedule a daily update for 10:00 P.M. every day, the statements should read:

```
channelObject.intervalTime = -5
channelObject.absoluteTime = 1320
```

You can create offsets in any amounts down to the minute. For example, if you decided you wanted to make the daily update time 10:45 P.M., rather than 10:00 P.M., you just add the additional 45 minutes to 1320 for a total of 1365.

Be sure to use the actual name for the variable representing the channelObject after you create a new instance of the object. For example, if you create a channelObject named channel_wow, substitute the variable name when specifying schedule data, as in:

```
channel_wow.intervalTime = 60
```

Designing an Interface

Channel content can be designed to operate within the boundaries of a normal browser window, relying on the standard navigation controls to move between documents, travel forward or backward in a viewed sequence, or jump to a specific page. In Netcaster Webtop view, however, your presentation occupies a windowless space on the user's desktop, and the only navigation controls are those that you provide as the content designer. Full-screen mode offers a similar design challenge, although you have a bit more access to standard navigational options; in many ways, even though you are working with HTML and JavaScript as your construction tools, you are building the equivalent of an application to run on the user's desktop. It may be a simple application—constructed to display several articles and graphics—but to be effective, your channel content must reflect solid design principles and a user interface that guides rather than confuses. Dynamic HTML, as we've said repeatedly throughout this book, makes it particularly easy to construct an intuitive, easy-to-navigate interface. Using the built-in capabilities of DHTML, you can craft a menu structure that displays popup hints, expands to expose nested content, uses animation to point out or highlight particular types of information, and takes advantage of cascading style sheet features to control page layout and provide dynamic interaction with content. Chapter 8, "Using DHTML for Netcaster Channels," illustrates some of the ways you can use DHTML with Netcaster, and Part Four of this book, "Case Studies," shows real-world examples through a series of case studies.

Webtop design in particular requires careful attention to the presentation. You are basically providing a surface upon which computer users will be running other applications with the Webtop anchored in a fixed position at the bottom layer. Since the Webtop will be highly visible, sometimes for hours at a stretch, you should spend a good deal of time developing a visually attractive setting with key interactive components easily visible without being intrusive. Flashy, graphically harsh Webtops will make it difficult for users to run other applications and will grow tiring after prolonged viewing. Flickering, blinking, animated objects dancing around the Webtop will make it difficult to read information in the windows of other applications or to focus on anything other than the desktop.

If you're not comfortable in the role of software interface designer, consult a good reference on design principles to get a solid grounding in the topic. Dynamic HTML lets you basically construct an interface from scratch and gives you the opportunity to make all the mistakes that beginning interface designers often fall prey to. Take a careful look at some of the better-designed channels on the Web and check out the examples in this book to get an idea of what works and what doesn't. Then build your own interface, keeping in mind the user's perspective and desire for clarity and simplicity.

Some recommended sources for design principles appear in Appendix B, "Resources."

Indicating a Channel Icon

The Channel object uses the cardURL property to determine the location of a graphic to represent the channel content. To specify the appropriate URL for the graphic, use the syntax:

```
channelObject.cardURL = "string"
```

The string should contain a valid URL address that points to the graphic to use in the Netcaster My Channels display when the mouse pointer moves into the area. If this optional value is not specified, Netcaster substitutes a generic graphic image to represent the channel.

Since this graphic can provide a way to distinguish your channel and clearly identify it among other channels listed in the My Channels area, it is worth developing an attractive graphic to make your listing stand out.

Working with Castanet

Netscape Netcaster includes a built-in Castanet tuner, which allows it to receive channels that are hosted through a Castanet Transmitter. While the functionality offered by a Castanet Transmitter is similar to the Web-server approach for channel delivery described in this chapter, Castanet offers a number of significant capabilities that improve the scope and promise of Webcasting. These improved capabilities let you use a Castanet Transmitter to:

- Create a channel consisting of a Java application or an applet that can be run on the user's desktop and updated automatically. This type of construct is called a *software channel.*

- Improve bandwidth usage by intelligent updating of only changed channel content and the ability to perform small edits to large channel files. These optimized delivery techniques are well suited to large sites that include frequently changing channel content.

- Support a distributed server architecture that scales gracefully to millions of subscribers. Castanet Transmitters can balance the server load of subscription updates by transferring update requests to a Transmitter with close geographic proximity to the subscriber.

- Provide personalized content delivery based on a history of user transactions and expressed user preferences.

- Perform more detailed logging of user interactions, including real-time feedback through the use of Transmitter plug-ins.

- Monitor each subscription update transaction for file transfer integrity and ensure that each subscriber receives a full update.

From the perspective of the individual subscriber, content delivered through Castanet channels looks identical to content delivered through Web-server techniques. The full Webtop-mode display is supported. The channel subscription process is the same and the method of accessing channels through the Channel Finder is the same. However, by delivering content through the Castanet Transmitter, all of the more powerful channel features can be enabled.

Along with the increased capabilities, the cost of implementing this approach to channel delivery escalates. You need dedicated server hardware and the Castanet Transmitter software to set up channels of this type. Two components—the transmitter component and the publisher component—are required to set up the channel for subscribers. Because of the cost considerations, these techniques are generally reserved for large corporations that are offering channel content for tens of thousands of subscribers, or even larger audiences. Marimba provides evaluation copies of these products on its Website:

www.marimba.com

Publishing a Castanet Channel

You don't need to abandon your conventional Web development tools to create and publish a Castanet channel. You can use familiar applications to develop Website documents or Java applications and then transfer these files to a base directory, which is designated when configuring the Castanet software as the channel's base location.

The base directory stores the full range of channel content files and a set of properties files. The properties file defines the characteristics of the Castanet channel, including the channel's name, the recommended update schedule, whether the channel is based on HTML documents or Java applications, and similar kinds of information. An optional plug-in subdirectory stores any plug-in files that are used in relation to the content.

Once you've assembled the content within the base directory, the Castanet publisher lets you complete the channel-creation process by copying the content to the area where the transmitter software performs its channel delivery tasks. Shared files that are used by multiple channels can be stored as a single copy in the transmitter channel directory. The publishing process makes the channel available for subscriptions. If the channel has a plug-in, the publishing operation also installs each necessary plug-in.

Whenever a channel needs to be updated, the Web developer replaces those files that have changed in the base directory defined for the channel and performs the publishing operation once more to equip the transmitter to serve the modified files. With an updated record of the current channel contents, the transmitter responds to subscription update requests by serving these new files—downloads that are already in process use the earlier set of files. The transmitter regularly purges any outdated files that are no longer included in the channel from its storage directories.

Levels of JavaScript

The JavaScript interpreters built into each new release of Netscape Navigator since version 2.0 have had a different and expanded set of capabilities. You can't automatically assume that JavaScript code written for recent browsers will run

Responding to Feedback

One of the most powerful capabilities of Castanet channels involves the capability of collecting data from the channel to the transmitter—providing a feedback loop that can be used to control the nature of the data delivered and to respond to personalized requirements. Developers can create transmitter plug-ins that are invoked whenever an update request is serviced by the transmitter. The plug-in processes and interacts with the data—which includes a list of the files sent to service the update request—and can perform customized operations to personalize the content, such as enabling a speech synthesis module to read content to a vision-impaired subscriber or producing the text in Swedish instead of English. Electronic commerce transactions can also be managed by plug-ins; for example, the feedback data might provide a user ID and password that could instruct the plug-in to access the user's account information from an online database. Plug-ins can also perform simple logging of user interactions.

Plug-ins can be generated using typical Java development applications. The files composing a plug-in are stored in the channel's base directory and published along with the rest of the channel content. The feedback mechanism offered by plug-ins makes it possible for the channel developer to perform many useful, real-time operations to improve the response of a channel to a user's expectations.

correctly (or at all) on earlier browsers. In particular, there are many new features incorporated in Navigator 4 that are designed to support JavaScript 1.2, but have no equivalent functionality in earlier versions of Navigator.

The <SCRIPT> tag is one means of protecting your site viewers from colliding with JavaScript sequences that are too advanced for their browsers. By specifying the level of JavaScript as a LANGUAGE attribute within the <SCRIPT> tags, you ensure that earlier browsers will ignore the code nested between the beginning and end tags. For example, the following entry identifies the language as JavaScript 1.2:

```
<SCRIPT LANGUAGE="JavaScript1.2">
```

When the Navigator 4 browser encounters this attribute, it automatically runs the code since it supports JavaScript 1.2. Navigator 3 and Navigator 2 browsers would skip over the enclosed code, since they cannot interpret it.

Similarly, if you specify that LANGUAGE="JavaScript1.1", Navigator 3 and Navigator 4 will both run the code. Navigator 2 won't. Navigator 2 only reads code if the LANGUAGE="JavaScript" attribute is encountered.

You can then use this attribute to shield earlier browsers from code sequences that would confuse them. Because channel content can only be delivered through Netcaster, and JavaScript 1.2 features are important to channel definitions, you can make HTML pages available for subscriptions through Netcaster (using the JavaScript setup explained in this chapter) and still allow earlier browsers to view the pages through standard means. As long as the LANGUAGE="JavaScript1.2" attribute encloses the channel description code, earlier browsers won't choke on it. Keep in mind that if you develop your site in this manner, any DHTML effects you place on common pages won't work with older browsers either.

Managing Security Issues

You can develop channel content for Netcaster that doesn't present any type of security concern for users accessing the pages. However, it is becoming more common for developers to distribute the equivalent to complete applications—constructed in JavaScript or Java—to run on the user's machine. Applications that have been designed to perform typical program functions, such as writing to a hard disk drive or modifying the interface to the system, present security concerns. Netscape has designed a technique called *digital signing* to address the security issue. An example of the types of actions that can only be performed through signed code are:

- Performing write operations to the hard disk drive

- Positioning a window in the offscreen area

- Opening a window with dimensions smaller than 100×100 pixels

- Opening windows that do not have integrated controls or borders

- Modifying or replacing the key browser elements, such as the title bar, status bar, menu bar, location bar, personal bar, or menu elements

The general term that applies to these kinds of operations is code that performs actions *outside of the sandbox*. The *sandbox* is a defined, restricted area recognized by the browser where certain secure application activities can take place.

Digital Certificates are a means of validating your identity or your company's identity and providing assurance that a block of code or application hasn't been tampered with in any way. Signing certificates can be attached to individual files or JavaScript code to present the attached item as being certified from the original source. Network administrators who set up browsers on a corporate basis may institute policies that restrict the running of applications that are unsigned; Netscape Communicator has features that support different levels of security. One of the options is choosing to only run applications that can be associated with a Digital Certificate. Digital Certificates are awarded and maintained by companies, such as Verisign, Inc., and they provide a sophisticated way to reduce the risks of rogue applications damaging or disrupting a user's system.

Netscape has developed an object-signing protocol that lets developers specify precisely the degree of access they want to a user's system within a particular script or application. The level of security set up by user's preferences in Communicator is matched to the type of activity that an application or script requests (through a JavaScript statement), and those activities that are restricted to verification through object signing can then be blocked if a valid digital certificate is not presented. This gives each individual user control over what he or she considers a trusted source of software, and gives Communicator the ability to discriminate between software sources to identify those that are assumed to be trusted providers. While not perfect, this system provides the benefits of cryptographic methods to authenticate software, reducing the dangers of running downloaded programs.

If an object is downloaded in Communicator that has an attached certificate, the browser displays a message identifying the source of the object and indicates those system services that the object wants to use. The user then responds by granting or denying the request. The dialog box that appears offers the option of automatically allowing signed objects from the same source to be run without question in the future. In this case, Communicator only displays the prompts when it encounters a signed object from a source that has not been previously confirmed.

Additional details on the security constraints that Netscape has developed appear at:

developer.netscape.com/library/documentation/communicator/jsguide/js1_2.htm

Summary

Depending on your background and experience, you may want to create your Netcaster channel description by directly producing the necessary JavaScript code, or create the code using the Add JavaScript Channel wizard described in this chapter. As with HTML, even if you normally work with a high-level editing tool, there are times you will want to drop down to the code level and inspect the statements one by one to ensure you're getting the precise results that you want. Understanding the individual JavaScript objects and methods relating to channel delivery can also be helpful for troubleshooting or fine-tuning your channel behavior.

Chapter 8, "Using DHTML for Netcaster Channels," goes beyond the mechanical aspects of creating the channel and explains how DHTML can be used to produce interactive content for delivery through Netcaster. Many of the techniques presented can be immediately applied to your own channel development projects.

Using **DHTML** for
Netcaster Channels

This chapter offers a number of ideas for constructing page content in DHTML for delivery through Netcaster channels. The examples provided cover each of the following topics:

- Animating layers for an opening page

- Creating a script that handles movement

- Building platform-independent scripts with mBed Interactor

- Adding rollover functions to a page with Dreamweaver

DHTML provides the ideal vehicle for delivering Web content through Netcaster channels, offering the tools to construct pages that suit the particular features available through Netcaster, such as the Webtop display. Since, for Webtop displays and full-screen channel content, the developer provides the primary navigational controls, DHTML's capabilities come into play. Rollover controls, expandable menu trees, layering of text descriptions, and style sheet attributes under script control all combine to contribute to a flexible, interactive authoring environment.

The Captive Netcaster Audience

If you are creating content designed for an audience running Netscape Netcaster, the problems of maintaining cross-browser compatibility vanish. You know that your audience is running a component of Netscape Communicator, so you can tailor your DHTML features to the Netscape-supported variations. You can also freely use proprietary tags, such as the Netscape <LAYER> tag. Pages constructed in this manner will undoubtedly degrade in a totally ungraceful way on versions of Navigator prior to 4.0 and other browsers, but you can be assured that if your audience is running Netcaster, it has Netscape's 4.0 software installed. Compatibility is guaranteed.

Given this latitude of freedom, you can create some impressive presentations within the Netscape arena. The examples provided in this chapter are Netscape-only examples. However, one of the examples is constructed using mBed Software's Interactor, which creates multimedia content that automatically supports the Netscape and Microsoft interpretations of DHTML. This multimedia content is produced in a form that allows it to be saved with Microsoft-compatible DHTML features (as well as Netscape).

Animating Layers for an Opening Page

Netscape introduced a concept referred to as *layers* in recent releases of its browser. Layers are essentially a series of planes—each with its own content, such as text and images—that can be rearranged, hidden, or repositioned in the browser window. If you're familiar with traditional cel animation, such as cartoonists use, the illusion of motion is created by progressively showing a series of images very rapidly. By moving a series of images in quick succession, the human eye blends together the sequence and sees it as real-time movement.

Animation using the <LAYER> tag follows this basic principle. If you create 24 individual layers, each with an image slightly out of position with the previous layer, and then cycle through them rapidly, you can produce very smooth, very well synchronized animated sequences. You also have the option of using a second method of manipulating and animating an image on a layer. You can reposition the layer itself incrementally over a series of steps to create a sense of movement. The image moves with the layer, following a course that you can specify through script-level controls.

While the <LAYER> tag is unapproved by any standards body, you can use it safely with pages that are delivered through Netcaster, since you're assured support through version 4 of Communicator (of which Netcaster is a component).

To support the use of the <LAYER> tag, Netscape incorporated some changes to JavaScript, allowing layers to be managed through script control.

JavaScript Extensions

To accommodate the concept of layers, Netscape added objects and methods to JavaScript. The Layer object has a set of properties that identify it, express whether it is hidden or visible, position it within a series of other layers, and define its position in relation to the browser window or other layers. Clipping rectangles can be used to control the display of a portion of a layer (while hiding the rest). Several new methods apply to the Layer object, including those shown in Table 8.1.

The properties of each layer are as shown in Table 8.2.

Each layer also has several clipping rectangles properties that specify a portion of a complete layer that is visible. Valid clipping rectangle properties include:

- clip.left
- clip.top
- clip.right
- clip.bottom
- clip.width
- clip.height

Table 8.1 Methods Used with the Layer Object

Method	Description
moveBy(x, y)	Repositions a layer by the x/y coordinates indicated in pixels added to the previous x/y position.
moveTo(x, y)	Moves the upper-left corner of the layer to the x/y position indicated (measured in pixels).
resizeTo(width, height)	Modifies the coordinates of a layer's lower-right corner clipping rectangle.
resizeBy(delta width, delta height)	Changes the current coordinates of a layer's clipping rectangle by the amount indicated.
moveAbove(layer)	Positions a layer directly above the layer identified by name.
moveBelow(layer)	Positions a layer directly below the layer identified by name.

Table 8.2 Properties of Layers

name	Identifies the name of the layer appearing between the <LAYER> tags.
left	Specifies the left edge of a layer in pixels. The reference is relative to the parameters of the layer that encloses it.
top	Specifies the vertical edge of a layer in pixels. The reference is relative to the parameters of the layer that encloses it.
visibility	Determines whether the layer is hidden or not.
siblingAbove	Identifies the layer directly above the one being referenced (using z-order). This value is null if the indicated layer is already on top of the stack.
siblingBelow	Identifies the layer directly below the one being referenced (using z-order). This value is null if the layer is already on the bottom of the stack.
parentLayer	Corresponds with a particular layer object that encloses the specified layer. This value is null if the layer is already at the root.
layers	Provides the index value position in an array (as well as the name) of each child layer that appears in a document.

Defining a Layer

To create a layer in a document, enclose the appropriate properties between a starting <LAYER> tag and an ending <LAYER> tag. For example, the following tags create a layer named squid_one that is offset from the upper left by 25 pixels and from the top by 50 pixels:

```
<LAYER NAME="squid_one" LEFT=25 TOP=50>
...layer contents...
</LAYER>
```

A layer can be referred to in JavaScript code by its name or index value. For example, you could reference the previous layer as:

```
document.squid_one
```

Or, if it was the first layer in the document, you would use the value:

```
document.layers[0]
```

Although the order in which the layers are indexed cannot be modified, you can use an indexed reference to assign properties, such as the position at which the layer appears. For example, this statement moves the layer indicated to 150 pixels from the left:

```
document.layers[1].left=150
```

One means of manipulating an animated sequence is to cycle through the index values of the `layers` array, displaying each layer for a specified duration. You can also move the layer itself and its contents, as described in the following section.

Moving a Layer

One of the simplest forms of animation available through layers consists of repositioning the entire layer and everything on it. One way to visualize this is to imagine that you have a piece of Plexiglas about the size of your computer screen with a stick-on image upon it. By default, the image appears in a fixed position—if you map the upper-left corner of the Plexiglas to the upper-left corner of the screen, the image will be within the boundaries of the screen. If you start moving the Plexiglas across the screen to the right, 10 pixels at a time, the image moves across the background presented on the computer screen. Layers can be positioned using the `moveTo()` or the `offset()` functions of JavaScript 1.2.

The number of increments and the speed at which each repositioning movement occurs need to be controlled so that the entire animation doesn't happen in the flash of a few milliseconds (too fast for the eye to even see the motion). The time between increments can be controlled using the JavaScript `setTimeout()` method, which lets you control the intervals (in milliseconds) between specific events in the sequence of JavaScript code.

You can also use the `setInterval()` method, which establishes a time period for calling the function indicated in the argument. When you use `setTimeout()`, the expression to be evaluated or function called by the argument is executed only once. You need to establish a recursive program flow, where the function calls itself until a particular condition is satisfied, ending the execution of the function. Using `setInterval()` lets you repeatedly call the same function at the interval that you specify. For example, the following code calls the function rotate_letter every second:

```
setInterval(rotate_letter, 1000)
```

This continues until the process is terminated by a `clearInterval()` method.

You'll see both the `setTimeout()` method and the `setInterval()` method used in JavaScripts that control DHTML elements. Just keep in mind that the `setTimeout()` method calls its function only once; the `setInterval()` method calls repeatedly. Both of these methods should be terminated by their complementary method: `clearTimeout()` or `clearInterval()`. Timing plays a crucial role in DHTML interactions, particularly where animation is involved, so understanding how to use these methods can improve your scripting efforts.

A Simple Banner Animation

You can implement a simple banner animation that results from the repositioning of a layer with a minimum of JavaScript code. The first step in the process is to place the layer and its content within the body of the HTML document. Layer positioning is based on the upper-left corner of the enclosing window or layer, measured in pixels. One nice feature about Netscape's Layers implementation is that you can position portions of the layer offscreen—content that appears in these areas will be concealed until the layer is moved into the viewing position.

For this example, a banner display for the fictional retail outlet Pogo World, we'll create a layer and assign it the name pogo1. Using a negative value for the LEFT property of the layer, we'll ensure that the graphic appearing on the layer is initially out of sight. The code to define the layer is as follows:

```
<LAYER NAME="pogo1" LEFT=-280 TOP=95>
<IMG SRC="pogo.gif" HEIGHT=80 WIDTH=280>
</LAYER>
```

Note that the left offset, −280, corresponds with the width of the graphic, essentially bumping it over to the left so that the rightmost edge is just out of the display region.

The next step is to create the script sequence that will dynamically move the layer. You can assign the layer to a variable for easy reference in the script with the following code:

```
banner=document.layers['pogo1']
```

This references the Layers array of the current document and uses the name of the layer—pogo1—for identification. Alternatively, you could use the index value of the layer; since it is the first layer in the document and index values start at 0, the line of code would read:

```
banner=document.layers[0]
```

We'll establish a variable for a counter called reps that will control the overall movement of the layer, as follows:

```
reps=1
```

We'll also control the rate at which the animation function will be called by using the setInterval() method and choosing a value of 20 milliseconds, as shown:

```
sliding_span=setInterval(scootPogo, 20)
```

The variable assignment, `sliding_span`, is used as an identification for the interval timer, which we can refer to later in the script when we want to terminate the timing function. Basically, this line of code instructs JavaScript to call the function `scootPogo()`—which we still need to create—every 20 milliseconds.

The `scootPogo` function executes when the reps value that we set to 1 earlier is less than 100. For each cycle through the following if clause, the left property of the layer (now called `banner`) is increased by 5 pixels. From its offscreen position, it will quickly move across the display until the reps counter reaches 100. At that point, the else clause is executed, clearing the interval timer and halting the animation. The code for the function follows:

```
function scootPogo() {
if (reps<100) {
    reps++
    banner.left += 5
    } else {
    clearInterval(sliding_span)
    }
}
```

If we add a bit of supporting HTML code to serve as infrastructure, the layer animation would appear as follows:

```
<HTML>
<TITLE>Pogo Sticks Make a Comeback</TITLE>
<BODY>
<H1>Are you willing to make the leap?<H1>
<LAYER NAME="pogo1" LEFT=-280 TOP=95>
<IMG SRC="pogo.gif" HEIGHT=80 WIDTH=280>
</LAYER>
<P>Welcome to Pogo World.</P>

<SCRIPT LANGUAGE="JavaScript1.2">
banner=document.layers['pogo1']
reps=1
sliding_span=setInterval(scootPogo, 20)
```

```
function scootPogo(){
    if (reps<100) {
        reps++
        banner.left += 5
    } else {
        clearInterval(sliding_span)
    }
}
</SCRIPT>
</BODY>
</HTML>
```

If you run this script, the banner emerges and scrolls smoothly across the screen until it reaches its final destination, as shown in Figure 8.1.

Even though the previous example doesn't require an enormous amount of code to implement, if you wanted to animate several different objects on the same page,

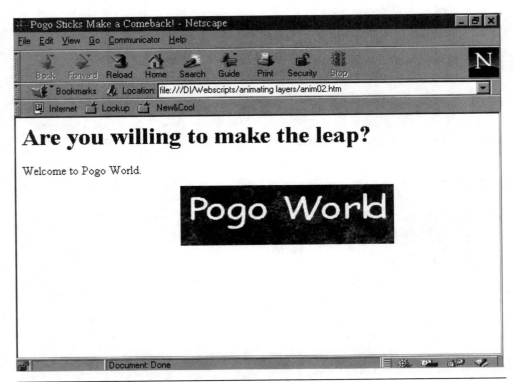

Figure 8.1 Scrolled-out banner from Pogo World.

you would end up doing a lot of hard-coding of values to control where the layers are positioned. To avoid this extra work, you can devise a general-purpose script to handle the basic positioning and movement characteristics of a layer and then supply values to the function through the arguments specified when the function is initially called.

Let's look at a script adapted from one of the examples given in the Netscape Developer's area.

Sliding a Layer with a Function

A function in JavaScript can serve as a kind of magical black box. You feed some numbers to the function and it performs a task for you without any further effort. By enclosing certain kinds of commonly used tasks within a function, you can create reusable sections of code that will simplify your scripting efforts in the future.

The following function—`slider()`—uses a series of variables that regulate the animated movement of a layer. The variables are:

lyr: Provides the identification of the layer.

xinc: Specifies the movement along the x-axis (horizontally) in pixels. Both positive and negative values can be used. Positive values move the layer to the right; negative, to the left.

yinc: Specifies the movement along the y-axis (vertically) in pixels. Both positive and negative values can be used. Positive values move the layer up; negative, down.

inctime: Indicates the number of milliseconds between each incremental movement of the layer. The combination of the number of movements and the distance of the movements (from the xinc and yinc) values determines how smooth or how choppy the animation will be.

xstop: Specifies a value along the x-axis where the animated movement will stop. The function obtains the value of the current position of the layer from the left each time it is run and performs a comparison to see if it should continue.

The basic contents of the script are as follows:

```
<SCRIPT LANGUAGE="JavaScript1.2">

function slider(lyr,xinc,yinc,inctime,xstop) {
    lyr.top += yinc
```

```
      lyr.left += xinc
      if (((xinc > 0) && (lyr.left < xstop)) ||
            ((xinc < 0) && (lyr.left > xstop))) {
      setTimeout('slider(document.layer["'+lyr.name+'"],'+xinc+','+yinc+','
└+inctime+','+xstop+')',inctime)
      }
}
</SCRIPT>
```

As you can see, the function accepts five arguments, and these determine the course of the layer animation. Each time through, the yinc and xinc values are used to modify the layer position, as indicated by lyr.top and lyr.left values.

The if clause in the function determines whether the recursive function call will be made again, as it appears in the setTimeout statement. The comparison looks at the value of xinc and determines if the position of the layer has reached the xstop limit.

Within setTimeout, the inctime variable specifies the delay before the function will be called again, which determines the rate at which the animated layer movement will be performed.

If you put this function to work in an actual HTML document, the code could be written as shown in the following example:

```
<HTML>
<HEAD>
<TITLE>Things are Jumping at Pogo World</TITLE>

<SCRIPT LANGUAGE="JavaScript1.2">

function slider(lyr,xinc,yinc,inctime,xstop) {
      lyr.top += yinc
      lyr.left += xinc
      if (((xinc > 0) && (lyr.left < xstop)) ||
            ((xinc < 0) && (lyr.left > xstop))) {
      setTimeout('slider(document.layer["'+lyr.name+'"],'+xinc+','+yinc+','
└+inctime+','+xstop+')',inctime)
      }
}
</SCRIPT>
</HEAD>
<BODY BGCOLOR="FFFFFF" onLoad=slider(document.layers['pogo1'], 20,10, 100, 450)">
```

```
<LAYER NAME="pogo1" TOP=80 LEFT=10 VISIBILITY=INHERIT>
<IMG SRC="pogo.gif" WIDTH=280 HEIGHT=80 ALT="Sliding Pogo Banner">
</LAYER>
</BODY>
</HTML>
```

When the body of the page is initially loaded, the onLoad reference to the slider function passes the values over to the JavaScript function slider in the <HEAD> region. These values determine the behavior of the animation.

In this case, the layer has an xinc value of 20 and a yinc value of 10, so the movement will be to the right and down. Using a different combination of xinc and yinc enables you to perform animation along a diagonal. The logo banner starts at the upper-left portion of the window and moves down to the lower right. The xstop value stops the whole process before the banner slips off the right side of the display area.

Using JavaScript in this manner allows you to create straightforward movement of layers. You can combine the movements of several objects at the same time using a similar process, but, as you can imagine, the scripts begin to get pretty elaborate. One way to create more intricate onscreen DHTML activities on your pages is to use a tool like mBed Interactor, which contains a prebuilt library of the necessary JavaScript functions to perform a wide range of onscreen effects. If you need to develop a path that contains a greater range of flexibility in the movement, Interactor can help you do that in a visual manner, as shown in the later section, *Cross-Platform Multimedia Delivery with Interactor*.

Effective Opening Sequences

Through television and film, we're used to a number of conventions commonly used in the opening of presentations—whether you're watching the start of the evening news or the beginning of the latest James Bond film. Dramatic use of color, sound, and motion sets the stage—so to speak—for the material to follow. Using DHTML, you have the ability to produce similar kinds of effects and build a sense of drama or anticipation in your audience. While the bandwidth limitations of dial-up connections on the Internet might prevent you from launching an animated extravaganza backed by a full orchestral score, channels offer you some significant advantages in this area: DHTML allows impressive effects without overloading the bandwidth, and channels are typically downloaded in the background so users are not so conditioned to receive immediate playback of the content.

To train yourself to the nuances of an effective opening presentation, pay attention to the broadcast media and to the Websites that have adopted DHTML to see how the professionals skillfully capture the attention of the eye, prepare the user for the content to follow, and lead smoothly into the opening of material to follow. A sense of timing is important, as are your choices of elements and their handling.

Cross-Platform Multimedia Delivery with Interactor

One of the more capable offerings in the current crop of DHTML authoring tools is mBed Interactor. This application has the capability of generating a single HTML file that branches to the appropriate DHTML content depending on whether it is accessed by Netscape Navigator or Microsoft Internet Explorer. Relying on a library of JavaScript functions for Navigator and a separate library for Explorer, Interactor adroitly bridges the gap between the differing DHTML implementations. As you author pages in a visual editing environment, Interactor uses its own language to represent the multimedia effects: animation, transitions, sound, and so on. As you save the content within the program, a parallel set of files is created: one for the Navigator crowd, with the multimedia effects performed by calls to the external JavaScript file; and another for the Internet Explorer gang, with a similar set of functions in a different Explorer-specific JavaScript file. These functions, of course, only call on those features and operations that are fully supported in the target browser. This simple yet elegant approach eliminates the vast majority of developers' problems in wrestling with incompatible feature sets.

If you want to hedge your bet even further, you can use Interactor to reach the pre-version 4 audience by either generating Java applets from mBed Interactor's native files or generating content that can be viewed through the use of the Interactor plug-in. In other words, from a single set of source files, you can create multimedia applications and presentations that can span the vast majority of existing browsers in use today. For authors interested in the design aspects of their pages rather than the programming intricacies, Interactor is better equipped for this approach than other tools on the market. The following example shows some of the authoring possibilities.

Animating along a Complex Path

As demonstrated in the earlier JavaScript examples in this chapter, animating a layer in a single direction to move a graphic or other content can be accomplished with reasonably compact code, but what do you do if you want to animate an object along a more complex path, such as a circle or a polygon? The JavaScript code to accomplish this kind of movement would be considerably more difficult.

mBed Interactor provides an authoring environment that divides the different kinds of multimedia content into 12 basic elements, called *players*. If you're working with an element in Interactor, by definition it has to be one of the following:

Sprite. A series of graphic images designed for sequential animation.

Picture. An image file to be included in an mBedlet.

Path. The trajectory to be followed by an object.

Button. A checkbox, pushbutton, or radio button used to control an interaction.

Text. A block of text that can be marked as visible or hidden.

Sound. An embedded sound that can be played directly or attached to handlers so it responds, for example, when a button is clicked. WAV and AU sound formats are supported.

Box. A rectangular player that can be positioned to block or highlight an area within an mBedlet.

Control. A slider or scroll bar that can be used to control an interactive event.

Effect. A transition that controls the appearance (or disappearance) of a player, such as a wipe or dissolve.

Score. A visual timeline that controls the occurrence of various events.

Audio Stream. A sound event based on a RealAudio format file.

Sublet. Another mBedlet that is called and used within the current mBedlet.

By skillful use of the data, the properties, and the handlers associated with each of these players, you can create elaborate multimedia applications that take full advantage of the various features of Dynamic HTML. The Score player is an exceptionally powerful feature that lets you orchestrate a number of events along a timeline, choosing the time that each event takes place and the conditions that will trigger its occurrence. Creative use of the Score player lets you design multimedia applications or complex presentations.

Objects can be moved along specified paths to produce animation. For example, Interactor lets us move a player, such as a Picture (the mBed reference for an image file) along a circular path. As an example, let's take the Pogo World logo from the prior examples in this chapter and animate it on a path.

Select New from the File menu to create an mBedlet. The Layout window and a single mBedlet player appears onscreen. To work with the mBedlet, you create additional players—sounds, pictures, paths, scores, and so on—and drag them from the Players toolbar to the Layout window. You then modify the data, properties, and handlers of each player to create the effects and interaction that you want. A Prototype window lets you view the interaction of events; you can also preview your production in your choice of browsers.

To insert the Pogo World GIF file into the mBedlet, select Picture from the Insert menu. Click the Data button on the Player toolbar to bring up a dialog box where you can choose, preview, and select graphics from storage. When you select the POGO.GIF file, a thumbnail of its image appears in the middle of the picture icon on the Players toolbar. To place it in the Layout window, drag it from the toolbar and position it within the window area.

In a similar manner, you can use the Insert Path option to add a path for the animation to follow. Figure 8.2 shows the Layout window with the Pogo World GIF inserted and the Players toolbar with the current players ready for use.

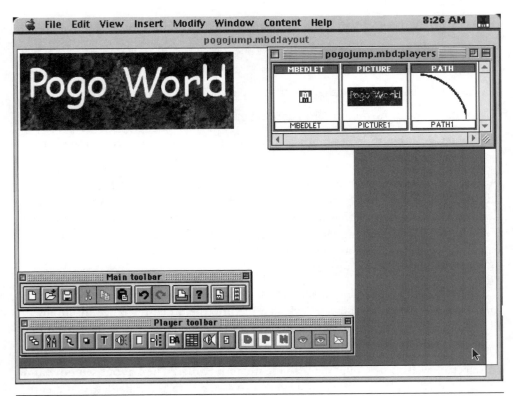

Figure 8.2 Pogo World logo placed in an mBedlet.

The properties of a player can be accessed by double-clicking the player. For example, if you double-click the Picture icon, the Properties control panel appears, as shown in Figure 8.3. The properties available vary for each player and some may be grayed out depending on which output format you have chosen for the mBedlet. Different options apply to DHTML, Java, and native mBedlet output formats. For a Picture player, you can choose whether it is initially visible, its size and location, whether it should be preloaded and cached, and whether it should be scaled for display.

Double-click on the Path player to display the properties that apply to the path. You can specify a Straight, Circular, or Bezier path to apply to the motion of the object that will be associated with the path, as shown in Figure 8.4. For this example, we'll use a Circular path. From the Path tab, you then select the player that will be used with the path; in this case, PICTURE1, the Pogo World logo. The EASEIN and EASEOUT values on the Path tab control how quickly the object on the path will accelerate towards its full speed, which is determined by the DURATION

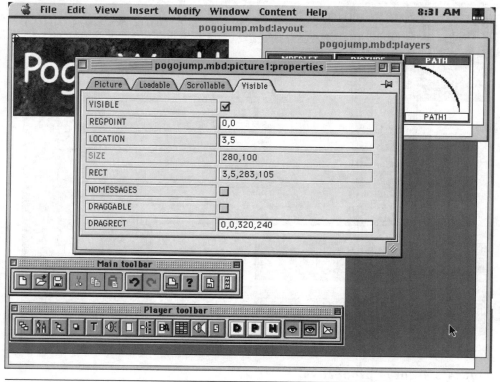

Figure 8.3 Properties control panel.

setting. Setting the EASEIN to 90 and the EASEOUT to 10 produces a springy effect such as you might see from a pogo stick. The AUTOREVERSE option, if checked, will return the player back to its source once it has reached the end of the path, as shown in Figure 8.5.

To get the Picture to start its movement when the mBedlet first loads, you need to modify the properties of the mBedlet itself, Double-clicking on the mBedlet player brings up the Handlers dialog box, shown in Figure 8.6. *Handlers* are short routines that control program flow based on events and conditions. Clicking on the Plus icon gives you an initial Message/Condition display; holding the Control key while clicking on Message displays those handlers available to the mBedlet. The available handlers, of course, will be different for each type of player and for each development platform (DHTML, Java, or native Interactor). Select the STARTUP message to start the animation when the mBedlet first loads.

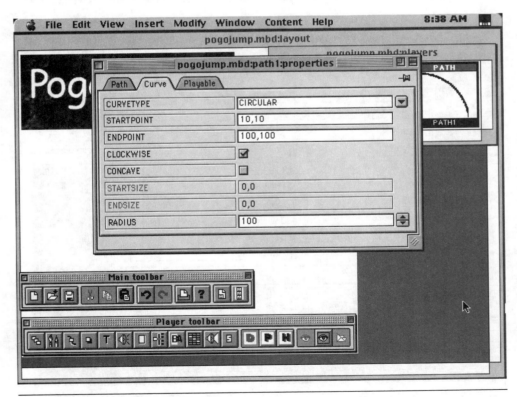

Figure 8.4 Curve properties.

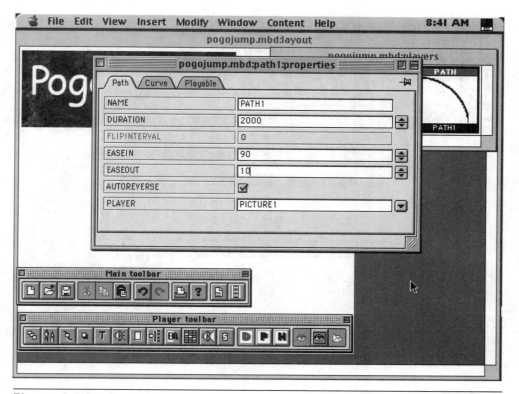

Figure 8.5 Path properties.

To add the PATH1 player to the STARTUP activities, click the Insert Line icon (that looks like a text edit symbol) and then use the Control key to scroll through the list of available players. For this example, we want to use PATH1, the Circular path that was chosen earlier. By following the drop-down option list, you can then select the ACTION, which is to PLAY when the mBedlet loads, and the PARAMETER, which is PICTURE1, the image to move along the path.

Save the mBedlet at this stage, using the Save As option from the File menu to choose a unique name. Once the content has been saved, you can open the Runtime window and use the control buttons on the Control toolbar to preview the animation and be sure that the effects you have chosen work well. Once you're satisfied with the results, you can preview the entire production in either Navigator or Internet Explorer.

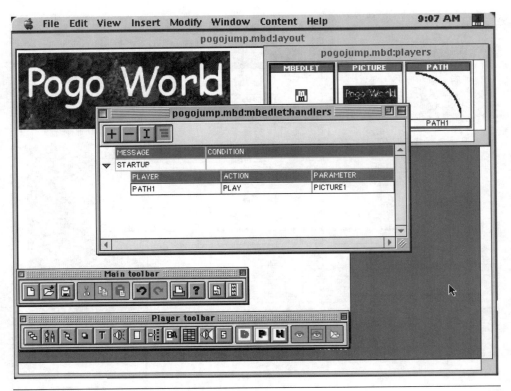

Figure 8.6 mBedlet handlers.

Creating a Framework for Presenting Topics

DHTML makes it easy to embed multiple slices of information within a single page, essentially producing content in layers (or storing it offscreen in an area outside the normal display area). You can then use various controls to display the content and slide it into place for viewing. The following example shows a simple means of creating layered content that can expose topics selectively. This simple example only uses two subject areas, but you could easily adopt this approach to accommodate eight or ten categories on a single page, providing a compact way of presenting large amounts of information for delivery through channels.

Text blocks that appear in an mBedlet can be either visible or hidden, and this Visibility property can be placed under control of typical events. Interactor recognizes the MOUSEENTER and MOUSELEAVE events (equivalent to the onMouseOver and onMouseOut events in JavaScript). For this example, let's take two text blocks that physically occupy the same space on a page and use buttons to control which block of text is visible.

From the Insert menu, select the Button option. Open up the Data dialog box for the newly created button, as shown in Figure 8.7. Interactor supplies a number of pre-made button graphics, many of which can be used in combination to show changes—such as a button that lights red when clicked or a button that glows when the pointer passes over it. The Default selection for the button represents the button at rest. You can also select a Mouse Down Bitmap to display when someone clicks on the button.

Next, you can create the text blocks that will occupy the same space but be alternately displayed and hidden. Interactor lets you create small text blocks up to 255 characters by entering a VALUE as one of the properties of a newly created Text player. You can also adjust the data options for the Text player to access a block of ASCII text up to 32K, which will be drawn in and displayed with the formatting options that you supply through the Properties selections. Text that overflows that indicated display area of the text field can be accessed by making the selection scrollable. Use the Insert Text option to create two new Text players.

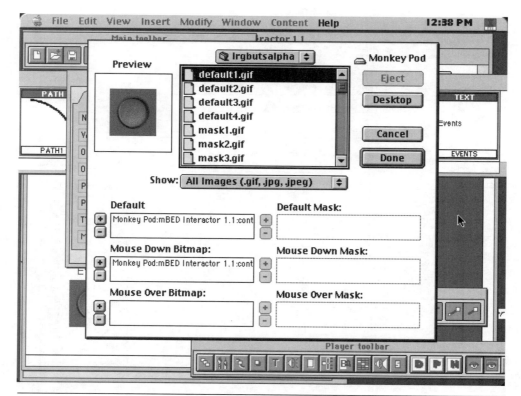

Figure 8.7 Interactor button selections.

For this example, we can enter short text entries in the VALUE field, which will serve as an abstract that pops up when the mouse pointer hovers over the appropriate button. Figure 8.8 shows the Properties dialog box for the Text player. Enter the appropriate text in the VALUE field. We also set the VISIBLE property to false (it appears on the Visible tab), so that the text will initially be hidden. Repeating this process for a second text field, we can then drag the two players into the Layout window and expand the dimensions to fit the area beside the two buttons, as shown in Figure 8.9. Note that you can use the Show in Layout option on the Player toolbar to temporarily display the text block for positioning.

Once you have the two overlapping Text players in position, both marked as initially hidden, you go back to the buttons that were created and modify the handlers for each.

For the first button (BUTTON1), select the Handlers icon from the Player toolbar. We want to use the MOUSEENTER event to control the TEXT1 player. Use

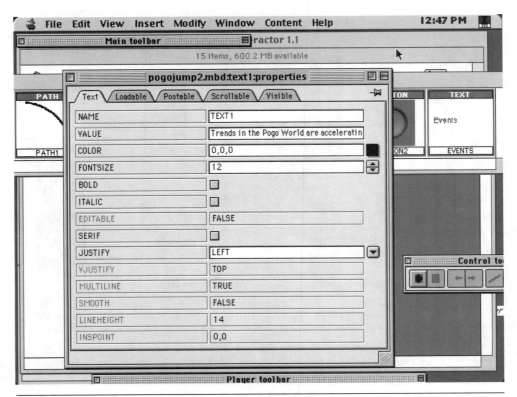

Figure 8.8 Properties dialog box for Text player.

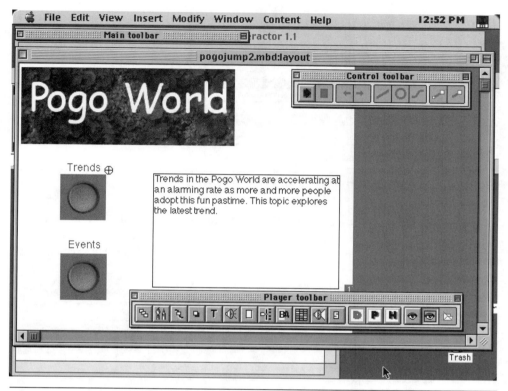

Figure 8.9 Text block moved into position.

the Control key on the Macintosh and the right button under Windows to view the valid options for each created handler. Use the Insert Line option to choose TEXT1 as the player and the action should be set to SET VISIBLE=TRUE, as shown in Figure 8.10. In a similar manner, set the MOUSELEAVE event to the same player, TEXT1, but in this case, set the Action to HIDE.

Perform the same procedure for the second button, but use the TEXT2 block for the VISIBLE=TRUE and HIDE parameters. With these handlers in place, two things happen now whenever the mouse pointer enters the region over the button:

- The selected MouseOver graphic displays, as was selected when you specified the data values for the button. In this case, a red glow appears in the center of the button.

- The text block becomes visible beside the button while the pointer is above it. The block then vanishes as soon as the pointer leaves the region. To see the final results as they appear in a browser window, refer to Figure 8.11.

MESSAGE	CONDITION	
▼ MOUSEENTER		
PLAYER	ACTION	PARAMETER
TEXT1	SET	VISIBLE=TRUE
▼ MOUSELEAVE		
PLAYER	ACTION	PARAMETER
TEXT1	HIDE	

pogojump2.mbd:button1:handlers

Figure 8.10 Button handlers for Text player.

This presentation could be extended to respond to the MOUSEDOWN event. Clicking on the button could trigger the display of another block of text consisting of the full topic contents in a scrollable field. If you wanted to get still fancier, you

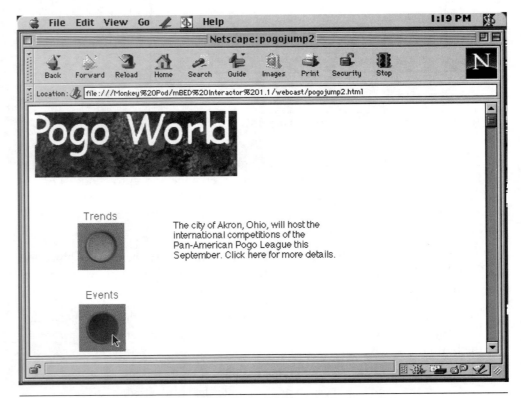

Figure 8.11 Pogo World text being displayed in browser.

could place the topic text block on a path that would slide into place when the button was clicked. Using the fundamental building blocks of Interactor—players, properties, and handlers—you can build very elaborate multimedia shows for conveying information in DHTML pages.

Creating Button Rollovers with Dreamweaver

Dynamic HTML excels at responding to user interactions quickly since the necessary logic and intelligence to carry out the interactions are resident in the downloaded document. Processing and script execution take place on the client side of the equation, rather than requiring lengthy trips to the server to execute CGI scripts or perform other kinds of processing. One of the more useful DHTML effects is the *button rollover*. An onscreen button or image changes dynamically whenever the mouse pointer passes over it. The button might darken, the button label may suddenly be highlighted, or the lighting on the button surface may appear to change. All of these effects help the user navigate a page effectively. From the response to the rollover, it is immediately clear that the button represents a live link, and the rollover change makes it evident that the pointer is positioned properly and ready to click. Small cues such as this may seem minor, but they really do assist users in navigating a document successfully.

Macromedia's Dreamweaver raises DHTML authors one level above the coding, allowing elaborate interactions to be constructed without relying on JavaScript or VBScript. By modifying properties and selecting events and interactions from browser-specific lists, you can generate the underlying code automatically when your project is saved. With Dreamweaver, however, you can go in and display the code and scripts, and work with the elements further if you need to—you can freely move back and forth between a visual editing environment and the underlying source code.

The button rollover uses the capability of DHTML to modify the SRC of an image tag in response to an event; in this case, the proximity of the mouse pointer. To produce this effect, you first need to assemble two separate images to represent a single button: one image that reflects the appearance while the button is at rest and another to show the rollover effect. You can produce the necessary GIF or JPEG image files using any of a number of graphics processing packages. Equilibrium DeBabelizer Pro, discussed in Appendix B, can quickly modify an existing graphic to show some type of graphic change for the rollover; you can change the color of the text on the button label, place a luminescent rectangle around the outer edges, or create the illusion of three-dimensional lighting. Many different types of effects will clearly indicate the rollover option.

The following two buttons were created using Fractal Design Painter, a flexible application that supports many different forms of masking, allowing you to layer images and add text in the form of floaters over the top of a background image. With certain masking of a floater, you can paint with a different pattern or color over the background image without affecting the text. Alternatively, you can reverse the mask and paint the text floaters a different color without affecting the background. Either one of these effects will work as the basis for a rollover.

For this example, I quickly used the Nozzle tool to spray a background down for the button, loading the nozzle first with images of coins and then with images of clover. Choosing a medium spray pattern, I completely filled two 90-pixel by 90-pixel squares with these background images. I then overlaid the text "Get Rich" and "Find Luck" as floaters, using white letters to stand out against the darker backgrounds. Once I had saved these two "at-rest" button images, I modified each of them by painting the backgrounds in dark red, keeping a mask on the text floaters so that they would not be affected by the paint. After saving both of these images in GIF format, I had a set of before-and-after button images for use as rollovers.

Figure 8.12 shows the Get Rich button in its at-rest state and in its rollover state. Figure 8.13 shows the Find Luck button in each of its two states.

To start a new document in Dreamweaver, you select New from the File menu and a blank document window appears for you to work in. For this example, we've added a couple of lines of text for the fictional company, Commodity Kingdom. Use the Insert menu to add each image to the document. These are the "before" button images that will be shown when the page loads. Figure 8.14 shows the page at this point.

Figure 8.12 Get Rich button before and after.

Figure 8.13 Find Luck button before and after.

Select the first image and choose Selection Properties from the Modify menu. The dialog box shown in Figure 8.15 appears. Use this box to enter a name for the

Figure 8.14 Images for buttons inserted in the page.

image (important for referencing it from JavaScript), the dimensions, and a link to be associated with the button. A link reference must be supplied if this image is to respond to onMouseOver events. You can also select borders, the type of alignment, and padding for the image from the set of options in this box.

Follow this same procedure for the second button image, making sure that you give it a name and an associated link.

Return to the first image, and with it selected, click on the anchor symbol (<a>) that appears in the status bar. From the Window menu, select the Behavior option and a dialog box providing the applicable behaviors available to the different browser environments appears, as shown in Figure 8.16.

The Plus button under the <a> Events column lets you select the appropriate event; in this case, the onMouseOver event. Moving to the Actions column, when you click the Plus button, Dreamweaver displays the valid options for the onMouseOver event.

Figure 8.15 Modify Properties items.

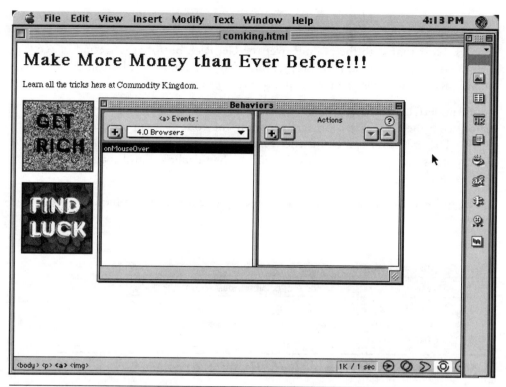

Figure 8.16 Behaviors window.

Choose the Swap Image action for the first of the two graphics, named get_rich. The dialog box that appears lets you browse through the available graphics and select the swap image for each of the image buttons. When you click OK, Dreamweaver returns you to the Behaviors window and records the swap image selections. Select the second image and repeat this same process, assigning the appropriate swap image for the onMouseOver event and using the onMouseOut event to trigger a Swap Image Restore.

Next select the onMouseOut event from the list of <a> Events. This determines what will happen when the mouse pointer moves out of the region occupied by the image. From the Actions column, click the Plus button and then select Swap Image Restore from the list. This ensures that the original image will be accessed as the SRC by DHTML when the mouse pointer exits. Basically, you're using the mouse pointer to toggle between two different image sources. Since the browser responds immediately to the interaction, the button changes appear to users almost instantaneously.

Dreamweaver provides an option that lets you jump to Preview mode in the browser of your choice. When you choose Preview, the screen shown in Figure 8.17 appears. Note that with the pointer over the Get Rich button, the second image with the dark background is displayed. Similarly, the Find Luck button displays its second SRC value when the mouse pointer is over it.

The underlying JavaScript code is always accessible by clicking the HTML option from the Launcher toolbar. Examining the code that is produced automatically by Dreamweaver can be instructive and suggests a number of ways you may want to consider solving problems that arise when dealing with browser compatibility issues.

The following code sequence is generated by Dreamweaver to handle the button rollovers:

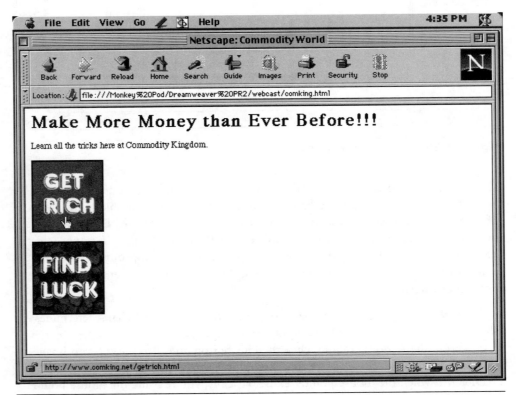

Figure 8.17 Get Rich button with rollover enabled.

```html
<html>
<head>
<title>Commodity World</title>
<meta http-equiv="Content-Type" content="text/html; charset=iso-8859-1">
  <script language="JavaScript">
function MM_swapImgRestore() {
  if (document.MM_swapImgData != null)
    for (var i=0; i<(document.MM_swapImgData.length-1); i+=2)
      document.MM_swapImgData[i].src = document.MM_swapImgData[i+1];
}
</script>
  <script language="JavaScript">
function MM_swapImage() {
  var i,theObj,j=0,swapArray=new Array,oldArray=document.MM_swapImgData;
  for (i=0; i < (MM_swapImage.arguments.length-2); i+=3) {
    theObj = eval(MM_swapImage.arguments[(navigator.appName ==
'Netscape')?i:i+1])
    if (theObj != null) {
      swapArray[j++] = theObj;
      swapArray[j++] = (oldArray==null || oldArray[j-
1]!=theObj)?theObj.src:oldArray[j];
      theObj.src = MM_swapImage.arguments[i+2];
  } }
  document.MM_swapImgData = swapArray; //used for restore
}
</script>
</head>

<body bgcolor="#FFFFFF">
<h1>Make More Money than Ever Before!!!</h1>
<p>Learn all the tricks here at Commodity Kingdom. </p>
<p><a href="http://www.comking.net/getrich.html" target="_blank"
onmouseout="MM_swapImgRestore()"
onmouseover="MM_swapImage('document.get_rich','document.get_rich','MNY1_ON.
GIF')"><img src="MNY1_OFF.GIF" name="get_rich" width="90" height="90"></a></p>
<p><a href="http://www.comking.net/find_luck.html"
onmouseover="MM_swapImage('document.find_luck','document.find_luck','GRN_ON.
GIF')" onmouseout="MM_swapImgRestore()"><img src="GRN_OFF.GIF" name="find_
luck" width="90" height="90"></a></p>
</body>
</html>
```

As shown in the JavaScript code, Dreamweaver generates individual JavaScript functions for the Swap Image operation (called `MM_swapImage()` in the code) that occurs during the onMouseOver events and a separate Swap Image Restore function (called `MM_swapImgRestore()` in the code) for the onMouseOut event. An array is created for storing the pointers to the SRC image to be used for each of these events, and the correct image accessed conditionally from within the functions.

Working Directly with the Code

Macromedia Dreamweaver actively encourages authors to get involved in working with the low-level code. The Roundtrip HTML feature provides a means of moving from existing code to the visual design environment and back again without any changes being inflicted on either the source HTML code or the JavaScripts that appear within documents. For this reason, the JavaScript code produced by Dreamweaver uses variable names, function names, and other identifying terms that can be clearly read and understood by programmers. Other products, such as mBed Interactor, deliberately choose to distance the author from the code generation. JavaScript that is generated by Interactor uses abstract variable and function names and it would be extremely difficult for anyone—even a seasoned JavaScript programmer—to determine what is taking place. Both of these approaches have their merits. Dreamweaver provides an editing and development environment that provides two views of the ultimate product; Interactor provides a platform-neutral multimedia authoring tool that can direct its output into Java applets, JavaScript-powered DHTML pages, or multimedia files for playback with the mBed plug-in. Interactor protects its investment in code design by adding a layer of abstraction to the scripts, but provides more flexibility for authors interested in design issues rather than the underlying programming.

Summary

You can see that it is relatively easy to author for either a selective audience consisting of Netcaster subscribers or to deliver the same DHTML content to audiences consisting of Microsoft and Netscape users by creating parallel platform-specific HTML documents (using a product such as mBed Interactor) or by conditional branches managed by means of JavaScript (using an approach similar to Macromedia Dreamweaver). While you can always author for one browser or the other, many developers will want to ensure their content can be directed into as many different browsers as possible, and with the effective use of scripting, you can certainly do this.

Part Four

Case Studies

Part Four

Lightspeed Publishing
Case Study

Lightspeed Publishing LLC is my own company, formed shortly after Vermont became the last state to sanction the Limited Liability Company as a valid business entity. I set up a Website as a focal point for my particular perspectives on the benevolent use of technology to create new businesses and to solve ongoing problems for existing businesses. The site showcases my technical writing services, techniques for the design and development of Web content, the trade computer books I have written, options available to businesses interested in electronic publishing, avenues for recycling, and the evolution of socially responsible businesses.

This chapter examines the path that I took to produce DHTML content suitable for channel delivery and then to set up the subscription mechanism to make the channel available as an Active Channel. The material within this chapter offers specific details on the decisions made during the process and the means I chose to implement this approach.

Starting Point

The lure of channels is a strong one. Delivering content through channels to a worldwide audience on a regular basis, rather than randomly as visitors drop by (perhaps distracted by other quests or research pursuits), seems like a much stronger way to form strong relationships with the networked community of business owners. With the addition of channel content, I hoped to establish a dependable audience that would tune in to learn about techniques and practices that could apply to its own business operations—to reduce costs, to incorporate recycling and reuse into daily practices, to discover resources that prove useful in running a socially responsible business. As it stands, the site includes areas devoted to alternative paper sources, telecommuting as a way of reducing automobile use, electronic publishing tips, and similar kinds of topics.

The initial Lightspeed Publishing site design was the usual compromise between high-minded design goals and scarcity of time. I had wanted to produce a site with impeccable page layout aesthetics, dazzling multimedia effects, and archives of useful content on every aspect of responsible business operation and environmental ethics. Instead, the site hints at some of the possibilities without quite reaching the intended goals. The design tool used was Symantec's Visual Café for the Macintosh, primarily for its ability to handle table creation and resizing visually—an important capability if you want to be able to position text for browsers prior to the version 4 releases from Microsoft and Netscape. With Dynamic HTML, of course, you can escape the layout problem issue through the use of Cascading Style Sheets.

Figure 9.1 shows the original entry page for Lightspeed Publishing, a compact entry page that provides a hint of the site contents for idle passersby before jumping to the next page that serves as the homepage.

The entry page unfolds to the primary homepage, with a text-based navigation toolbar leading to the nested levels of content (see Figure 9.2). The icons at the left side of the page access Adobe Acrobat documents, an approach that I had never been quite comfortable with, knowing that many users probably click on the icons thinking they lead to HTML pages and are surprised to encounter Acrobat documents (which display in your browser if your have the Acrobat plug-in or ActiveX component loaded, and provide a file download message if you don't). Some reorganization of the navigational paths on the site would be one objective with the site makeover.

The first step was to figure out how channel delivery techniques could best be integrated into my existing site. Given available time, I needed to develop an approach that would refine and improve the existing content, include new content for channel delivery, and make sure site visitors could find their way around without confusion.

Figure 9.1 Lightspeed Publishing's entry page.

Design Goals

The design goals for revamping the Lightspeed Publishing site were to:

- Provide an area designed for channel delivery that can be updated on a weekly basis.

- Improve the structure of the existing site and provide separation between HTML and DHTML areas of the site (to avoid restricting users with earlier browsers).

- Create additional content in DHTML to include in the new channel.

- Find ways to showcase the more interesting possibilities offered by both Web channels and DHTML.

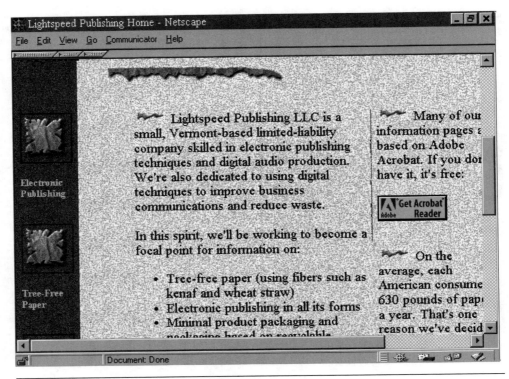

Figure 9.2 Lightspeed Publishing's homepage.

It strikes me that the approach to this problem is not unlike the one taken in television home restoration programs—such as *This Old House*. You go through the site carefully to determine what parts are most in need of modernization, what timbers contain dry rot and need replacement, what features add the most character and personality to the building and should be preserved.

Parts of my Website showing decay needed to be ripped out, some parts needed to be strengthened and modernized, and some essential characteristics needed to be expanded, refined, and showcased.

Site Makeover: The Approach

After grappling with the possibilities for about a week, I reached some decisions, realizing that during the course of implementing the approach that I had in mind, I would undoubtedly make adjustments and reconsider parts of the plan. The most critical aspect of developing the channel would be coming up with content that would be worthwhile enough that subscribers would look forward to the weekly updates. Certainly, news and information about recycling issues, discussions about electronic publishing tools and approaches, and business ideas embracing digital communication would be worthwhile, but a newsletter alone didn't seem like a strong enough hook to build a subscriber base. I felt as though I needed something that would build anticipation and perhaps even spread interest in the site through word of mouth and Web exchanges. That's when I came up with the idea of serializing a novel and presenting it in audio form. The ancient art of storytelling meets the electronic muse of digital communication.

Serializing a Novel in Audio Form

Serial storytelling has a long and illustrious history; if you can present a story with characters developed vividly enough that your audience grows to care about them, nothing can be a stronger incentive to tune in to the next episode than to find out what happens to the hero or heroine. Charles Dickens was wildly successful at this game, attracting throngs of English readers to his serialized exploits in nineteenth-century England. Installments were folded into magazines or bound into small books called *chapbooks*. Readers clamored for the new installments each month.

In the 1930s, filmgoers came back week after week for new episodes of Flash Gordon, and each week the current story would end with a cliffhanger, usually with Flash facing imminent death from his latest adversary. The Green Hornet, Zorro, Captain Video, and others occupied a niche within this genre as well. Modern daytime television with its emphasis on the soap opera is more evidence that ongoing interest in the fictional lives of a group of characters can draw an audience to the television screen on a daily basis.

Novelist Stephen King has also experimented and succeeded with this literary form in the recent past. His serial novel, *The Green Mile*, was released in a series of six installments and became a *New York Times* bestseller. The story takes place in Cold Mountain Penitentiary—a fictional Southern prison—around 1932 and includes characters that range from an assortment of psychopathic killers to a falsely imprisoned murderer facing "Old Sparky," the electric chair. Each individual installment ended with—in King's words—a "mini-climax." Millions of book readers bought all six installments—which together totaled about $19—and the book was subsequently reissued as a single volume.

I decided to take a novel and present it in serial form—a chapter at a time—and release it in RealAudio file format. Each weekly installment could be bundled into a DHTML wrapper, so to speak, surrounded with other news highlights and short articles. Since my site is largely focused on the benefits of electronic publishing, releasing audio chapters in this form would demonstrate the feasibility of this aspect of technology and, hopefully, build a sense of drama around the arrival of each weekly installment as listeners were drawn into the story.

Clearly, the work chosen would have to be something in the public domain. Scouting around through the books of the past century, I came across a work by Edgar Allen Poe called *The Narrative of Arthur Gordon Pym of Nantucket*. Originally published in 1850, this work is one of Poe's lesser-known novels and also one of his strangest. Novelist and travel-writer Paul Theroux called it one of the most frightening novels he had ever read and the book literally gave him nightmares. The combination of a little-known work from a well-known author seemed a good blend for the serialization.

To test the concept, I decided to create the first installment and find out how large the resulting RealAudio file would be. The whole idea would be useless if the file sizes for installments were too large to conveniently deliver through a channel. My feeling was that if I couldn't keep the channel content files under 2Mb, it would be a losing game. But I also knew that compression techniques for audio have been improving rapidly in recent months and I had been impressed with the fidelity of sound playback under RealPlayer 5 from RealNetworks (formerly, Progressive Networks).

With the Preface and Chapter 1 of *The Narrative of Arthur Gordon Pym of Nantucket* in hand, I set up an Audio Technica Pro 5 microphone through a Mackie 1202 mixer into the audio input lines of a Panasonic SV-3700 Digital Audio Tape recorder. I mention the actual equipment primarily to make a point: It is difficult to do digital recording directly into a computer sound board, particularly if you are doing vocal work through a microphone. The combination of computer fan noise and whirring hard disk drives will intrude on your recording, and it's very difficult to isolate the microphone from this noise. The SV-3700 is virtually silent and when the recording is complete, I transfer the resulting digital signals through the SV-3700's AES-EBU connector into a Zefiro Acoustics board into the digital sound processing application of my choice; in this case, Sonic Foundry's Sound Forge 4.0.

I recorded the Preface and Chapter 1 to DAT in a single session, repeated any words or phrases that I stumbled on during the recording. Using digital editing tools it would be easy to snip those gaffes out later. Once the recording was complete, I transferred the file digitally to my computer, setting the input sample rate at 22KHz, monaural. Even though the transfer takes place digitally (there are no additional Digital-to-Analog or Analog-to-Digital conversions between the DAT unit and the computer), you have the option of performing digital downsampling as the file is brought across. This would keep the file to a more manageable size for editing, and since a voice recording stays within a very narrow frequency range, any higher sampling rate would simply be overkill.

The Preface and Chapter took up 28 minutes of recording time. This seemed a reasonable length for an installment, but I was worried that the encoder would not be able to reduce this much content to a small enough size to distribute. In uncompressed size at a 44.1KHz sampling rate (the resolution you normally hear on an audio CD), this 28 minutes of recording would occupy more than 280Mb of storage space. Could this much audio be reduced to an Internet-distributable size?

Editing the Audio File

As it was brought into Sound Forge (downsampled to 44.1KHz), the audio narration of the *Pym* novel occupied 71Mb of storage space. While Sound Forge is fairly adept at working with large file sizes, this 71Mb monster caused a few problems until I disabled the Undo/Redo option, which keeps a parallel copy of the content to use in Undo operations. Nonetheless, I would recommend that for lengthy readings of audio material, you break the content down into 8- to 10-minute segments that can then be spliced together into one file once you've made all necessary corrections.

Compared to the days of manually cutting and splicing segments of magnetic audio tape, as was the practice for many years in the recording and radio industries, working with sound in digital format is a breeze. As shown in Figure 9.3, Sound Forge allows you to zoom in on a particular portion of the waveform and select any part of it. You can play the selected segment to be sure that it is the word or phrase that you want, and cut it completely from the file without any audio artifacts remaining behind. So, if you make a mistake while reading into the microphone, just reread the passage again and remove the mistake from the digital sound file as part of the editing process.

Make sure that you trim any blank space from the beginning and end of the sound file. Every byte that you can save will help keep the final encoded file size down for RealAudio delivery.

Once I finished with the sound processing and cleanup, I fired up RealPublisher 5, shown in Figure 9.4, an inexpensive utility from RealNetworks that lets you produce encoded files for delivering audio or video content. The program is extremely simple to operate. You select the file or files that you want to encode and then choose the template that matches the intended delivery mechanism; for example, voice over a 28.8Kbps modem.

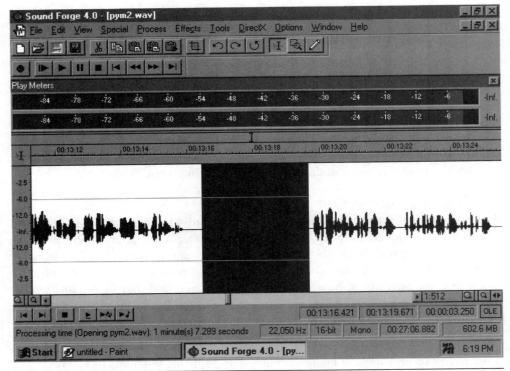

Figure 9.3 Snipping a mistake from the digital audio file.

Because I wanted to wring every byte of compression out of the encoder, I went in and tweaked the settings through the Advanced Settings dialog box, shown in Figure 9.5. The normal template for voice delivery over a 28.8Kbps modem is based on an assumed streaming rate of 16Kbps (since streaming delivery rarely achieves a rate equal to the modem's connect rate—Internet traffic and other factors reduce the effective data transfer rate). I reduced the compression further by choosing the lowest audio setting, 5Kbps. I assumed that the audio quality would be terrible, but I thought it would be a good test of file size versus audio fidelity.

The resulting file output amounted to 1Mb—an amazing amount of compression for 28 minutes worth of audio content. Equally amazing, the quality of the audio was fully acceptable. The voice had a slight amount of the metallic, submarine flanger sound that is characteristic of extreme audio compression, but was clear and entirely understandable. You might want to experiment with the audio fidelity at different settings—such as 6.5Kbps, 8Kbps, 12Kbps, and 16Kbps—to achieve a

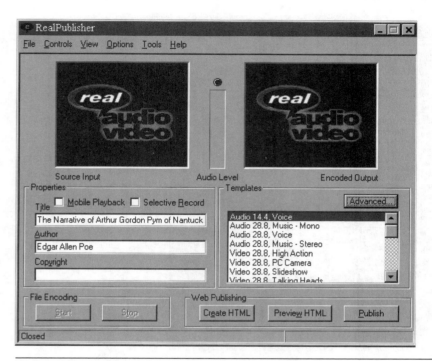

Figure 9.4 RealPublisher 5.0 opening screen.

balance of file size and sound quality that is acceptable to you. For my purposes, 28 minutes of sound in a 1Mb package was ideal for serving audio over a Web channel.

With the audio content in a form suitable for delivery through channels, I next needed to devise the structure by which I would deliver the files, ideally creating a reusable template using Dynamic HTML into which I could place new articles and provide links to the unfolding *Pym* episodes.

Site Architecture

The challenge for Web developers authoring for the version 4 platforms of Internet Explorer and Communicator is the inconsistency between DHTML implementations and special Navigator features not supported under Internet Explorer, such as the <LAYER> tag. If I wanted to make my channel content available for subscription under both Netcaster and Active Channels, I would need a mechanism to provide separate pathways for users running each browser.

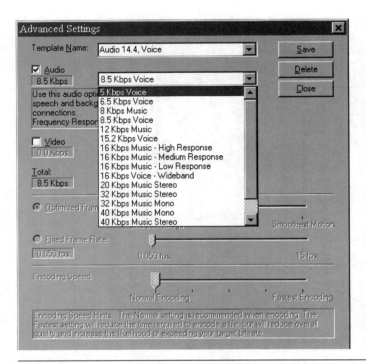

Figure 9.5 Advanced RealPublisher encoder settings.

Running the RealPublisher Wizard

If your goal is to generate a simple HTML page that can be bundled with your Web channel content, RealPublisher includes a simple wizard that walks you through a series of questions and generates the appropriate HTML, including your choice of RealPlayer controls, to serve up your audio or video content. Both audio and video are excellent additions to Web channel content. Though video tends to quickly get out of control with large file sizes, you can do some very interesting things using a slide-show type approach backed by music and narration. The encoding takes advantage of the fact that the still images in the slide show are remaining unchanged onscreen for a certain period, and the degree of compression for this type of presentation is generally much greater than for equivalent full-motion video content. Once you've made your choices through the wizard, you can link the resulting page to the rest of your Web channel content and have it in perfect shape for delivery. For example, using the embedded player option offered by the wizard, I generated the HTML document shown in Figure 9.6. A Publish wizard also included

Figure 9.6 HTML output from the RealPublisher wizard.

with the program provides the means for uploading the file and content to your Web server and inserting the appropriate commands to enable either HTTP streaming or streaming through a RealNetworks server.

More on Digital Sound Recording

If you're interested in learning more about digital sound recording and distributing audio content on the Web, one possibility is a book that I co-authored with Jordan Hemphill for John Wiley & Sons, the *Internet Audio Sourcebook*, which was released in September 1997. It includes a number of techniques for effective digital sound recording and includes trial versions of many of the leading sound processing applicatons. We wrote it to address the needs of Webmasters venturing into the audio domain, as well as musicians and audio enthusiasts looking to the Internet for a new distribution medium.

The easiest tool I have found to do this is mBed Interactor, which isolates the authoring process from the output format. You can choose a mode of delivery (Dynamic HTML, Java, or native mBed) and then construct the page content you want with the features available to your selection. When you save the project—called an mBedlet by the program—three individual HTML files are created to handle the content. The first file is a small HTML that serves as a traffic director—it detects the browser accessing it and reroutes the path to the appropriate HTML content; one HTML file includes Internet Explorer content and the other, Communicator content.

Using this approach, I could set up individual subscription mechanisms for delivering the weekly updates. The CDF file for Internet Explorer would point to the Microsoft-specific files; the JavaScript enabler under Netcaster would point to the Netscape-specific files. Universal content, such as the actual RealAudio file containing the *Pym* epic, could be placed in a directory below the channel content using root-relative references.

The structure would be organized as shown in Figure 9.7.

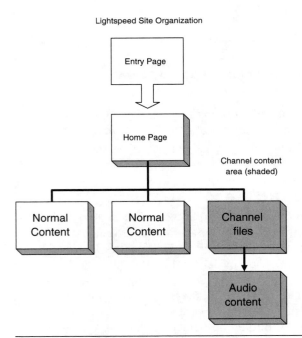

Figure 9.7 Lightspeed Publishing's site organization.

RealPlayer 5 Installation

The audio files at the Lightspeed Publishing site are encoded using RealNetworks' RealPublisher utility, an encoding program that handles both audio and video files. Consequently, playback requires a version of RealPlayer at a level equal to the encoded format; in this case, RealPlayer 5. The free downloadable installer available on the RealNetworks' Website includes an ActiveX component for Internet Explorer installations and a plug-in for Netscape Communicator installations. Both browsers can be equipped for RealAudio playback from the same installer. You might also note that Internet Explorer 4 is equipped with a built-in version of an earlier release of the RealAudio player; if you try to play back files encoded under RealAudio version 5 formats without first updating Internet Explorer, the player displays an error message explaining that the file format is not a RealAudio file. This is a cue to upgrade the ActiveX component. If you place RealAudio content on your Website, you might want to point this out to your audience.

Site Makeover: The Design Process

The process of redesigning my site to accommodate channel delivery involved creating an area of the site file directory that would be the repository of the channel content. I simply created a directory off the root directory of my site: www.lp-vt.com/Channel. The initial subscription page and the basic content would reside in the Channel directory and a subdirectory called audio would be used to hold the RealAudio file content and associated page.

I decided to incorporate three primary elements on the main page with a link leading to the page containing the RealAudio file content. The elements are:

- A description of the RealAudio content and the novel serialization that would display as a popup message over an image of Edgar Allan Poe.

- A slowly cycling background sequence of the first stanza of Poe's poem, *The Raven.*

- A button for controlling a series of articles that would be individually occupying their own layer and displayed and hidden as needed.

The procedures for accomplishing these goals appear in the following sections.

Switching from mBed Interactor to Dreamweaver

The multimedia design program mBed Interactor has a number of powerful features that break down platform incompatibilities, and an outstanding design architecture that isolates multimedia implementations from the quirks of individual browsers; but I ran into a problem that forced me to abandon Interactor during the design process. For some unknown reason, the Data button for the Text player was grayed out and unavailable on the PowerPC Macintosh I was using, so I was unable to generate text blocks of a reasonable size for the articles and essays I planned to include through the channel. Each Text player directly supports a text value of up to 255 characters, but this was not sufficient for holding the story content.

Switching over to Macromedia Dreamweaver was a fairly easy transition. Dreamweaver brings to this product one of the foundations of its popular Director multimedia application: the timeline. Timelines serve as the basis for coordinating events in the program; you can quickly set up many different kinds of interactions visually using the timeline as a guide. Animation and the alternate hiding and displaying of layers adapts well to this design framework. Any of the objects within your page can be viewed at any point in time (as measured by the timeline) and their properties (such as hidden or visible) noted or modified easily.

I also decided at this point to limit the initial release of the content to Active Channel format, for simplicity, and then to append the necessary Netcaster data. Since Dreamweaver creates content that is platform independent, this approach should work without difficulty.

Cycling through Three Layers

For the introduction to the page, I created three JPEG images, each containing two lines of Poe's poem, *The Raven*. Layers can be positioned anywhere on a page. Figure 9.8 shows the initial layer, Layer1, on the page with its properties displayed in the Property Inspector panel below it. Using the Insert Layer command, I created two more layers, positioned them each in the same place, and made them exactly the same size.

Layers, like an HTML document, can contain images, text, controls, and so on. For this example, I took the three JPEG images created earlier and dropped one onto each layer in sequence.

The Z-Index property of a layer indicates what position it occupies within a stack of layers. The Visibility property determines if it is to be displayed or hidden. Either of these properties could be used to progressively display the contents of several layers, either by bringing the layer you wanted to display to the top of the heap using the Z-Index value, or by changing the Visibility property as needed. For this example, I used the Visibility property.

The Layers inspector, shown in Figure 9.9, indicates which layers are visible and which are hidden, and also the Z-Index value. You can use this inspector to change

Figure 9.8 Initial layer in Dreamweaver.

values in relation to the timeline, clicking on the Eye symbol to hide or display any one of the listed layers. This is a fast and effective means of setting up properties over time, but you can also use the Layers inspector during the design process to display only those layers you want to work with or view at any one point. With 10 or 12 overlapping layers situated about the workspace, you can't really see what you're working on.

The next step is to open up a new timeline: From the Modify menu, choose Timeline and then Add New Timeline. Dreamweaver displays the Timelines inspector. Layers can be added to the timeline using drag-and-drop techniques. Select a layer in the Layers inspector, and when it appears onscreen, drag the grab handle in the upper-left corner of the layer object and move it onto one of the channels in the Timelines inspector.

Keyframes are points in the display of any object in the timeline that can be linked to events; minimally, you have a starting and ending keyframe—displayed as

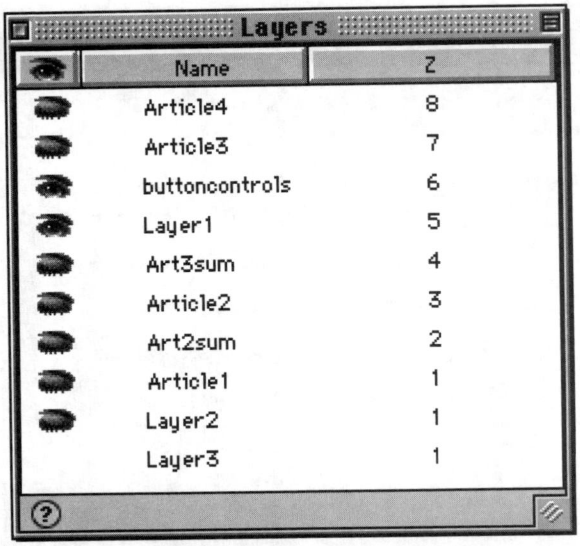

Figure 9.9 The Layers inspector.

an empty circle—for each object you create. You can stretch or shorten an object's duration on the timeline by grabbing one of the keyframes and dragging it in the appropriate direction a number of frames.

If you drag each of the three layers into the Timelines inspector, the onscreen display will appear similar to Figure 9.10.

If you select a layer, you can use the Timeline options menu to Add a Keyframe. If you extend each of the layers to occupy 60 frames, we want each layer to be displayed for an equal length of time, so the first keyframe on Layer1 should be added to frame 20.

If you select the keyframe on frame 20 with the Layers inspector open, the Visibility properties of each of the layers will be displayed. Click on the Eye symbol for Layer1 to change it from visible to hidden. You can then add a keyframe to frame 20 for Layer2 and change the Layer2 Visibility property from hidden to visible. As the timeline plays back, when it reaches this point it will hide Layer1 and display Layer2.

In a similar manner, you embed a keyframe for Layer3 at frame 40 and another for Layer2 at frame 40. Set the Visibility property for Layer2 to hidden through the Layers inspector and the Visibility property for Layer3 to visible.

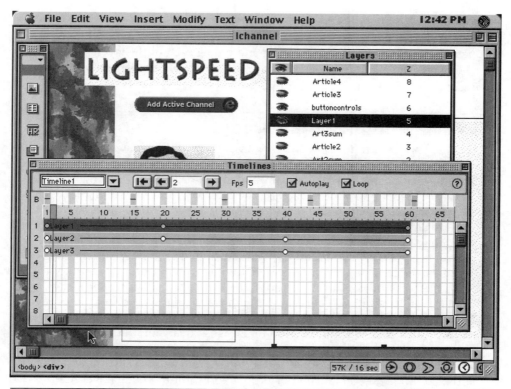

Figure 9.10 Layers shown in the timeline.

Use the ending keyframe for Layer3 to make it hidden so that it will vanish just before Layer1 becomes active on frame 1. You might want to double-check the starting keyframes for each layer at frame 1 to ensure that Layer1 is set to visible and the other layers are set to hidden.

To ensure that the sequence will play automatically when the page loads in a browser, click the Autoplay option button to select it in the Timelines inspector. Also, click the Loop button so that the sequence will loop around and continue playing from the beginning after frame 60. The fps setting lets you determine the number of frames per second that will play. This is normally set to 15 frames per second for animation, but since we're only displaying static images and want to allow enough time for someone to read the text, the fps value is set to 5. You can adjust this setting after previewing the content playback to make sure the speed is appropriate.

To get a sense of how the sequence will look during playback, hold down the right arrow button, Play, on the Timelines inspector. Dreamweaver will cycle through the frames alternately displaying and hiding each of the layers. When the page loads in someone's browser, each page of *The Raven* will remain visible for a few seconds before the next page is displayed.

Previewing in Dreamweaver

Ideally, you want to preview the results of your Dreamweaver production in a browser. If you are using the Site-root Relative option for establishing the relationships of files and links, this can present a problem. The Site-root Relative method, based on the directory root of your server, is recommended for professional sites, since it allows you to move and modify content without breaking links. Dreamweaver lets you establish a local development site that matches the structure of your actual site, so that files can be easily passed back and forth by FTP during site management activities. The problem is that if you fire up your browser and try to view files created with the Site-root Relative option active, the browser won't be able to retrieve content using these relative references, since it has no way of determining what the site root is. Windows users can employ the Preview Online option to access a local site that they set up for test purposes, but Macintosh users can't really properly preview the content unless it is first transferred to the remote server. This may make it difficult to test and launch your productions. Putting untested content on the remote site may cause errors by anyone viewing the material before you have a chance to correct it. A better method for previewing content for Macintosh users would improve this situation.

Displaying a Popup Description

One of the advantages to Dynamic HTML is being able to keep page designs compact and only display information when it is needed. To provide access to the Poe Real-Audio file, I took the clip-art Poe image and created a link to the page with the RealAudio content. To explain the audio content, I decided to create a message that would appear in response to the mouse pointer being placed over the Poe image. That would allow someone to get a sense of the content of the page connected by the link and decide whether he or she wanted to follow it, before actually clicking.

The technique to do this once again takes advantage of layers. The text for the popup description was embedded in a newly created layer, as shown in Figure 9.11. The next step was to create a behavior to be associated with the mouse pointer passing over the image.

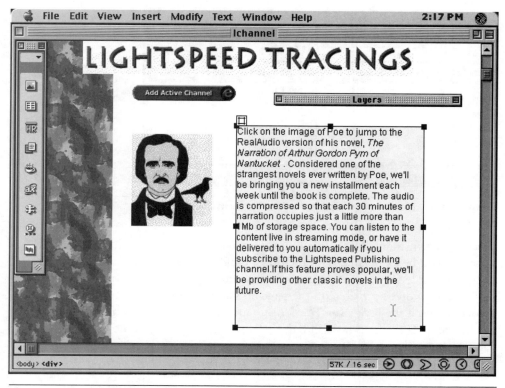

Figure 9.11 Text field to be associated with the Poe image.

As with the other layers, the layer with this descriptive text can be hidden through the Layers inspector. Initially, you want the text layer hidden, so clicking on the Eye symbol in the Layers inspector changes the property accordingly.

With the text layer hidden, the only thing left to do is create a behavior for the image that responds to the onMouseOver event. If you select the image and view its Properties inspector, you can see that it has a link to the HTML file that contains the RealAudio. From the Window menu, select the Behaviors inspector while the image is still selected. The Behaviors options by default are set to 4.0 browsers, but you can also model your content to fit earlier browsers or one platform or the other. To add an <img> event, click the plus (+) button and choose (onMouseOver) from the list that appears (see Figure 9.12).

Then, with this event selected, click the Actions plus (+) button in the next column. Select the Show-Hide Layers option and double-click on this option to display the available layers, as shown in Figure 9.13. If you select the layer containing the

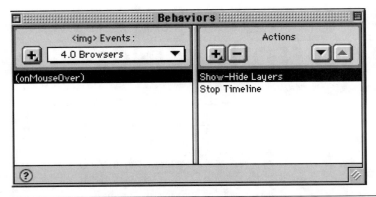

Figure 9.12 Behaviors options for an <img> event.

descriptive text (named Article1 in this example) and click the Hide button, this behavior will be associated with the onMouseOver event for the image. You can also select Hide for each of the three layers containing the pages from *The Raven*, so that they won't be visible on the page any longer. Finally, to stop the timeline associated with the layers for *The Raven*, add another Action to the column from the list: Stop Timeline. This will halt the continuous cycling of the timeline events for *The Raven* layers.

At this point, you've completed the basic work to cause a descriptive message to appear whenever the user points at the Poe image. If he or she wants to continue after reading the message, a click launches the page containing the RealAudio segment.

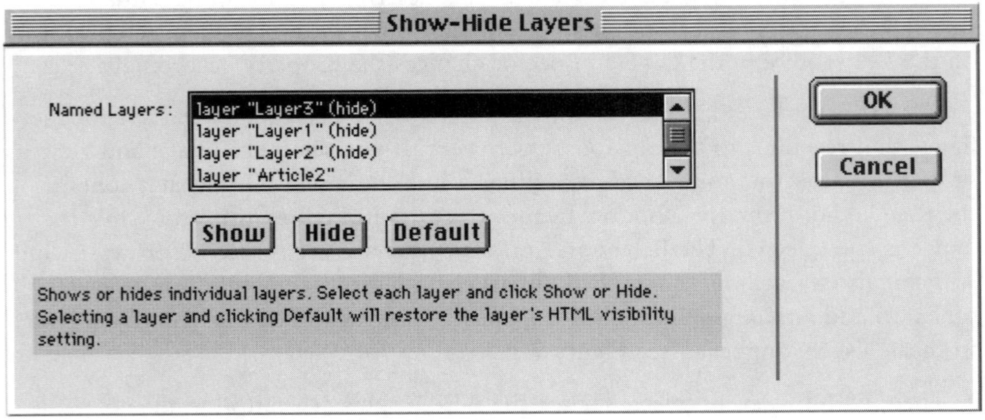

Figure 9.13 Show-Hide Layers.

Displaying the Articles

I decided to place three articles in each weekly issue of Lightspeed Tracings, and these would appear in layers as well. Unlike the popup description for the Poe image, Dreamweaver makes it a bit easier to display Show and Hide properties when they occur in combination with keyframes on a timeline. So, to drive the article playback, I embedded a button image in its own layer to control the sequence. The steps to display the articles sequentially are discussed next.

For improved readability, I decided to create a custom style sheet entry that would display the article contents in somewhat oversized type. Custom tags can be created and applied to text through the range of DHTML handled by Dreamweaver, and the program provides easy management and editing of your tag collections. Figure 9.14 shows the Style definition dialog box for the newly created .topic style sheet entry, distinguished by a 14-point Times New Roman font. You can apply the style sheet attributes to text within the document you are working on simply by selecting it from the Text menu in Dreamweaver.

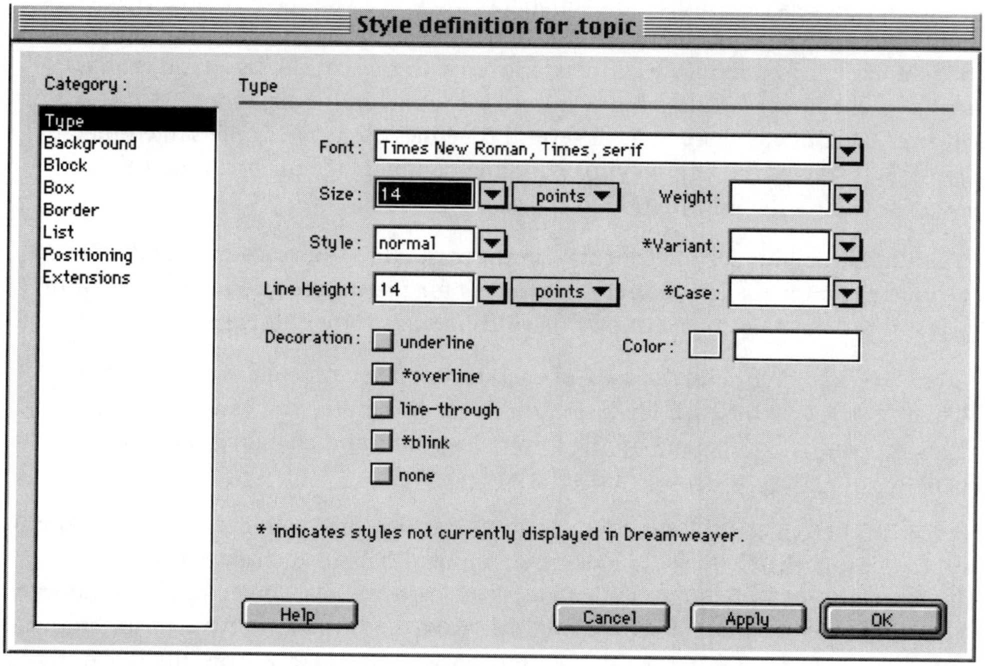

Figure 9.14 Style definition for .topic entry.

As in the first example, the text for the stories will appear in separate layers, but instead of cycling on a continuous running timeline, the story display will be driven by clicking a button to advance the display one item at a time.

First, create the three layers in identical overlapping positions. Then, enter the text you intend to display in each layer. If the text is lengthy and may overflow the boundaries of the layer that you create, make sure that you select the Scrolling property for the layer.

For the text, I used the custom .topic style sheet tag in each layer. Dreamweaver also contains a feature that helps maintain and update material over time: the Library. A Library contains elements that can be reused or edited and replaced globally. So, to change the content of each story, you can create a Library entry with a designated name and then just change the text whenever it's time for an update.

Create a new timeline by opening the Modify menu, selecting Timeline, and then choosing the Add Timeline option. Edit the name for the timeline so you'll remember its use; in this case, I used the name Stories. Once you have created the layers and their contents, enter them into the new timeline using the drag-and-drop method explained previously (display a layer with the Layers inspector, grab its handle in the upper left, and move it onto a channel in the timeline). A Dreamweaver document can have several timelines all active at the same time; in many cases, this is the best way for handling complex documents, rather than trying to embed all the information in the same timeline.

Multiply the number of elements—in this case, three stories—by 2 and add 1. Use this value for the total number of frames for the sequence. Extend each of the layers in the timeline so it occupies seven frames, as shown in Figure 9.15.

For the first keyframe, the start of each layer on the timeline, you want the Visibility property for each layer set to hidden. As before, you can check the properties very easily by opening up the Layers inspector and changing the setting of the Visibility property on the list of displayed layers.

Create keyframes for Article2 and Article3 at the third frame. Set Article3 to visible and ensure that Article3 is hidden. At frame 5, create keyframes for Article3 and Article4. Set Article3 to hidden and Article4 to visible. At the final keyframe, the end of the timeline, Article2 should be visible and the other two stories hidden. Check the Loop option setting so that the stories can advance from the last to the first in a continuous cycle, but make sure that the Autoplay option is deselected.

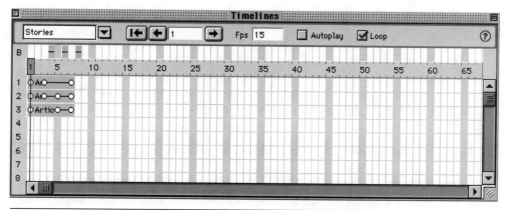

Figure 9.15 Stories timeline.

Now, we want to set a Behavior at specific frames to prevent the timeline from being free-running; in other words, we want it to pause following each click of the Advance button. To do this, select frame 4 and double-click in the top row of the timeline, marked with a B (for Behaviors). The Behaviors inspector appears, as shown in Figure 9.16.

The selected frame is already displayed—onFrame4—so click the plus (+) button in the Actions column to bring up a list of actions that can take place for this event. From the choices under the Timelines option, choose Stop Timeline. This causes the timeline playback to pause when it reaches this frame. It will advance again when

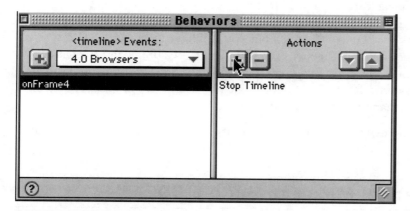

Figure 9.16 Behaviors inspector.

the Advance button, to be created in the next step, is clicked. Insert identical behaviors on frames 6 and 8.

Add the image of a button (from any convenient library of Web icons) to a newly created layer. Position the layer where you want the button to appear. In the button image Properties inspector, add a pound sign (#) to the Link field. Even though you don't want to jump to another point, the pound sign represents a null link and enables you to attach behaviors to specific events such as a mouse click.

Click the anchor symbol <a> in the status bar (with the button image still selected) to bring up the Behaviors for the image. From the Behaviors options, choose the onClick event from the first column. In the Actions column, add a new action by clicking the plus (+) symbol and then choosing Timeline followed by Play Timeline. A dialog box will ask you to select the appropriate timeline; in our example, it is the timeline named Stories.

You've just created a behavior for the button image so that each time it is clicked, it will start the timeline running. The timeline will run just a couple of frames until it encounters the next Pause in its Behavior row, but that will be enough to turn one layer on and another off, displaying the next story in sequence. Figure 9.17 shows the initial page with the first layer in *The Raven* presented for display.

If you don't have a copy of Macromedia Dreamweaver, Macromedia offers a trial version on its site that is good for 30 days. You might want to download a copy and try these examples as well as others to see if Dreamweaver seems to be a comfortable fit for your development needs.

With the Poe image carefully linked to the page that contains the HTML automatically created by RealPublisher, you now have a collection of material appropriate for delivery over an Active Channel, but you still have more work to do to prepare the content for use. The next step is to design a CDF file and to create icons to display in the Internet Explorer Channel pane, and—if you choose to participate—in the Microsoft Channel Guide, which provides listings of all registered Active Channels organized by the type of content.

The next section describes the use of the utility, Channel Maker, mentioned earlier in the book.

Using Channel Maker to Build a CDF File

You have several methods available to you for creating a CDF file to support your Active Channel, including hand-coding the file or using the Microsoft Creation

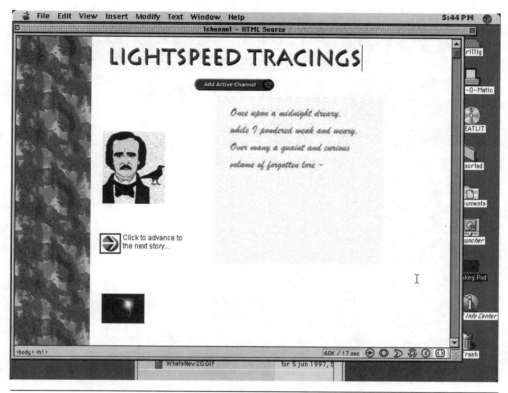

Figure 9.17 Lightspeed Tracings' opening page.

wizard, but Channel Maker from AnyWare Ltd. not only handles CDF file creation, but simplifies the long-term management and updates of the CDF file. Channel Maker also provides a number of tools for testing your channel links and content. This section provides a tour through the creation mechanism offered by Channel Maker.

Channel Maker uses a sequential series of tabbed panels to enter the key information required for CDF file creation, as shown in Figure 9.18.

The URL of the channel's cover page points to the first page that opens when someone accesses your channel. The Base URL is used as a reference to make sure that relative links can be properly resolved.

The General tab, shown in Figure 9.19, includes the channel title and the abstract that defines the channel contents to potential subscribers. This abstract is particularly important if you plan to get listed in the Microsoft Active Channel Guide. It pops up in response to the mouse pointer being positioned over your list-

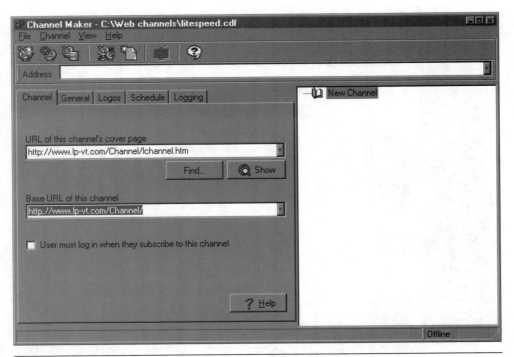

Figure 9.18 Starting point: The Channel tab in Channel Maker.

ing. Spend some time developing a short yet descriptive abstract that clearly identifies your content.

The checkbox, Instruct browser to precache content, indicates that your channel includes items that perform more effectively if they are cached before access. The subscriber has the option of overriding this recommendation, however. You can also specify how many extra levels of channel content to precache.

The Logos tab, shown in Figure 9.20, is particularly important to your channel presentation. If you don't supply icons and images, Microsoft uses generic text references in the Channel pane and Active Channel Guide, which can look very uninspired next to full-color images from *Wired* or Snap! Basically, you need three individual images to satisfy your channel presentation requirements:

- 16 × 16 icon (either in ICO or GIF format)

- 32 × 80 logo image (in GIF or JPEG format)

- 32 × 194 image (in GIF or JPEG format)

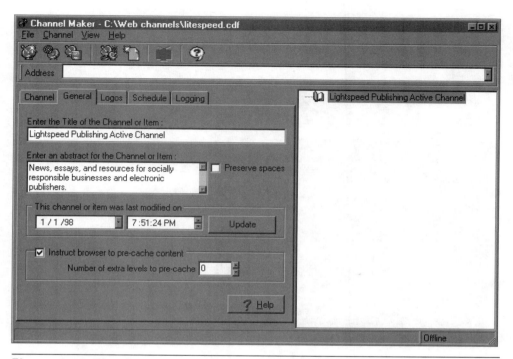

Figure 9.19 The General tab of Channel Maker.

You don't have much real estate to work with when designing these images. Scaling down an existing image with your logo or trademark may or may not work depending on the complexity of the image. Simplify the image content as much as you can; it will be unrecognizable at these small sizes if you try to pack too much information into it. Spend some time studying the images designed by the big companies and note how these work in combination with the Channel pane (which appears inside the browser) and the floating Channel Guide (that floats over the active desktop). If you supply a 32×80 pixel image but no wide image, the browser will compensate for the extra width and adapt the smaller image as much as possible. Convention has it that all logo images should use a pure black background; once again, take a look at how the pros have done it before you create your own image.

The three fields in this pane let you specify the locations of the images that are to be used for each one of these requirements.

The Schedule tab is your recommended update schedule, offered as a guide to your subscribers. The subscriber has the last word on when updates will actually

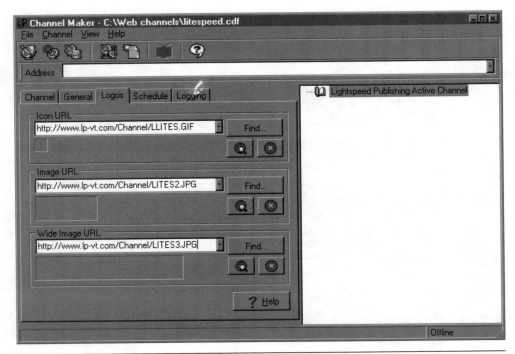

Figure 9.20 The Logos tab in Channel Maker.

take place, but your schedule at the very least indicates your commitment to provide new material for the channel. Busy commercial sites may want to use a daily or even hourly update schedule. Smaller channels with less activity will generally find weekly or biweekly update schedules more reasonable. Figure 9.21 shows the Schedule tab.

You also have the option of specifying a period of time in which the update will take place. This feature prevents all of the updates to all your subscribers from being performed at the same time. Instead, each individual client will perform an update at some random time within the period that you specify. If you indicate a period with a range of six hours, Internet Explorer may attempt to grab new content at any time within that six-hour period when the update time is reached. This, obviously, distributes update activity over a wide enough range to prevent the Web server and network from being overwhelmed.

The final tab, Logging (shown in Figure 9.22), is an optional feature that you may want to use to monitor a user's interest in different areas of your channel. Each browser running your channel keeps track of the links followed even when

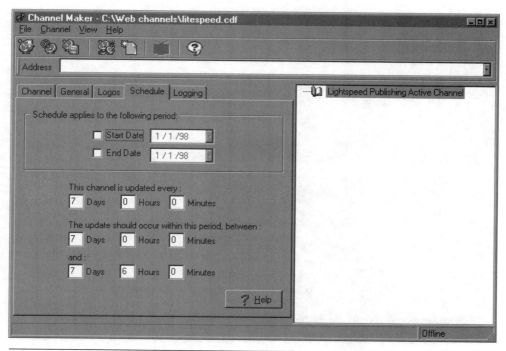

Figure 9.21 The Schedule tab in Channel Maker.

the user is running offline. Time logged in various areas is also tracked. This information can then be delivered to the URL that you specify the next time the person logs on. You need a CGI script or some other mechanism to handle the incoming data. This can be a useful way to see just what areas of your channel have elicited the most interest so you can redesign any areas that don't seem compelling to your subscribers.

Channel Maker includes a facility for checking that all your links are correct before completing the CDF file creation. You can base this link check on a locally stored repository of your channel content or on the actual remote site that is your Web server. This feature can ensure that your channel content is delivered in cohesive form with all of the necessary elements plugged in and ready to view by subscribers.

Channel Maker also makes it easy to add subchannels (content areas beneath your primary channel) and items (which appear in nested form in the Internet Explorer Channel pane). Dividing your content up into subchannels and items helps subscribers find areas of particular interest. If you have a good deal of content, take

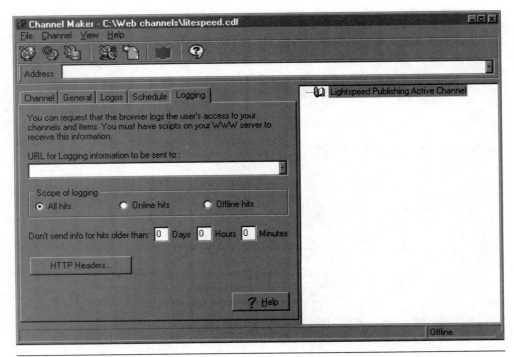

Figure 9.22 The Logging tab in Channel Maker.

advantage of this form of hierarchical listing to subdivide the various areas for easier access. Figure 9.23 shows a typical hierarchical listing of a channel's contents. Content can also be designated for the various types of uses that Internet Explorer offers, such as Screensavers and Active Desktop items.

If you plan to do a lot of ongoing work on your channel, Channel Maker greatly simplifies the day-to-day tasks and helps you create error-free CDF files that take advantage of all the options offered by Internet Explorer.

Building from the Simple to the Complex

While the pages created in the examples in this chapter are fairly simple, you can combine different effects and achieve much more elaborate page structures. For example, The Discovery Channel uses the Hide and Visible properties effectively on its channel topics page, shown in Figure 9.24, to highlight the individual articles

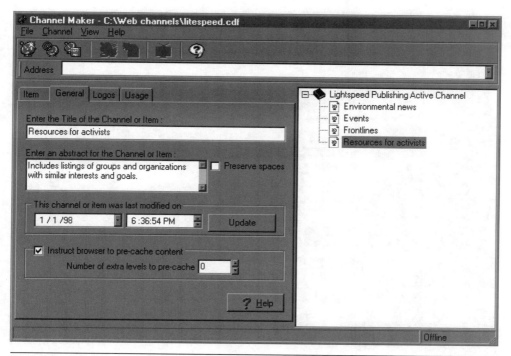

Figure 9.23 Item listings in Channel Maker.

and topics in each channel-updated issue. When the mouse pointer is positioned over a category, a topic abstract appears beside it with an accompanying graphic. You already have the experience to produce this same effect, as described in this chapter, although The Discovery Channel uses more graphics in its presentation. Even the most impressive DHTML pages are generally just collections of several different principles applied to a number of different objects on the page.

The Discovery Channel offers imaginative uses of RealAudio in its content. In a game in the History area of its site where it presents clues about a historical figure, whose identity you then try to guess, clicking on the telephone on a page (shown in Figure 9.25) brings up a RealAudio file, featuring an actor reading a quote from the mystery figure. Subscribers have the option to read quotes and transcripts as well, but having the audio option available—as it is in several other places in this guessing game—is an imaginative touch and brings the viewer quickly into the spirit of the game.

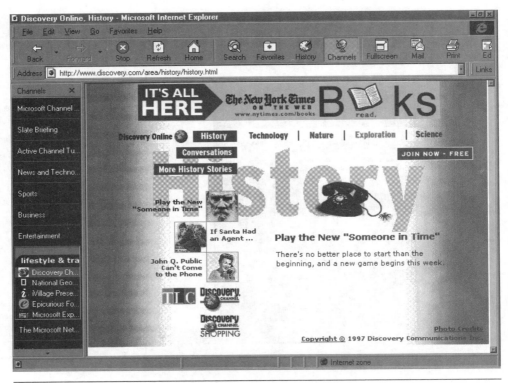

Figure 9.24 The Discovery Channel's channel topics page.

Downloading Subscriptions

Once a user has subscribed to several different channels, he or she can perform a large-scale update to all the channels at the same time using the Update All Subscriptions option on the Favorites menu. The Downloading Subscriptions dialog box provides a running commentary on the download process, displaying which subscriptions have been updated, which are pending, and which are in the process of being updated. Depending on how many different channels you subscribe to, the update process can take anywhere from a few minutes to well over an hour. The channels shown in the dialog box in Figure 9.26 took approximately 15 minutes to update.

Summary

The channel site design ended up taking much longer than I expected, resulted in my switching design tools midstream, and generally proved more challenging than I

Figure 9.25 Telephone linked to RealAudio playback.

had anticipated. Leave yourself sufficient time for dealing with new design tools and mastering the process—if you think it will take about a week to get your channel launched, give yourself two.

With the right design techniques, you can create a framework into which it should be easy to plug new content on a regular basis. For example, using the Library feature through Macromedia Dreamweaver, I can update the audio files and topic files on a weekly basis and then perform an automatic file update using the Site Management feature. The CDF file information also needs to be updated on a weekly basis, even though filenames are not actually changing, just to announce that more current files have been added to the site. The Channel Maker utility from AnyWare Ltd., proved ideal in that respect, automating and simplifying the update process of the CDF contents.

Once you've produced your initial channel release, you have the continuing challenge of adding new material on a regular basis. Plan ahead and try to get a

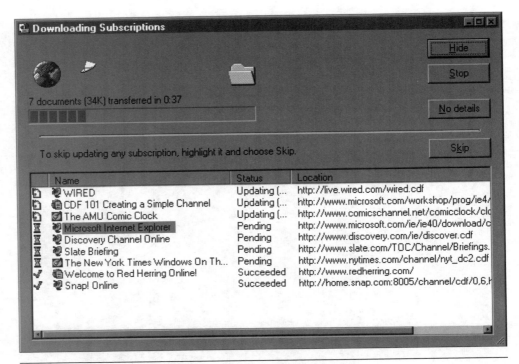

Figure 9.26 Downloading Subscriptions dialog box.

significant amount of material ready for content updates. The daily or weekly demands of supplying new material to your subscribers can introduce deadlines and pressures familiar to any magazine or television producer faced with supplying fresh material on a regular basis. Keep your channel lively by focusing on the quality of the content and the originality of your ideas.

AnyWare Ltd.
Case Study

Channels are not only a tool for large organizations to distribute entertainment or information to a worldwide audience, but also an effective means for small companies to attain a loyal, reliable subscriber base and build a business that is based on regular communication with customers. AnyWare Ltd. is a small software development company located in the United Kingdom specializing in development of standalone applications as well as components for Borland Delphi, Borland C++ Builder, and Borland JavaBuilder.

One of the current applications is Channel Maker, a program for accelerating the creation of CDF files for Active Channels and maintaining files for ongoing site updates and scheduling. With a philosophy that most software is far too expensive for typical users, AnyWare Ltd. concentrates on delivering high-quality, practical software economically—the Web serves as the perfect delivery mechanism. Trial versions are available through the AnyWare Website and preparations are under way to provide automated software updates using the Open Software Description (OSD) format.

This chapter looks at the upcoming OSD mechanism and the evolution of the AnyWare Ltd. Website to include more elements and features of an Active Channel.

Starting Point

Marc Palmer, the founder of AnyWare Ltd., spent a couple of years developing Internet Access software for the Windows platform where he was first exposed to the Borland Delphi development environment. Impressed by the ease with which Delphi reduced software development times, he began working with two other developers in his spare time to create shareware Winsock components. The fact that the other developers were spread out across the planet—one in Sweden and the other in the United States—makes it clear that the Internet serves as a highly effective collaborative tool. The three developers initially communicated using email, but then adopted teleconferencing tools as they became available. The shareware product was eventually released through a Canadian firm and made available through a secure online ordering system, achieving respectable sales in a fairly short time and also demonstrating the possibilities of electronic commerce.

Marc convinced his employer to let him continue telecommuting after he relocated to Bristol, England. Connecting to the workplace through a 28.8Kbps modem, he continued to work on Internet Access software, communicating through email and transferring interim file releases to his company through uploads.

His interest in a U.K. band called the Cardiacs got him started doing Website design, creating a site for the band that was hosted by his employer. As befits a music site, the Cardiacs' music could be downloaded in WAV file format or RealAudio files. Further site work was done on a volunteer basis for a group called Project Seahorse that was working to preserve dwindling populations of seahorses, and another U.K. band called The Monsoon Bassoon.

While in the process of looking for new job prospects, Marc became intrigued by the pending release of Internet Explorer 4, with its support for Dynamic HTML and channels. After studying the CDF specification for some time, he saw the potential for achieving all the benefits of channel delivery and push for everyone—including subscribers restricted by low-bandwidth connections. It was clear that while using CDF files, anyone with a Website could set up his or her own channel; however, the difficulties in constructing and maintaining the necessary CDF files would discourage many users. The regular scheduling and updating requirements would also be a burden, so Marc set about designing a tool to take the work out of CDF file creation and simplify the ongoing maintenance as site pages were modified.

Site Modifications

In examining his existing site, Marc decided to add more detail to the channel content by expanding the number of ITEMs available. Each defined item in a CDF file becomes a hierarchical option that can be selected from the Channel pane in the IE4 browser. The more entry points that you provide to the channel content, the easier it is for a site viewer to jump immediately to an area of interest.

Figure 10.1 shows the initial page of the AnyWare Ltd. Website. The use of a hidden ITEM tag makes it possible to pop up the subscription prompt if someone clicks anywhere on the site contents.

If you examine the contents of the channel in the IE4 Channel pane, you can see the nesting of the individual items and the use of subchannels to cluster related items together under a single heading (as shown in Figure 10.2). Note that the small icons that appear as a part of the item listing can either be a generic channel

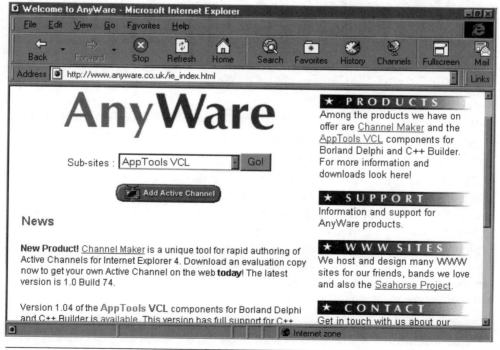

Figure 10.1 AnyWare Ltd. entry page.

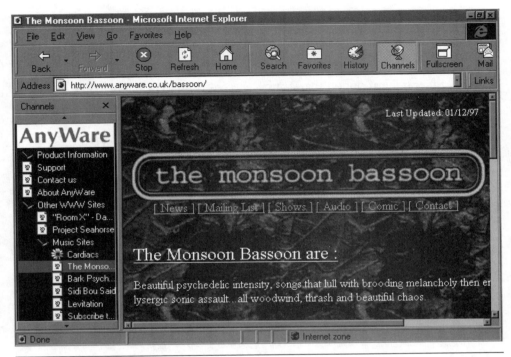

Figure 10.2 Items that appear for AnyWare Channel.

icon or a unique icon based on a pointer for that item that appears in the CDF file. To see how this nested structure is achieved, take a look at the CDF file for the site that appears in the next section.

The channel listing also includes links to a number of music-related sites and other sites that Marc has done the development work for, such as Project Seahorse (shown in Figure 10.3). Project Seahorse, in association with the Zoological Society of London/McGill University Conservation Programme, is working to prevent the exploitation of seahorses and pipefishes around the world. By collecting and correlating data about seahorse populations, they hope to prevent overfishing of these unique animals by cultures who use seahorses for medicinal uses, for aquarium sales, or (in the most callous use) as dried souvenir trinkets.

Marc also serves as Webmaster for an independent band in the U.K. called the Cardiacs (shown in Figure 10.4). This additional channel content isn't central to the software development theme of AnyWare Ltd., but helps characterize and personalize the site and also showcases Marc's skills in Website development. The Cardiacs site includes downloadable WAV files and real-time RealAudio samples of songs

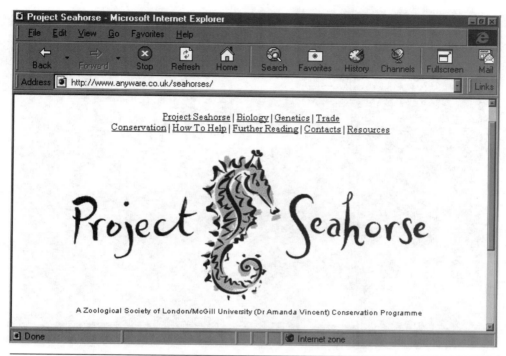

Figure 10.3 Project Seahorse site.

from the albums this group has released over the past several years. Despite shunning the mainstream labels, the Cardiacs have gained recognition through many gigs in and around London, and they have a strong underground following. Marc is looking into offering downloadable MPEG3 clips of songs and automating the online sales of the group's CDs as well.

AnyWare CDF File Contents

The current CDF file for the site appears as shown. Note the relation of the individual item entries to the structure shown in Figure 10.2.

```
<?XML VERSION="1.0" ENCODING="windows-1252" ?>
<!-- created by Marc Palmer -->



<Channel Base="http://www.anyware.co.uk" HREF="/index.html" LastMod="1997-12-
  04T11:11">
```

Figure 10.4 Entry page for the Cardiacs site.

```
<Channel HREF="/anyware/products.html" LastMod="1997-12-04T11:11">
  <Title>Product Information</Title>
  <Abstract XML-Space="Preserve">Information about our Software and
  Software Development components</Abstract>

  <Item LastMod="1997-12-04T11:11" HREF="/anyware/cm/index.html">
    <Title>Channel Maker</Title>
    <Abstract>High productivity CDF file creation tool</Abstract>
    <Logo Style="Icon" HREF="http://www.anyware.co.uk/images/cm.ico" />
  </Item>


  <Item HREF="/anyware/apptools" Precache="NO" LastMod="1997-12-04T11:11">
    <Title>AppTools Components for Delphi and C++ Builder</Title>
    <Abstract>Useful Delphi VCL for adding Splash Screens, Tip Of The Day,
    Wizards and Browse buttons to your applications</Abstract>
  </Item>
```

```
</Channel>


<Item HREF="/anyware/support.html" LastMod="1997-12-04T11:11">
  <Title>Support</Title>
  <Abstract>Get technical support for AnyWare Ltd. products</Abstract>
</Item>


<Item HREF="/anyware/contact.html" LastMod="1997-12-04T11:11">
  <Title>Contact us</Title>
  <Abstract>Get in touch with us about our software or WWW sites -
  we&apos;d love to hear from you!</Abstract>
</Item>


<Item HREF="/anyware/about.html" LastMod="1997-12-04T11:11">
  <Title>About AnyWare</Title>
  <Abstract>What is all this crap, and why?!</Abstract>
</Item>

<Title>AnyWare Ltd.</Title>
<Abstract XML-Space="Preserve">Software and WWW sites!</Abstract>
<Logo Style="Image" HREF="/images/aw_chan.gif" />

<Channel LastMod="1997-07-17T18:07" HREF="/starrysky">
  <Title>Other WWW Sites</Title>

  <Item Precache="NO" LastMod="1997-04-27T23:06" HREF="/dave">
    <Title>&quot;Room X&quot; - Dave&apos;s 3D Graphics</Title>
    <Abstract>Stunning 3D graphics drawn by the man behind the graphics
    for the Alien Resurrection game</Abstract>
  </Item>


  <Item Precache="NO" LastMod="1997-08-25T00:01" HREF="/seahorses">
    <Title>Project Seahorse</Title>
    <Abstract>Global Seahorse and pipefish conservation initiative.</Abstract>
  </Item>
```

```
<Abstract>Other WWW sites that AnyWare hosts and authors</Abstract>

<Channel Precache="NO" HREF="/starrysky" LastMod="1997-07-17T18:07">
  <Title>Music Sites</Title>
  <Abstract>Official sites for the bands we love... Cardiacs, The Monsoon
Bassoon, Levitation, Sidi Bou Said, Bark Psychosis</Abstract>

  <Item Precache="NO" HREF="/cardiacs" LastMod="1997-12-03T14:07">
    <Title>Cardiacs</Title>
    <Abstract>Simply the best band in the world! They have 13 full length
    CDs available and a huge underground following. Some reference points
    to describe their music are (in no particular order); Punky-Prog,
    Zappa, Madness, Gentle Giant... Check them out - there are 13 entire
    tracks for you to hear in RealAudio!</Abstract>
    <Logo Style="Icon" HREF="/cardiacs/images/channel_icon.gif" />
  </Item>


  <Item Precache="NO" HREF="/bassoon" LastMod="1997-12-01T18:18">
    <Title>The Monsoon Bassoon</Title>
    <Abstract>A fantastic band from London. They combine frenetic
    and complex rhythms with some voodoo funk and little touch of
    prog!</Abstract>
  </Item>


  <Item Precache="NO" HREF="/bp" LastMod="1997-09-01T17:22">
    <Title>Bark Psychosis</Title>
    <Abstract>Sadly defunct now. Their music was brooding and
    atmospheric, and you can find out more about their history
    and recordings on this official posthumous site</Abstract>
  </Item>


  <Item Precache="NO" HREF="/sbs" LastMod="1997-09-01T17:00">
    <Title>Sidi Bou Said</Title>
    <Abstract>Independent UK band with 3 albums to date. Their site
    includes material provided by the band members, including collages
    to accompany each song from their new album, and detailed instructions
    on how to build a dish rack!</Abstract>
  </Item>
```

```
<Item HREF="/levitation" LastMod="1997-07-08T16:48">
  <Title>Levitation</Title>
  <Abstract>Were sadly defunct but have recently regrouped minus Terry!
  This site has been compiled to provide information for fans of
  Levitation, containing rare interviews and sound samples, as well
  as news of the band members&apos; new projects</Abstract>
</Item>


<Item LastMod="1997-10-23T19:05" HREF="/music.cdf">
  <Title>Subscribe to our Music Channel</Title>
  <Abstract>This channel will notify you of changes to any of our
  music sites</Abstract>
</Item>

</Channel>

</Channel>

<Schedule EndDate="1998-05-09" TimeZone="+0000" StartDate="1997-10-31">
  <IntervalTime Day="1" />
  <EarliestTime Hour="1" />
  <LatestTime Hour="5" /></Schedule>
<Logo Style="Image-Wide" HREF="/images/aw_chanw.gif" />
<Logo Style="Icon" HREF="/images/cm.ico" />
<LogTarget HREF="/anyware/apptools" Scope="All" Method="Post"></LogTarget>
</Channel>
```

Automating Site Contents through JavaScript

Dynamic HTML is not the only way to provide variety and keep site visitors entertained and amused. Another way of ensuring that your site content changes on a regular basis is to use JavaScript to write different document entries depending on an external factor, such as the day of the week. This technique will even work for channels where the content is downloaded and then viewed offline at different periods during the week. Each day, a different selection will be displayed by the JavaScript functions included within the HTML file. This approach is used on the AnyWare Ltd. site to showcase a different Website each day.

The script to accomplish this on the AnyWare Ltd. site is not extremely complex, as shown by the following code. Comments from Marc Palmer have been added throughout to explain individual segments of the code.

```
<HTML>
<HEAD>
<META NAME="Keywords" CONTENT="AnyWare Ltd., Channel Maker, AppTools, dWinsock,
Cardiacs, Active Channels, CDF, Channel Definition Format, Levitation,
Monsoon Bassoon, Sidi Bou Said">
<META NAME="Description" CONTENT="AnyWare Ltd. - Authors of Channel Maker and
AppTools, we also host official Web sites for UK bands Cardiacs, The Monsoon
Bassoon, Sidi Bou Said, Levitation and Bark Psychosis">
<STYLE>
<!--
  P { font-family: arial, sans-serif; font-size: 9pt }
  UL { font-family: arial, sans-serif; font-size: 9pt }
  TABLE { font-family: arial, sans-serif; font-size: 9pt }
-->
</STYLE>

<TITLE>Welcome to AnyWare</TITLE>


//This section begins the TextOfTheDay code. It's
//designed to be self-contained; changing the parameters
//passed to the TextOfTheDayAdd() function will change
//the content in the document accordingly.


//The general-purpose MakeArray() function returns an
//array with the specified number of elements. The array
//is used to store references to objects created in the
//script; for example, the DayData() function uses it.
//The array is designed so that the starting index value is
//1 (rather than 0).
<SCRIPT LANGUAGE="JavaScript">
<!--
function MakeArray(n) {
  this.length = n;
  for (var i = 1; i <= n; i++) {
```

```
    this[i] = 0
  }
  return this;
}
// -->
</SCRIPT>

<SCRIPT LANGUAGE="JavaScript">
<!--
//The TextOfTheDayData acts as a global variable
//to store the array of text entries that will be used
//to supply content for each day. Other functions access
//it to retrieve the text that has been provided.
TextOfTheDayData = new MakeArray(7);

//This function is similar to a C++ constructor. It
//defines an object type called DayData with a single
//property: Text. Minimally, it can be used with a text
//string, but you could also choose to embed other
//properties, such as a Font property with attributes to
//be used with the <FONT> tag.
function DayData( t) {
  this.Text = t;
  return this;
}

//This function is called from within the document to
//retrieve the text for the specific day of the week.

function TextOfTheDayAdd(day, text) {
  TextOfTheDayData[day+1] = new DayData(text);
}

//This function is called from within the document to
//embed the appropriate text corresponding with the
//current day of the week.

function TextOfTheDay() {
  d = new Date();
  theday = d.getDay();
```

```
      document.write( TextOfTheDayData[theday+1].Text);
  }
  // -->
  </SCRIPT>

  //The following code creates the JavaScript-managed
  //drop-down list box that lets the user select from
  //an assortment of URLs to follow upon clicking the
  //"Go" button. This provides a concise, high-speed way
  //to offer links to a number of different URLs.

  <SCRIPT LANGUAGE="JavaScript">
  <!--
  curjump = 1;
  numjumps = 0;

  function MakeJump( name, url) {
    this.Name = name;
    this.URL = url;
    return this;
  }
  function AddJump( name, url) {
    if (curjump > numjumps) return;
    jumps[curjump] = new MakeJump( name,url);
    curjump++;
  }
  function DoJump(idx) {
    ShowUrl(jumps[idx+1].URL);
  }
  function InitJumps( num) {
    jumps = new MakeArray(num);
    numjumps = num;
  }
  function JumpList() {
    document.write('<FORM NAME="QuickJumpForm">');
    document.write('Sub-sites : <SELECT NAME="JumpList" SIZE=1>');
    for (var i = 1; i <= numjumps; i++) {
      document.write( "<OPTION>"+jumps[i].Name);
    }
    document.write('</SELECT><INPUT TYPE="button" VALUE=" Go! "
```

```
ↄonClick="DoJump(JumpList.selectedIndex)"></FORM>');
}
// -->
</SCRIPT>


<SCRIPT LANGUAGE="JavaScript">
<!--
InitJumps(13);
AddJump( "AppTools VCL", "anyware/apptools/index.html");
AddJump( "Bark Psychosis", "bp/index.html");
AddJump( "Cardiacs", "cardiacs/index.html");
AddJump( "Channel Maker", "anyware/cm/index.html");
AddJump( "Dave's Graphics", "dave/index.html");
AddJump( "dWinsock", "http://www.aait.com/dwinsock");
AddJump( "Fizgig Web Design", "fizgig/index.html");
AddJump( "Flesh Farm", "ff/index.html");
AddJump( "Levitation", "levitation/index.html");
AddJump( "Marc's Black Hole", "marc/index.html");
AddJump( "Project Seahorse", "seahorses/index.html");
AddJump( "Sidi Bou Said", "sbs/index.html");
AddJump( "The Monsoon Bassoon", "bassoon/index.html");
AddJump( "The Starry Sky", "starrysky/index.html");
AddJump( "The Maresnest", "laura/index.html");

TextOfTheDayAdd( 0,
   '<A HREF="sbs/index.html">Sidi Bou Said</A> are an '+
   'independent UK band with 3 albums to date. Their site includes '+
   'material provided by the band members, including collages to '+
   'accompany each song from their new album, and detailed instructions '+
   'on how to build a dish rack!');
TextOfTheDayAdd( 1,
   '<A HREF="cardiacs/index.html">Cardiacs</A> are simply '+
   'the best band in the world! They have 13 full length CDs available '+
   'and a huge underground following. The closest reference points  '+
   'to describe their music are (in no particular order); Punky-Prog, '+
   'Zappa, Madness, Gentle Giant... Check them out - there are 13  '+
   'entire tracks for you to hear in real-time!' );
TextOfTheDayAdd( 2,
   '<A HREF="seahorses/index.html">Project Seahorse</A> is a conservation '+
```

```
'and research project. We know very little about Seahorses and we need '+
'to know more if we are to effectively conserve them. Populations that '+
'have been studied are suffering rapid decline and action must be taken '+
'as soon as possible.');
TextOfTheDayAdd( 3,
'<A HREF="bassoon/index.html">The Monsoon Bassoon</A> are a fantastic '+
'band from London. They combine frenetic and complex rhythms with some '+
'voodoo funk and little touch of prog! There are real-time audio files '+
'on the site so that you can hear them, and you may even be able to get '+
'on to a guest list for one of their gigs by checking out their site.');
TextOfTheDayAdd( 4,
'<A HREF="levitation/index.html">Levitation</A> were sadly defunct '+
'but have recently regrouped minus Terry! This site has been compiled '+
'to provide information for fans of Levitation, containing rare '+
'interviews and sound samples, as well as news of the band '+
'members\' new projects');
TextOfTheDayAdd( 5,
'<A HREF="dave/index.html">Dave\'s Graphics</A> is a site containing '+
'3D computer artwork produced by our friend David Moss. He is a graphic '+
'artist for the game developers Argonaut Software, but he also does '+
'a lot of work in his spare time.');
TextOfTheDayAdd( 6,
'<A HREF="bp/index.html">Bark Psychosis</A> are sadly '+
'defunct now. Their music was brooding and atmospheric, and you can '+
'find out more about their history and recordings on this official '+
'posthumous site');
// -->
</SCRIPT>

</HEAD>

<BODY BGCOLOR=#FFFFFF TEXT=#000000 VLINK=#40805C LINK=#B700B7 LEFTMARGIN=0
TOPMARGIN=0>



<TABLE WIDTH=100% BGCOLOR=#000000 BORDER=0>
<TR>
  <TD ALIGN=CENTER><NOBR><A
HREF="http://www.anyware.co.uk/anyware/cm/download.html"><FONT COLOR=#FFFFFF
```

```
SIZE=-1>Channel Maker 1.0 released! Click here to download</FONT></A></NOBR>
</TD>
</TR>
</TABLE>

<CENTER>
<TABLE WIDTH=600 BORDER=0>
<TR>
  <TD>



<BR>
<BR>

<TABLE BORDER=0 WIDTH=100%>
  <TR>
    <TD VALIGN=TOP ALIGN=LEFT WIDTH=390><CENTER><IMG SRC="images/anyware.gif"
WIDTH=276 HEIGHT=62 ALT="AnyWare"></CENTER>
    <BR>

      <CENTER>
      <FONT SIZE=-1 FACE=ARIAL>
      <SCRIPT LANGUAGE="JavaScript">
        <!--
        JumpList();
        // -->
      </SCRIPT>
      </FONT>
      <A
HREF="javascript:external.addchannel('http://www.anyware.co.uk/anyware.cdf');">
<IMG SRC="images/add_active_channel.gif" BORDER=0 WIDTH=138 HEIGHT=24 ALT="Add
Active Channel"></A>
      </CENTER>
    <BR>
      <FONT COLOR=#7B5A86 FACE=ARIAL SIZE=3><B>News</B></FONT><BR>
      <BR>
      <FONT SIZE=-1 FACE=ARIAL><P>
<FONT COLOR=#FF0000><B>New Product!</B></FONT>
<A HREF="anyware/cm/index.html">Channel Maker</A> is a unique tool
```

for rapid authoring of Active Channels for Internet Explorer 4.
Download an evaluation copy now to get your own Active Channel
on the web <B>today</B>! The latest version is 1.0 Build 74.
</P>

<P>
Version 1.04 of the <font color="#FC7938" size="2"
face="Arial"><strong>AppTools</strong></font><font size="2"
face="Arial"><strong> </strong></font><font color="#3874FC" size="2"
face="Arial"><strong>VCL</strong></font> components for Borland Delphi
and C++ Builder is <A HREF="anyware/apptools/index.html">available</A>.
This version has full support for C++ Builder and is also 100% Delphi 3
compatible, with a compiled package file included in the trial and
registered releases. Registered users are entitled to free
<A HREF="anyware/apptools/upgrade.html">upgrades</A>.
</P>

</FONT>
        <FONT COLOR=#7B5A86 FACE=ARIAL SIZE=3><B>Site Of The Day</B></FONT>

        <FONT SIZE=-1 FACE=ARIAL>
        <SCRIPT LANGUAGE="JavaScript">
          <!--
          TextOfTheDay();
          // -->
        </SCRIPT>
        </FONT>
    </TD>
    <TD VALIGN=TOP WIDTH=199>

        <A HREF="anyware/products.html"><IMG SRC="images/products.gif" HEIGHT=19
        WIDTH=199 ALT="* Products" BORDER=0></A>
        <FONT SIZE=-1 FACE=ARIAL>Among the products we have on offer are
        <A HREF="anyware/cm/index.html">Channel Maker</A> and
        the <A HREF="anyware/apptools/index.html">AppTools VCL</A>
        components for Borland Delphi and C++ Builder.
        For more information and downloads look here!</FONT>

        <A HREF="anyware/support.html"><IMG SRC="images/support.gif" HEIGHT=19
        WIDTH=199 ALT="* Support" BORDER=0></A>

```
            <FONT SIZE=-1 FACE=ARIAL>Information and support for AnyWare
            products.</FONT><BR>
            <BR>
            <A HREF="starrysky/index.html"><IMG SRC="images/wwwsites.gif" HEIGHT=19
            WIDTH=199 ALT="* WWW Sites" BORDER=0></A><BR>
            <FONT SIZE=-1 FACE=ARIAL>We host and design many WWW sites for our
            friends, bands we love and
            also the <A HREF="seahorses/index.html">Seahorse Project</A>.</FONT><BR>
            <BR>
            <A HREF="anyware/contact.html"><IMG SRC="images/contact.gif" HEIGHT=19
            WIDTH=199 ALT="* Contact" BORDER=0></A><BR>
            <FONT SIZE=-1 FACE=ARIAL>Get in touch with us about our software or
            WWW sites - we'd love to hear from you!</FONT><BR>
            <BR>
            <A HREF="anyware/about.html"><IMG SRC="images/about.gif" HEIGHT=19
            WIDTH=199 ALT="* About" BORDER=0></A><BR>
            <FONT SIZE=-1 FACE=ARIAL>What is all this crap, and why?!</FONT><BR>
        </TD>
    </TR>
</TABLE>
<BR>
<BR>


    </TD>
</TR>
</TABLE>

<TABLE WIDTH=600>
    <TR>
        <TD COLSPAN=2><HR></TD>
    </TR>
    <TR>
        <TD VALIGN=TOP ALIGN=LEFT WIDTH=50%>
        <FONT SIZE=-2 FACE=ARIAL>&copy; 1997 <A
HREF="mailto:info@anyware.co.uk">AnyWare Ltd.</A></FONT></TD>
        <TD VALIGN=TOP ALIGN=RIGHT WIDTH=50%><A HREF="http://www.anyware.co.uk/
        anyware/cm"><IMG SRC="../../images/created_with_cm.gif" WIDTH=119 HEIGHT=31
        ALT="Created with Channel Maker" BORDER=0></A></TD>
    </TR>
```

```
</TABLE>
</CENTER>


</BODY>

</HTML>
```

Distributing Software through Channels

One of the more promising aspects of channel delivery is the ability to perform software updates for channel subscribers as soon as the latest version of a software product is available. Marc has grappled with several different methods for previewing and distributing software for sale on the Internet, and decided to utilize the Open Software Description to ensure that people who purchase his products will have immediate access to newly developed releases.

The Open Software Description specification is based on a set of particular XML tags that indicate the structure and relationships of various software components. Much as XML is a flexible tool for providing a framework and context to Web pages, OSD makes it easy to determine the version of a piece of software, the relationships between individual software components, the software requirements, and the underlying structure of an application. Using OSD, you can reference and describe components from a wide variety of platforms and deal with different types of components, whether they are based on ActiveX, Java, or native Macintosh applications. Using OSD simplifies the push delivery of software components, ensuring that end users get the appropriate product for their needs, and improves the installation process.

The OSD specification was co-authored by Microsoft and Marimba. One of Microsoft's stated end goals is to reduce the overall cost of PC ownership, by providing a mechanism for the automatic installation of applications (as well as other administrative functions). The combination of CDF and OSD provides an integrated means of developing an automated software installation system based on push principles. XML provides the structure within which both these specifications express the details of channel delivery and software packaging—this close integration ensures that software updates can be successfully managed.

AnyWare Ltd.'s Future Use of OSD for Updates

Marc Palmer is currently engineering his code and site to accommodate support for OSD in future releases. Fairly significant changes were introduced in the release of the Internet Explorer 4.01 software as to the handling of software updates through OSD and more changes are expected as this new technology is refined for large-scale use. As Microsoft continues to fine tune this feature, expect to see more and more companies offering software upgrades using the features available through OSD. OSD removes the burden from the customer, who no longer has to check back to the software producer's site to find out when a new release has taken place. Instead, OSD provides the mechanism for employing channel methods to automate and simplify software upgrades and make the entire process much less painful for anyone who wants to ensure they have the latest version of a product.

Shareware on the Internet

In reflecting on the abundance of shareware on the Internet, Marc observes, "I have always felt that, in general, software is *too expensive*. The shareware phenomenon, along with the Internet, is the best thing that could have happened to the software industry. Unfortunately, it is still hard to get people to pay for your software even if it is brilliant. I'm not sure why that is, but it does depend on what the shareware restrictions are. I'm of the opinion that no matter how good your software is and how cheap it is, if users can use it indefinitely for free, most of them will. This isn't because I don't believe that people are honest—it's just that to them there is no need to pay. We all do it."

The product as it is currently distributed in its trial version limits the functionality slightly (limiting the use of the ITEM tags to indicate multiple levels) unless you request additional functionality by registering with AnyWare. You have a 30-day window to run the program before it times out; you can pay for a copy to receive a license key that provides full access to the software. The price at press time was $59.95. Documentation consists of a thorough HTML-based user manual for all of the program procedures.

Summary

Channels have multiple uses and can support the goals of both large and small companies. As more and more independent developers continue to offer software products through the Internet, the Web channel makes it easier for each independent to stay in touch with his or her customers and provide a mechanism by which software can be automatically updated as soon as newly released versions are available. Also, through creative use of JavaScript, content management on small sites can be changed automatically based on changing factors, such as the current day of the week, and used to present new material to keep visitors' interest high.

Fast Company
Case Study

Fast *Company* is a different kind of business magazine with a unique perspective and a position that has garnered increasing respect in the business community. Focusing on the evolution of business as we move into the twenty-first century, *Fast Company* runs articles that highlight the benevolent aspects of technology, the keystones of entrepreneurial creativity, and the empowerment of the individual within an organization, while never losing its awareness of social issues. *Fast Company* looks carefully and then reports thoughtfully on the forces that are shaping the nature and the future of business in this country and around the world.

When Netscape offered *Fast Company* the opportunity to become one of the first companies with a premier spot on the Netcaster Channel Finder, *Fast Company* saw it as a chance to reach a new audience, occupy the computer desktops of its existing audience, build its subscriber base, and experiment with an intriguing new technology. This chapter explores the process by which the *Fast Company* Netcaster channel came into existence and the underlying architecture that makes it work.

Starting Point

In just a couple of years, *Fast Company* has successfully established itself as one of the most forward-thinking, provocative business magazines around. In a global economy linked with a worldwide computer network and characterized by rapidly changing societies, the old rules don't work anymore. Headquartered on the fringes of Boston, Massachusetts, *Fast Company* casts a steady eye on the maelstrom of business change, and showcases the companies and individuals that are forging new paths through the changing landscapes, not with the starry-eyed perspective of a visionary, but with a practical-minded, hard-nosed Yankee forthrightness.

A glance at some of the recent articles hints at the underpinnings of the *Fast Company* ideology. The lead article in the December/January 1998 issue examines the *Free Agent Nation*, the 25-million Americans who have slipped free from corporate shackles and now operate independently as consultants, small business owners, and contractors. The premise is that in a world of corporate downsizing and highly competitive business change, compact, fast-moving business organizations can run rings around staid, unimaginative corporate megaliths. A series of articles in this issue explore this trend, offer practical advice to those who want to become free agents, and look at the tools and techniques that support the survival of the new breed of independents.

The same issue includes an article titled "The Web Can Make You a Star!," providing a glimpse into the lives of four business people who successfully used the Internet to propel their businesses to higher levels. Other profiles include a look at how Kinko's provides self-employed professionals the infrastructure to run an independent business; a new model for retail sales being pioneered by REI in Seattle; the rise of Monorail, Inc., a computer company with virtual roots; and an article on how business people can give back to the communities in which they reside.

Fast Company operated a Website before the channel opportunity came along, posting archived articles, news announcements, and similar material at:

www.fastcompany.com

I spoke with David Searson, an Australian computer programmer who emigrated to the Boston area to become the Web architect for *Fast Company*'s site. He offered his insights on the development process and described the structure on which the channel is based.

Moving to Boston

After accumulating a number of years' experience with computers in Australia, doing everything from programming mainframes to developing Websites, David Searson set his sights toward the computer mecca, California's Silicon Valley, in pursuit of challenging projects. He describes the connection with *Fast Company* and the move from Australia as follows:

"I was working on the Net, producing Websites, everything from corner stores to government departments. I'd been doing it for a couple of years and thought it would be nice to go to Silicon Valley to work, mainly because in Australia only 10 percent of the people know what a computer is, let alone what the Internet is. I was finding it difficult to implement some of my ideas.

"I was looking around for production work and, for some peculiar reason, I happened to cross a listing on Guy Kawasaki's email newsletter: *Fast Company* is looking for a Webmaster. I vaguely knew where Boston was—all I knew was that it wasn't anywhere near Silicon Valley. I sent *Fast Company* an email message and got into a conversation with the current Webmaster at *Fast Company*. After a couple of phone interviews, they sent me a magazine. There was a basic Website set up for *Fast Company*. I read the magazine online, saw the kind of content it was, and read their manifesto. I saw they were people who were interested in the New Economy and the way that business and work and technology were shaping the future and were being shaped by the future. I thought, here are some people who actually think the way I do. I got into some conversations and they sent over some of the print magazines. As soon as I saw the magazine, I bought an airline ticket and came over for a visit. I haven't looked back. Brought the family and settled in very nicely.

"It was basically seeing *Fast Company* across the Internet that changed the direction in which I was headed."

Planning the Site

As the planning sessions began, David and the staff members were fairly clear early on that they were addressing a particular audience: people with high-end machines. It was a fairly well-defined demographic that represented about 60 percent of their readers.

Netscape approached the magazine and asked *Fast Company* to participate as one of the premier channels. As David describes it, "They were asking a lot of money so we had to give it some serious thought. They were telling us at the time that 8 gazillion people a day were going to come through the channel and it would be bundled as a part of the Netscape release. At the time, it was the new release of Netscape Communicator bundled sometime around late August 1997. We took a look at what they were talking about and thought, 'Yeah, it sounds fine.' It was certainly what we were looking for—a way of driving traffic to our mainstream Website. It was also an opportunity to demonstrate *Fast Company* on what would ultimately be the broadband channel."

As a basic principle, the main Website had been deliberately designed to be really low tech. Java and proprietary tags were kept out of it completely. The site almost universally was constructed around HTML 2 conventions. The Netscape channel offer provided the opportunity for the staff to play with a new technology that offered more control over the layout and typesetting on the page—the look and feel and action. The channel offer also provided the opportunity to work with JavaScript in an environment that was totally controlled.

From David's perspective, if you build a Netcaster channel, you know exactly who is going to be using it: people who have Netcaster. The parameters are well defined. You know what tags are going to work and what tags are *not* going to work. You know what parts of JavaScript have been implemented and what parts don't work as advertised. In comparison, on a normal Website, you are wide open to the audience; by necessity, you've got to accommodate everybody from LYNX clients up to the latest beta version of every browser that is coming to the market.

Fast Company was fully aware that whenever you experiment on the Web with any technology, you blow people off. There will always be people coming to your Website and finding that it just doesn't work. This has been the driving reason behind the simplicity of the existing site. But, with a Netcaster channel, the audience was assured of compatibility. "The channel approach gave us the opportunity to do some playing around, to do some high-end stuff, do some noise and action, without blowing people off," David said.

A Look at the Channel

Before going any further, it might be instructive to take a look at the actual *Fast Company* channel and its organization. After this overview, the following sections will describe how the content was chosen and prepared and how the actual components were put together for channel delivery.

Once you subscribe to the *Fast Company* channel, updates are on a daily basis. Optionally, of course, the individual user can set a schedule that is different from the one specified in the channel object as it is constructed in JavaScript. If you're online and running Netcaster, when you choose the *Fast Company* channel from the Channel Finder, a full-page screen appears, while the updated channel content is downloaded.

The same framework for the channel content, as shown in Figure 11.1, appears from week to week, so only the material that has changed needs to be downloaded for storage in the Netcaster cache. Prior content can be retrieved from the cache (unless it has been refreshed or overwritten with additional channel content), so the channel framework and large files (such as the audio file used as background music and a periodically updated QuickTime movie composing the FCTV section) can be readily retrieved for offline channel browsing.

The menu structure along the left side of the channel window displays the categories for recurring content. As you move the mouse pointer over each individual

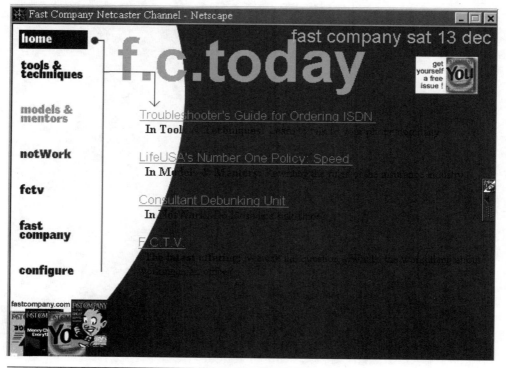

Figure 11.1 Framework for the channel content.

item, a message box appears below giving a capsule description of the type of content that appears under that category. Home is the general summary of the current channel highlights. Tools & Techniques provides topics that explain how to work and what to use. Models & Mentors profiles people who are driving the change in the business world. notWork is about keeping your sense of balance. FCTV includes video clips and short interviews. The *Fast Company* option can be used to access the standard *Fast Company* Website while you're online to learn about magazine subscription rates and upcoming seminars. The Configure option at the bottom of the menu lets you set up various channel options to your preferences.

If you select one of the major categories by clicking on it, the Dynamic HTML scrolls the next level of choices into view, usually three or four articles under the category. For example, under the Models & Mentors category, the options shown in Figure 11.2 appear, including Zen and the Art of Managerial Maintenance, Job Titles of the Future, and the Voice of the Tiananmen Generation.

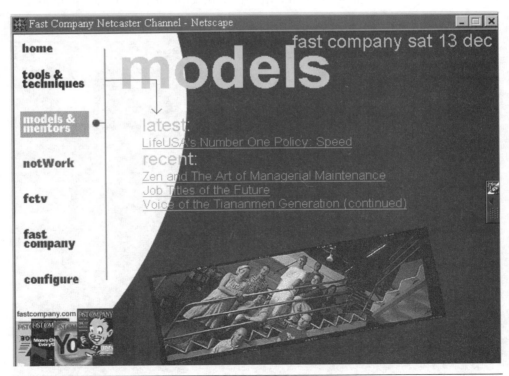

Figure 11.2 Models & Mentors selections.

The central content is all in Dynamic HTML format within a frame. Clicking on one of the topics causes a text window to slide into place (using DHTML positioning techniques). The content, shown in Figure 11.3, is accessed through two scroll controls—the upward and downward arrows to the right side of the text box. When you're finished reading, clicking the Close button causes the text box to slide out of the frame and the previous set of options are displayed.

The channel content can be personalized to some degree by choosing the Configure option, which brings up the screen shown in Figure 11.4. You can choose the Light setting, which reduces the amount of material downloaded to compensate for slower Internet connections. You can also set the Sound Off, which prevents the background music from playing—essential if you're using the channel in a typical office environment. The Standard setting enables all the normal options, which includes loading past articles from three or four days back if you haven't updated recently.

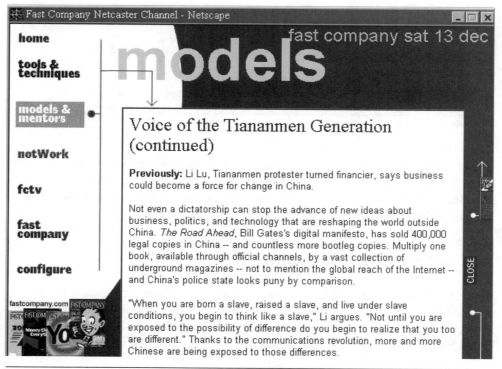

Figure 11.3 Text box in the *Fast Company* channel.

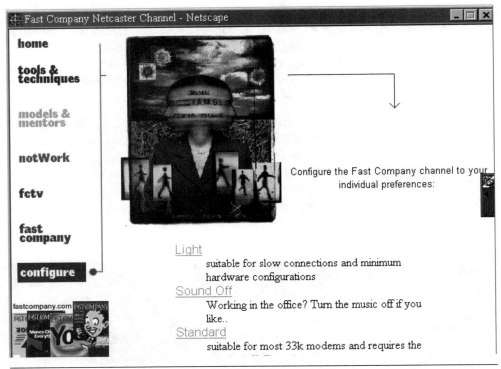

Figure 11.4 Configuration options for the channel.

The content downloading and display is controlled by a combination of JavaScript, a server-side CGI script in Perl, and DHTML pages assembled on-the-fly by the server that delivers the channel content. The manner in which all of these elements are coordinated and transferred is described in the following sections.

Implementing the Channel

Deadline pressures kept the *Fast Company* staff under the gun throughout the month-long development process. The first two weeks or so were occupied with lively discussions as to what to put on the channel and how it should be designed. The actual work of scripting took place largely within a single week.

Shaping the Content

According to David Searson, deciding the appropriate content was the biggest part of the decision-making process. The staff found it was harder to reach agreements on those details than to work the technology out. Discussion involved sitting down and basically trying to understand who it was that they were talking to and what sort of content they were going to be delivering, knowing that there was no intention to turn the channel into a news site. As David describes it, "We didn't have the five feeds a day. We aren't really interested in getting into that whole arena. We like to think that the content of the magazine that we are putting out is—within reason—pretty well timeless. So, whether you get it at two o'clock in the morning or three o'clock in the afternoon is pretty much immaterial."

After the prolonged debate, the staff decided on a daily schedule for channel delivery. They initially started off with five areas of interest and then narrowed the topic areas down to three: Tools & Techniques—things people can do on a daily basis in their business and their work environment to make change; Models & Mentors—providing cases studies of people doing business in different ways; and notWork—offering lifestyle and social topics that don't revolve around the workplace.

Once the categories were worked out, the staff decided that there would be some new writing that was done specifically for the channel and some that could be taken directly out of the archives of the magazines or repositioned—chopped and changed around to produce the size pieces that they wanted to deliver as channel content. David put a fairly tight restriction on the editorial, limiting the content to two-minute segments. His feeling was that if people couldn't read the content on a daily basis and get some ideas within a couple of minutes, then there was something seriously wrong with the approach.

The staff divided the channel into two paths. One path involved the headlines and the stories; this was designed to present to readers what they can do on a daily basis—dive straight into it, get what they want, and go. This content was designed to be either graphics-free or to take advantage of reused graphics that appeared on the Website or in the magazine. In essence, the audience would just pull down some text on a daily basis through the channel, always presented in a familiar format—framed with color and movement and all the requisite, flashy, crowd-pleasing stuff.

Expanding Menu Structure

The main display screen for the *Fast Company* channel is in three frames—traditional HTML frame sets. The menu bar located on the left side of the channel window can be customized; it is built from pure JavaScript. The script for accomplishing this was adapted from a standard Netscape JavaScript library. The menu system is flexible since it reads the number of links that are required and then builds the menu display on-the-fly.

The center part of the screen is where the Dynamic HTML appears—the Netscape layers and animated content appear in this region. This material does use the proprietary Netscape <LAYER> tag, since it is safe to assume that Netcaster users are basically a captive Netscape audience. The only risk, from David's perspective, is if Netscape decides to change its specifications for the implementation of layers. From a development standpoint, the channel content was constructed fully within the Netscape range of tag sets and parameters. The content pretty much falls apart if you try to feed the DHTML documents to any browser other than Netscape's. From the beginning, the DHTML content was specifically designed only for Netcaster.

Separating Data-Heavy Topics

As a design decision, the staff deliberately tried to divide any heavy graphics or movie files—anything requiring intensive download time and storage space—into a different area. One area that contains periodic QuickTime movies is titled FCTV; this content comes up in a different frame. Viewers can bypass it if they want on a daily basis. The underlying idea was to separate the occasionally viewed topics from the daily fare.

This approach was decided upon after studying a number of other channels. On this topic, David said, "One of the things that annoyed me about the other channels that I was looking at while we were trying to figure out what we were doing, was that if all you wanted to do was read a particular story, you had to go through the whole song-and-dance routine. While it might be very clever and very picturesque, it didn't help if all you wanted to do was read a story. That is why we decided to divide our content up. You hit the everyday stuff, and then FCTV; the *Fast Company* song-and-dance show is separated from the daily content."

The Content-Handling System

The text that is supplied by writers and editors is relayed through an email application that parses the material for HTML delivery. Writers and editors are linked through a Macintosh local area network. A Frontier database uses object-oriented techniques to organize textual content. The content-handling process uses scripting to allow the database to accept email input from the writers.

The process works this way: The writer sends an email message using plain ASCII text to the Email Server from his or her Macintosh computer. The email message contains the body of the story for the day and some tags explaining the date that it is to appear. The Subject field of the message is translated into the filename for the submission.

For example, if a writer wants to write a story to appear next Friday, she puts it in with the appropriate date for the story to run, and sends it by email to the system. Individual stories are extracted from their holding directories; the Frontier database residing on the Content Server pulls out the textual content and translates the text files into database objects. The database then supplies the HTML markup necessary to post the story and also writes about six header lines that are needed to define what layer the story is going to be in and the page titles that apply. Notification is sent back to the writer from the Email Server indicating that the incoming story has been processed. Since the stories are stored in holding tables, changes to the content can be accommodated up to the actual release date associated with the file.

The Content Server is designed to construct generic layers on a scheduled basis. The templates that are used to process database entries are easily customizable to produce content suitable for other channel formats. This offers the potential to create several different formatted story files—each tailored to a specific channel use— for a single email story submission.

A mirroring script sends the material to the Unix Server as a flat file in a directory residing outside the Web space. Three directories are used to separate the content; for example, the Models & Mentors stories are stored in a directory titled /models. Filenames assigned to each story correspond with the release data; for example, a story slated for release on 30DEC97 has the filename 19971230. All of the files stored in the Unix directories are accessible by Perl scripts.

When somebody calls up the channel on the browser through the subscription mechanism, the content retrieval is automated. The channel calls for an index page and the Unix Server calls a Perl script that looks through all the entries for the Tools & Techniques, all the entries for the notWork sections, all the entries for the Models & Mentors, and picks up the latest story to be readied in the queue. From this input, the server builds a hyperlinked directory. It also constructs the layers separately for each of the documents.

Figure 11.5 shows the organization of the key components in this system.

When you press the Tool & Techniques button on the channel page, it calls up the appropriate page from the server (if you've got a live connection) and it asks for the most recent document in that section. For example, on Friday the 12th it will pick up the Friday the 12th story and the four previous stories. It won't pick up tomorrow's story or next week's story. So, the staff can put stories in the directory in advance and not have to worry about uploading material just before the scheduled delivery.

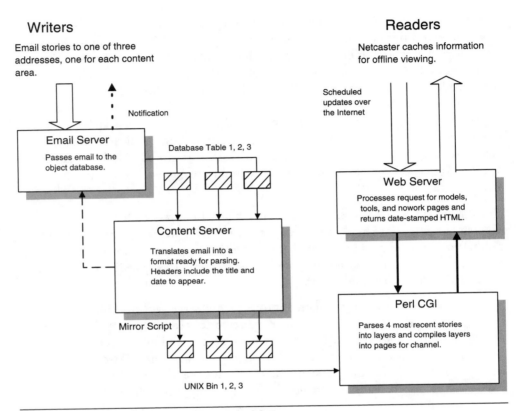

Figure 11.5 *Fast Company* networking.

The script pulls in the four stories and then assigns a layer to each. The writer or editor doesn't need to specify which layer the story is going into. The script builds those four layers at the time the content is pulled down from the server. The HTML page output is produced dynamically.

In other words, depending on the time of day and the schedule, the Perl script assembles the material for offline viewing. The script to accomplish this process is fairly simple, and is shown later in the chapter. But, as David describes it, as they were working on the design, they had no idea how they were going to make the whole process work. The development took place over three or four weeks of planning and experimentation, followed by a week to actually construct all the necessary scripts in JavaScript and Perl to make the story retrieval and channel page construction automatic.

Automating the entire process was essential. As David describes it, "I didn't want to build something that I would have to go back to every day—sit down and clack out another page of HTML. The mechanism has run flawlessly since we started it and hasn't required any fixes. When we want to put a new story into the system, it is just a case of: write it out in plain text, email it in with a date tag, and it goes straight into the schedule where it can be pulled up as needed, depending on what time people do the update of their channel."

The content can be viewed through the ordinary browser as long as you are using Netscape Communicator 4, so the content works as a live site as well.

David also included some options that were never really used in the actual production. The channel offers the option of turning sound on and off. You can also choose whether or not to bring in the FCTV pages at all. The music was incorporated as a downloadable QuickTime sound-only file that plays in the background. The file size for the sound content is around 700Kb. The FCTV consists of a short QuickTime video sequence that is not updated as frequently as the daily content. The logic behind using an audio wave file rather than MIDI or another format was that this resource gets lodged in the Netcaster cache, where it will be resident and can be accessed in the future—even two weeks later if the cache is not cleared. The download time, which is not that significant, is a reasonable trade-off for the predictability of standard WAV content embedded in a QuickTime file.

The feeling was that the single music piece would be used as background music and remain unchanged during several days of daily updates. The downside of this approach is that the music cycles over and over in an endless loop and—although it's an enjoyable piece of music—the repetition gets monotonous and annoying after several playings. Ambient background music and sound fields, such as can be enabled using the Headspace Beatnik plug-in or the Sseyo Koan plug-in, offer changing music landscapes at a less-significant download burden. Koan, in particular, can compose several hours' worth of generative music based on a 30K instruction file.

In theory, with Netcaster channels you design content and resources to be pulled down overnight or in the background. Under those circumstances, large sound files or video don't present a download problem. Some users, however, expect that the content should be streamlined to download in the foreground and react negatively to long download times.

Having worked with Netcaster for awhile, David looks at it to some degree as another form of offline browser—an application that pulls down sites for later viewing. The technology has existed for a fairly long period (by Web standards). If you put a glossy front end on it and say, "here we'll integrate our offline browser into our suite of programs and give it a name—Netcaster—and call it a channel." The subscription mechanism itself has helped people relate to the idea. The technology, however, is not a radical departure from what has existed for quite some time.

Fast Company gets some feedback from end users expressing confusion as to how to set up their subscription, how to run it, exactly what the channel is, and what it is supposed to be doing. Similar confusion has been seen with the introduction of most other forms of push technology as well.

Fast Company isn't using the Castanet tuner approach at the moment, but the underlying architecture of the channel content has been designed so that it can be parsed out to any other form of channel delivery as needed. With minimal extensions to the current structure, the *Fast Company* content could be delivered using Active Channel distribution. "Once we've captured the content and run it through the templates, it can be used in any format," David said.

This effort would require the redistribution of the content as parallel channels. The method would be fairly easy to implement by modifying the output of the layers to generate a DHTML z-Index tag for the story content, rather than using the Netscape <LAYERS> tag. The logic behind the delivery would stay the same; only the details would have to be tweaked. This level of change could be implemented entirely through the CGI Perl scripts that handle the page construction. The primary *Fast Company* Website is already set up to be sensitive to whatever browser a visitor is using.

Scripts and Code

Several of the important scripts—including JavaScripts and Perl scripts—that are used to implement the content-handling process are provided in this section.

Introductory Page in DHTML

The intro screen for the *Fast Company* channel makes heavy use of Dynamic HTML. Animated graphics and text move across the screen at different speeds, some images jitter and shake before your eyes. The effects that appear as part of the introduction are based on a series of JavaScript functions that move objects in combination with layers. The introduction screen is shown in Figure 11.6.

The code used to accomplish this page follows.

Figure 11.6 *Fast Company* **intro page.**

```
<html><head><title>intro</title>

<SCRIPT LANGUAGE="JavaScript1.2">

var swishspeed = 0.1
var maxswish = 30
var z=0
var flashtime=0

function swish(lyr,xdest,ydest,maxswish){

        xtogo = ( xdest - lyr.left ) * swishspeed
        if (xtogo>maxswish){xtogo=maxswish}
        if (xtogo<-maxswish){xtogo=-maxswish}
        if ((xtogo * xtogo) < 1) { lyr.left = xdest ; }
        else { lyr.left += xtogo ; toMove = 'yes' ; }

        ytogo = ( ydest - lyr.top ) * swishspeed
        if (ytogo>maxswish){ytogo=maxswish}
```

```
            if (ytogo<-maxswish){ytogo=-maxswish}
            if ((ytogo * ytogo) < 1) { lyr.top = ydest ; }
            else { lyr.top += ytogo ; toMove = 'yes' ; }

            if (toMove == 'yes'){
            toMove='no'

setTimeout('swish(document.layers["'+lyr.name+'"],'+xdest+','+ydest+','+maxswish
 +')',5)
            }
}


function
 sq6a(){swish(document.layers["graphic6"],640,100,50);setTimeout('sq1a()',2000)}
function
 sq1a(){swish(document.layers["graphic1"],1840,100,500);setTimeout('wd4c()',2000)}
        function
 wd4c(){swish(document.layers["words4"],400,600,35);setTimeout('wd5c()',2000)}
        function
 wd5c(){swish(document.layers["words5"],350,350,80);setTimeout('sq5a()',2000)}
function
 sq5a(){swish(document.layers["graphic5"],100,200,60);setTimeout('sq4a()',2000)}
function
 sq4a(){swish(document.layers["graphic4"],400,200,40);setTimeout('wd1a()',2000)}
        function wd1a(){swish(document.layers["words1"],-
 900,100,35);setTimeout('wd2a()',2000)}
        function wd2a(){swish(document.layers["words2"],-800,-
 100,80);setTimeout('sq6b()',2000)}
function sq6b(){document.layers["graphic6"].top=200;
swish(document.layers["graphic6"],-250,200,30);setTimeout('wd3a()',2000)}
        function
 wd3a(){swish(document.layers["words3"],700,0,35);setTimeout('wd4a()',2000)}
        function wd4a(){swish(document.layers["words4"],-
 1300,200,60);setTimeout('sq1b()',2000)}
function sq1b(){swish(document.layers["graphic1"],-
 240,400,500);setTimeout('sq3a()',2000)}
function
 sq3a(){swish(document.layers["graphic3"],700,300,20);setTimeout('wd3a()',2000)}
```

```
          function
⌐wd3a(){swish(document.layers["words3"],700,0,35);setTimeout('wd4a()',2000)}
          function wd4a(){swish(document.layers["words4"],-
⌐1300,200,60);setTimeout('sq2a()',2000)}
function
⌐sq2a(){swish(document.layers["graphic2"],500,300,100);setTimeout('sq5b()',2000)}
function sq5b(){swish(document.layers["graphic5"],100,-
⌐300,30);setTimeout('wd1b()',2000)}
          function
⌐wd1b(){swish(document.layers["words1"],700,100,50);setTimeout('wd5a()',2000)}
          function wd5a(){swish(document.layers["words5"],20,-
⌐100,60);setTimeout('sq1c()',2000)}
function
⌐sq1c(){swish(document.layers["graphic1"],1840,100,500);setTimeout('sq4b()',2000)}
function sq4b(){swish(document.layers["graphic4"],-
⌐160,200,40);setTimeout('wd2b()',2000)}
          function
⌐wd2b(){swish(document.layers["words2"],150,200,200);setTimeout('wd3b()',2000)}
          function
⌐wd3b(){swish(document.layers["words3"],0,250,80);setTimeout('sq3b()',2000)}
function sq3b(){swish(document.layers["graphic3"],-
⌐340,300,20);setTimeout('sq2b()',2000)}
function
⌐sq2b(){swish(document.layers["graphic2"],500,100,100);setTimeout('wd4b()',2000)}
          function
⌐wd4b(){swish(document.layers["words4"],400,200,35);setTimeout('wd5b()',2000)}
          function
⌐wd5b(){swish(document.layers["words5"],20,350,50);setTimeout('sq1d()',2000)}
function sq1d(){swish(document.layers["graphic1"],-
⌐340,400,500);setTimeout('wd1c()',2000)}
          function wd1c(){swish(document.layers["words1"],300,-
⌐100,90);setTimeout('wd2c()',2000)}
          function
⌐wd2c(){swish(document.layers["words2"],150,600,35);setTimeout('wd3c()',2000)}
          function
⌐wd3c(){swish(document.layers["words3"],700,250,305);setTimeout('sq5c()',2000)}
function sq5c(){document.layers["graphic5"].top=500;setTimeout('sq6c()',1000)}
function
⌐sq6c(){swish(document.layers["graphic6"],700,500,100);setTimeout('sq2c()',2000)}
```

```
function sq2c(){swish(document.layers["graphic2"],-
300,100,35);setTimeout('sq6a()',2000)}




function swapthem(lyroff,lyron){
lyroff.visibility='hide'
lyron.visibility='show'
while (flashtime < 10000){flashtime++}
}

</SCRIPT>

</head>
<body bgcolor="000000" onLoad="javascript:sq6a()">

<layer name="biglogo" left=90 top=110>
<IMG SRC="circuspix/logo.gif" WIDTH="402" HEIGHT="66" BORDER="0">
</layer>
<layer name="graphic2" left=400 top=-120>
<IMG SRC="circuspix/034b.gif" WIDTH="120" HEIGHT="99" BORDER="0">
</layer>
<layer name="graphic3" left=-500 top=300>
<IMG SRC="circuspix/freefood.gif" WIDTH="121" HEIGHT="155" BORDER="0">
</layer>
<layer name="graphic4" left=400 top=500>
<IMG SRC="circuspix/cafe.gif" WIDTH="140" HEIGHT="140" BORDER="0">
</layer>
<layer name="graphic5" left=100 top=500>
<IMG SRC="circuspix/storm.gif" WIDTH="213" HEIGHT="140" BORDER="0">
</layer>
<layer name="graphic1" left=-500 top=60>
<IMG SRC="circuspix/redbook.gif" WIDTH="105" HEIGHT="94" BORDER="0">
</layer>
<layer name="graphic6" left=-250 top=100>
<IMG SRC="circuspix/poker.gif" WIDTH="236" HEIGHT="151" BORDER="0">
</layer>
```

```
<layer name="words1" left=-450 top=100>
<font face='arial' point-size=70 color=white>relevant</font>
</layer>
<layer name="words2" left=150 top=600>
<font face='times' point-size=50 color=grey>case studies</font>
</layer>
<layer name="words3" left=-450 top=100>
<font face='arial' point-size=40 color=green>working solutions</font>
</layer>
<layer name="words4" left=-450 top=100>
<font face='times' point-size=30 color=red>real life stories</font>
</layer>
<layer name="words5" left=-450 top=100>
<font face='arial' point-size=50 color=blue>real people</font>
</layer>

<layer name=music left=0 top=0>
<A HREF="stage.html" TARGET="_top">
<IMG SRC="pix/toc_head_pick.gif" WIDTH="85" HEIGHT="40" BORDER="0"></A>
<embed src="media/dealqt.MOV" loop="true" controller="false" autoplay="true">
</layer>
</body></html>
```

Table of Contents in JavaScript

The Table of Contents used to access the daily *Fast Company* items was adapted from a JavaScript provided by Netscape that scales itself to the number and organization of items listed. The script, commented for easy understanding, is as follows:

```
<xmp><HTML>
<HEAD>
<SCRIPT LANGUAGE="JavaScript1.1">


// Title:       JavaScript-enabled Table of Contents
// Date:        1-13-96
// Author:      Robert W. Husted (husted@netscape.com)
// Modified By:


// GET BASE URL (http://machine.company.com/directorypath/)
with (this.location) {baseURL = href.substring (0,href.lastIndexOf ("/") + 1)}
```

```
var totalGraphics=0;          // TOTAL NUMBER OF GRAPHIC OBJECTS CREATED
var graphic = new Array();    // ARRAY OF IMAGE OBJECTS


// CREATE NEW GRAPHIC OBJECT
function tocGraphic (width, height, name, statusText, link) {

    // SET GRAPHIC DIMENSIONS (DECREASES LOAD ON WEB SERVER)
    this.height    = height;
    this.width     = width;


    // GRAPHIC NAME PREFIX - USED FOR SEARCHING
    this.name      = name;


    // HREF URL - PAGE TO WHICH GRAPHIC LINKS
    this.link      = link;


    // PLAIN VERSION OF THE GRAPHIC - "off"
    this.off       = new Image (width, height);
    this.off.src   = imageSubdirectory + imagePrefix + name + offSuffix;
    this.offname   = imageSubdirectory + imagePrefix + name + offSuffix;


    // IF MOUSEOVER IS NOT DISABLED FOR THIS GRAPHIC, ASSIGN 'ON' AND
    //  'PICK' VERSIONS OF THE GRAPHIC AND SET THE STATUS BAR TEXT
    if (link != "") {

        // HIGHLIGHTED (MOUSEOVER) VERSION OF GRAPHIC - "on"
        this.on        = new Image (width, height);
        this.on.src    = imageSubdirectory + imagePrefix + name + onSuffix;


        // SELECTED (MOUSECLICK) VERSION OF GRAPHIC - "pick"
        this.pick      = new Image (width, height);
        this.pick.src  = imageSubdirectory + imagePrefix + name + pickSuffix;


        // TEXT TO DISPLAY ON THE STATUS LINE (DURING MOUSEOVER)
        this.statusText = statusText;
    }
}
```

```
// BUILD ARRAY OF GRAPHIC OBJECTS (OFF, ON, PICK)
function createTocGraphic (width, height, name, statusText, link) {

    // CREATE NEW GRAPHIC ARRAY OBJECT AND ASSIGN PROPERTIES
    graphic[totalGraphics] = new tocGraphic(width, height, name, statusText, link);

    // KEEP TRACK OF TOTAL NUMBER OF GRAPHIC ARRAY OBJECTS
    totalGraphics++;
}



// CHANGE GRAPHIC TO 'PICKED' STATE WHEN MOUSE IS CLICKED
//   CALL THIS FUNCTION IF YOU WANT TO SET A MENU ITEM
//   CALL THE FUNCTION FROM THE NEW PAGE LIKE SO:
//   <BODY ... onLoad="parent.toc.doClick(5)">
//
//   NOTE: IF YOU DO NOT USE A STANDARD NAMING CONVENTION (BY INCLUDING
//   THE NAME OF THE GRAPHIC OBJECT (graphic[num].name) IN YOUR URL
//   THEN WHEN THE USER PRESSES THE RELOAD BUTTON ON THEIR BROWSER THE
//   TOC WILL RESET TO AN IMPROPER STATE AND THE WRONG IMAGE WILL SET TO
//   "PICK"
//
//   E.G.  IF YOUR TOC CATEGORY IS "mail" THEN THE URL FOR ALL THE
//   DOCUMENTS ASSOCIATED WITH THAT CATEGORY SHOULD CONTAIN THE WORD
//   "mail" EITHER 'http://www.company.com/path/mail/page.html'
//   OR 'http://www.company.com/path/page_mail.html'

function doClick (num) {

    document.images[graphic[num].name].src = graphic[num].pick.src;

    if (num != picked) {
        document.images[graphic[picked].name].src = graphic[picked].off.src;
    }
    picked = num;
}



// ON MOUSEOVER, REPLACE THE GRAPHIC OVER WHICH THE MOUSE IS POSITIONED
```

```
//   WITH THE "on" VERSION OF THAT GRAPHIC.   IF GRAPHIC IS CURRENTLY IN A
//   "PICKED" STATE, LEAVE IT ALONE.
//   ADDITIONALLY, CHANGE THE STATUS LINE TO REFLECT THE TEXT FOR THIS MENU
//   ITEM.

function doMouseOver(num) {
  if (num != picked) {

    // REPLACE DOCUMENT GRAPHIC WITH "on" GRAPHIC
    document.images[graphic[num].name].src = graphic[num].on.src;
  }


  // IF GRAPHIC (OVER WHICH THE POINTER IS HOVERING) IS IN A 'PICKED'
  //  OR 'ON' STATE, LEAVE IT ALONE.
  if (highlighted != picked && highlighted != num) {
    document.images[graphic[highlighted].name].src =
graphic[highlighted].off.src;
  }
  highlighted = num;

  // CHANGE STATUS LINE TEXT
  self.status = graphic[num].statusText;
}


//   THIS FUNCTION WILL ENSURE THAT WHEN THE POINTER LEAVES THE TOC
//   NOTHING WILL BE HIGHLIGHTED.   BE SURE TO ALLOW ADDITIONAL ROOM
//   (ABOUT 10 PIXELS) ON THE RIGHT SIDE OF YOUR TOC SO THAT THE BROWSER
//   WILL RECOGNIZE THAT THE POINTER IS NOT OVER A GRAPHIC *BEFORE* THE
//   POINTER ENTERS THE OTHER FRAME.   OTHERWISE, THE BROWSER WILL LEAVE
//   A TOC OPTION HIGHLIGHTED WHEN THE POINTER ENTERS THE OTHER FRAME.

function doMouseOut (num) {

  //  IF GRAPHIC (OVER WHICH THE POINTER IS HOVERING) IS IN A 'PICKED'
  //   OR 'ON' STATE, LEAVE IT ALONE.
  if (highlighted != picked) {
    document.images[graphic[highlighted].name].src =
```

```
⌐graphic[highlighted].off.src;
    }

}


// CHANGE TABLE OF CONTENTS TO DISPLAY PROPER 'PICKED' IMAGE IF USER
//   HITS THE RELOAD BUTTON.
//
//   IMPORTANT: DO *NOT* USE THIS FUNCTION TO SET THE TOC FROM ANOTHER
//   PAGE... USE doClick() INSTEAD.

function doOnLoad (num) {

  // GET URL FOR PAGE IN "content" FRAME - CHANGE NAME IF YOUR FRAME
  // HAS A NAME OTHER THAN "content"
  currentPage =  top.frames[frameTarget].location.href;

  // FIND GRAPHIC THAT CORRESPONDS WITH CURRENT PAGE AND ADJUST HEADER
  //   (SEARCH FOR "name" TEXT IN URL... IF FOUND, THEN THAT'S THE GRAPHIC
  //    WE SHOULD MAKE "PICKED")
  for (i = 1; i < totalGraphics; i++) {
    // IF "name" TEXT FOUND IN URL, SWITCH GRAPHIC TO "PICKED" VERSION
    if (currentPage.indexOf(graphic[i].name) > 0) {

      // CALL MOUSECLICK() FUNCTION TO SET GRAPHIC TO 'ON'
      doClick(i);
      return(1);

    }
  }
  // NOTHING FOUND, SET TO DEFAULT TOC OPTION SPECIFIED BY tocNumber
  if (i >= totalGraphics) {
    doClick(num);
  }
  return(-1);
}


// ----------------------- IMPORTANT NOTE -----------------------------
```

```
//
// TO GET THIS JAVASCRIPT TO WORK.... YOU SHOULD ONLY NEED TO CHANGE THE
//  CODE BELOW THIS POINT... CREATE EACH GRAPHIC YOU NEED (CREATE THEM
//  IN THE ORDER IN WHICH THEY SHOULD APPEAR ON THE PAGE), ADJUST THE
//  TARGET... AND EVERYTHING SHOULD WORK.
//
// ----------------------------------------------------------------------


// ----------------- CHANGE THIS INFORMATION -----------------------------

//  TARGET FRAME WHERE HTML DOCUMENTS WILL DISPLAY AFTER CLICKING THE
//  CORRESPONDING TOC IMAGE
var frameTarget = "right";

var picked=0;        // PICKED GRAPHIC - SET INITIAL VALUE
var highlighted=0;    // HIGHLIGHTED GRAPHIC - SET INITIAL VALUE

//  IMAGE NAME DEFAULTS - ENSURE THAT THE GRAPHICS YOU USE ARE UNDER
//  imageSubdirectory AND THAT THEY START WITH imagePrefix AND END
//  WITH offSuffix, onSuffix, and pickSuffix.  IT IS BEST TO USE
//  CONSISTENT NAMING CONVENTIONS - FOR THE 'help' PAGE (help.html)
//  AND CORRESPONDING GRAPHICS YOU SHOULD USE THE NAMES
//  toc_help_off.gif, toc_help_on.gif, toc_help_pick.gif
imageSubdirectory = "pix/";
imagePrefix       = "toc_";
offSuffix         = "_off.gif";
onSuffix          = "_on.gif";
pickSuffix        = "_pick.gif";


// ------------------------ EXPLANATION ----------------------------------
//
// createTocGraphic(width, height, name, text, link)
//
// EXPLANATION: creates a Table of Contents Graphic Object for use with
//                mouseOver and mouseClick functionality.
//
```

```
// width:        the width of the graphic in pixels.
//
// height:       the height of the graphic in pixels.
//
// name:         the name assigned to the object.  Please ensure that
//               your graphics and pages all have this name in them.
//               For instance, if you use the name "mozilla" then your
//               graphics should be called "toc_mozilla_off.gif",
//               "toc_mozilla_on.gif", and "toc_mozilla_pick.gif".
//               Additionally, your page should have the word "mozilla"
//               somewhere in the URL because this is the text that the
//               doOnLoad() function will search for to determine which
//               page is currently loaded and which corresponding graphic
//               to highlight.
//               E.G. 'http://www.company.com/path/mozilla/page.html'
//               or 'http://www.company.com/path/mozilla_cool.html'.
//
// text:         the text to be displayed when the pointer moves over
//               a graphic.
//
// link:         the URL for the page that will appear when the user
//               clicks on this graphic.  If the link is left blank
//               ("") then the graphic will not be assigned an 'on' or
//               'picked' state and will not be assigned a URL.  This
//               allows you to include title graphics or other graphics
//               that do not link to anything.  Please remember that even
//               though these 'title' graphics do not have an 'on' or
//               'picked' state... the name of the graphic must follow
//               the same naming convention as the other 'off' graphics
//               in the TOC.  I.E; if your 'off' images end in "_off.gif"
//               then your title graphic must likewise end in "_off.gif".
//
// -------------------------------------------------------------------

createTocGraphic(120, 35, "home", "Todays Headlines", "headlines.cgi");
createTocGraphic(120, 62, "tool", "Tools", "tools.cgi");
createTocGraphic(120, 58, "model", "Models", "models.cgi");
createTocGraphic(120, 48, "not", "Notwork", "notwork.cgi");
```

```
createTocGraphic(120, 48, "tv", "FCTV", "tv.html");
createTocGraphic(120, 59, "fc", "Multimedia Circus", "circus.html");
createTocGraphic(120, 48, "conf", "Configure", "config.html");


// -------------------- END CHANGES -------------------------------------



// NOW WRITE OUT TABLE OF CONTENTS WITH GRAPHICS... THIS IS TO MAKE THIS
//  JAVASCRIPT ROUTINE PLUG-N-PLAY ... ADD FORMATTING CHANGES HERE TO MAKE
//  YOUR TOC LOOK APPROPRIATE.

with (top.left.document) {

  // START WRITING TABLE OF CONTENTS
  open ('text/html');

  // WRITE TITLE INFORMATION
  write ("<TITLE>Table of Contents</TITLE>\n</HEAD>\n");

  // WRITE BODY TAG - doOnLoad() WILL BE RUN WHEN PAGE IS FIRST LOADED
  write ('<BODY bgcolor="ffffff" TEXT="#000000" onLoad="doOnLoad(0)">\n');

  // WRITE OUT CODE FOR TABLE OF CONTENTS
  for(i = 0; i < totalGraphics; i++) {

    // DISPLAY ENABLED GRAPHICS ONLY
    if (graphic[i].link != "") {

      // START ANCHOR
      if (graphic[i].link != "circus.html")  { write ('<A TARGET="' +
 ⌐frameTarget );}
        else { write ('<A TARGET="_top' );}
      // DISPLAY GRAPHIC IMAGE
      write ('" HREF="' + graphic[i].link + '" onMouseOver="doMouseOver(' + i + ');
return true" onMouseOut="doMouseOut(' + i + ')" onClick="doClick(' + i + ')">');
      write ('<IMG NAME="' + graphic[i].name + '" SRC="' + graphic[i].offname +
 ⌐'" WIDTH=' + graphic[i].width + ' HEIGHT=' + graphic[i].height + ' BORDER=0>');
```

```
    // END ANCHOR AND LINE
      write ('</A><BR>\n');
    }


    // DISPLAY NON-ENABLED GRAPHICS
    else {

      // DISPLAY GRAPHIC IMAGE
      write ('<IMG SRC="' + graphic[i].offname + '" WIDTH=' + graphic[i].width
  + ' HEIGHT=' + graphic[i].height + ' BORDER=0> <BR>\n');
    }
  }
}


</SCRIPT>

<embed src="media/houseqt.MOV" loop="true" controller="false" autoplay="true">

</BODY>
</HTML>
</xmp>
```

Headline Compiling in CGI

The CGI script that extracts the appropriate headlines and then compiles the
Headlines page from the current stories in each of the categories appears as follows:

```
#!/usr/bin/perl
$| = 1;


sub CompilePage {


print "Content-type: text/html\n\n";
# -----------------------------------------------------------------
# GET TODAY'S DATE AND THEN
# -----------------------------------------------------------------
$this_century_prefix = "19"; ##Y2000 workaround
          ## what's the time, Mister Wolf ?
local ($sec,$min,$hour,$mday,$mon,$year,$wday,$yday,$isdst,$date); local (@days,
```

```
↳@months);
@days = (sun,mon,tues,wed,thurs,fri,sat);
@months =
↳('jan','feb','mar','apr','may','jun','jul','aug','sep','oct','nov','dec');
($sec,$min,$hour,$mday,$mon,$year,$wday,$yday,$isdst) = localtime(time);
$date_words = $days[$wday]." ".$mday." ".$months[$mon];
$mon++; if ($mon < 10) { $mon = "0$mon"; } if ($mday < 10) { $mday = "0$mday"; }
$date_numbers = $this_century_prefix.$year.$mon.$mday ;


# --------------------------------------------------------------
# BUILD THE STANDARD HEADLINE LAYER HERE
# --------------------------------------------------------------
$compile = qq!
<HTML><HEAD><TITLE>$hopper_title_bar</TITLE>
<STYLE TYPE="text/javascript">
window.document.ids.section.color = "#$headcolor";
window.document.ids.section.fontFamily = "arial,arial ms,helvetica,sans serif";
window.document.ids.section.fontSize = "80";

window.document.ids.menu.fontFamily = "arial,arial ms,helvetica,sans serif";
window.document.ids.menu.fontSize = "18";
window.document.ids.menu.color = "#9999ff";

window.document.ids.menudate.fontFamily = "arial,arial ms,helvetica,sans serif";
window.document.ids.menudate.fontSize = "24";
window.document.ids.menudate.color = "#cccccc";

window.document.ids.headline.fontFamily = "arial bold,arial ms,helvetica,sans
↳serif";
window.document.ids.headline.fontSize = "24";
window.document.ids.headline.fontStyle = "bold";

window.document.ids.storyline.fontFamily = "arial,arial ms,helvetica,sans
↳serif";
window.document.ids.storyline.fontSize = "14";
window.document.ids.storyline.color = "#000000";

window.document.tags.em.fontFamily = "arial,arial ms,helvetica,sans serif";
```

```
window.document.tags.em.fontSize = "12";
window.document.tags.em.color = "#999999";
window.document.tags.EM.fontStyle = "bold";
</STYLE>
<SCRIPT LANGUAGE="JavaScript1.2">
var startposition = 112 ;
var offscreen = 1000 ;

function swish(lyr,xdest,ydest){
     xtogo = ( xdest - lyr.left ) * 0.3
     if ((xtogo * xtogo) < 1) { lyr.left = xdest ; }
     else { lyr.left += xtogo ; toMove = 'yes' ; }
     ytogo = ( ydest - lyr.top ) * 0.3
     if ((ytogo * ytogo) < 1) { lyr.top = ydest ; }
     else { lyr.top += ytogo ; toMove = 'yes' ; }
     if (toMove == 'yes'){
toMove='no';setTimeout('swish(document.layers["'+lyr.name+'"],'+xdest+','+ydest+'
)',10) ; }
     }

function swishOff(lyr){
     xtogo = ( -500 - lyr.left ) * 0.3
     if ((xtogo * xtogo) < 1) {
     lyr.left = -500
     }
     else {
     lyr.left += xtogo
     toMove = 'yes'
     }
     if (toMove == 'yes'){
toMove='no';setTimeout('swishOff(document.layers["'+lyr.name+'"])',10) ; }
     else {intro()
     }
     }

function intro() {
     hideAll()
     document.layers["SECTION"].left = -3000
```

```
        document.layers["SECTION"].top = 0
        document.layers["SECTION"].visibility = 'show'
        document.layers["MENU"].left = 40
        document.layers["MENU"].top = offscreen
        document.layers["MENU"].visibility = 'show'
        swish(document.layers["SECTION"],10,0)
        setTimeout('intro2()',180)
        }

function intro2() {
        swish(document.layers["MENU"],40,startposition)
        }

function nothing() { ; }

function readit(lyrR,butup,butdn,clos) {
        hideAll()
        butup.visibility = 'show'
        butdn.visibility = 'show'
        lyrR.visibility = 'show'
        clos.visibility = 'show'
        swish(lyrR,20,startposition)
        }

function scrollup(lyr) {
        if (lyr.top < (startposition - 1)) { lyr.top += 70 ;}
        }

function scrolldown(lyr) {
        lyr.top -= 70 ;
        }

function hideAll() {

        document.layers["MENU"].visibility = 'hide'
        document.layers["SCREEN1"].visibility = 'hide'
        document.layers["SCREEN2"].visibility = 'hide'
        document.layers["SCREEN3"].visibility = 'hide'
        document.layers["SCREEN4"].visibility = 'hide'
```

```
        document.layers["MENU"].top = offscreen
        document.layers["SCREEN1"].top = offscreen
        document.layers["SCREEN2"].top = offscreen
        document.layers["SCREEN3"].top = offscreen
        document.layers["SCREEN4"].top = offscreen

        document.layers["CLOSE1"].visibility = 'hide'
        document.layers["CLOSE2"].visibility = 'hide'
        document.layers["CLOSE3"].visibility = 'hide'
        document.layers["CLOSE4"].visibility = 'hide'
        document.layers["MOVEUP1"].visibility = 'hide'
        document.layers["MOVEDN1"].visibility = 'hide'
        document.layers["MOVEUP2"].visibility = 'hide'
        document.layers["MOVEDN2"].visibility = 'hide'
        document.layers["MOVEUP3"].visibility = 'hide'
        document.layers["MOVEDN3"].visibility = 'hide'
        document.layers["MOVEUP4"].visibility = 'hide'
        document.layers["MOVEDN4"].visibility = 'hide'
        }
</SCRIPT>
</HEAD><BODY bgcolor="#990000" onLoad="javascript:intro()">
!;


# --------------------------------------------------------------
# LOOK IN EACH DIRECTORY FOR THE 4 MOST RECENT DOCUMENTS
# --------------------------------------------------------------
opendir(STORIES,"$this_hopper");@choices=readdir(STORIES);closedir(STORIES);
@choices = reverse sort @choices;$x=1;foreach $choice(@choices){
if(($choice le $date_numbers)&&($choice !~ /\./))
{&ExtractDetails;$x++;if($x >=5){last;}}}


# --------------------------------------------------------------
# BUILD THE WHOLE PAGE
# --------------------------------------------------------------
$compile .= qq!
<LAYER NAME=swoosh VISIBILITY=show top=0 left=-3><IMG SRC="pix/swooshb.gif"
WIDTH="130" HEIGHT="375" BORDER="0">
</layer>
```

```
<LAYER NAME=MENU LEFT=40 TOP=620 VISIBILITY=hide>
!;

$compile .= "<SPAN ID=menudate>latest\:</SPAN><br>$compile_current <SPAN
⌐ID=menudate>recent\:</SPAN><br>" ;

$compile .= $compile_title;
$compile .= qq!<p align=left><IMG SRC="pix/$menugraphic"
WIDTH="$graphic_width" HEIGHT="$graphic_height" BORDER="0"></LAYER>!;
$compile .= $compile_story;

$compile .= qq!
<LAYER bgcolor="990000" NAME=swoosh2 VISIBILITY=show top=0 left=-3 clip=800,110>
<IMG SRC="pix/swooshb.gif" WIDTH="130" HEIGHT="375" BORDER="0">
</layer>
<LAYER NAME=SECTION LEFT=-5000 TOP=10 VISIBILITY=hide >
<span ID=section><B>$hopper_title_bar</B></span></LAYER>
<LAYER NAME=blank VISIBILITY=show top=0 left=0>
<p align=right><SPAN ID=menudate>fast company $date_words</SPAN></layer>
<LAYER NAME=arrow VISIBILITY=show top=63 left=-80>
<IMG SRC="pix/14748.gif" WIDTH="147" HEIGHT="48" BORDER="0"></layer>
!;

print $compile ;
print $compilebuttons ;

}

# --------------------------------------------------------------
# EXTRACT THE DETAILS FROM EACH
# --------------------------------------------------------------
sub ExtractDetails {
$tablestart = qq!<LAYER NAME=SCREEN$x LEFT=650 TOP=200 VISIBILITY=hide>
<table border=1 width=450 bgcolor=eeeeff cellspacing=0 cellpadding=8><TR><TD
⌐width=450>\n!;
open(STORY,"$this_hopper/$choice");@lines=<STORY>;close(STORY);
foreach $line(@lines) {
## ------- CHECK FOR CUSTOM STYLE TAGS
if ($line =~ /<FC-story>/i){$compile_story .= $tablestart
⌐;$section="story";next;}
```

```
elsif ($line =~ /<FC-title>/i){$section="title";next;}
elsif ($line =~ /<FC-headline>/i){$section="headline";next;}
## ------- COMPILE THE SECTIONS
if ($section eq "story") {
    $line =~ s/SCREENyyy/SCREEN$x/g;
    $line =~ s/current channel listings/$hopper_title_bar/g;
    $compile_story .= $line ;}
elsif ($section eq "title") {
    $line =~ s/SCREENyyy/SCREEN$x/g;
    $line =~ s/MOVEUPyyy/MOVEUP$x/g;
    $line =~ s/MOVEDNyyy/MOVEDN$x/g;
    $line =~ s/CLOSEyyy/CLOSE$x/g;
    if ($x eq 1){$compile_current .= $line ;}
    else{$compile_title .= $line ;}
    }
}
$compilebuttons .= qq!
<LAYER NAME=MOVEUP$x LEFT=477 TOP=180 VISIBILITY=hide>
<A HREF="javascript: scrollup(document.layers['SCREEN$x'])"><IMG SRC="pix/UP.GIF"
WIDTH="23" HEIGHT="80" BORDER="0"></A>
</LAYER>
<LAYER NAME=MOVEDN$x LEFT=477 TOP=380 VISIBILITY=hide>
<A HREF="javascript: scrolldown(document.layers['SCREEN$x'])"><IMG
SRC="pix/DOWN.GIF"
WIDTH="23" HEIGHT="80" BORDER="0"></A>
</LAYER>
<LAYER NAME=CLOSE$x LEFT=470 TOP=310 VISIBILITY=hide>
<A HREF="javascript: swishOff(document.layers['SCREEN$x'])"><IMG
SRC="pix/close.gif" BORDER="0" width=17 height=38></a>
</LAYER>
!;
}

1;
```

Net Results

David sees a lot of confusion among new users, especially considering that at any one time some 70 percent of Internet users are people who have only been on the

Net for two or three months. These people still haven't quite figured out what the Internet is, what exactly a browser can do, where their local resources end and where the browser content begins. Implementations such as the Webtop mode of display confuse users even more as to where the Internet begins and what is really residing on their own machines. Trying to figure out exactly what a channel is—as viewed from within a browser—only compounds this confusion.

David remembers, "When desktop publishing was first available on a wide scale, you'd get letters and memos and things written in 17 different typefaces—a horrible mishmash. People were doing things simply because they could. Push technology has suffered exactly the same fate during introduction. Developers are saying, 'Wow, we've got all these tools; let's use every single one of them at the same time.' Keeping restrained within an environment that allows you to do anything is a hard lesson to learn for many developers."

The *Fast Company* channel approach deliberately avoids these excesses. The focus is on story content and provocative ideas, instead of multimedia bells and whistles. The framework uses DHTML and JavaScript to its advantage to provide an ongoing orientation to the subject areas and a consistent mechanism for accessing the stories.

The staff at *Fast Company* is watching carefully to see what kind of long-term response is generated by its highly visible channel. With its logo positioned on a comfortable perch on the Netscape Channel Finder, and this easy subscription link going out with every full-edition copy of Netscape Communicator that is distributed, it's still too early to see if channel subscribers will stay around and become magazine subscribers. Push technology is still new enough that discussions about the ultimate purpose of the channel generate lively debate. As David Searson said, "We wonder about just what the longevity of a subscriber's attention is—what any one person's experience with the channel is. Are push channels destined to be an introduction to a service or a product or a Website? Are they a way for people to be immersed in a particular viewpoint. For example, in our situation the presentation suggests, 'Here's *Fast Company*. This is what we have to offer. This is our look and feel. This is our attitude to life.' You try to do a few different things that you can't do on static Web pages or on low-bandwidth Web pages. What you're really saying is, 'This is what we're all about.'"

As a final commentary on the state of the technology, David said, "I still think channels are ahead of the game. Which is great. I can still remember when Netscape was ahead of the game. When the whole concept of using email was new and exciting. Most of the new technologies only get a chance to mature when a lot of people understand them and a lot of people use them. There has to be some straightforward, basic, everyday uses for the technology. Until that happens, the technology is just an interesting pastime."

Summary

While creating and targeting content using DHTML effects specifically for Netcaster users, *Fast Company* has created a structure and a system that adapts easily to producing formatted content for other channel delivery applications. This design architecture suggests techniques that other developers may want to adopt to construct a system that can support any of the leading Web channels as needed.

NewsEDGE/BackWeb
Case Study

This chapter takes a slightly different approach from the model established with the earlier case studies chapters. In this case, we're going to progressively create a solution to a hypothetical problem using a set of tools in a product that at press time was too new to yet have any real-world examples. The product is an enterprise-level offering from BackWeb Technologies that combines the BackWeb channel delivery with content supplied by two recently merged companies: Individual and Desktop Data.

In this hypothetical example, we'll show how a fictional high-tech consulting firm can keep staff members up to date on rapidly changing information that is critical to the firm's operation. The companion Website to this book will also offer additional tips and guidelines for working with news content distributed through channels to a staff with differing personal requirements. We hope that in this manner we can give you the valuable information on a product that is too new to yet have a history, but that promises to be increasingly important in the months to come. On the companion site, we'll continue to cover recent developments, giving you up-to-the-minute information on the use and creation of Web channels throughout the Internet.

The Fictional Scenario

Strategic Visions is the name of a fictional consulting firm that we'll use to illuminate the processes by which filtered and personalized news information can be delivered through channels to staff members to support their work. Though this company is fictional, the product they will be working with is real: NewsEDGE content combines the strengths of two pioneering companies—Desktop Data, Inc., and Individual, Inc.—whose merger makes them one of the largest news providers in the industry. The newly formed NewsEDGE Corporation will offer content from more than 2000 information sources. More than 50,000 stories a day will be generated by the merged corporations. Through a partnership with BackWeb Technologies, all of this content can be segmented and personalized for delivery through push channels. The case study will illustrate a number of ways that the BackWeb tools can be used to present relevant content to a group within a company.

The staff members of Strategic Visions LLC, located in San Jose, California, occupy the bleeding edge of the high-tech world, preparing reports, projections, and forecasts for venture capitalists, marketing organizations, government agencies, and others involved in emerging technologies. From the heart of Silicon Valley, 32 staff members cull through hundreds of information sources to obtain key information as a part of their ongoing research efforts. The term *information overload* is as familiar to the staff as is the daily commuter traffic on Route 237. Fully dependent on a stream of news sources for the raw material with which Strategic Visions bases its reports, the management of this small company is constantly on the lookout for new technologies that can solve the problems they face each day. Among the most pressing problems is devising an effective way to deal with the flood of content that must be retrieved and sorted each day. Every staff member spends several hours a day searching online news services, reading industry trade publications, scanning the wire services output, and so on. Keeping abreast of the latest industry developments requires investigative skills, diligence, and heavy use of the latest computer tools.

Roland Spencer, founder and CTO of Strategic Visions, has been dealing with information systems issues since 1986, when he worked on an expert system application to calculate and suggest strategies for futures trading in the commodities marketplace. He's determined to find a more effective way to deal with managing information gathered from the Internet beyond the hit-or-miss approach that has been used up to this point. His overworked and harried staff is in full agreement with this goal.

A Wealth of Information Sources

The Internet abounds with quality information sources; many news services and companies have already set up highly successful distribution systems for news and information, including Reuters, Dow Jones, PointCast, and so on. Part of the problem has been the sheer volume of information and the problems associated with sorting and filtering the incoming content. There is no problem with the quantity of information, but for someone seeking specific types of content, the emphasis must be on *relevant* information.

With their headquarters located within eyesight of each other in Burlington, Massachusetts, Individual, Inc. and Desktop Data had been arch rivals until the merger brought them together to form the largest news integration organization in the country. Each one of these companies brings its own particular strengths into the new organization. Since 1989, Individual has focused on refining the filtering and processing of news and information—the term you see again and again in its descriptive literature is *relevant* content. The relevance comes from a combination of software tools, based on expert system principles, that group incoming news stories into various categories. This expert system is combined with a highly trained staff of editors and news processors who further filter, extract, sort, and evaluate the content and fit it into a delivery system designed to present concise, focused information to its audience. The audience consists of over 2 million paid, registered, or licensed readers around the world.

While Individual has excelled at providing highly focused content, Desktop Data has put its emphasis on real-time feeds of information and the dispersal of customized information to large organizations. In business since 1988, Desktop Data offers content collected from over 200 individual sources, and manages this information to produce authoritative, up-to-the-minute news delivery to business professionals seeking a competitive edge. Its most important product, NewsEDGE, reaches an audience of nearly 170,000 business people in more than 400 organizations internationally. The merger with Individual provides the opportunity for both companies to combine their resources and specific strengths to produce a unique combination of focused content and real-time content.

The third element in this powerful emerging structure is BackWeb Technology. BackWeb has formed a partnership with the new NewsEDGE Corporation to deliver its content to enterprises through push technology and channels. This service promises to be a highly effective means of placing very specific kinds of data and information onto the desktops of workgroup members within organizations.

Beyond the consolidation and filtering of information that is performed on the content by NewsEDGE Corporation, BackWeb products offer the means to further channel and direct this information to specific individuals through the personalization and segmentation features built into its software. If a particular staff member requires information about fluctuations in Integrated Chip prices and availability in the Asian markets, BackWeb can create an individualized channel that feeds news stories of this type directly to the individual.

The BackWeb Console is the software application that handles the setup and creation of content delivery modes, managing the database of information in the form of InfoPaks that are stored on the BackWeb Server. Since this system can be highly automated, some setup and configuration may be all that is needed to form highly focused channels for information professionals. BackWeb Technologies increasingly is targeting enterprise-level applications, a shift from its original channel activities in the open commercial Internet marketplace. Within the more controlled confines of a corporate intranet, sensitive database information from corporate operations can be combined with externally retrieved data, such as the incoming news feeds from NewsEDGE, to produce a selective, individualized set of channels to keep staff members well informed and tuned to the corporate goals and mission.

Individual's Solution to Infoglut

The wildly successful growth of the Web has led to a problem of information saturation, or *infoglut*. While the Web provides access to an incredible range of information, collecting and assimilating that information has become more and more difficult, partly due to the volume of information and partly due to the diverse nature of the sources and the difficultly in retrieving relevant information.

At the same time, the market for business and professional information is growing rapidly; Forrester Research Inc. predicts that by the year 2001, the market in this area will reach $800,000,000. Individual, Inc. has built its business around the concept that there is value to sorting and categorizing all this information and delivering it to an audience in easily digestible nuggets.

Individual acquires information from a wide assortment of sources: wire services, newspapers, trade magazines, satellite systems, monthly periodicals, and so on. All in all, the company uses approximately 600 information sources. The diverse incoming content is processed to put it in a single common format that can be stored and delivered on the computer. Once the information is in the system, it is sent through a filtering process using a computer tool known as SMART (System for the Manipulation and Retrieval of Text). SMART was initially developed at

Cornell University and then used to form the core of the Individual information management scheme.

The SMART expert system is rule based and runs off a huge thesaurus that has been constructed over the last nine years. The thesaurus knows company names. It can determine relationships between words. It has no trouble equating International Business Machines with IBM with Big Blue. It knows what a browser is, and what companies produce browsers. All together, hundreds of thousands of hours of expertise have been embedded in the rule system that drives SMART. From this collection of information, a set of categories has been created based on industry topics. Specialists in the editorial department come from a wide assortment of disciplines—health care, energy, storage technologies, government, communications, and so on.

News stories are segmented into a range of topics. The SMART system may successfully complete about 80 or 90 percent of the job, but the human editorial staff takes over from there and further refines the content. Duplicate stories are tossed out. Some stories are moved from one category to another or included in multiple categories. Some stories that ran in a slightly different form a couple of weeks ago are eliminated. By the time the editors are finished, the remaining content is categorized and concentrated and directed towards very specific topics.

End users of the information are often interested in a distilled, concise delivery of information—something they can read in 20 or 30 minutes in the morning to get an edge on their competitors in the industry. Each end user can set up his or her own profile, which contains those topics he or she is primarily interested in, and then scan the stories that have the most interest from sets of headlines.

Physically, the information gets fed through a fairly complex network system. Incoming news streams are captured on a collection of NT servers and then processed to get the data into the common format. A series of Unix servers that run the SMART expert system then perform the first pass on the categorization. The editors who process and refine data at night work from a centralized news database contained in a set of SQL server tables running on NT systems. Most workstations accessing the NT databases are Windows95 based. The entire system is dependent on this mutliserver, highly distributed architecture tuned to the needs of information processing.

Paul Pinella, the Director of Enterprise Programs and Partnerships, sees the NewsEDGE merger and the partnership with BackWeb as a means of offering even more control over the type and nature of information that is delivered to the desktop. Paul said, "The systems that are going to be implemented—the workflow and procedures—are going to be different in every company. I would think that an effective use of BackWeb would be for the people who are running the business, the executives, to set the ground rules. These are the people who will build the channels. Here are the people who will deliver content to those channels. This is the audience that we want to target this information towards. It is then the job of the implementors to take over from there—the gatekeepers who actually provide the information. To be effective, it needs to be adapted in a company and it needs to be updated. There should be people who are assigned to the role of keeping the content fresh. If none of this happens, the approach won't be effective. But if it does, from what I can tell with the BackWeb v4.0 release, there are a lot of good tools that are given to the channel implementor, or, if you will, the content person—the gatekeeper. So, people can upload information even on a daily basis to keep the content set fresh."

Content being packaged by Individual for use with BackWeb is delivered in SGML format. Each individual story is first encapsulated in SGML format and then stored in a database. As part of the alliance, BackWeb and Individual put together a system by which each subscribing customer site can automatically connect to the central database at a defined hour—for example, 3:00 A.M.—to retrieve the SGML data from the Individual FTP site. Once the data is transferred to a BackWeb Server, the SGML content is automatically converted into a format for delivery through BackWeb channels. The SGML tags are used to identify topic areas that apply to specific data items so that they can be tagged for delivery. A user who subscribes to a channel, for example, designated for Electronic Commerce, receives all of the news stories that have the corresponding tag.

There are a multitude of steps involved in processing hundreds of stories every day and then converting them into a format that can be conveniently delivered as channel content. For the subscriber, however, it is a simple matter of turning on the computer, accessing the channel, and viewing the information each day. Given the way the information is sorted and categorized, the odds are in favor of the content being on target and relevant to the end user's needs.

The Alliance

The alliance between BackWeb Technologies and the newly formed company composed of Individual and Desktop Data seems to be a natural melding of the strengths of each organization. With this partnership and the release of BackWeb Infocenter v4.0, BackWeb's enterprise customers have a vehicle to obtain filtered and structured information directly to the desktop throughout the business day. The two key content-based products are Individual's First!, based on a Topic Library consisting of 2500 industry topics, and Desktop Data's NewsEDGE, real-time news and information from up to 2000 different sources.

Both of these forms of filtered content are mapped into the BackWeb channel delivery mode where they can be selectively directed to users or workgroups. Users also have significant control over both the type of information and the delivery mode, with a sophisticated search agent that allows news and content to be sifted and evaluated, and an alert system that triggers user notifications when details in certain preselected topics become available or specific kinds of information are fed into the system. Users who are working under deadline pressures or dependent on receiving certain kinds of information for research or studies can take maximum advantage of the information delivery modes available.

The enterprise solutions to information delivery have been bundled into several different packages that have been made available to BackWeb corporate customers. Entry-level packages include fewer news sources and a more restricted range of topics. Higher-end product offerings increase the range of coverage to a full comprehensive assortment of sources and stories. Corporate customers can choose an appropriate level of content and sources to meet their requirements.

Applying Push to Content Delivery

After watching his staff members at work for several months, our fictional CTO, Roland, became convinced that the previous Internet model was not working. Researchers were spending far too much time trying to locate critical kinds of information and often failing to get the kinds of content that they needed to do their jobs. The problem was a dual issue of targeted information retrieval and carefully tuned delivery of that information. The push technology model and the channel delivery method seemed to offer a fitting solution to the difficulties.

Looking carefully at the problem, Roland Spencer realizes that he needs to segment the information from the various sources into several specific categories. He has one staff specialist who focuses on recordable CD and other optical storage technologies. Another concentrates on information systems tools. One of his junior staff members has become specialized in distribution of audio content over the Internet and emerging electronic commerce models in this area; since this person has a closer touch to the younger music buyers, Roland would like to channel content in this area to this eager researcher. Another staff member is perpetually involved in research on alternative energy systems and techniques for applying these to corporate cost-savings programs. Having a wide supply of information sources in these narrow market segments makes the consulting services that Strategic Visions offers much more valuable to clients and customers. The whole system is largely dependent on the quality and the nature of information that is available to the staff members.

The person administering the BackWeb Console—in this case, Roland—becomes, in essence, the gatekeeper controlling the flow of information into the company. Though BackWeb offers flexibility and can be configured to also access outside commercial channels, Roland wants to ensure that the primary kinds of content reaching the researchers' desks are relevant to the problem at hand.

One of the first goals to be met within the group would be to designate one person as the channel architect. In this case, the channel architect would require training in BALI (the BackWeb Authoring Language Interface) to obtain the necessary skills to generate channels. Channel creation can be a simple matter of just funneling text and content to users, or it can involve multimedia creation and production, including audio and video content. Since many corporate sites will be using intranets for content delivery, with high-speed continuous connections for workgroup members, more elaborate channel content can be distributed than could be reasonably accomplished on the Internet.

The next area to consider is the management of the information that will be automatically lodged in the BackWeb Server and the regular channel delivery of that information to groups and individuals within the organization. A thorough understanding of the BackWeb architecture is important to this goal, as well as familiarity with the capabilities of the BackWeb Console component. The BackWeb model is reasonably flexible in this area, and accessing the necessary technologies does not require a long learning curve.

The BackWeb Components

The BackWeb Technologies software components include Server software that stores and delivers InfoPaks, a Console utility that manages the Server operation and also controls distribution and scheduling of content, and customizable Client software that provides viewing and accessing of InfoPaks and also supports the display of the many different types of alerts and notices that BackWeb uses. All of these components are necessary parts of this form of push technology.

BackWeb also offers a number of other software components that increase the range of channel publishing options: an authoring toolkit that supports the creation of original multimedia channel content, automation utilities that simplify the performance of repetitive operations, and proxy server software that allows channel integration of content retrieved from outside corporate firewalls.

Content delivered through the BackWeb InfoCenter approach can originate from four distinct sources:

A BackWeb Channel Server. InfoPaks stored on a BackWeb Server can be routed to channel subscribers over the Internet, intranets, or extranets. InfoPaks are created using the authoring language, BALI, provided by BackWeb.

World Wide Web resources. Documents that have been profiled using BackWeb software utilities can be distributed as part of a BackWeb channel. This type of content can either be distributed directly from the Web or through a BackWeb Channel Server.

Channel Definition Format channels. BackWeb channel delivery can be accomplished using the scheduling and structuring data included in a standard CDF file.

File distribution. Files containing a wide variety of content, including software applications and multimedia content, can be delivered using the channel approach. The files can be transferred from a shared resource on a LAN or from a designated location on the Web.

Each of these different types of content exists in independent channels, though all the different types can be accessed through the standard BackWeb channel. Much of the work to offer the various types of content to channel subscribers is carried out through the BackWeb Console component.

While many of the software tools provided by BackWeb can simplify various administrative and content development tasks, the most commonly used tool in most situations will be the BackWeb Console. As demonstrated in the next section, the Console provides the means for determining the nature and characteristics of each individual channel.

Filtering Content through the Console

If you will be administering a BackWeb Server, much of your work will be accomplished through the use of the BackWeb Console. The Server installation and setup are straightforward and reasonably simple. Once you have installed the server software to run under either Solaris 2.5 or above, Windows NT, or Irix 6.2 or above, the Console software is used to manage the InfoPaks to be installed on the Server and to be distributed through channels.

You can personalize and segment the information distributed in a variety of ways, as shown in the examples that appear in the following sections.

Segmentation through Workgroups

The BackWeb Console lets you define and create individual workgroup clients that have been presubscribed to a set of channels and that have distinct characteristics. Through the Console, you select those channels that are to be included with the client and then create a customized executeable file consisting of the BackWeb InfoCenter Client software defined according to your parameters. Each person who is to be a member of the workgroup installs the custom Client on his or her workstation, and he or she can immediately begin receiving InfoPaks from the channels that have been configured for the workgroup client.

For the purposes of our example, Roland decides to create two specific workgroups: one called *Strategic*, which will include a broad selection of channels and content, and the other called *Hightech*, which will be focused on a narrow range of content delivered through the NewsEDGE database.

The Workgroups window consists of two panes: one on the left that shows the full range of categories available on the Server, and one on the right that shows the channels that appear within the selected category. The first step in tailoring the content to a specific workgroup is to select those categories and channels to include or exclude. Figure 12.1 shows the selections for the Strategic workgroup, which includes a broad-based selection of computer-oriented channels.

The Hightech selections are limited to those channels specific to NewsEDGE categories (See Figure 12.2). Roland has chosen this more limited range of news items to keep a small group of staff members focused on certain specific technology issues. The same technique could be used to choose any set or subset of the channels and categories stored on the BackWeb Server.

Once you've tailored the content to your needs, you choose the New option from the Workgroup menu and a dialog box appears, as shown in Figure 12.3, that lets you assign a name to the new workgroup. Once you launch BackWeb to create the workgroup, the software creates a version of the installable client utility containing those channels and characteristics that you assigned. The Settings option on the Workgroup menu offers further means for defining the behavior and parameters that apply to the newly created workgroup. You can allow individual subscribers to further customize the installation of the client or to prevent any changes from taking place to the client setup. You can also change the appearance of the client, place limits on the type or number of channels that can be accessed, control access options through proxy servers, specify automatic updating of the BackWeb software, and

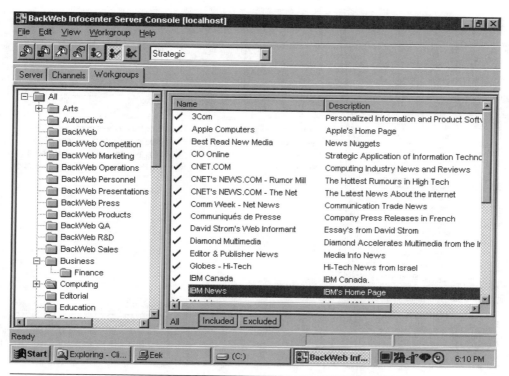

Figure 12.1 Workgroups window showing Strategic selections.

control many other features of the client. The administrator can essentially choose the degree of control over the individual subscribers who will be running the client. In some circumstances, it may be necessary to carefully restrict operation of the client; in other cases, it may make sense to give subscribers a good deal of latitude in setting up the client options themselves.

Once you distribute the client software to the members of the new workgroup, they install it on their individual workstations. When the client is run, it appears with the selected channels ready to start receiving InfoPaks from the Server. Figure 12.4 shows the Hightech workgroup client with the available NewsEDGE channels after it has been installed.

Based on the workgroup settings you establish, the BackWeb software creates a set of segmentation rules that determine what content is directed to what clients. From the Server tab of the Console, you can view the current list of segmentation rules that apply to the Server. Figure 12.5 shows the segmentation rules for the two workgroups, Strategic and Hightech, as they appear following the workgroup creation.

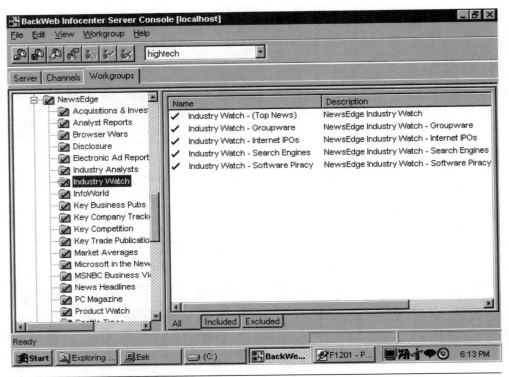

Figure 12.2 Workgroups window showing Hightech selections.

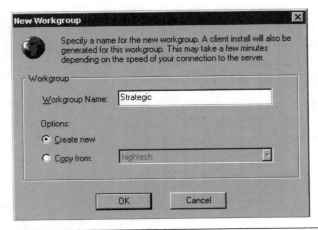

Figure 12.3 Creation of a new workgroup.

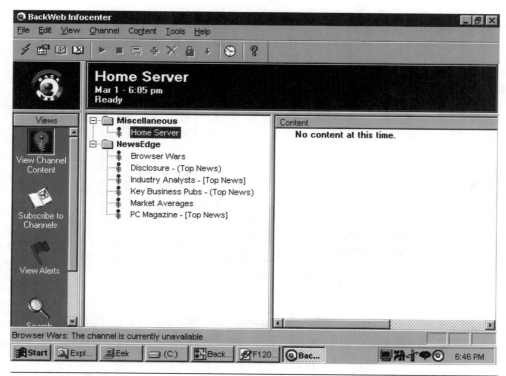

Figure 12.4 Hightech workgroup client.

You can create as many workgroups as is appropriate for your organization and use the resulting workgroup clients to control the routing and delivery of InfoPaks. Some workgroup members may need access to a large selection of channels, while others may find it more effective to survey and monitor just a few carefully chosen channels.

Content Management through Structuring

One powerful tool that the system administrator has available when using BackWeb push solutions is the ability to structure the channel display as it appears to subscribers, grouping and prioritizing the content areas according to any scheme that is appropriate. The hierarchical organization of InfoPaks in this manner can guide and influence selections and adapt different types of material to a variety of potential uses.

The use of subchannels is one means by which the content within a single channel can be arranged and organized for presentation to the subscriber. A subchannel

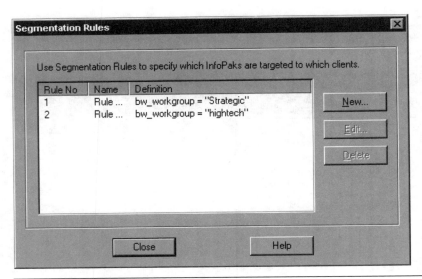

Figure 12.5 Segmentation rules.

can be assigned a weighting value that determines what combination of InfoPaks the end user receives. Another technique is the creation of Exposure Groups, a technique that controls the order in which InfoPaks are sent. For example, the most recent InfoPaks can be sent first, or InfoPaks can be sent out in random order.

Roland could use this capability to control the mix of content from the NewsEDGE delivery. To a group of staff members that he wants to focus on technology issues over marketing issues, he could create a technology-oriented subchannel with a weight of 7, and then create a marketing perspective subchannel with a weight of 3. The weighting of the subchannels affects the mix of content that is delivered.

This level of management of InfoPaks is accomplished through the Console using the Server tab. InfoPaks that have been listed on the Server can be individually selected. Right-clicking on the InfoPak name displays its properties, as shown in Figure 12.6. The tabs available through the Properties let you control all characteristics on an InfoPak, including setting the weighted values and choosing the display options, time sensitivity, corresponding exposure groups, segmentation rules, and so on.

Profiling Websites

The Channel Profiler tool allows external Website pages to be integrated into the channel model used by BackWeb. This allows diverse types of material to be presented

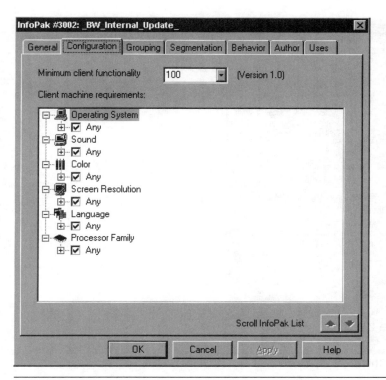

Figure 12.6 Properties options for an InfoPak.

through the BackWeb channel directory. Each new type of content that is manipulated in this manner must have a channel agent constructed for it; the task of constructing a custom channel agent is simplified through BackWeb's Web Channel Agent wizard, which makes the process a step-by-step sequence. The Channel Agent communicates the structure of the channel content so that it can be delivered from the BackWeb Server to any number of clients.

To create a custom channel agent based on Web pages, access the Channels tab from within the BackWeb Console. Select the Add Channel option from the Channel menu and the dialog box shown in Figure 12.7 appears.

Since in this case we want to construct a channel based on Web pages, select the Web Channel option from the existing choices. This launches the wizard that prepares the Channel Agent file.

One way to indicate a Web page to profile is to bring up that page in your Web browser and then, as the wizard proceeds, select the page in the browser as the

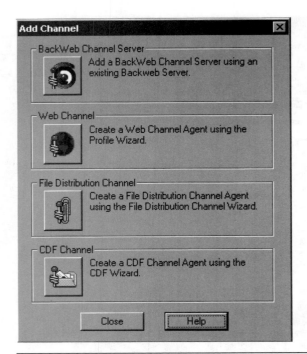

Figure 12.7 Add Channel options.

source for the profiled content. For our example, let's assume that Roland decides to channel content to the member of his staff who is interested in CD-recordable developments. Roland brings up the table of contents page for The CD-Info Company and selects this page through the wizard to use as a channel. With the browser pointed to the TOC page (www.cd-info.com/new_index.html), the page displayed in the Profile Wizard appears, as shown in Figure 12.8.

This window provides the tools to determine how the content from the Web page will be integrated into the channel and presented in a hierarchical view in the StoryView pane, shown on the right side of the window. The first few times you use this window, you can take advantage of step-by-step instructions that appear at the top of the window that guide you through the profiling process. You can change the settings that apply to the Profile Wizard window to control the toolbars and panes that appear and the overall appearance of the options.

Once you choose those items from the selected Web page that you want to appear as stories and you give them titles through the wizard, you can validate the newly created Web Channel Agent to ensure that the output is what you expected.

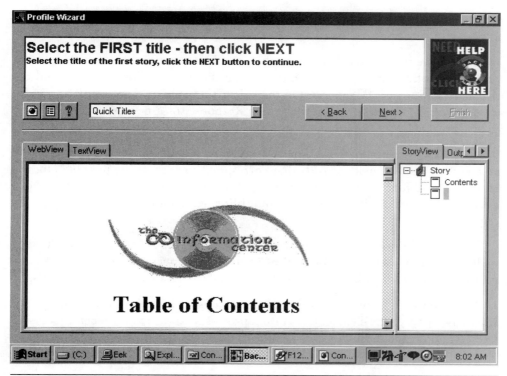

Figure 12.8 The CD-Info Company table of contents page.

Once created, the agent allows the Web page content to be listed in the BackWeb channel directory with the title you have assigned to it, and the corresponding information can be retrieved through standard channel methods.

Other channel agents handle different types of content, such as files intended for distribution through channels, and channels that are based on the Channel Definition Format files.

Creating Custom Responses through Hooks

The term *Hook* applies to a mechanism by which a BackWeb Server can deliver custom InfoPak selections dynamically based on data included in a Match Request packet. Hooks used with BackWeb Servers somewhat resemble CGI scripts as used on Web servers, basically extending the capabilities of the server to respond to incoming requests. The Hook can be used to construct an InfoPak that contains specific kinds of data, or to make a selection from the existing InfoPaks that are available in the server database.

In response to a Match Request packet, the Server returns a Match Response packet that offers suggestions as to the InfoPaks that most closely correspond to the specifications of the request. On the Client side, one or more InfoPaks can be chosen from those presented in the Match Response, or a new Match Request can be initiated.

Hooks are programmed in C++ language using a collection of entry points and structure defined by a set of APIs that correspond to each of the possible types of Hooks. The C functions designed to be used with Hooks take advantage of the BackWeb Server's ability to carry out multithreaded handling of processes and requests.

Personalized InfoPaks aren't sent through a channel that is using the TIBCO multicast method of delivery, but a TIBCO-enabled channel can be set up to support pesonalized InfoPaks by increasing the poll delay to an appropriate interval.

A typical use of a Hook might be to retrieve a user's Frequent Flier number, stored as a part of the channel registration process, and then use it when processing a reservation made through a channel interaction.

Summary

As the Internet and push technologies mature, the key issue is no longer simply providing information to corporate workers through the vast resources of the Internet, but providing useful, filtered information in a timely way. Efficiency and precision have become more important than sheer volume and unlimited access. To accomplish the goals of equipping staff members with the data they need to do their jobs effectively requires tools to shape, structure, and deliver information to the computer desktop. The alliance of BackWeb Technologies and NewsEDGE offers a powerful combination of focused channel delivery and quality, sorted news content.

Trial versions of the BackWeb Server software and supporting programs can be downloaded from BackWeb Technologies to get a sense of how this product operates. There are also 30-day trial subscriptions for the NewsEDGE content that administrators may want to sample to see if the technology is well worth considering for corporations and organizations looking for a way to tame the flood of information, circulating the kinds of information that they can build into channels for intranet subscribers.

HTML 4.0 and XML

This appendix provides an overview of HTML 4.0 and XML, two important standards that provide the framework for data structures and page content on the Web. This appendix highlights those key aspects of the standards that will be of the most interest for developers creating channel content.

Working within the Framework

Designers and developers over the past four years have struggled to keep pace with the never-ending fluctuating and metamorphosing standards upon which all content presentation on the Web depends. Two primary schools of thought have emerged for dealing with this rapid-growth phenomena. One, the conservative school, designs content only for those standards that have been around for awhile, even if it means using HTML 2.0 for months (or years) after everyone else has adopted HTML 3.2. Users take a long time to adapt to newly introduced browsers, and without the appropriate browser to handle the content, you might as well be looking at bacteria cultures in a petri dish.

The second school—for lack of a better name, let's call it the *advanced* school—embraces the latest techno-wizardry as soon as there is a hint that a standard will become official, designing content to take advantage of every whiz-bang effect that is available. In some cases, developers provide a secondary, parallel course of content to accommodate users with earlier browsers, but often-times they are brushed aside with terse messages that version 99 of the Excalibur WebDancer browser is required to venture any further. With a bit of work, more elegant solutions can be crafted in JavaScript that dynamically present the appropri-ate links for users on different platforms, or otherwise modify the page displays to accommodate everyone, but, of course, creating the necessary scripts and testing them against half a dozen different browsers can be a tedious and time-consuming pursuit.

Everyone agrees that it would be far better to get everyone to agree to a common set of standards, and it probably wouldn't hurt to slow down the development cycles for new browser releases a bit. That wish may come true, as the World Wide Web Consortium (W3C) appears to be doing a great deal to unify the fractious Web software development community and implement a series of standards that will eliminate the large majority of platform-related developer headaches. Recently, Netscape announced that it would be lengthening its software development cycles as a cost reduction measure (to help make up for a significant financial loss in 1997); so far, there is no indication whether Microsoft intends to similarly curb the frantic pace of new browser releases.

Software producers often begin incorporating new standards before they have officially been through the approval process. Microsoft, for example, made Internet Explorer 4.0 fully compliant with the pending HTML 4.0 standard, six months before HTML 4.0 was released as a standard. Microsoft also incorporated elements of XML 1.0 in its design of the CDF file format, either as a show of confidence in the emergence of XML 1.0 in the near future or Microsoft's own assuredness that it could help sway passage of XML 1.0. We also know that software producers some-times shape their products to include features that haven't been approved by any standards body. For example, Netscape's use of its proprietary <LAYER> tag flew in the face of any standards approval process, since the tag had already been rejected by the W3C. The tag is supported in Netscape's version 4 of Communicator and devel-opers continue to use it, but its popularity hasn't reached the point yet that you might consider it a *de facto* standard.

From most vantage points, the news looks encouraging and standards develop-ment may solidify to the point where developers don't have to learn a whole new set of standards every six months. In the meantime, here are two new standards, HTML 4.0 and XML 1.0, that will form the bedrock of the Web development foundation, hopefully, for some time to come. XML 1.0 and HTML 4.0 are already here. HTML has been through the final approval stage and has been recommended by the W3C as a bona fide standard. XML is in the final stage of the standards approval process, having been submitted for final comments by member organizations. It could still change significantly, going back to working-draft status before being approved, but most indications seem to point towards quick approval and acceptance as a standard in 1998.

HTML 4.0 Overview

On December 18, 1997, after more than a year of development, the W3C released version 4.0 of the HTML specification. Produced by the collective efforts of the members of the W3C HTML working group, HTML 4.0 consolidates a number of features to make HTML documents more accessible, more readable, and more usable. The member bodies of the W3C HTML working group include most of the primary players in Web software development and content development, including staff members from HotWired, PathFinder, Sun Microsystems, Netscape Communications, Novell, Adobe Systems, IBM, Hewlett-Packard, Microsoft, SoftQuad, Reuters, Verso, Spyglass, and others.

The W3C HTML working group took into account the changing landscape of the Web, including such factors as the increasing number of devices being designed to provide Web access (such as smart TVs, handheld computers, and cellular phones), the increasing internationalization of the Web, and the growing use of the Web as an information transfer mechanism for networked corporations and other organizations. The new features added as a part of HTML 4.0 reflect consideration of each one of these factors. This newest release of the standard also focused on unifying and improving use and presentation of forms and tables, providing better support for script-level interactions, and standardizing the approach to style sheets, which were first presented in HTML 3.2.

New and Improved Features in HTML 4.0

While the new features of HTML 4.0 are not revolutionary in scope, they address a number of different areas where standardization has been needed, and extend the existing HTML framework to better serve handicapped users, to support diverse access devices, to handle metadata constructs, and to improve the onscreen layout of text and graphics in a flexible and modifiable way.

The following items summarize the changes:

Standardized support for document objects. Script-level control of HTML 4.0 documents will be improved by the refinements to the object model. Dynamic HTML effects are better supported through script-level controls, and style sheet handling has been enhanced and improved. Authoring DHTML documents for

Web channel use will be an easier and more consistent process with the enhancements that have been made in this area.

Online forms-handling improvements. Many different enhancements have been made to support the processing and appearance of forms within HTML documents, including support for keyboard shortcuts to form controls, rich HTML text use in buttons, read-only controls, labels for form controls, and grouping of form controls.

Frame enhancements. A number of features have been added to support frame creation and use, including support for inline frames.

Table-handling improvements. Changes in the way that table borders can be managed and techniques for grouping rows and columns will make it easier to present attractive, complex tables in HTML documents. Table data can now be associated with headers to simplify access to browsers that perform text-to-speech translation and for Braille readers.

Expanded symbol, character, and language support. Presenting mathematical formulas and international content will be enhanced through the addition of support for an expanded set of symbols, including mathematical, markup, and international characters. Full support for the ISO 10646 character set lets Web authors adapt content for a variety of languages, supporting mixed direction or right-to-left text flow and many different character-encoding schemes. The goal was to provide full support for multilingual documents and ensure that any international language can be handled in documents.

What Does This Mean for Developers?

How will these changes to the HTML specifications make a difference to Web authors and developers? Several of the improvements included as a part of the HTML 4.0 should cause significant changes in the way that documents are created and presented. You can expect the following shifts in the way content is handled and presented on the Web:

Page formatting will increasingly be handled through the use of style sheets, rather than by forcing text into table cells and resizing table columns. Standardization and wider acceptance of style sheets will also bring about more varied onscreen layouts, incorporating a wider selection of fonts and embracing more of the design techniques that have proven effective in both the broadcast media and print media.

Web documents will contain more hooks to make it possible to describe elements to nongraphical browsers. For example, images will be able to be easily described using text-to-speech techniques; Web authors will become accustomed to the techniques for embedding the necessary elements to make all documents more widely accessible.

HTML documents will more often be designed for international audiences. Through the use of multilingual techniques and the Unicode character set to handle a wide variety of languages, including many that have previously been ignored because of the difficulty in representing them in standard HTML documents, documents will be accessible to a much larger, worldwide audience.

When tables are used in documents (rather than style sheets), the designer will have more control over the table presentation. Recommended column widths will be supported, allowing data to be displayed incrementally during downloading, rather than causing an extended wait for the entire table contents to be downloaded. The use of column groups in tables will provide more intricate and complex table structures with more consistent presentation.

The standardization of the <OBJECT> element in HTML documents will support a wider variety of embedded content, including mathematical content, many different forms of multimedia, special-purpose applications, and other page enhancements. This will ultimately provide a richer viewing experience for users and a simplified development environment for page authors.

Scripting the behavior of internal HTML elements will become more commonplace and dynamic HTML content will become the normal presentation medium, rather than a rarity on the Web. Earlier disparities in the handling of dynamic HTML will be largely eliminated, as long as the browser producers comply with the specification.

All of these different techniques and processes will be made fully accessible to nonprogrammers through a wide variety of authoring and content creation tools. Style sheets, DHTML effects, page transitions, filters, and other content enhancements are already handled well in a variety of authoring tools, such as Macromedia Dreamweaver, ExperTelligence WebberActive, SoftQuad HotMetalPro 4, mBed Interactor, and other applications. The visual authoring environment will become increasingly sophisticated, allowing more designers and novice page authors to produce impressive and complex onscreen works.

While there will no doubt be an adjustment period while authors get used to all the new capabilities and users begin installing the most current HTML 4.0-capable browsers, Web content on even modest sites should soon begin showing features made possible by the latest HTML standard. The promise is for more interesting and informative sites for everyone.

> # W3C Web Accessibility Initiative Guidelines
> The W3C Web Accessibility Initiative (WAI) has been working to develop
> a set of guidelines to help Web developers produce content that is more
> universally accessible. The goal is to reach the millions of Web users
> who may rely on nongraphical browsers (employing text-to-speech
> browsers, Braille readers, or text-based browsers), and to ensure the
> widest possible dispersal of information contained in HTML documents.
> Detailed authoring guidelines as they are released can be obtained from
> the W3C Website (www.w3.org).

XML 1.0 Overview

The Extensible Markup Language (XML) has made its way through a series of
committees and working groups and has been released as a W3C Proposed
Recommendation. This indicates that the W3C XML Working Group believes that
the standard is solid, ready for peer-group review, and a useful addition to the standards framework that supports communication on the Web. Before the standard
can be finalized, it must be reviewed and voted on by the W3C member organizations (which number 229 organizations worldwide).

There is always a chance that a standard at this stage will return to the working-
draft level (if enough W3C members feel that changes are warranted), but many
observers feel that XML 1.0 will achieve final approval with only minor modifications.

XML is an adaptation of the full SGML specification that has been optimized
for the handling and accessing of data on the Web. XML is characterized by a formal structure that establishes fixed relationships among objects and the ability to
support author-created tags for special-purpose situations. Some working group
members refer to it jokingly as SGML-Lite, but—despite the joking—it's clear that
from the beginning, the intent of XML was to streamline SGML and make it practical
for widespread use on the Web. There is a layer of abstraction about the manner in
which the structure is handled and presented that may be initially intimidating to users
who haven't been exposed to structured languages of this type, but most authors
should be able to quickly adapt to the environment once they've had some exposure to
the architectural framework composing XML.

Designers and programmers look at XML as a *metalanguage*. In other words, it's
a language that lets you construct your own language. The term *extensible* refers to
the fact that XML supports the creation of additional tags that serve to classify,
extend, and define the elements they represent. A good example of the use of XML

is the CDF file that has been discussed throughout this book. The CDF file contains a series of tags, constructed in XML format, that have specific meanings when applied to Web channels. The content, organizational structure, recommended delivery schedule, channel icons, and other elements can all be clearly specified by the information presented in the CDF file. The tags used in the CDF file did not exist for general HTML implementations, but were created explicitly for conveying information about channels. Since the Internet Explorer 4 browser includes the built-in capability to parse XML file content, the browser can properly interpret the channel information and apply it towards retrieving and presenting the data associated with the channel.

As a developer, how can you take advantage of XML? By being able to define relationships between various data elements in a document, you're able to extend the range of interactivity possible and create applications—using Java or a scripting language—that deal intelligently with the different kinds of data within the document. For example, you might have tags to define and characterize different types of online merchandise so that it can be previewed or purchased using electronic commerce mechanisms. This capability basically lets you create your own document types, just as the original designers used SGML to create HTML, a simple markup language for presenting basic information on the Web. You might want to design a document type to support an electronic catalog, provide access to a library of multimedia sound effects, establish links to an ODBC database for extracting certain kinds of information, or create a means of sorting and evaluating data about blues musicians from the 1930s. The flexibility of XML opens many creative possibilities.

Fundamental XML Architecture

Learning about XML requires absorbing a whole new set of terms that define the essential concepts and structure used in XML. Beyond the vocabulary, the syntax of the language ventures into some areas well beyond the boundaries of HTML, although anyone familiar with SGML will immediately recognize the parentage. This section offers a brief picture of the fundamental XML architecture.

XML documents are considered a class of data objects within the framework of SGML. They are composed of basic units that are referred to as *entities*. Each entity can include text or binary data. Entities form the physical structure of an XML document; an individual document may include entities that reference other entities that are to be included in the document. Each document contains a root that consists of the document entity.

As with HTML, the text portion of a document is broken down into two separate types:

- Text that represents actual content of the document as expressed by strings of characters.

- Text that is used for markup purposes to delineate the logical structure of a document and its basic layout.

Apart from the physical structure, an XML document also has a logical structure that is composed of a set of declarations, comments, processing instructions, elements, and character references—these items are identified within the document through the markup language.

To read the contents of a file containing XML elements, an additional software component is required: an XML processor. The XML processor can interpret the structure established in the XML document and provide access to the underlying content. Without an appropriate XML processor, the content of an XML document cannot be accessed or used (a conventional browser without a built-in XML parser won't know how to read or interpret the structure).

Building Blocks

XML documents consist of a set of well-defined constructs, divided between markup and content. Those portions of a document that are used for markup fit into six distinct markup types:

- Elements
- Entity References
- Processing Instructions
- Comments
- Marked Sections
- Document Type Declarations

Each of these markup types is defined in the following sections.

Elements

Elements serve to characterize the content of an item appearing within the XML document. As in HTML, start tags and end tags surrounded by angle brackets (< >) are used to distinguish the internal content, but empty elements can be specified as well. These are expressed using a single end tag, such as </element>.

Elements proliferate throughout XML documents—in most documents, they will be the most abundant item in it. Attributes are used to specify values with the starting element tag. For example, to create a class titled intro within a div element, you would use the entry:

```
<div class="intro">
```

XML requires that all attribute values must be surrounded by quotations.

Entity References

Any markup language defines a set of characters that have precisely defined meanings within the markup structure. However, you will frequently want to use these characters within the content as well. To do so, the convention of *Entity References* was established; an alternate character string is used to specify an item that would otherwise be interpreted as a markup character. An example is the left angle bracket—the character that signifies the starting point of an element's tag. The only way you can use a left angle bracket within the content of a document is to create an Entity Reference.

Each Entity Reference begins with an ampersand character (&) and is terminated with a semicolon (;). In between these two characters, you can embed either a decimal or a hexadecimal character reference. Entities are given unique names within an Entity Declaration section in the document.

For example, one of the predefined Entity References is lt, used to represent the left angle bracket (<). With this Entity Reference, you can then use the bracket within a document by using the name and identifying characters, as shown in the following line:

```
When the temperature is &lt; 32 degrees F, ice forms.
```

Entity References also allow you to embed characters that you would not otherwise be able to enter into a document, since they don't exist as the normal set of characters available on your keyboard. However, using Entity References and the appropriate decimal or hexadecimal character code, you can access the full range of Unicode characters and symbols for use in your documents.

Processing Instructions

Processing Instructions contain information to be passed to an application. The syntax for this type of entry is as follows:

```
<?name pidata?>
```

The name `value` identifies the particular Processing Instruction to the application; this is referred to as the PI target. The `pidata` that follows the name is passed to any application that recognizes the PI target provided. Names should be specified as formal notations to provide unique identification.

Comments

Comments, as in any programming language, provide information apart from the content and markup in the document. These can be embedded throughout the XML content to clarify or characterize particular entries. Each Comment string should begin with the characters <!-- and end with -->. The only string that can't be legally contained within a Comment is the literal string "--".

The following line illustrates the proper formatting of an embedded Comment:

```
<!--The following section includes the electronic commerce mechanism.-->
```

Marked Sections

Within an XML document, if you want to include characters that are normally interpreted as markup characters, you can include them within a marked section. The XML parser ignores markup characters within this type of section. For example, you can create a CDATA section by using the opening CDATA tag <![CDATA[and the closing tag]]> to enclose those portions of text that you want displayed as is.

Document Type Declarations

Document Type Declarations (DTD) are optional with XML, but are required for certain types of documents. If you're working in an authoring environment, using tools that work from a particular content model, the Document Type Declaration may be needed to clarify the structure.

Typically, declarations within an XML document convey meta-information about the document content to those applications that will be parsing and interpreting the information. The kinds of information that fit into this category include:

- Names of external files that may be referenced from within the body of the document

- The acceptable organization for nested tags and the sequence within which they may appear

- Entities that are included within the document structure

- Attribute values, including the normal defaults and types that apply

- Formats of any non-XML data that may appear in a document

Declarations can be expressed in one of four different categories:

Element Declarations: Specify the names of individual elements and characterize their internal content.

Attribute Declarations: Indicate which of the elements in a document may have associated attributes and the values that are related to the attributes. Default values are also included as a part of this type of declaration.

Entity Declarations: Form a relationship between a name and some portion of the document content. The declaration can refer to a segment of text, externally referenced data, or a part of the Document Type Declaration.

Notation Declarations: Identify particular kinds of data that are external to the document.

The later section, *Examining the OSD Tags Used in a CDF File*, shows a series of declarations referring to the different elements and attributes that can be included in a CDF file designed to automatically process software updates online.

Well-Formed Documents

XML documents are said to be *well-formed* when they can be handled by any application that doesn't require a Document Type Definition. Since XML documents by default don't require a DTD, this criteria essentially requires that each of the elements contained in the document have the proper syntax and order, and that the contents adhere to the grammar specified within the standard. One of the requirements of an XML processor is that it must, at a minimum, check to see if an XML document is well-formed. The term *validity checking* is applied to inspecting documents that do contain a DTD to ensure that the structural requirements, as expressed by the DTD, are consistent throughout the document. XML documents are capable of being *self-described* containers; their definition is inherent in the organization of their contents.

From its conception, XML was intended to be less difficult to use for document production than SGML; the minimal constraints required to construct well-formed documents are vastly simpler than the work surrounding validation of fully SGML-compliant documents using a DTD. Becoming an author of XML documents does not require becoming fully proficient in SGML techniques; XML is a step removed from the rigorous requirements of SGML.

Linking Model in XML

A separate specification, XML Linking Specification (XLL), defines the model that applies to links created in XML documents. Links in XLL terms indicate a relationship between two or more resources. Any location that is specified within a link can be considered a resource. The relationship between the resources is defined by a number of factors, including the semantic information that you include as a part of the link reference and the characteristics of the application that processes the link. XLL allows you to create Extended Links, which can involve more than two resources, and also introduces a new concept referred to as *Extended Pointers*, which provides a more complex model for specifying and locating individual resources.

The simplest links in XML look almost identical to a typical link as expressed in HTML. For example, the following link shows the similarity:

```
<LINK XML-LINK="SIMPLE"  HREF="http://www.someplace.net"> Go someplace
soon.</LINK>
```

Extended links establish a relationship between several different resources. For example, you could create extended links that identify a collection of resources associated with data and information involving a particular aircraft.

```
<ELINK XML-LINK="EXTENDED"
    ROLE="CUB_SPECS">
<LOCATOR XML-LINK="LOCATOR"
    HREF="www.cub.net/charac">Flight Characteristics
</LOCATOR>
<LOCATOR XML-LINK="LOCATOR"
    HREF="www.cub.net/weight">Weight and Loading
</LOCATOR>
<LOCATOR XML-LINK="LOCATOR"'
    HREF="www.cub.net/history:>History
</LOCATOR>
</ELINK>
```

By this construction, you've established a relationship between each of the different resources offered for the specifications associated with a Piper Cub.

XSL and XML

XML documents by definition can take advantage of user-defined tag sets, which creates a problem when determining the presentation of the document content. Unlike HTML, which has some broadly defined default for the display of various

XML in Commerce

One of the promising applications for XML, which has excited interest throughout the computer industry, is its use in electronic commerce applications. CommerceNet, a coalition of corporations and organizations dedicated to developing solutions for electronic commerce on the Internet, has begun a global initiative to illustrate practical applications of XML in a variety of electronic commerce areas. The key feature behind this initiative is the capability of XML to construct tags that not only can be keyed to particular products in a vendor's catalog, but can be used to facilitate searches across the Internet. For example, if you're a consumer hunting through the Internet to find a speedometer cable for your 1975 Morgan +8 Roadster, a properly tagged item in an XML document could positively identify this rare item. XML can help change the Web from a chaotic assortment of unrelated HTML documents to a carefully charted terrain that makes locating things somewhat akin to finding a book in the library by using the card catalog. As XML proliferates, so the expectation goes, you'll be able to send out shopping agents or robots to locate specialized products or merchandise with a precision that has been impossible given the weaknesses in current search mechanisms and HTML content specifications. CommerceNet's XML/EDI task force has been preparing sample catalogs based on XML to demonstrate some of the basc techniques and to begin working towards standardization of a common Document Type Definition that would fit the commerce model. The eagerness with which many companies are approaching electronic commerce, and the role that XML can play in simplifying the process, should hasten its adoption and use throughout the Web.

elements, such as an <H2> tag or <BLOCKQUOTE> tag, a browser is liable to encounter any type of tag within the context of an XML document.

The way around this problem is through style sheet references that attach certain display properties to the elements of an XML document. The XSL specification is under way to establish the relationship of styles to internal XML elements, but this specification is still a work in progress and the final implementation has not yet been established. The approach taken is likely to include the use of Cascading Style Sheets, much as they are used in HTML 4.0, as well as another international style sheet language referred to as DSSSL, the Document Style Semantics and Specification Language. Whatever final approach is chosen, it is clear that some mechanism needs to be applied to allow XML content to be displayed in a consistent way in browsers and applications.

Examining the OSD Tags Used in a CDF File

Like CDF, the Open Software Definition (OSD) is based on the Extensible Markup Language, providing a unique set of tags that fully describe a set of software components, the associated software dependencies, specific version information, and the structure and relationships to other components. One of the key uses of OSD is to facilitate automated software updating through push technology. OSD is equipped to describe and reference software specific to various platforms; it can handle Java packages and applications, as well as Macintosh, Windows 32-bit, and ActiveX components.

The Channel Definition Format, as defined by Microsoft and supported by Internet Explorer 4, recognizes a subset of the full range of OSD tags. This allows software updates to be initiated and controlled through CDF file entries, as long as the complexities of the update process do not require the full OSD tag set.

The structure of the OSD tags as represented in CDF illustrates some of the basic concepts that have been presented in this appendix. The following code segment covers the range of CDF-compatible tags:

```
<!-- OSD tags -->
<!ELEMENT SoftPkg (Title, Abstract, Logo, Language, Usage, Implementation,
DeleteOnInstall, Dependency, Java, NativeCode)* >
<!ATTLIST SoftPkg AUTOINSTALL (YES | NO) "NO">
<!ATTLIST SoftPkg HREF CDATA #REQUIRED>
<!ATTLIST SoftPkg NAME CDATA #REQUIRED>
<!ATTLIST SoftPkg PRECACHE (YES | NO) "NO">
<!ATTLIST SoftPkg VERSION CDATA>
<!-- this for CDF files only -->
<!ATTLIST SoftPkg STYLE (ACTIVESETUP | MSICD)>
<!ELEMENT Class (Icon, IsBean, TypeLib)* >
<!ATTLIST Class CLASSID CDATA>
<!ATTLIST Class NAME CDATA #REQUIRED>
<!ELEMENT Code (Implementation, System) >
<!ATTLIST Code CLASSID CDATA>
<!ATTLIST Code NAME CDATA #REQUIRED>
<!ATTLIST Code VERSION CDATA #REQUIRED "0,0,0,0">
<!ELEMENT CodeBase EMPTY>
<!ATTLIST CodeBase FILENAME CDATA>
<!ATTLIST CodeBase HREF CDATA>
<!ATTLIST CodeBase SIZE CDATA>
```

```
<!ATTLIST CodeBase STYLE (ActiveSetup | MSICD)>
<!ELEMENT DeleteOnInstall EMPTY>
<!ELEMENT Dependency (SoftPkg, Language)*>
<!ATTLIST Dependency ACTION (Assert | Install) "Assert">
<!ELEMENT Icon>
<!ATTLIST Icon FILENAME CDATA>
<!ELEMENT Implementation (CodeBase, Language, OS, Processor)*>
<!ELEMENT IsBean EMPTY>
<!ELEMENT Java (Package, Namespace)*>
<!ELEMENT Language EMPTY>
<!ATTLIST Language VALUE CDATA #REQUIRED>
<!ELEMENT Namespace>
<!ELEMENT NativeCode (Code)>
<!ELEMENT NeedsTrustedSource EMPTY>
<!ELEMENT OS (OSVersion)>
<!ATTLIST OS VALUE (Mac | Win95 | Winnt) #REQUIRED>
<!ELEMENT OSVersion EMPTY>
<!ATTLIST OSVersion VALUE CDATA #REQUIRED>
<!ELEMENT Package (Implementation, Class, NeedsTrustedSource, System)*>
<!ATTLIST Package NAME CDATA #REQUIRED>
<!ATTLIST Package VERSION CDATA #REQUIRED>
<!ELEMENT Processor EMPTY>
<!ATTLIST Processor VALUE (Alpha | MIPS | PPC | x86) #REQUIRED>
<!ELEMENT System EMPTY>
<!ELEMENT TypeLib EMPTY>
<!ATTLIST TypeLib CLASSID CDATA #REQUIRED>
```

Summary

This appendix only hints at the capabilities and possibilities offered through XML and HTML 4.0. You can obtain additional information about both of these standards through the World Wide Web Consortium site:

www.w3.org

The full text of the proposed XML 1.0 standard can be retrieved from:

www.w3.org/TR/PR-xml-971208

We recommend that you check the site to see if any more recent versions have been issued since this book went to press.

You can see from the material in this appendix that, as a developer, choosing to use XML or HTML 4.0 is not an *either-or* choice. HTML will continue to be a widely used option for basic documents and simple information that needs to be presented and distributed across the Web, but XML will begin to be used more frequently in certain kinds of specialized information transfers where the internal content of a document or a set of documents needs to be precisely described. As more and more authoring tools encompass the structures that compose these two standards, and provide utilities for validating the document structures, we'll begin to see expanded capabilities appearing more commonly in XML-based documents. This process is bound to be a very slow, incremental change, so authors and developers don't have to plan on immediately tossing out their favorite editing applications and purchasing completely new toolkits. An awareness of what can be accomplished within each of these standards should help guide your development efforts.

Resources

This appendix profiles a number of resources that can help you in the development of DHTML content for channel delivery. The areas covered include:

- DHTML authoring tools
- Channel creation tools
- Useful accessory applications
- Organizations
- Online resources

Dynamic HTML Authoring Tools

This chapter examines the leading DHTML authoring tools. Some of these are mentioned and described briefly in earlier chapters; this appendix pulls together the information about these tools into one common area where they can be evaluated and compared.

mBed Interactor

mBed Software builds tools for presenting multimedia on the Web. Since late 1995, this small San Francisco-based company has been working on ways to overcome the limitations of the Internet for handling the grist of multimedia: animation, interactive controls and navigation aids, sound, transitions, and so on. mBed Interactor is an application that manages traditional multimedia elements in a visual environment.

Dynamic content can be scaled to fit specific browser platforms; for example, if you select the Dynamic HTML options, the program enables the feature set that matches the capabilities of Netscape Communicator and Microsoft Internet Explorer 4. If you select the Java feature set, the application uses elements in the form of embedded Java applets—the minimum target platform in this case is Internet Explorer 3 or Navigator 2. You also have the option of using the full mBed Interactor feature set, which then requires a plug-in or ActiveX control for use with Netscape Navigator 2 and later, or Internet Explorer 3 or later. Depending on the feature set, the multimedia content is handled differently, but the differences are largely transparent to the author working within the visual development environment.

You can reselect the feature set through the Edit menu even while in the middle of a multimedia production, and mBed Interactor will automatically tailor the output to fit the target platform. However, if you have chosen effects that aren't supported on the newly selected platform, these will be disabled by the edit selection. Some of the more interesting effects, such as the ability to control embedded RealAudio content, are only available when using the full mBed Interactor feature set (not through DHTML).

You can, however, use the application solely as a Dynamic HTML authoring tool. Once you've created the effects that you want, you can access the source code from the multimedia elements (which mBed refers to as *mBedlets*) and cut and paste the clearly marked code segments into your HTML document. Copy the supporting files over to your Website and the publishing operation is complete. By default, the program references the embedded libraries of JavaScript—that actually produce the DHTML effects—at its own Website, but you can also simply move the required JavaScript files to your own Website and modify the external references to the appropriate location. A single HTML file is used to field incoming page accesses, detect the client browser, and automatically direct the link to an HTML file that is tailored either for Internet Explorer or Navigator implementations of DHTML.

Optionally, you can use this development tool to produce DHTML documents that are optimized for one platform or the other—Netscape or Microsoft—but the product's strength is the ability to support both platforms. Since this ability overcomes one of the major obstacles of DHTML development, it offers one of the most painless solutions for dealing with this particular problem.

A trial version can be downloaded from the mBed Software Website at:

www.mbed.com

It provides full functionality for 30 days and then can be extended by purchasing the license key from the company to unlock the software for nonrestricted use.

SoftQuad HoTMetaL PRO 4.0

HoTMetaL PRO 4.0 has been among the leading HTML authoring packages since its introduction several years ago. The latest version includes a number of features that incorporate elements of both Dynamic HTML and XML to provide unique capabilities to developers.

A recent upgrade to HoTMetaL PRO includes a feature called Live Database Pages (LDP), which combines DHTML and XML for increased control over online database accesses. Creation and management of online databases is fully supported by the tool. Developers can very simply produce forms that allow data collected through forms or queries to be returned in either table format or as a single database record for inclusion in the created database.

LDPs are available through the HoTMetaL FX Chooser, a utility included with the program that provides easy access to different elements that can be used on pages, such as multimedia objects, background textures, Dynamic HTML effects, and other features. LDPs can be customized through the use of DHTML so that Internet Explorer 4 users can sort and filter the data that appears in an onscreen data display without requiring server-side interactions. The FX Chooser selections have been significantly expanded to include many different database-related objects.

The LDP feature upgrade provides the necessary software to implement an online database either through the program's own database engine and server-side middleware or through another ODBC-compliant database. Support for common databases, such as Microsoft Access, is built in, and LDP can also be used to support interactions with Microsoft's Internet Information Server 4.0 (IIS) and Active Server Pages (ASP).

The editing environment supported by HoTMetaL PRO offers three different tiers, depending on the user's expertise in page layout and design:

- WYSIWYG editing mode allows beginners to construct pages without referring to code.

- Tags On mode supports tag selection based on the current selected output mode (displaying only those tags that make sense for the current environment).

- Source Code mode allows the experts to drop down to the line-by-line code level and perform any additions or changes to the HTML source code.

Users can freely switch between the different modes and choose their level of interaction with the code, or avoid working with it at all. The creation and management of style sheets is very well handled within the program, allowing external style sheets to be produced and accessed, as well as internal style sheet attributes applied wherever they are needed.

HoTMetaL PRO comes bundled with some excellent accessories, including the Infuse JavaScript editing utility from Acadia Software and Ulead's PhotoImpact SE for graphics work. The PhotoImpact GIF animator makes it a simple matter to produce effective animations in GIF format, and the SmartSaver utility is one of the most effective (and simple) utilities for reducing the size of JPEG and GIF images, while being able to continuously view the before and after images. The application also includes a simple site management utility and tools for performing frames editing. You can even run a utility to locate and repair broken links that occur within a set of HTML documents included in your site. To round out the already robust package, SoftQuad includes JambaPE software, a program that allows multimedia Java applets to be easily created and embedded within documents.

The Site Maker feature lets you pick and choose from an assortment of styles that can then be applied on a global basis to a collection of HTML documents. Because the process is visual and guided by a wizard, it removes the user from the intricacies of style-sheet creation; Site Maker allows even beginners to quickly take advantage of the stylistic options.

HoTMetaL PRO offers developers a very wide range of options and an authoring environment well supported with a number of accessories and utilities that will prove very useful in day-to-day development. Although the number of DHTML effects directly supported by the FX Chooser is minimal at this point, indications are that SoftQuad will be strengthening this area of the program in the near future. The database handling supported by LDP should prove an extremely useful feature in the long term.

Additional details can be obtained from:

www.softquad.com

Astound WebCast Professional

Astound Incorporated has produced a very interesting tool for developing both DHTML content and Web channels: WebCast Professional. This software supports Netscape Netcaster and Microsoft Active Channel design, but also includes a proprietary channel player that can handle the multimedia content within companies that may not have yet adopted the latest browser technology. The ChannelAgent technology incorporated in Webcast Professional operates over any HTTP server network; the agent can extract data and information down to the text and graphic levels from collections of HTML documents located either inside or outside a corporate firewall.

The core of the content creation offered by the program is very similar to Astound's DHTML production software: Dynamite. Dynamite is one of the most intuitive and well-rounded applications for creating pages that incorporate DHTML effects. It automatically creates necessary scripts to shield content from incompatible browsers. The program also makes the developer fully aware of which effects can be applied for which browsers, so as you create your pages, you can pick and choose from those features you want to use depending on which platforms you intend to support.

WebCast Professional includes an NT-compatible server that can be used to provide automatic updates of Web content for a number of different channels. It includes features that make it especially useful in an intranet environment, where a single folder can be used to store channel updates and subscribers receive new content without having to install or use the individual ChannelAgent. Published content can be circulated throughout a company even if an Internet connection is not available. However, the WebCast Server can also publish directly to an HTTP server to supply updated channel information for distribution through conventional Netcaster or Active Channel channels. You can also establish connections through the use of a proxy server.

The capabilities of the DHTML editor and content creation tools alone (called WebCast Studio within the application) make this program worth serious consideration. Object manipulation, path handling, layer shuffling, text editing, and all the other tasks that need to be performed frequently to create useful DHTML content can be handled simply and previewed immediately through the appropriate browser. Chapter 5, "Using Dynamic HTML for Active Channels," provides an example of constructing a Preview Page for an Active Channel using Astound Dynamite. All of the same authoring capabilities are present in Astound WebCast Professional, as well as the additional server software and channel management tools.

For additional information, refer to:

www.astound.com

Macromedia Dreamweaver

Macromedia has applied its considerable multimedia development expertise to the task of creating and managing Website content. The result is a very well-balanced, useful application that could easily become your tool of choice as a site developer. The full range of DHTML effects can be handled from within Dreamweaver, using a series of properties settings and a timeline facility that can be used to coordinate many different objects and layers throughout a DHTML document. The authoring environment is completely visual and is similar enough to Macromedia Director that most Director users should feel immediately comfortable working in this framework.

One of the key features of the program is Roundtrip HTML; Macromedia feels strongly enough about this feature that it has trademarked the term. This feature addresses one of the most serious reservations that developers and designers have had with visual editing tools—the inability to jump back and forth between the visual editing environment and the actual HTML source code. Many visual editing applications produce code that is completely inscrutable due to complex table constructions, embedded positioning elements, or other factors. The programs often modify incoming HTML that is opened in the editing environment and inject inappropriate or unwanted lines of code into the content. Many developers avoid visual editing completely because of the concern that a program will alter preexisting code or inject problems into mature, well-tested code.

Dreamweaver's Roundtrip HTML feature ensures that you can maintain code integrity as you alternate between visual editing and code-level editing. Dreamweaver won't modify your existing code and lets you preview the creation of new code, even as you are working in the visual editing mode. The program includes versions of two popular editing applications—HomeSite for Windows users and BBEdit for Mac users. You can call up these programs while working within Dreamweaver, perform any necessary edits, and immediately return to the visual editing environment.

Dynamic HTML is supported through a number of built-in JavaScript functions, which you can specify and preview while constructing pages. The coded script is constructed to handle platform differences between Microsoft and Netscape. Among the built-in effects supported are layers animation, button rollovers, image swapping, form validation, and sound playing; the existing behaviors can also be extended with your own JavaScript functions and then added to the Behavior Library of the program where they can be applied to elements on your pages.

Cascading Style Sheets with Positioning are well supported by the program, which offers authors the ability to create custom style sheet tags as needed and to reference external sheets. Style sheet changes can be viewed immediately in the application window. Previewing some effects, however, can be difficult for Macintosh users, particularly if you use site-relative links in your pages, which is the preferred method for professional site development. While Windows users have a mode that allows them to preview pages locally even when they include site-relative references, Macintosh users lack the same capability. If you want to see your pages exactly as they will appear in a browser, your only real option is to set up an area on a remote server to perform the testing. This can be something of a handicap, since authors will invariably want to preview pages before posting them to the Web. It's an area that Macromedia might want to improve in future releases.

Through an Object palette, you can easily plug external elements into your Web pages, such as Java applets, Shockwave plug-ins, and ActiveX components. The available objects can also be extended to include additional elements.

The Site manager included with Dreamweaver is a particularly well-considered implementation. With a built-in FTP client to access the remote site (the destination for your authored content), you can display the remote site content and local site equivalent side by side. Several different mechanisms exist for moving updated content back and forth—the process is simple and very easy to visualize. Collaborative work can be handled with a check-out feature that monitors files that have been checked out of the remote site for local editing. The product also supports a Library feature, where repeated content can be stored and then updated during a remote connection, even if it is contained in multiple areas on the site. The Library feature can also be used to consolidate material that changes frequently. Changing the content as it appears in the Library will cue Dreamweaver to automatically update the corresponding content throughout any Web pages wherever the Library reference appears.

An example of Dreamweaver in action appears in Chapter 8 of this book, "Using DHTML for Netcaster Channels," where the program is used to produce a rollover effect. Additional coverage appears in Chapter 9, "Lightspeed Publishing Case Study," where Dreamweaver's ability to manage layers is utilized to design a compact, easily updateable channel page as a part of one of the case studies.

A trial version of Dreamweaver is available from:

www.macromedia.com

ExperTelligence WebberActive
WebberActive is unique in that it not only provides good support for DHTML content creation, but it features a built-in channel creation tool, which makes it easy to

direct newly created content to a subscriber base. The program lets you work directly and specify the characteristics of the most common channel tags—a very useful feature if you are responsible for handling the day-to-day maintenance issues involving channel creation and updating.

A number of wizard-like sequences, called Assistants in WebberActive, simplify the creation of certain types of content. A Script Assistant provides full support for the IE 4.0 object model and lets you work dynamically with the properties and structure. The Tag Assistant correlates tag use to selected browser platforms so you can target the audience for created content.

This program is heavily weighted towards the Internet Explorer 4 view of the universe, but it is flexible enough that you can create content for both platforms. In fact, you can plug in the DTD of your choice to equip WebberActive to work with tags either from past browsers or those that will be coming down the pike in the near future. This may make it possible to work with evolving XML implementations that are developed as the XML specification reaches the approval state. Another nice feature is WebberActive's full support for the Document Object Model, which allows you to work with all of the elements of an HTML page. Since DOM is supported more thoroughly in Internet Explorer 4 than in Netscape Communicator, many of the effects offered by access to the DOM model will only work in the Explorer mode. The pledge by both software producers to fully support DOM in their next releases, however, will make this an even more valuable asset in the program.

The CDF file management features are a strong plus, and the previewing functions make it fairly easy to construct pages as you are learning the intricacies of style sheets and DHTML. WebberActive includes many features that can help guide you through content creation and tweak your pages to achieve precisely the effects that you want. There is a depth and sophistication to this application that will prevent you from learning it overnight, but it offers features that you can grow into over time, and its capabilities ensure it will become an indispensable tool for many Web developers.

Preview versions of this product can be downloaded from:

www.webbase.com/webberA/

Pictorius iNet Developer

Pictorius, located in Halifax, Nova Scotia, Canada, has produced an application targeted at corporate intranet developers who want to quickly adopt channel technology and use it to deliver information to workgroup members. The program provides single-click channel creation and a robust set of DHTML features. Network members can designate channel content by surveying a sitemap and selecting any branch or page to be accessible as a channel. The idea is that simple channel creation allows an intranet to be set up that supports a systematic flow of key organizational information; for example, network members could regularly receive policy information from the Human Resources department, product updates and comparative analyses from the Marketing group, development updates and schedules from the Research and Development department, and software updates through Information Services. Group calendars, company news, collaborative project information, corporate publications, and similar material can all be delivered through channels with a minimum setup effort.

Using iNet Developer, you can incorporate DHTML features into page content without programming; many functions can be enabled through simple drag-and-drop controls, including the ability to integrate ActiveX controls into channel content. Other DHTML features that can be used without requiring programming include page transitions, absolute and relative positioning of content, and object animation. Positioning can be performed by means of a grid system that includes a snap-to-grid option. DHTML output can be directed to Microsoft-compatible or Netscape-compatible implementations.

Online surveys and database links can be incorporated into channel content with a minimum of effort using an assortment of predesigned agents. The program also has the capability of vastly simplifying site management, reducing the fundamental details of a site with hundreds of HTML documents to only two files. The entire site is represented through a visual map; components can be moved and rearranged through drag-and-drop techniques. The program also provides the unique ability to integrate and test new applications on a live system, without having to shut down any of the components.

A demonstration version of iNet Developer 2.0 can be downloaded from:

www.pictorius.com

This tool is priced at a level that won't surprise IS managers, but might tend to discourage small businesses and independent users. The range of features and integrated tool set, however, justify the cost. iNet Developer includes an application server, a Web server, a fully integrated programming environment, a site management utility, and HTML and DHTML page editors. With a focus on supporting the activities of a corporate intranet, iNet Developer provides an industrial-strength solution for delivering information through channels to an organization and managing the ongoing activities of an internal Website.

Useful Accessory Applications

This section describes some of the most important accessory tools that can support your channel development efforts.

Equilibrium DeBabelizer

A large part of content preparation for Web development involves graphics—handling graphic formats, compression, palettes, sizing, and so on. An indispensable tool for this purpose is Equilibrium DeBabelizer, with seamless handling of any graphic format you can think of and the tools to prep graphics in an almost endless variety of ways. From its initial release as a Macintosh-only application, Equilibrium has created DeBabelizer Pro to bring its wide range of features to Windows users.

The fact that the program includes abundant support for scripted operations and batch processing emphasizes its role as a time-saving tool for professionals who handle large amounts of graphics on a daily basis. If you do much Web development, you undoubtedly find yourself in that position on a frequent basis, and a tool like DeBabelizer can be a bright light in a never-ending spiral of graphics.

While tools such as Photoshop can perform small-scale image processing, they are impractical for the demands of large volumes of graphics—the area in which DeBabelizer excels. Imagine that you're working with a Photo CD of images, all of which need to be scaled and converted to medium-quality PNG format. Such a feat in Photoshop would take days; DeBabelizer can be set up to automate the browser and convert the graphics as fast as your processor can retrieve them.

DeBabelizer also has a number of techniques for manipulating Image palettes, which can be essential when trimming down graphic images to achieve the best balance between image fidelity and file size. Palettes can also be optimized in other ways for Web delivery; DeBabelizer includes a feature called the SuperPalette that can extract an optimal palette from a specified number of images automatically. The program also lets you produce a replacement for the common 216-color palette used by the majority of Web browsers; the replacement palette consists of only 128 colors, an effect that works well for many types of images that aren't particularly well-rendered in the standard 216-color palette.

Your first exposure to DeBabelizer might be a bit intimidating; the program has so many options and file conversion features that it takes a fair amount of time to become comfortable with the use of the application. The Windows version includes a newly modeled interface that is actually less confusing than the Macintosh interface (which is overdue for a thorough redesign). To effectively use DeBabelizer, you need to become well versed in a number of different graphic-oriented terms and concepts. The Reference Guide included with the Macintosh is a bit more difficult to work with then the User Manual for the Windows version of the product. Both manuals do a pretty good job, however, of explaining the underlying concepts and presenting the key tasks available through the program.

Script creation is simplified through the use of a wizard, the ProScripts Wizard, that handles a number of the most useful automated processes. Further types of scripts, of course, can be custom designed to support almost any conceivable use of the program. Equilibrium also includes some boilerplate scripts that perform automatic conversions of graphics to Web-ready formats, using a preselected palette, if that is your wish.

If your Web duties include producing digital video content or animations, DeBabelizer's processing tools can be put to work in this area as well. Optimized 8-bit palettes can be generated for a series of images encountered in an animation or digital video sequence. The result can be a significant improvement in the appearance of digital video material that is compressed for speedier Web presentation. You can also use DeBabelizer's Filter Interpolation to progressively add special effects to an image series, creating some very spectacular animation effects.

More information on DeBabelizer and DeBabelizer Pro can be obtained from:

www.equilibrium.com

Fractal Design Painter and Expression

If you're looking for a way to distinguish your Web graphic design efforts from the mainstream, Fractal Design has two tools worthy of serious consideration. Fractal Design Painter was the original natural media application that applied traditional materials—such as paint, ink, and canvas—to a computer-rendered environment. Painter gets better and better with each subsequent release, and many of its features are tailored to Web presentation output, such as the creation of image maps and the creation of Web-ready graphics in different formats and compression rates. What distinguishes this program, however, is the incredibly stunning effects that you can create by use of the media tools and techniques provided by the program. Custom textures, different lighting effects, modified surfaces and paper patterns, a wide assortment of brushes, pencils, crayons, chalk, ink—all of these ingredients give Painter the ability to produce totally unique renderings. A tool called the Image Hose produces complex images composed of different source material that you provide it; for example, you can spray an image full of jungle foliage, with full shadow effects and clever integration, by loading up the appropriate source image and using the Image Hose.

Fractal Design Expression applies the same essential natural media look with a vector-based environment, giving you the ability to infinitely edit complex creations that have the appearance of natural-media artwork. Choosing from a library of paint strokes, you can produce text or graphic shapes and then modify their appearance by stretching or repositioning nodes, much as you would in a program such as Adobe Illustrator. The difference, of course, is that with the strokes and media look applied to the strokes, you gain a final piece of artwork that is much more distinctive than something constructed in a simple paint program.

Expression gives you the ability to adjust and redesign strokes, and to add your own strokes to the library that already contains some 350 different variations. If you did nothing other than use Expression to generate titles and captions for your Web page content, it would be easily worth the purchase price. But given the range of capabilities that the program has, you can generate effects and art that are unlike anything that can be done with any other program.

Together, these two programs can stimulate the artistic instincts even in those who are not professional artists or designers. More information on Fractal Design products can be obtained from:

www.fractaldesign.com

Organizations

The following organizations provide an assortment of resources to support your channel development goals.

World Wide Web Consortium

The World Wide Web Consortium (W3C) has become the reigning standards body and has helped reduce the dissension and infighting between various companies struggling to leverage their view to market. The bedrock foundation of Web channel delivery is built on an interlocking collection of standards, as described in Part One of this book, including: CDF, RDF, XML, XSL, CSS1, CSS-P, DOM, and so on.

The W3C Website offers a wealth of descriptive information about these new standards and their uses, often authored by the same people who have been the members of the working groups hammering out the specifications, negotiating the changes and improvements, and releasing the final drafts to the industry.

ISO

ISO, the International Standards Organization, plays a major role in coordinating the activities of technological development in approximately 100 member nations. One of the key areas in which ISO is working is the standardization of information technology on a global level. If your Web development efforts are aimed toward reaching an international community, ISO provides a valuable resource in understanding and adapting your content so that it will be accessible to the world. Standards released by ISO often parallel those originally authored by other standards bodies, such as the W3C. It's good to keep track of developments in this area if your market is international.

The entry page for ISO appears at:

www.iso.ch

ECMA

Headquartered in Switzerland, ECMA is an international organization devoted to standardizing information and communication systems. Their significance to channel development is that this organization authored ECMAScript, the vendor-neutral version of JavaScript that attempts to circumvent the Microsoft and Netscape dissension and present a global version of this scripting language. ECMA is also involved with standardizing technologies relating to DVD, Internet telephony, CD-ROM, and ISDN, as well as other important standards affecting communications technology.

The ECMAScript standard can be examined at:

www.ecma.ch

Online Resources

The following resources should prove helpful in obtaining additional information about channel technology and related topics.

Companion Website

To provide up-to-the-minute information about the rapidly evolving topics discussed in this book, we've constructed a companion Website where you will find articles, tips, and resources to increase your skills and knowledge in channel development. The site will also include a channel-based newsletter to which you can subscribe to obtain articles and news delivered to your desktop on a regularly scheduled basis.

To sample the site contents, point your browser to:

www.wiley.com/compbooks/purcell

Dynamic HTML Zone

Macromedia, the developer of the authoring tool Dreamweaver, has constructed a Website devoted to conveying the most current information about DHTML, including suggestions on use and solutions for common obstacles encountered by DHTML developers. The site includes a link to an area where you can download a trial version of Dreamweaver and experiment with its authoring capabilities yourself.

The site incorporates a wealth of DHTML effects, so it is a good place to go to get a sense of what can be accomplished in this new medium. There is also a set of tutorials that can help you get started learning how to implement DHTML on your own pages. Discussion groups hosted here provide a good place to share experiences with other developers and learn from both their successes and failures.

To reach the Dynamic HTML zone, point your browser to:

www.dhtmlzone.com

Inside DHTML

Inside DHTML, part of the Webmonkey Network (affiliated with HotWired), offers a wealth of information about DHTML. You'll find toolkits, a number of tutorials, sample code, and numerous examples of DHMTL in action. The topics presented cover a wide range and should satisfy the needs of both beginning DHTML authors and seasoned professional developers.

To sample the wares at Inside DHTML, fire up your browser and cruise to:

www.insidedhtml.com/home.htm

C/NET BUILDER.COM

The extensive resources at C/NET can help you master the new standards, such as HTML 4.0, XML, and Dynamic HTML. The site handles the full range of topics of primary interest to developers, including authoring techniques, programming for the Web, constructing Web graphics, managing Web servers, and conducting business over the Web. You also have quick access to downloads of many leading Web development tools, such as HomeSite, HotDog Professional, WebxBase, and Channel Maker. You can also sample C/NET's take on the current crop of development tools, with a selection of reviews covering the leading applications.

The Builder Buzz area of the site offers a place to exchange ideas with fellow developers and tap into some of the best techniques growing out of this community. C/NET also posts regular news items and articles of interest to developers and has a collection of additional resources and links to keep the Web information tree expanding.

The BUILDER.COM site can be accessed at:

www.cnet.com/Content/Builder

The Companion
Website

Way back in 1965, Gordon Moore, the cofounder of Intel, formulated the general principle that computer processing power would double every 18 months, based on continual improvements in the ability to embed more and more transistors into tiny slices of silicon. Moore's Law has become the prevailing axiom in the industry and we've all witnessed the accelerated pace of computer development, particularly as it applies to the phenomenon of the Internet. Tools and processes continue to change, and the situation for Web channels is no different. By the time this book reaches your hands, you can expect that there will be a number of changes in the way channels are created and used, and the pioneers who lead the pack in this area will be moving the boundaries of the medium and coming up with new and interesting ways to communicate through channels.

To keep you informed of the latest changes and developments in the Web channel field, we've designed a companion Website for this book. You can access the site by pointing your browser to:

www.wiley.com/compbooks/purcell

You'll find the following kinds of material at the companion Website:

- A newsletter designed for distribution using Microsoft's Active Channels approach to Webcasting. By subscribing to the newsletter, you'll receive periodic information on Web channel development tools, techniques for improving your channel development efforts, the latest news and trends in this dynamic area, and pointers to many examples of the best Webcasting models. The newsletter is, of course, free, and will be delivered to your desktop on the schedule that you select during the subscription process. This is an easy, painless way to keep up to date on the current trends, especially if you plan on creating channels yourself.

- Short articles showcasing:
  - New Web channel developments from Microsoft and Netscape.
  - The status of emerging standards that affect your page authoring (such as DHTML, DOM, XML, XSS, and so on).
  - Reviews of software tools as they are introduced.
  - Interviews with creative Web channel architects.
  - Ideas that you can incorporate into your design efforts.
  - News bytes and trivia from the world of Webcasting.

- A *Resources* section that points you toward other online sources of Web channel development information. Resources will focus on areas such as online tutorials to improve your authoring skills, specifications and standards to refine your page development goals, and Websites developed by leading software producers to present their Web channel related products.

- A frequently changing channel survey that steers you toward the more innovative channels that are being introduced on the Web. This survey will encompass particular areas of interest, highlighting emerging computer technologies, digital music, popular culture, Web oddities, and other categories. Channels that spark your imagination and stimulate your creative powers will be showcased.

- A *Tips and Techniques* section that provides step-by-step guidelines for incorporating different types of effects into your Web channel pages. Techniques supported by DHTML and specific authoring tools, such as the ALAPI plug-ins for Macromedia's Dreamweaver, will be offered.

We hope that this book has given you the necessary information and incentive to set up Web channels and communicate to a new audience across the Internet. The companion Website will extend the information presented in the book and keep you informed, entertained, and inspired as you work on your individual projects. Good luck in your development efforts!

Glossary

This Glossary provides definitions of terms relating to Web channels, Dynamic HTML, XML, CSS1, CSS-P, RDF, and CDF.

Absolute positioning A method of precisely specifying the position of Web elements—such as text, images, plug-ins, and links—through coordinates. Dynamic HTML supports absolute positioning, providing more control over Web page layout than has been available in earlier versions of HTML. Absolute positioning locates an object based on a horizontal and vertical offset from the upper-left corner of the container within which it resides.

ActiveX A Microsoft-specific technology that supports linking to application documents and files. For example, the ActiveX features of Netscape Communicator allow you to open up a Word document from within the browser.

ActiveX Streaming Format Abbreviated as ASF. A format that supports streaming multimedia delivery for different server types and networks. Using this format, you can synchronize transmission of audio material, video, still images, and so on, in a scalable, reliable manner.

Applet A program that is largely self-contained, designed to be run within a specific environment, such as a browser window.

API Short for Application Programmer's Interface. The set of conventions that apply to accessing particular services within a piece of software. For example, Netcaster has an API developed by Netscape that allows developers to control the characteristics of channel operation.

Argument In programming terms, a parameter that is passed from one portion of a program to another. For example, a reference to a function in an expression often contains one or more arguments, which are values passed to the function to serve as data when the function executes.

Array A collection of items contained in an ordered list and accessed by an index value corresponding to their position in the list. For example, JavaScript recognizes and accesses the images in an HTML document through an array that lists the images in the order in which they occur in the document file.

Auto authentication A feature of Internet Explorer 4 by which the software can automatically present a user ID and password from the cache. This facilitates access to premium subscription sites that require authenticated access.

Basic Webcasting A term that Microsoft uses to describe the most fundamental form of Webcasting in Internet Explorer 4, where subscriptions to any Website can be established through site crawling—without requiring any modifications to the original site content.

BinHex A compression format commonly used for transferring large files over the Internet. Many email applications, such as Netscape Messenger and Eudora Mail, provide automatic handling of message components (including attachments) in BinHex format.

Bookmark A reference to a previously visited Website, storing the URL under a title and category selected by the user. Major browsers, such as Microsoft Internet Explorer and Netscape Navigator, include flexible bookmarking features, as do third-party products, such as DataViz WebBuddy.

Boolean A data type consisting of only two values: true and false. Boolean logic represents the basic decision-making mechanism used with digital computers, and Boolean values are used frequently in Java and JavaScript.

Branch A place within a program where the execution can proceed down two or more separate paths. Conditions detected by the program generally determine which path will be followed.

Broadcast address An IP- or media-specific address that includes an entire range of target stations to which data will be delivered.

Built-in objects Objects available to a script author for use in developing a program. For example, JavaScript recognizes a wide range of built-in objects that appear in HTML documents, such as windows, frames, checkboxes, radio buttons, forms, and so on.

Cache A region on the storage media of a local or client computer dedicated to persistent data storage. By storing some types of data locally, the information can be quickly accessed without downloading from the network. Netcaster uses a separate cache for channel data than does Communicator. Microsoft Internet Explorer uses a single cache for offline viewing of browser content and channel content.

Cascading Style Sheets (CSS) A collection of style definitions that controls the appearance of HTML documents, including text size, colors, margins, flow, and so on. Variations of this standard include CSS1, Cascading Style Sheets Level 1 (the initial specification), CSS2, Cascading Style Sheets Level 2 (based on the Document Object Model), and CSS-P, Cascading Style Sheets with Positioning, which is particularly valuable for moving objects in DHTML.

Castanet Transmitter The component of a Castanet channel that resides on a server and delivers the channel content through push technology.

Castanet Tuner A software component that allows specific Web Channels compatible with Marimba Software's Web delivery technique to be selected and accessed. Netscape's Netcaster includes a built-in version of the Castanet Tuner.

Certificate An authentication mechanism implemented in the form of a cryptographic code and key that is used to verify the source and credibility of a company, individual, or file. Certificates are issued by an organization that maintains the registration and verification process. Also sometimes called a *digital certificate*.

Channel The generic term that applies to a Website that has structured its content for dynamic delivery to subscribers through push techniques. This term encompasses sites set up for use with Microsoft's Active Channels, as well as channels developed for delivery using Netscape's Netcaster.

Channel Definition Format (CDF) An open standard developed by Microsoft that allows the contents of a site to selectively be made available for channel delivery. The CDF file contains the key characteristics of the site, including the proposed update schedule, the type of content, the pages available to the site crawler, and the hierarchical organization of the material. Creation of a single CDF file can transform any Website into a Microsoft Active Channel.

Channel Finder Netscape's guide to a selected range of Web channels compatible with its Netcaster technology. Accessing the Channel Finder requires registering with Netscape's Netcenter, after which subscriptions to a variety of information providers become accessible.

Conditional behavior In programming terms, the branching of program flow depending on changing conditions available to the program. For example, a JavaScript could use conditional behavior to select one path through a Website when the Internet Explorer browser was detected as being active, and another path when Netscape Navigator was found.

Container A means of storing and presenting items related in some manner within a particular area in an application, such as Netscape Communicator.

Cookie A piece of data that can be written to a user's hard disk drive to store pertinent information for later use (such as a user identification code that allows someone to log in to an online newspaper each time he or she accesses it).

Crawling Also known as *site crawling*. The operation performed by a channel applicaton as it revisits a site and examines channel contents link by link to retrieve updated material for downloading to the subscriber.

Crossware Applications built around open Internet standards that are designed to work on a variety of operating systems and across different networks.

Customizable toolbar An application feature that allows a user to designate buttons for special-purpose functions. For example, Netscape Navigator allows users to drag and drop page icons to a toolbar to create buttons that point to selected favorite Websites.

Digital Certificate An identification document based on digitally stored codes that can be used to verify a site or user's identity. Digital Certificates are issued and maintained by an agency or company, such as VeriSign, and sometimes incorporated into browser and Web channel software. For example, Netscape's Netcaster includes an option to attach a Digital Certificate to the browser for identification.

Digital signature A means of providing user-specific identification to a document or file through a unique code. This technique allows positive confirmation of the authenticity of a document by someone who receives it.

Dotted decimal notation The means by which IP addresses are constructed using four 8-bit numbers, each represented as base-10 values, with dots between each value. Dotted decimal notation is used to indicate specific nodes on the Internet; each node representing a computer, printer, router, or other device that is identifiable by an address.

Dynamic binding A mechanism for checking object references and verifying them when a program is actually being run. For example, JavaScript uses dynamic binding to check object references through the interpreter during program execution.

Dynamic Hypertext Markup Language (DHTML) A variation of standard HTML that includes absolute positioning and layering of text and images on a Web page. Dynamic HTML specifications have been standardized in HTML 4.0, but both Microsoft and Netscape released browsers supporting implementations of Dynamic HTML before the actual approval of the standard. Components in a Dynamic HTML page can be manipulated through scripting or coding to change position, undergo transitions, or change the display of a layer. Pages can respond swiftly to user interactions without requiring interaction with a server. DHTML makes it possible to design complete applications and multimedia presentations that run on the user's desktop without server interaction—making them ideal for offline viewing.

Encryption A method of privacy protection that encapsulates the data in a file in a specially coded form that can only be opened with a software key. Encryption is used to keep the contents of email messages private and to support the electronic commerce sales of software products over the Internet.

Event handler A piece of code that responds to some action taking place. Scripting languages, such as JavaScript, use event handlers to control program flow. Actions such as a page loading, a user clicking the mouse, or a page unloading are used to trigger operations within a program.

Extensible Markup Language (XML) A simplified version of the Standard Generalized Markup Language tailored for the design of Web documents. The XML standard encompasses both the structure of a document and its content, allowing important information about the content of a site to be distributed. XML provides developers with the capability of creating their own special-purpose tags that can be defined for a variety of purposes, including the creation of large technical information libraries and the support of various kinds of electronic commerce.

File Transfer Protocol Abbreviated to FTP. A protocol designed to manage the efficient exchange of files across the Internet.

Host A computer system—from a simple PC to a supercomputer—that connects to a network.

Host identifier The segment of a dot-separated IP address that distinguishes a particular host on the Internet.

HTML editor A software application designed to simplify the creation of HTML documents and the insertion of tags. Most HTML editors let you preview Web page content as it will appear in the browser window. A new generation of HTML editors that support Dynamic HTML has appeared on the market, including Xpertelligence's WebberActive and Macromedia's Dreamweaver.

HTTP A protocol for delivering Web content from server to client. HTTP is the standard means for transferring files on the Web.

Inheritance The transfer of properties from a higher-level object to a lower-level object without the need to formally declare the properties.

Inline link In XML terms, a link designed to act as a resource for itself. The linking element's content becomes the resource.

Instance In object terms, a single representation of a particular object type. For example, when you create a channel object in Netcaster, you are constructing an occurrence of a single channel that has all the characteristics of that data type.

Internet Definition Language (IDL) A generalized language designed to specify the techniques for communicating with the Document Object Model (or similar-type construct). The IDL is designed to accommodate a number of popular programming languages, such as C, C++, Perl, Java, JavaScript, and so on.

Internet Service Provider (ISP) An organization that provides space on a network server for customers to set up personal or business Websites. Website content is uploaded to a storage location on an assigned server where it then becomes accessible to the Web community.

IP address A 32-bit quantity, expressed in a dot-separated format, that indicates a single point of attachment on the Internet.

IP datagram The fundamental unit of information transfer within a TCP/IP network. Each datagram consists of a packet of data with a destination address and source identification.

JAR Short for Java Archive. An archiving format allowing Java developers to archive and distribute complete applications across the Internet or within an intranet.

JAR packager An application designed to produce Java archives by consolidating all of the required files into a single package. A certificate is often used to verify the source of the contents of the Java archive, so the users may run the application stored in the archive without concern for the applicaton misusing their system resources.

Keywords Terms that are reserved for use within a programming language. These terms cannot be used for variable names or object names, since the programming language recognizes them for specific purposes.

LDAP Lightweight Directory Access Protocol (LDAP) provides a means for storing and accessing information from within an industry-standard, networked directory. Information such as names and addresses, email account numbers, telephone numbers, and so on, can be accessed through LDAP. Netscape Communicator includes built-in support for LDAP.

Linking element In XML terms, a description of link characteristics associated with an element contained within a document.

Literal An explicit value that appears within an expression, such as the number of feet in a mile.

Locator A string of characters that appears in relation to a link used to identify the location of a resource.

Managed Webcasting A term that Microsoft applies to content delivered from a site equipped for channel delivery through a CDF file. The CDF file indicates the key characteristics of the site, including those pages to include in the channel delivery, and sets up the subscription mechanism.

Metadata Data that describes other data. The RDF specification is an attempt to create a system of metadata that can be used to classify various types of content on the Web. While metadata is a form of data itself, it extends the usefulness of other forms of data by expressing its content in machine-understandable terms.

Methods The techniques by which you can interact with an object through a program. For example, the Netcaster component in JavaScript has an activate method that sets up a channel object for use under Netcaster.

Multicast Backbone (MBONE) A virtual network that runs on top of the Internet using a series of multicast islands to transfer packets using multicast techniques. This approach takes advantage of a technique known as *tunneling* to relay data (by means of a unicast approach) between multicast islands.

Multicasting A form of transferring Web content designed to minimize bandwidth issues. Web resources being transferred to multiple sites are sent out singly and then replicated by a multicast-capable server closer to their destination node. Compare this to unicast techniques, which require that a server broadcast a copy of each resource file for every destination node.

Multicast routing The means by which a network creates packet distribution trees to distribute multicast packets to each and every receiver.

Multidirectional link In XML terms, a link that is set up for traversal from more than one resource.

Multipurpose Internet Mail Extension (MIME) A means for identifying files containing specific kinds of content. MIME extensions control how an HTTP server handles certain kinds of content, such as email attachments, streaming audio and video, applications, portable document files, and so on. Most email packages, such as Netscape Messenger, can handle a variety of content transferred using MIME.

Nesting The hierarchical organization of a number of elements with lower-order elements progressively positioned beneath higher-order elements. Nesting, for example, is used for items listed as a part of channel content in CDF files to determine the tree structure that allows users to navigate through an outline of site contents.

Netcaster A separately installable component of Netscape Communicator that provides access to channel content through site crawling and periodic updates. Netcaster also contains a Castanet Tuner for receiving channel content delivered through true push technology by a Castanet Transmitter.

Netcasting The term applied to the delivery of HTML documents and other Web content on a regularly scheduled basis using push techniques.

Netscape Capabilities Model A protocol used to differentiate between different levels of access to the system resources of a computer and to control access based on the use of signed objects, verified through digital certificates.

Object A collection of properties describing an item that are organized to provide access through a program. For example, an object in JavaScript can be a collection of items contained in an array or the properties that compose a Netcaster channel.

Offline cache A feature of Netscape Netcaster that lets users retrieve information from a broadcast channel and store it locally in a cache. The information can then be accessed offline at a later time—the essential structure is maintained so it appears the same as during online access.

Offline site A Website organized so that it can be downloaded in the background for viewing when there is not an active Internet connection. Most channel content is designed so that it can be retrieved and accessed in this manner.

Out-of-line link In XML terms, a link that is not associated with its particular resource, as in the case of a link group that indicates to an application where to locate links. Multidirectional traversal requires the use of out-of-line links.

Plug-ins Compact, special-purpose applications that add additional capabilities to an application, such as Netscape Communicator. A plug-in can provide multimedia effects (Macromedia Shockwave), streaming audio playback (RealAudio), streaming video (VIVO), or other kinds of functionality.

Public key cryptography A technique used to control access to data by the use of two keys: one public and one private. The public key is distributed to anyone for use, but the private key is held secretly. Both keys are required to decode and access data that has been encoded.

Push technology A delivery mechanism for Web content that relies on the Web server distributing updated content on a scheduled basis and presenting it to clients without their explicit action.

Resource In XML parlance, a unit of information that is accessible by means of a locator and a linking element. A resource can be a file, image, application, document, or the returned information from a database query.

Robots control A means of indicating a range of URLs on a Website that are not intended to be retrieved by a site crawler.

Route In Internet terms, the path that a network packet takes as it travels from source to destination. Under the TCP/IP protocol, packets are routed independently and a series of them may take different paths to their end destination, depending on network traffic and other factors.

Router A specialized computer device that provides a link between several networks and facilitates the exchange of packets between networks. For example, an IP router is designed to handle incoming IP datagrams and distribute them to other networks to which it is connected. Each journey of a packet from one router to the next is referred to as a *hop*.

Scripting language A higher-level of programming language that allows many operations to be carried out with a minimum of code. Both JavaScript and VBScript are scripting languages.

Secure Multipurpose Internet Mail Extension (S/MIME) A standard for transferring mail and mail attachments using encryption. S/MIME, incorporated into mail applications such as Netscape Messenger, allows the originator of a message to be positively identified and authenticated, and protects the message contents from being viewed by unauthorized individuals.

Secure Socket Layers version 3.0 (SSL 3.0) A Netscape-developed security protocol that performs encryption of data being exchanged across the Internet or a corporate intranet. SSL 3.0 has been submitted as an open standard to several standards organizations and has been adopted by a number of organizations.

Session Description Protocol Abbreviated to SDP. In MBONE implementations, a technique for announcing multicasted data in advance of its arrival. The protocol specifies a full description of the upcoming multicast, including IP addresses, ports, and particular protocols in use.

Signing certificate A means of verifying the source of a file, application, or script through association with a digital certificate. A certification organization issues and maintains the encrypted verification tools.

Simple Mail Transfer Protocol (SMTP) The message handling protocol that determines the handling and exchange of mail and attachments over the Internet using the TCP/IP protocol. SMTP controls interactions between different mail systems and specifies the formatting of control messages.

Snippets Very short scripts designed to perform a simple task or carry out an operation on a Web page. Because of their inherent simplicity, snippets can often be added to HTML documents with a simple cut-and-paste operation, where they then perform a designated task.

Standard Generalized Markup Language (SGML) The predecessor to HTML and XML, SGML is a complex, formalized means of authoring document content for computer management and distribution.

Statement A line in a program that assigns value to a variable, performs a task, or completes an operation. Statements generally are the individual lines that compose a program or a script.

Streaming media A technology by which large files containing audio or video content can be delivered in real time by buffering a portion of the incoming file and presenting it to the user while the rest of the file is being downloaded. RealNetworks provides support for this technology both through dedicated servers that stream large volumes of files and HTTP transfers for smaller sites without server software installed.

String A line of characters consisting of numeric values or ASCII characters.

Style sheets Collections of page and text formatting information organized by tags. Style sheets allow "templates" to be applied to page design, controlling the layout in a consistent manner. Style sheet elements can also be manipulated under script control to allow dynamic control of the appearance of a document. Dynamic HTML takes advantage of this capability of style sheets.

Subscription The act of selecting a channel for regularly scheduled delivery. Both Microsoft Internet Explorer and Netscape Netcaster have single-click access to channel subscriptions and the option of adding new channels to a selection bar for quickly opening the channel content.

Syntax The rules by which different elements—as in a programming language— are combined to construct meaningful messages. Syntax allows elements to be combined in precise ways to avoid any confusion in the interpretation of the message string.

Title In XML terms, the caption describing a resource intended to illustrate the significance of a link's association with that resource.

Traversal In XML terms, the accessing of a resource by means of a link. A traversal may be initiated under program control, or it may occur when someone clicks the displayed content of a linking element.

True Webcasting A term that Microsoft uses to apply to scalable, high-volume Webcasting as implemented using multicasting technology. True Webcasting requires a server equipped to deliver channel material using the necessary protocols, such as a Microsoft NetShow Server. Other third-party push applications can also be used in combination with Internet Explorer to achieve true Webcasting.

Tunneling A process by which data contained in a packet is passed through a transport system in encapsulated form. For example, MBONE uses tunneling to transfer IP multicast datagrams within standard datagrams.

Unicasting The current predominant means of transferring data on the Internet, characterized by its inefficient use of bandwidth. A individual copy of a data packet is generated and sent to each client that makes a request for it, resulting in multiple copies being produced. Compare to multicasting, where a single data packet is distributed across the network to be replicated and passed on by servers closer to the packet destination.

Variable The means of representing data in symbolic form within a program. Variables often are assigned several different values during the course of program execution.

Webcasting The delivery of HTML-based content through a Web channel based on a set of subscription settings. This term is also applied to the real-time delivery of audio and video content, either through unicasting or multicasting protocols on the Internet.

Web-server channel A Webcasting channel that delivers content using the hypertext transfer protocol (HTTP) through a server.

Webtop anchor Netscape's approach to opening up the desktop for access to channel delivery of information. Channel content appears on the desktop according to the schedule set by the individual and the update schedule adopted by the channel provider. Microsoft calls its approach to this technique "Active Desktop."

Working group A term applied to a group of individuals, usually part of a committee, who are responsible for developing and finalizing a standard, protocol, or design issue. For example, the IETF and the W3C have working groups devoted to resolving TCP/IP protocols and new World Wide Web standards.

Index

ndex